THE OLD NORTHWEST

Studies in Regional History, 1787–1910

Edited by

HARRY N. SCHEIBER

UNIVERSITY OF NEBRASKA PRESS · LINCOLN

For P. W. G.

List of Abbreviations

The following abbreviations have been used in the notes to regularize the reference style employed in this volume:

HPSO	Historical and Philosophical Society of Ohio
IMH	*Indiana Magazine of History*
JISHS	*Journal* of the *Illinois State Historical Society*
MVHR	*Mississippi Valley Historical Review*
OAHQ	*Ohio Archaeological and Historical Quarterly*
OH	*Ohio History*
OHQ	*Ohio Historical Quarterly*
WHC	Wisconsin State Historical Society *Collections*
WMH	*Wisconsin Magazine of History*

Preface: On the Concepts of "Regionalism" and "Frontier"

THE present-day states of Ohio, Indiana, Illinois, Michigan, and Wisconsin are all part of the region won from the British in the American Revolution, later governed as a Federal territory under the famous Northwest Ordinance. But usually when historians speak of this area as "the Old Northwest," they mean to connote something more than the common political genesis. For despite differences within the area, and despite similarities between the Old Northwest and other sections of the United States and Canada, historically the Old Northwest comprised an areal component of the nation whose people, institutions, and politics were relatively homogeneous. In significant aspects, moreover, its distinctive characteristics differentiated the Old Northwest from the rest of the nation—enough so to justify, on this score alone, denominating it "a region." But regional identity is not exclusively a matter of objective homogeneity: it is also, as Louis Wirth has written, a matter of self-identification—a "state of mind," "a sense of common belonging." On this count, perhaps even more than on the first, the Old Northwest is a legitimate unit for historical analysis in terms of regionalism.[1]

The objective interdependence and commonality of the Old Northwest was first defined by the political instrument that established the Northwest Territory. The 1787 Ordinance decreed that there was to be no slavery in the region; and thus it was mandated that society in the new lands north of the Ohio would need to build communities on a different basis from that which characterized settlement south of the river, where the "peculiar institution" would suffuse all social arrangements with special problems and impose a different framework for political behavior.[2] It was not merely a

[1] Louis Wirth, "The Limitations of Regionalism," *Regionalism in America*, ed. Merrill Jensen (Madison, 1951), pp. 386 ff.

[2] Of course, vestiges of slavery survived in the Old Northwest, as did powerful

naïve chauvinism that prompted men of the Old Northwest to speak of their region as "the free west." The word "free" denoted the key difference, as they perceived it, between their social order and the order in communities being planted in the new Southwest.

The sources and composition of population were not the same in all the states of the Old Northwest. But in the first three states to be settled—Ohio, Indiana, and Illinois—there was a striking similarity, as the culture of the upland South mingled with the cultures of New England, the Middle Atlantic States, and northern Europe. The uplanders made their imprint first, and then came an invasion of Yankees "determined to refashion the men of the West." [3] This cultural drama became an important part of the history of all three states; and because Wisconsin and Michigan interacted with the older three in other respects, they felt the impact of this drama as well.

The institutions of economic life manifested a more thorough-going homogeneity in all five states. For in all of them an agriculture based on small-scale farming took hold. Commercial farm production centered on wheat, corn, and livestock, all of which were cash crops that required access to outside markets. In the lower half of the Old Northwest, which was settled at first mainly by uplanders from the South, farmers sought markets for their crops at New Orleans; but as settlement slowly penetrated the central and Great Lakes areas of the region, the New Englanders and Middle Staters who made farms there looked instead to New York and the other eastern seaboard ports. Despite this difference, there was a common interest in better transportation—a recognition in both the lower and the upper Northwest that the fiscal resources of government would have to be mobilized to provide transport facilities. As a result, the region spoke with one voice in national politics for Federal subsidies and for river and harbor improvements. But more im-

---

anti-Negro sentiment. See Merton Lynn Dillon, "The Antislavery Movement in Illinois," in this volume; Francis S. Philbrick (ed.), *Laws of the Illinois Territory, 1809–1818* ("Illinois State Historical Library Collections," Vol. XXV, 1950), introduction, pp. ccxl *et seq.*; Leon Litwak, *North of Slavery: The Negro in the Free States, 1790–1860* (Chicago, 1961); H. N. Scheiber, "The Thirteenth Amendment . . . A Reappraisal," *Cornell Law Quarterly*, XLIX (Spring, 1964), 508–514.

[3] Richard Lyle Power, *Planting Corn Belt Culture* (Indianapolis, 1953), p. 3. Further compounding the drama was the influence of a considerable foreign-born or non-English-speaking group, even in the early years.

portant still, the general commitment to government-sponsored transportation projects forced otherwise diverse local groups into statewide coalitions. It force-fed in all five states what has been termed the "commonwealth tradition," the essentially mercantilistic view that the interests of each state *as a single community* demanded men's loyalties and men's energies; and it produced a commitment to vigorous governmental enterprise throughout the region.[4]

This movement for better transportation—for "internal improvements," in the parlance of the day—blended the economic interests of commercialized agriculture with political and idealistic concepts of commonwealth. An important force impelling this development was the role of towns and cities, which epitomized the business civilization of the region. For cash-crop farming required efficient marketing facilities, centers for wholesale and retail distribution of "imported" goods from the East and abroad, and urban-based banking institutions, just as it required adequate transportation. Thus in the Old Northwest there developed far more urban centers, in relation to total population, than appeared in the contemporary Southwest. The town was "the natural focus for the exchange of goods and services." But it also became the focus of political life: the welfare of merchants, bankers, and the urban work force depended upon prosperity in the respective hinterlands of their towns, and so urban leaders became the spokesmen in state politics for their local subregions. Development was regarded as a struggle— a race for the prizes of material growth—and the towns were the leading actors in it, especially when it came to statewide rivalries over patronage and distribution of the public largesse.[5]

In all the states of the Old Northwest, moreover, there was a high degree of participation in the affairs of government. This was partly a matter of institutions: the formal structure of local government

[4] Arthur L. Kohlmeier, *The Old Northwest as the Keystone of the Arch of American Federal Union* (Bloomington, 1938). See also Carter Goodrich, *Government Promotion of American Canals and Railroads, 1800–1890* (New York, 1960), pp. 134 ff.; Oscar and Mary Handlin, *The Dimensions of Liberty* (Cambridge, 1961), pp. 53 ff.

[5] Stanley Elkins and Eric McKitrick, "A Meaning for Turner's Frontier: Part I—Democracy in the Old Northwest," *Political Science Quarterly*, LXIX (September, 1954), 342. See also H. N. Scheiber, "Urban Rivalry and Internal Improvements in the Old Northwest, 1820–1860," in this volume, and Daniel J. Boorstin, *The Americans: The National Experience* (New York, 1965), pp. 113 ff.

required the services of many officials. But it was also a matter of "style" and a larger question of political behavior—for men felt they had a stake in what their governments did, and they had faith that their participation mattered. Such institutions and behavior were not unique, to be sure; they had become familiar enough in New England and in the British experience.[6] Yet this common element in their political life probably contributed to the sense of the people that they all shared something important—and notions of sharing bring us to regionalism as "a state of mind."

Well into the Civil War era, in the forum of national policy debate, the Senators and Representatives from the Old Northwest behaved as though the region had important common interests. On some issues they allied themselves with the South, on others with the Northeast; on some matters, of course, they split among themselves. But always they were conscious of their identity as spokesmen of the "free West"; they forged their *ad hoc* interregional coalitions in a manner calculated to promote what they regarded as their common regional interest; and when they failed to unite on a major question, they expressed concern about such division.[7] As early as 1820, one of the Congressmen from Ohio perceived "from the south & even from the east . . . a strong jealousy of the rising prosperity of the northwest." Similarly, Ohio's governor spoke of "the people N. W. of the River Ohio, whose strength is growing too mighty to be treated with contempt."[8] Modern historians have perceived that during the crisis of disunion in the 1840's and 1850's, the position of the Old Northwest was a pivotal factor in the struggle

[6] Elkins and McKitrick, "A Meaning for Turner's Frontier: Part II—The Southwest Frontier and New England," *Political Science Quarterly*, LXIX (December, 1954), 565 ff. See also Sumner Chilton Powell, *Puritan Village* (New York, 1965). The degree to which men dominant in the private sector of western communities held political office, and the consequences for power structure, are issues pursued in the case study by Robert O. Schulze, "The Role of Economic Dominants in Community Power Structure," *American Sociological Review*, LXIV (November, 1958), 251–261, reprinted in Lewis A. Coser (ed.), *Political Sociology* (New York, 1967).

[7] See Frederick Jackson Turner, *Rise of the New West, 1819–1829* (New York, 1962), pp. 160 ff.; and Curtis P. Nettels, "The Mississippi Valley and the Constitution, 1815–1829," *MVHR*, XI (December, 1924), 332–357.

[8] William A. Trimble to E. A. Brown, April 29, 1820, and reply, May 12, 1820, Ethan Allen Brown Papers, Ohio State Library and Ohio Historical Society.

for power between slavery and antislavery advocates. If such a view gives too much emphasis to a simple three-way North-West-South split, or if it exaggerates the homogeneity of the Old Northwest, still it must be recognized that the western leaders of the time were fully conscious of the possibility—many saw it as a moral necessity—of defining a regional interest and a regional position in the struggle.[9]

No less expressive of the regional ethos of the Old Northwest were political efforts to make the region autonomous economically. Even before 1810 there was a much-publicized movement to foster "home manufactures"—a planned development of manufacturing for local markets, with agriculture adjusting by producing raw materials for manufactures instead of only foodstuffs. "We must choose one of two alternatives," declared a typical spokesman for the movement, "either to be in a state of dependence, with foreign manufactures, or be independent, clothed in homespun, the products of our own labor."[10] From the standpoint of such parochial ambitions, the movement for internal improvements succeeded too well: for when new transportation facilities increased the profitability of commercial farming, as intended, the policy of home manufactures quickly was pushed into the background. But it was not long before the mercantile men and bankers who profited from such developments looked for new investment outlets: food processing industries appeared, and as capital accumulation went forward the other natural resources of the region—especially her mineral wealth—opened possibilities for heavy manufacturing. A few of the old industries, once protected by the barriers of high-cost transportation from outside competition, fell victim to the influx of eastern goods. But others served the rapidly expanding local farm markets for agricultural implements, stoves and ironware, glass, furniture, and lumber: exploiting the region's ample resource base, enjoying access to a relatively educated labor force, and aided by the railroad revolution of the 1850's, they

---

[9] Henry C. Hubbart, *The Older Middle West, 1840–1880* (New York, 1936). See also Frank L. Klement, "Middle Western Copperheadism," in this volume.

[10] Quoted in Alfred B. Sears, *Thomas Worthington, Father of Ohio Statehood* (Columbus, 1958), p. 213. On the early movement for home manufactures, which affected Kentucky no less than the Old Northwest states, see George Rogers Taylor, "Agrarian Discontent in the Mississippi Valley," in this volume; and E. M. Coulter, "The Genesis of Henry Clay's American System," *South Atlantic Quarterly*, XXV (1926), 45 ff.

made the Old Northwest a major manufacturing region of the
nation. Indeed, the new industrialism caused a dramatic con-
vergence of the West with the older East in economic structure.[11]

Yet men had not forgotten early hopes for regional economic
autonomy. Even while they sought capital from the East with which
to build factories, establish banks, and finance townsite speculations,
western entrepreneurs remained sensitive to "the importance of
keeping Eastern influence out of view" in such matters.[12] In western
common speech, the word "foreign" included the East; and "our
people," an Indiana politician wrote in the mid-1840's, "are
jealous of foreign and out-door influence."[13] This jealousy of their
economic independence led the western states to limit the branch-
banking activities of eastern financial institutions. Defending Ohio's
prohibition against establishment of a Bank of the United States
branch in Ohio, for instance, one prominent member of the legislature at Columbus asserted: "Yes, he was governed, in some degree,
by feelings of State pride. He would oppose the entrance of a foreign
foe, in whatever garb he might appear. He cared not whether he
was armed with the ordinary implements of death, or the seductive
and no less formidable weapon of monetary influence."[14]

The cultural leaders of the West shared fully this sense of identity
with the region. When one of Cincinnati's leading writers wrote in
1830 to a friend in Massachusetts, urging him to migrate and found
a western literary review in his city, he declared that the free West
was a place that stood apart: "The whole Union is looking with
interest to the West," he asserted. "Again, all the Western institutions are in a forming state. If you desire *influence*, here is your
place."[15] Three years earlier, another Cincinnati enthusiast for a
regional literature had announced that the time had come "when

[11] See editor's preface to Part VII, and notes, in this volume.

[12] Arthur Bronson to Lucius Lyon, September 7, 1833, Lucius Lyon Papers,
Clements Library, University of Michigan.

[13] C. J. Hammond to George Griswold, quoted in Charles L. Prentiss, *The Union
Theological Seminary* . . . (Asbury Park, N. J., 1899).

[14] William Medill, reported in Columbus *Ohio Statesman*, January 16, 1838. As
Frank L. Klement argues, in the article reprinted in this volume, such sentiments
persisted well into the 1860's and colored western politics in the Civil War era.

[15] Timothy Walker to George Bancroft, December 8, 1830, George Bancroft
Papers, Massachusetts Historical Society.

the political and moral claims of this great region, will be as well understood, and as promptly admitted, as its physical extent and resources are."[16] Again, there were ironies in such regional self-consciousness. For when western men of letters organized to promote their cultural creed, they built on familiar lines: as Merle Curti has written, "the rapid spread of agencies of intellectual life on the frontier was a reflection of the fact that on the whole Westerners were merely Easterners who had emigrated."[17] That they were more imitative than innovative, that they tried mainly to emulate eastern culture and institutions, is perhaps less important than the fact that the western regionalists in arts and letters considered the regional culture of the Old Northwest as something different from that of the East or the slave country south of the Ohio River.[18]

To say that the Old Northwest had a coherent identity in objective terms, and also a strong regional self-consciousness, is not to say that it was "unique" in all respects. Nor does it imply that its character and institutions reflected mainly the impact of the same environmental forces that conditioned development on all the American frontiers. Such caveats may appear commonplace; but still it seems worthwhile to state them explicitly, for confusion on these two points has long bedeviled historical writings on the Old Northwest.

On the matter of alleged uniqueness: some historians have argued that the frontier stage of development in the Old Northwest produced a "distinctive civilization."[19] At a simple level this is true enough, every community being unique. But it is the combination of characteristics and of developmental patterns that must interest the

[16] Timothy Flint (1827), quoted in Merle Curti, *The Growth of American Thought* (2d ed.; New York, 1951), p. 288.

[17] Curti, *Growth of American Thought*, p. 289. See also John T. Flanagan, *James Hall: Literary Pioneer of the Ohio Valley* (Minneapolis, 1941); and David Donald and F. E. Palmer, "Toward a Western Literature, 1820–1860," *MVHR*, XXXV (December, 1948), 416.

[18] It is hardly surprising that they should have viewed western culture as distinctive: so too did a host of foreign observers who wrote on the American scene in that period.

[19] For example, see Beverley W. Bond, Jr., *The Civilization of the Old Northwest, . . . 1788–1812* (New York, 1934).

historian. Attention to such patterns, as we have seen, indicates that in erecting cultural institutions the men of letters sought mainly to duplicate what was already familiar in the East. Similarly, the movement for home manufactures and regional economic autonomy had a vigorous (though short-lived and less influential) counterpart in the Old South. Even the West's political institutions and "style" reflected, in many essential respects, the patterns and combinations that had marked political development in older regions; in many ways, especially the interplay of local with national-party politics, the West was but an extension of established political behavior and forms. Thus we may find that "conservatism, inheritance, and continuity bulked at least as large . . . as radicalism and environment."[20]

The subject of the frontier influence is a more profound source of confusion than assertions of alleged uniqueness. In broad outline, the argument often accepted is that the Old Northwest may be viewed as one case among many of American frontier societies, all of which responded in the same way—at least in "basically" the same way—to identical environmental forces.

This persisting notion is the best known and least useful legacy of Frederick Jackson Turner, the founder of academic studies in American frontier history. In his famous 1893 essay on "The Significance of the Frontier in American History," and in most of his subsequent writings, Turner postulated that in each successive American frontier, from the seventeenth century to the 1890's, environmental forces evoked essentially the same patterns of social change, the same traits in men, the same kinds of institutional development. To be sure, Turner paid lip service to "the essential differences due to the place element and the time element" on frontiers separated spatially and temporally.[21] (Had he not recognized differences, he could not even have begun a logical exposition of sectionalism and its impact on American life, which became the

[20] Earl Pomeroy, "Toward a Reorientation of Western History: Continuity and Environment," *MVHR*, XLI (March, 1955), 581. See also Louis B. Wright, *Culture on the Moving Frontier* (Bloomington, Ind., 1955).

[21] Turner, *The Frontier in American History* (New York, 1920), pp. 9–10 *et passim*. See also the important critique by Robert Berkhofer, "Space, Time, Culture and the New Frontier," *Agricultural History*, XXXVIII (January, 1964), 21–30.

framework for some of his best historical studies.) And yet the essence of Turner's famous Frontier Thesis is his contention that successive frontier experiences—as America expanded—produced the democratic social order, the democratic styles of political behavior, and the distinctive national characteristics and traits that differentiated America from the Old World.

At "the outer margin of the settled area," Turner wrote, society had to grapple with the rude and naked forces of environment. There, the frontier transformed men, their psychology, their ideals, and their social relationships; the environment "called forth" a social order that he termed "the western democracy." This social order was more fluid and open than the society of older-settled regions; its men were idealistic, materialistic too, innovative and energetic, individualistic, optimistic, and restless. "Coarseness and strength combined with acuteness and acquisitiveness" marked the frontier man; extremes of "manly exertion" were required of him. But the frontier was also liberating: it provided "the chance for indefinite ascent in the scale of social advance." On each successive frontier, society experienced a "rebirth," and the result was the uniquely American culture and its political order.[22] Compared with these common products of successive frontier experiences, differences of place and time appear relatively unimportant in Turner's interpretation.

Also essential to Turner's interpretation is an alleged identity between frontier traits and national traits. In his view, this identity was forged, first of all, because each successive frontier "reacted on the East" by continually reminding men in the older-settled region of their "morning wishes"—the democratic ideals that had been evoked by environment in their own frontier period.[23] Moreover, frontiers offered havens for the dissatisfied and the restless; the West kept the nation as a whole "in touch with primitive conditions"; and with Andrew Jackson's election, "these Western forces of aggressive nationalism and democracy took possession of the government." Acting as a "gate of escape," what Turner called the "free lands" of the West meant that opportunity was always open. On the

[22] Turner, *Frontier in American History*, pp. 256, 37, 261. See also *ibid.*, pp. 68, 77, 107.

[23] *Ibid.*, pp. 301, 205.

frontier, then, there was always "an opportunity for a new order of things"—but the new order was in essential respects a duplicate of the order built in earlier frontiers.[24]

In addition, the identity between frontier and national traits came about because "long after the frontier period of a particular region . . . has passed away," its legacy leaves a permanent imprint on ensuing generations: "the conception of society, the ideals and aspirations which it produced, persist in the minds of the people." Because each frontier, from 1607 to the 1890's, contained "free land" —and because free land always "promoted individualism, economic equality, freedom to rise, democracy"—the succession of frontier experiences had a cumulative influence, reinforcing the same ideational, institutional, and psychological impacts in each instance.[25]

Only on the assumptions that frontier environment (including free land) always produced fundamentally the same kind of society, and that each frontier reinforced identical traits, differentiating American society and politics from Europe's, could Turner's thesis stand up. It was the similarity of development in successive Wests that "vitalized all American democracy" by reinvigorating and continually strengthening egalitarian, democratic traditions.

When Turner considered the Old Northwest, then, he treated it as one case among many in a long progression, from the seventeenth century to the 1890's, revealing the universal influence of frontier environment. Indeed, it was the region from which Turner drew most of his historical evidence for his theory that on the frontier "freedom of opportunity is opened, the cake of custom is broken, and new activities, new lines of growth, new institutions, and new ideals, are brought into existence."[26] Even though several generations of American historians have attacked Turner's postulates, some students

[24] *Ibid.*, pp. 259–261, 216.

[25] *Ibid.*, pp. 266, 259.

[26] *Ibid.*, p. 205. In a series of brilliant critical essays, George W. Pierson made it abundantly clear long ago that Turner slipped back and forth among various definitions of "the West" and of "frontier." But the statement here quoted, with all its normative implications, can be applied consistently, I think, to nearly all Turner's interpretations. See Pierson, "The Frontier and the Frontiersmen of Turner's Essays," *Pennsylvania Magazine of History and Biography*, Vol. LXIV (October, 1940); and "The Frontier and American Institutions," *New England Quarterly*, Vol. XV (June, 1942).

of the West today employ definitions of frontier impact that are no less value-laden than Turner's. For example, in Ray Allen Billington's recent reformulation of the Turner Thesis, he writes:

> The frontier as place . . . may be defined as a geographic region adjacent to the unsettled portions of the continent in which a low man-land ratio and unusually abundant, unexploited, natural resources provide an exceptional opportunity for social and economic betterment to the small-propertied individual.[27]

Such a definition of "frontier as place" will distort, I think, any attempts at analysis of the frontier impact on subsequent development of the Old Northwest, or indeed any other region, because important questions have been foreclosed by the definition itself. For instance, some frontier regions (or local subregions) were relatively *lacking* in natural resources; and in any case, where resources were abundant, the "opportunity for social and economic betterment" was a function of government resource-use policy, of the level of technology required to exploit resources, and of the structure of law as it favored capitalistic entrepreneurs as opposed to (say) workers. In theory, certainly, it is possible to conceive of frontier areas —"adjacent. to the unsettled portions of the continent"—that offered men *less* opportunity than did contemporaneous older-settled areas. And empirically, certainly in the history of the Old Northwest, there were periods when the region as a whole or localities within it did not conform by any means to the Billington formulation—nor to Turner's.[28]

[27] Ray Allen Billington, *America's Frontier Heritage* (New York, 1966), p. 25. Billington's book is a most provocative and illuminating reappraisal of the frontier hypothesis in light of contemporary studies in social science. For a summary of frontier historical scholarship at an earlier date, see Gene M. Gressley, "The Turner Thesis: A Problem in Historiography," *Agricultural History*, XXXII (October, 1958), 227–249.

[28] See, for instance, Paul W. Gates, "Frontier Landlords and Pioneer Tenants," *JISHS*, XXXVIII (June, 1945), 143–206; H. N. Scheiber, "State Policy and the Public Domain: The Ohio Canal Lands," *Journal of Economic History*, XXV (March, 1965), 86–113; and the article by Rudolf Freund, in this volume. A striking case study of frontier environment in interplay with forces impelling early growth of large-scale corporations and governing the institutional framework of early development is Rodman W. Paul, *Mining Frontiers of the Far West, 1848–1880* (New York, 1963).

For purposes of historical analysis, it seems preferable to strip the definition of frontier of all such value implications. Whether or not new communities were abundant in resources or offered exceptional opportunity are questions best treated as subjects for investigation, not as definitional postulates. In this context, the distinctive characteristic of the "frontier" is that it is *the site, bordering unsettled areas, in which new communities are founded.* This may be on the fringes of settlement, or it may be in a location widely separated from the metropolitan nation's main body of settlement, as with Oregon in the 1840's or Utah during the Mormon influx. Considered in these terms, the frontier environment becomes one variable among many, in a multi-variable analysis of social, political, and intellectual development. Furthermore, such a framework permits comparison of the community-building process in frontier locations with patterns of development on other frontiers separated by time and space; it permits, too, comparison of patterns of change between frontier communities and contemporaneous older-settled communities; and it also expedites isolation of the "fresh start"—the initial phase of community-building processes—for comparison with the social process in new communities (e.g., the mining towns built up in the East in the 1870's) that were *not* situated in a frontier setting.[29]

Instead of searching as Turner did in the history of the early Atlantic frontier for "the germs of processes repeated at each successive frontier," the historian is free to analyze the Old Northwest —or any other region in its frontier and post-frontier phases—as a case study in American community-building. Once having divorced from the definition of "frontier" such normative concepts as Turner and Billington introduce, the analysis need not be cast in terms of repetitive processes, continual reinforcement of identical impacts, and the like. Instead of insisting, as Turner did,[30] that the historian

[29] For an alternative view of fruitful redefinition of "frontier," stressing demographic and land-use aspects, see Willis F. Dunbar, "Frontiersmanship in Michigan," *Michigan History*, L (June, 1966), 97–110.

[30] Turner, *Frontier in American History*, p. 258. In chapter vii of his *People of Plenty: Economic Abundance and the American Character* (Chicago, 1954), David Potter argues brilliantly the importance of technology in determining opportunity on the frontier. Allan G. Bogue, "Social Theory and the Pioneer," *Agricultural History*, XXXIV (1960), 21–34, is a path-breaking behavioralist reappraisal of the Turner Thesis.

focus on the pioneer *as builder of "a new society"*—with different norms, different psychological traits "called out," different responses to environment, than were characteristic of life in older regions—the historian need only concern himself with the pioneer as *builder of new communities*. The impact of both the frontier environment and of the community-building process may then be treated as part of a larger complex of influences which—together with changing technology and communications, shifting economic and political relationships, and the like—operated to shape the subsequent course of regional development.

Each of the essays in this volume treats aspects of development in the Old Northwest, either in the frontier or post-frontier stages. Some of the selections are "Turnerian" in their concerns, concentrating upon manifestations of the impact of environment. Most of them are written entirely outside the framework Turner set out; that is, they do not concern themselves much with the "frontier heritage," yet they have an important bearing on the questions of community-building and of distinctive Old-Northwest regionalism. One essay—Arthur Bestor's—is explicitly critical of Turner. They all have in common, however, a concern for the central issues that must be treated by the student of western history undertaking systematic comparison of social process on various frontiers, and as between frontier and non-frontier communities.

The specific themes treated here range from received law and institutions in pre-statehood days to the origins of LaFollette-style progressivism. The coverage of topics is not comprehensive; rather, the essays have been selected mainly for the distinctiveness of their contributions to our understanding of community-building processes in general and in this particular western region. As such, they illuminate the larger question that Turner posed so brilliantly, whether properly "the West" may be viewed as a major integrating theme of American history.

H. N. S.

Acknowledgments

SINCERE appreciation is due individual authors and the editors and publishers of the publications from which essays in this volume are drawn. Their enthusiasm was no less important than their cooperation. Students in my seminars on the West at Dartmouth College played a major role in working out the themes of community-building and community development, discussed in the Preface and forming the conceptual framework for the collection. Finally, Bruce H. Nicoll of the University of Nebraska Press encouraged work on this book—cheerfully but never uncritically. He shared my hope that the volume would make conveniently available some of the interesting scholarly writings on the Old Northwest that have appeared in journals that are often relatively inaccessible to students and lay readers. My thanks go to those listed below for their permission to reprint the material specified.

H. N. S.

In Part One:
"Military Bounty Lands and the Origins of the Public Domain," by Rudolf Freund. Reprinted from *Agricultural History*, XX (January, 1946), 8–18, by permission of the Agricultural History Society.

"Agrarian Discontent in the Mississippi Valley Preceding the War of 1812," by George Rogers Taylor. Reprinted from the *Journal of Political Economy*, XXXIX, 471–505, by permission of the University of Chicago Press. Copyright 1931 by the University of Chicago Press.

In Part Two:
"Patent-Office Models of the Good Society: Some Relationships Between Social Reform and Westward Expansion," by Arthur E. Bestor, Jr. Reprinted from *The American Historical Review*, LVIII,

No. 3 (April, 1953), 505–526, by permission of the author and the American Historical Association.

"Social Relationships in Trempealeau County," by Merle Curti. Reprinted from *The Making of an American Community: A Case Study of Democracy in a Frontier County*, by Merle Curti, with the permission of the publishers, Stanford University Press. Copyright © 1959 by the Board of Trustees of the Leland Stanford Junior University.

"Disease and Sickness on the Wisconsin Frontier: Cholera," by Peter T. Harstad. Reprinted with permission from the *Wisconsin Magazine of History*, XLIII (Spring, 1960), 203–220.

In Part Three:

"Farming in the Prairie Peninsula, 1830–1890," by Allan G. Bogue. Reprinted with permission from *The Journal of Economic History*, XXIII, No. 1 (March, 1963), 3–29.

"The Dairy Industry in Ohio Prior to the Civil War," by Robert Leslie Jones. Reprinted from the *Ohio Archaeological and Historical Quarterly*, LVI (1947), 46–69, by permission of the Ohio Historical Society.

In Part Four:

"Urban Life in Western America, 1790–1830," by Richard C. Wade. Reprinted from the *American Historical Review*, LXIV (1959), 14–30, by permission of the author and the American Historical Association.

"Urban Rivalry and Internal Improvements, 1820–1860," by Harry N. Scheiber. Reprinted from *Ohio History*, LXXI, No. 3 (October, 1962), 227–239, by permission of the Ohio Historical Society.

In Part Five:

"Who Were the Lumberjacks?" by George B. Engberg. Reprinted from *Michigan History*, XXXIII (1948), 238–246, by permission of the Michigan Department of State: Historical Commission Section.

"Restless Grant County: Americans on the Move," by Peter J. Coleman. Reprinted with permission from the *Wisconsin Magazine of History*, XLVI (1962), 16–20.

In Part Six:

"The Antislavery Movement in Illinois: 1824–1835," by Merton Lynn Dillon. Reprinted with permission from the *Journal of the Illinois State Historical Society*, XLVII (1954), 149–166.

"Agrarian Radicalism in Illinois' Constitutional Convention of 1862," by Stanley L. Jones. Reprinted with permission from the *Journal of the Illinois State Historical Society*, XLVIII (1955), 271–282.

"Middle Western Copperheadism and the Genesis of the Granger Movement," by Frank L. Klement. Reprinted from the *Mississippi Valley Historical Review*, XXXVIII (March, 1952), 679–694, by permission of the Organization of American Historians.

"The Origin and Early Development of the Wisconsin Idea," by Vernon Carstensen. Reprinted with permission from the *Wisconsin Magazine of History*, XXXIX (1956), 181–188.

In Part Seven:

"The Workers' Search for Power: Labor in the Gilded Age," by Herbert G. Gutman. Reprinted by permission from *The Gilded Age*, edited by H. Wayne Morgan. Copyright © 1963 by Syracuse University Press, Syracuse, New York. All rights reserved.

Contents

V. The People—Moving

VI. Government and Politics

VII. The Tensions of Industrialization

I
PIONEER PERIOD: EARLY INSTITUTIONS
AND PROBLEMS

Part I
Pioneer Period: Early Institutions and Problems

IT was a central theme in Frederick Jackson Turner's writings that the West kept alive America's "morning wishes." The democracy, the egalitarianism, and the vitality of successive frontier societies continually reminded Americans in older-settled areas of the ideals that frontier environment had "called forth" in their own pioneering days.[1] As we have noted already, if one discards the notion that all frontier regions had the same egalitarian, democratizing effects on the communities that settled them—and also the same effects on older-settled areas of the nation—then this idea loses its logical force. But surely there was some causal connection between the history of community-building in successive Wests and popular thought in the United States on such problems as democracy and social equality. Arthur Bestor has suggested a new approach to this connection: he argues that the very fact that new communities were being founded in frontier areas, in the nineteenth century, lent plausibility to the view (common among reformers) that "human choice could play its part in determining the character of the small beginnings from which great institutions would in future" develop. Thus Bestor quotes Lincoln, who declared that "in our new free territories, a state of nature *does* exist," and he cites Lincoln's belief that the political and social institutions that Congress mandated in the territories would be vitally important in determining the kind of society that would emerge in those regions as settlement poured in.[2]

Perhaps at no time in the history of the nation was this feeling, that the future of a continent and its society was being determined

---

[1] Turner, *The Frontier in American History* (New York, 1920), p. 301; the theme is elaborated in *ibid.*, pp. 214, 259–264.

[2] Arthur E. Bestor, Jr., "Patent-Office Models of the Good Society," in this volume.

by policy decisions affecting the territories, so strong as when Congress debated the problems of land disposal and governance for the Old Northwest in the 1780's. In the first of the following essays, Rudolph Freund, who until his death was an economist at the University of Virginia, argues that pressure from disaffected Revolutionary Army officers was one of the major political forces that conditioned contemporary thought and policy-making affecting the Old Northwest. As he makes clear, land hunger, political ideology, and new concepts of nation-building all must be examined in any effort to explain the policies that were finally written into law. And indeed subsequent history proved that such decisions as those to sell the public lands on terms progressively more attractive to small-scale settlers, to grant a high degree of self-government at a relatively early period in development, and to ban slavery, all did contribute in vital ways to the framework in which western community-building went forward. Members of the Continental Congress who treated these issues as though they held in their power much of the region's future proved not far wrong in their assessment of how important their decisions would be.[3]

George Rogers Taylor's essay draws our attention to some of the economic factors that conditioned early western development, to some extent independently of conscious policy-making by Congress and the early settlers themselves. Professor Taylor, an eminent economic historian, provides a cogent analysis of the marketing and transportation problems of the early West.[4] He treats the settlements of the Old Northwest as part of the larger Mississippi Valley (or

[3] Francis S. Philbrick, *The Rise of the West, 1754–1830* ("The New American Nation Series," ed. H. S. Commager and R. B. Morris [New York, 1965]), pp. 104–133; see also Staughton Lynd, "The Compromise of 1787," *Political Science Quarterly*, Vol. LXXXI (June, 1966), an article that stresses contemporary assumptions of northern and southern Congressmen concerning the future course of development in the Ohio country. Robert F. Berkhofer, Jr., of the University of Minnesota, has in progress a full revaluation of the Northwest Ordinance of 1787.

[4] Professor Taylor is professor emeritus at Amherst College and presently a senior research associate of the Eleutherian Mills-Hagley Foundation. His *Transportation Revolution, 1815–1860* ("The Economic History of the United States," ed. Henry David *et al.*, Vol. IV [New York, 1951]), treats the post-1815 development of transportation as it affected interregional relationships, and gives full attention to the Old Northwest.

trans-Appalachian) community of the pre-1812 period; but he also provides important evidence of the emergent differentiation of the western and southern economies, and of the differential impact of price changes on the regions north and south of the Ohio River. It is today a matter of lively dispute among historians whether Taylor was correct in ascribing so much weight to economic conditions in the region as a factor governing the western response to war issues.[5] But whatever the resolution of that particular controversy, his article remains—more than thirty years after its initial publication—one of the most vivid, systematic available analyses of the early western economy and its problems.[6]

[5] See Roger Hamilton Brown, *The Republic in Peril: 1812* (New York, 1964); and Reginald Horsman, *The Causes of the War of 1812* (Philadelphia, 1962).

[6] Charles Ambler, *A History of Transportation in the Ohio Valley* (Glendale, Calif., 1942); and L. D. Baldwin, *The Keelboat Age on Western Waters* (Pittsburgh, 1941), treat the flatboat trade in detail.

RUDOLF FREUND

1. Military Bounty Lands and the Origins of the Public Domain

THE bounty-land policy of the Revolutionary War has often been criticized on two accounts.[1] Historians seem to agree that the measures adopted did not serve their primary purpose of establishing deserving and needy veterans on farms of their own. Almost 20 years of peace went by before the first titles to bounty lands could be conveyed, and during this long delay most of the land warrants had found their way into the hands of speculators and land scouts. Only those veterans who could afford to wait or had pooled their claims were able to reap at least some of the intended benefits. Regarding its second objective, namely an orderly advance of settlement into the new western lands, the military bounty land policy of the United States is held to have failed just as signally. The insistent demands of old veterans and their heirs and assignees forced practically every administration between 1812 and 1862 to relax the stipulations and extend the date lines for the establishment of military claims. The central land office continued to honor these claims up to the end of the nineteenth century in considerable numbers. By that time, between 70 and 100 million acres had been assigned for army warrants of the Revolutionary war and that of 1812 alone, largely on the basis of laws passed as late as 1847 and 1855. If the total of "All Land in Farms" within the four "central" State groups as given in the Census of 1900 is fairly indicative of the farm acreage occupied during the previous hundred years of westward expansion, the military bounty lands alone comprise one-seventh to one-sixth of this acreage.[2] All these lands were acquired, of course, by the bounty claimants without cost.

[1] This article is a reduction of a paper presented at the joint meeting of the Agricultural History Society with the American Historical Association at Chicago on December 28, 1944.

[2] The land-bounty policy of the Revolutionary War is treated in a general way

The incipient stages in the development of this system are said to have had the effect of accustoming the people to "the idea of the government giving away public land."[3] This statement bespeaks the widely held opinion that the westward movement was caused by economic and social forces of overwhelming strength. Consequently, laws and administrative acts are accorded only secondary importance; they must either suit the interests of the pioneer, or be abandoned, or rendered ineffective in some other way. Bounty-land legislation may be viewed as an instance where the original purpose of rewarding the veteran for his services was transformed gradually and unwittingly into a means for helping the people of the frontier to achieve their goal of "free land."

It may be doubted, however, whether this interpretation does not oversimplify the matter. Although the bounty-land policy failed to achieve its intended purposes, nevertheless it contributed to a really remarkable degree toward setting the patterns and erecting the signposts for at least the earlier stages of the westward movement. The cession of western lands, the rules governing the administration of the Northwest Territory and its lands, the preferment of the survey principle over indiscriminate location, and last but not least the first settlements on the Ohio River are cases in point. Furthermore, the question may be raised whether the final stages of the westward movement permit a proper perspective concerning legislation which was forged in the crucible of a fateful war and its hardly less fateful aftermath. Are we to believe that the framers of these laws failed to appraise properly the character and the strength of the forces destined to push open the gate to the promised lands of the west? Did they try to impede these forces by virtue of a narrow and "eastern" conception of the future? And can the colorful and

in Payson Jackson Treat, *The National Land System, 1785–1820* (New York, 1910), pp. 232–246, 260–262; Benjamin H. Hibbard, *A History of the Public Land Policies* (New York, 1924), pp. 117–118, 126–129; and Thomas Donaldson, *The Public Domain* (Washington, 1884), pp. 232–234. The only exhaustive and penetrating study is that of William Thomas Hutchinson, "The Bounty Lands of the Revolution in Ohio" (Unpublished Ph.D. dissertation, University of Chicago, June, 1927). It is deeply to be regretted that this work is not available in print. The author had access to it only after most of his own research was completed.

[3] Amelia C. Ford, *Colonial Precedents of Our National Land System as It Existed in 1800* (Madison, 1910), p. 108.

fascinating interplay of personalities, ideas, and events which marked the incipient steps of the land policy of the United States be accorded its proper weight when viewed as but an awkward prelude to the grandiose spectacle of the westward movement?

The recent war [World War II] and victory have made all Americans conscious of the grave problem of the returning veteran. It is easier for us, therefore, than for peacetime generations to understand the anxiety felt by the Founding Fathers and their helpers on this account. But a still more vexing problem which has no present-day counterpart confronted them and called for immediate solution. Independence had thrown into the lap of a none-too-perfect union the vast and unsettled area between the Great Lakes and the Mississippi and Ohio rivers. It was but natural that the deserving and needy soldiers should expect to receive land in this region. But this prospect was by no means the only stake which the veteran hoped to have in the opening of the west. In the newly won territory, a novel type of colonial government and administration was to be established, in which the veterans, and especially the officers, claimed their due share. Some of them, chiefly from New England, held decided opinions as to the principles which they wished to see incorporated in the new western set-up for their own benefit and that of a strong federal union. Their views were certain to be challenged by Southerners, though adherence to either camp was not necessarily determined by regional interests and outlooks alone. However, some of the basic issues involved in the future administration and land policies of the new west had been tackled, and in part decided, long before the war ended. An early promise of the Continental Congress to the rank and file of its army brought them to a head.

Curiously enough, land was first promised by Congress, in August 1776, to Hessians and other foreigners if they would desert from the English army, but nothing much came of it.[4] The story of the military bounty lands really began somewhat later when

---

[4] Worthington C. Ford (ed.), *Journals of the Continental Congress, 1774–1789* (34 vols.; Washington, 1904-1937), V, 653–655. Hereafter cited as *Journals*. Benjamin Franklin to Thomas McKean, August 24, 1776, and to Horatio Gates, August 28, 1776, in Edmund C. Burnett (ed.), *Letters of Members of the Continental Congress* (8 vols.; Washington, 1921-1936), II, 59–60, 63. Hereafter cited as *Letters*.

Congress decided to offer land to its own nationals as an inducement for enlisting in the new army and for permanent service. The ill-fated summer campaigns of 1776 made it depressingly clear to everybody concerned that the war could not be waged successfully unless the militia was replaced, at least for the purposes of sustained warfare, by an army of regulars who were willing to serve without interruption until victory was won. This was a radical departure from previous practices, and it was clear that substantial rewards had to be offered to achieve the change from temporary to permanent enlistment. Therefore, when Congress decided in September 1776 to establish 88 regiments on State lines to serve during the war, the former money bounty of $20 was augmented by promises of land, ranging from 100 acres for a private to 500 acres for a colonel. The land was to be provided by the United States, and the expenses connected therewith were to be borne by the States in the same proportion as the other expenses of the war.[5]

These resolutions had been contested hotly in Congress before they were passed, but their execution caused still greater concern. The New England States believed that the land bonus was not sufficient to overcome the aversion to enlistment; civilians and soldiers complained, it was said, of the long engagement as a contract of servitude. These States wanted, therefore, to raise the money bounty, especially for privates, and passed acts to this effect in their assemblies.[6] Maryland protested that it had no land of its own and thought that it would have to buy land for bounties from other States. Its council of safety proposed to raise the money bounty to the Maryland line by $10 instead of offering land. This caused consternation in the Continental Congress where it was feared that this precedent might break the back of all North America. Maryland was officially assured that it would not have to make good the

[5] Resolution of September 16, 1776, in *Journals*, V, 762–763. For an appraisal of the military events leading to these steps, see especially the circular letter of the President of Congress (John Hancock) to the New Hampshire Assembly, September 24, 1776, in *Letters*, II, 98–100; and the special plea for the land bounty in the letter of Washington, September 2, 1776, to the President of Congress, in Peter Force (ed.), *American Archives, Series 5* (Washington, 1851), II, 120–121.

[6] William Hooper to the President of the North Carolina Convention, November 16, 1776, in *Letters*, II, 154–155. See also the letters of John Adams, William Williams, and Josiah Bartlett, in *ibid.*, pp. 57, 61, 85, 89.

bounty grants in its individual capacity because it was the intention
of Congress to provide the bounty lands at the expense of the United
States. But Maryland would not recant; and in order to mollify it
as well as the New England States, Congress finally permitted enlistment for 3 years under the money bounty system and reserved
the land bounty to those soldiers and officers who signed up for the
full duration of the war or until they were honorably discharged.[7]

Maryland's decided stand against the land bounty was by no
means motivated by petty considerations; this State made it
abundantly clear that much larger issues were involved. To an
earlier suggestion that land might be bought for $3 per hundred,
Maryland's delegates had replied "that an Expectation was formed
by the People of our State that what was conquered from an Enemy
at the joint Expence of Blood and Treasure of the whole should
become their joint property but as Claims had been set up opposite
to our Ideas of natural Justice it became a wise people rather to
prepare for the worst by giving ten Dollars now than trust to the
mercy of a few Venders from whom they would be obliged to
purchase . . . at any price, the Case of all Monopolies . . . ." And
shortly after the compromise of a 3-year alternative enlistment had
been reached, Maryland urged Congress not to close the door on its
request "that the back lands acquired from the Crown of *Great
Britain* in the present war, should be a common stock for the benefit
of the *United States*. . . ."[8]

Though this motion was not carried, the long struggle over the
cession of western lands had commenced. While it lasted, Maryland's
and even more so Virginia's moves were largely motivated and
conditioned by the bounty-land question. In order to "remove the
ostensible cause" of Maryland's anxiety to share in the common
property of the western lands and its subsequent refusal to join the

---

[7] Resolutions of Congress, October 30 and November 12, 1776, in *Journals*,
VI, 912–913, 145. New Jersey and Delaware soon fell in line with Maryland for the
same reasons. (*Letters*, III, 450.)

[8] See Benjamin Rumsey's letter to James Tilghman, October 24, 1776, in
Letters, II, 140 n.; Sam'l Chase's letter to the Council of Safety of Maryland,
in *American Archives*, *Series 5*, III, 787–788. As to the suggestion that Maryland
should buy land, presumably from Virginia, see Jefferson to Edmund Pendleton,
August 13, 1776, in *Letters*, II, 48; and the excerpt of a letter from Pendleton to
James Madison, in *Journals*, V, 505 n.

Confederation, the Virginia Assembly offered in December 1779 "to furnish lands out of their territory on the north west side of the Ohio river, without purchase money, to the troops on continental establishment of such of the confederated states as had not unappropriated lands for that purpose. . . ."[9] This offer hardly substantiates Maryland's suspicion of the grasping ambition of its big neighbor. Regardless of whether Virginia's generosity or Maryland's insistence can rightly be called the keystone of the Confederation, there is little doubt that the bounty resolutions of Congress in 1776 must be credited with having inaugurated the train of events which eventually led to perpetual union.[10]

Virginia's "Remonstrance" was only the first step toward actual cession. In the long haggling over the terms under which Virginia was to renounce its claims to the territory across the Ohio River, the bounty lands proved one of the main stumbling blocks. Holding immense tracts of unappropriated land, Virginia had very soon adopted the idea suggested by Congress of granting land bounties to its officers and soldiers, both on the State and continental establishment. And being more able to do so, Virginia was more liberal than Congress with grants. By October 1779, all its officers had been granted ten times, noncoms four times, and privates two times as much land as Congress had stipulated; a year later all

[9] William W. Hening, *The Statutes-at-Large, Being a Collection of All the Laws of Virginia*, X (Richmond, 1822), 559. Hereafter cited as Hening, *Statutes*. The word "ostensible" is italicized in the original, the less ostensible causes of Maryland's stand being, in the opinion of the Virginia Assembly, its backing of the land claims of several big land companies. For the part played by the land question in the Virginia Assembly in 1778–1779, see Kate Mason Rowland, *The Life of George Mason, 1752–1792* (New York, 1892), I, 320–329, 340–344, 359–367. Also, Thomas Perkins Abernethy, *Western Lands and the American Revolution* (New York, 1937), 242–247; and Shaw Livermore, *Early American Land Companies* (New York, 1939), 109–110. [EDITOR'S NOTE: See also Merrill Jensen, *The Articles of Confederation* (Madison, 1940), pp. 211–224.]

[10] Herbert Baxter Adams, *Maryland's Influence upon Land Cessions to the United States* (Baltimore, 1885), pp. 22–40, where the "ostensible cause" is also discussed. Hutchinson, "The Bounty Lands," p. 21, says that the very important consequences of Maryland's stand have often been emphasized but that its inception of the resistance to the Military Bounty Act of 1776 seems to have been overlooked. Treat, *National Land System*, p. 234, and Adams, *Maryland's Influence*, p. 48, hint at this connection without, however, developing its importance.

bounties were increased by one-third, and new ones were added for generals (following congressional precedent); and in 1782 further increases and bounties for 3-year enlistments were granted. George Rogers Clark and his men had been promised lands in the trans-Ohio region that they were to wrest from the English. Finally, a land office created at Richmond in 1779 was charged with the administration and execution of military bounty warrants and of all other claims pertaining to the unappropriated lands of the State. This step had been greatly resented by Maryland and the other landless States because any definite arrangements made by Virginia might render it still more difficult to obtain its consent to the cession of the northwestern territory under reasonable terms.[11]

Most important of all, as early as December 1778, Virginia had set aside an extensive tract in western Kentucky from which to supply its line officers and soldiers with land.[12] This military reserve became the source of many vexations. When the boundary between Virginia and North Carolina was extended, part of this district fell south of the line. In its final cession offer on January 2, 1781, Virginia stipulated, therefore, that in case the quantity of good lands which it had reserved southeast of the Ohio River proved insufficient, the deficiency should be made up in good lands to be laid off between the Scioto and Little Miami rivers northwest of the Ohio. Even after this clause and the cession had been accepted on March 1, 1784, Congress delayed final action in the matter, until Virginia could prove that its supply of "good land" southeast of the Ohio had really been exhausted. The Senate and the House finally settled the matter by an act of August 10, 1790; the first titles to land in the Military Reserve of Virginia northwest of the Ohio were conveyed in 1791, almost 8 years after peace had been declared and more than 6 years after Virginia had ceded its northwestern territories.[13]

[11] For the bounty laws, see Hening, *Statutes*, X, 24, 27, 160, 331, 375; *ibid.*, XI, 559–565. On Clark, see *ibid.*, X, 26; and Rowland, *George Mason*, I, 290, for the first land promise to Clark. On the land office, see Hening, *Statutes*, X, 50–65; and Abernethy, *Western Lands*, pp. 217–229.

[12] Hening, *Statutes*, X, 55 n.; Rowland, *George Mason*, I, 310.

[13] For Virginia's offer, see Hening, *Statutes*, X, 564–566. Hening claims that the term "Virginia" troops included all troops, both on continental and Virginia's own establishment. For Virginia's cession and the opening of the Virginia Military Reserve to Virginia claimants, see Clarence E. Carter, compiler and editor, *The*

In the protracted struggle over Virginia's claims to bounty lands across the Ohio River, two major issues were involved. The first related to the methods of locating warrants. According to the Land Ordinance of 1785, the lands of the Northwest Territory had to be surveyed and subdivided into rectangular townships and sections before warrants could be located and titles conveyed. An exception was the Virginia Military Reserve,[14] because it was to be settled under Virginia laws which allowed the warrant holder to locate his land himself and to have it surveyed afterward in any shape he and the surveyor thought suitable. Under this practice, good lands, especially the river bottoms, were taken up rapidly. Newcomers pushed farther and farther into the wilderness in search of good lands without bothering about the nearer but second-rate stretches. Thus, new regions quickly became dotted with widely scattered and often unconnected settlements. Determined to give its soldiers the full advantages of "indiscriminate location," Virginia needed large areas in order to satisfy them. This explains why Virginia insisted on making "good land" the measure of its claims to large tracts on both sides of the Ohio and why it grew impatient over the long delay in admitting claimants to its reserve northwest of the river.

In these clashes the ever-present conflict between the North and the South played an important part, though mostly behind the scenes. The Land Ordinance of 1785, just as the famed Ordinance of 1787 for the northwestern territory, was widely hailed as a victory for the decided preference of New Englanders for compact settlement and rectangular surveys. Certain groups of New England officers took the lead in the settlement and administration of the new territory, largely through the Ohio Company. These men feared that the Virginians and their ways would prove a disturbing element once they took up lands in the reserve under the laws of their Mother State. The settlers who eventually entered the Virginia Reserve from the south quickly succeeded in taking up the best lands and soon began to play their full and vigorous part in the political life of the territory and the ascendancy of Ohio to

Territorial Papers of the United States, II (Washington, 1934), 296–298. Hereafter cited as *Territorial Papers*. For the documents relating to the "good land" issue, see *American State Papers: Lands*, I (Washington, 1834), 1–3, 12–13, 17.

[14] *Territorial Papers*, II, 18.

statehood.[15] However, the veterans of the Revolutionary War had a comparatively small share in all this because many of them had tired of the long delay and sold their claims to enterprising Easterners who in time did a thriving business in locating and selling Ohio lands.

Only a few days after the terms of the preliminary peace had been ratified, a shrewd observer in Congress wrote to an eminent officer: "Our circumstances afford an odd Contrast to those we have heretofore experienced. The Difficulty which heretofore oppres'd us was how to raise an Army. The one which now embarrasses is how to dissolve it."[16] Two months later, mutinous soldiers forced Congress to flee from Philadelphia to Princeton. In this open revolt, the officers had not taken part, but they too were discontented and irritable. They hesitated to resort to desperate means, at least as long as there was hope that Congress would act in their favor. In December 1782 they had presented the last of a long list of memorials to that body. This petition demanded the prompt settlement of arrearages and the commutation of half pay for life, promised in 1780, into a lump sum of money to be paid on discharge. Congress had sent a committee to investigate, but having no resources of its own it could only recommend speedy action to the States; but they were slow in adopting appropriate measures. Deeply disturbed by rumors of the approaching peace, even the officers' restraint threatened to give way to open rebellion.

Matters came to a head in early March 1783 at Newburgh. An anonymous officer addressed his comrades in these incendiary terms: ". . . while the swords you wear are necessary for the defence of America, what have you to expect from peace, when your voice shall sink, and your strength dissipate by division? . . . . Can you then consent to be the only sufferers by this revolution, and retiring from the field, grow old in poverty, wretchedness and contempt?. . . . If you can—GO—and carry with you the jest of Tories, and the scorn of Whigs—the ridicule, and what is worse, the pity of the

[15] The literature and source material pertaining to the early phases of political life in the Northwest Territory is too extensive to be cited here. For two excellent and comprehensive treatments with copious references, see Beverley W. Bond, Jr., *The Civilization of the Old Northwest* (New York, 1934); and Bond, *The Foundations of Ohio* ("The History of the State of Ohio," ed. Carl Wittke, Vol. I [Columbus, 1941]).

[16] Richard Peters to Baron Steuben, April 23, 1783, in *Letters*, VII, 150.

world. Go, starve, and be forgotten!" And then followed a dire threat: ". . . the slightest mark of indignity from Congress now, must operate like the grave, and part you [and Congress] forever: that in any political event, the army has its alternative. If peace, that nothing shall separate you from your arms but death: if war, that . . . you will retire to some unsettled country, smile in your turn, and 'mock when their fear cometh on.'"

Here indeed were the seeds of a serious revolt. The officers were exhorted not to lay down their arms until Congress granted their demands; and if Congress refused an exodus into the western lands was to be the ultimate answer. No doubt, the addresses made a deep impression upon the officers of the cantonment. But at a meeting of their delegates Washington himself unexpectedly appeared. In a speech which moved some of his hearers to tears he reiterated his belief that Congress, though moving slowly, would eventually do full justice to the wishes of the army. He then solemnly pledged his own support in every way which was consistent with his duty to his country. This appeal dissuaded the officers from their dangerous course and set them once more upon the road to orderly appeal, strongly seconded by their commander in chief.[17]

Congress acted quickly and agreed to commute the promise of half pay for life into a sum in gross amounting to 5 years' full pay in money or securities such as those given to the other creditors of the United States. By virtue of this last clause which shows Alexander Hamilton's hand in drawing up the resolutions, the money and pension claims of the army would be treated in exactly the same way as the claims of any other creditor upon the exchequer of the United States. One month later, the proceeds from special imposts on foreign liquors, sugar, etc., a general duty of 5 percent on imports, and contributions from the States were assigned to the service of the total public debt; it is significant that a proposal to appropriate the 5-percent duty to the army claims alone was not adopted at the time. Neither were any provisions made to satisfy the land bounties, the

[17] For the Newburgh addresses, see *Journals*, XXIV, 291–311. See also Louis C. Hatch, *The Administration of the American Revolutionary Army* (New York, 1904), pp. 142–181, 198–199. Octavius Pickering, *The Life of Timothy Pickering* (Boston, 1867), I, 406–429, contains correspondence concerning John Armstrong's authorship of the addresses. Hereafter cited as *Pickering*.

obvious reason being that the cessions of western lands had not been completed. Their consummation was urged in order to hasten the extinguishment of the debts.[18]

Indeed, the officers themselves had not asked Congress to attend to the land-bounty matter; they had concentrated on obtaining the commutation of their pensions into hard cash. The seeds of the Newburgh addresses were to ripen in this respect also. The appeal to migrate to the west and begin a new semimilitary life there had not fallen on deaf ears, for this idea had been talked about previously,[19] and its combination with the bounty-land question produced a move which was destined to have far reaching, if slowly maturing, consequences. Soon after the Newburgh incident, two of the main actors on the scene, Quartermaster Timothy Pickering and Brigadier General Rufus Putnam, together with Brigadier General Jedediah Huntington, were hard at work trying to turn the insidious counsel of the "fellow soldier" into a positive scheme which would utilize the promised bounty lands and other land grants for the establishment of a new state for veterans on the Ohio. By April 1783, elaborate propositions for the settling of such a commonwealth were drawn up for the benefit of those officers and men who were willing to join an association to be founded for the purpose. These propositions called for concerted action along the following lines: purchase by the United States of a tract corresponding roughly to the present State of Ohio; prompt assignment of the bounty lands promised by Congress during the war; grants of additional and larger tracts but with the same scaling as the bounty lands to actual settlers in the purchased district; payment of the initial expenses of settlement and subsistence for 3 years from arrearages due to the members of the association; the preparation of a constitution previous to going west which would exclude slavery; and prompt admittance of this state to the Confederation.[20]

This ambitious plan drew from the supposed author of the

[18] *Journals*, XXIV, 257–261.

[19] *Pickering*, I, 456–461, 546–549. The merits of the Ohio country as a military refuge had been discussed by Washington and his officers during the war. See William P. Cutler and Julia P. Cutler, *Life, Journals, and Correspondence of Rev. Manasseh Cutler* (Cincinnati, 1888), I, 141–144. Hereafter cited as *Cutler*.

[20] *Pickering*, I, 546–549; *Cutler*, I, 149, 156–159.

Newburgh addresses the caustic remark: ". . . this quixotic idea. It originates with men who wish only to amuse and divert the army from the consideration of more important concerns. They ask, what can not be granted. 'Tis absurd."[21] Whatever sentiments John Armstrong harbored, he was right. Pickering and Putnam had simply proposed that the United States should purchase the tract for the new state from the natives, thereby ignoring, probably intentionally, the thorny problem of the cession of Virginia's northwestern claims. For this and perhaps other reasons, the final petition, signed in June 1783 by almost three hundred officers from New England, merely asked Congress to "assign and mark it out as a Tract or Territory suitable to form a distinct Government (or Colony of the United States) in time to be admitted" to the Confederation and to make provisions for the location and survey of the bounty lands promised.[22]

The petition was sent properly to the commander in chief first, accompanied by a lengthy letter from Putnam. The rugged soldier and pioneer stressed the paramount importance of the Ohio River region as a bastion against England and Spain and the necessity of securing the frontier by a string of forts in order to keep the Indians in check. He then proceeded to voice the expectations of the officers which had been deemed improper to mention in the petition. His comrades, Putnam explained, did not expect to be under any obligation to settle on the bounty lands; if, however, Congress made further and larger grants of land, many were determined to become actual settlers on the Ohio. Putnam went on to emphasize that at least some of the officers held rather decided views as to the manner in which these new lands should be distributed and administered. They were, he declared, much opposed to monopoly and wished to guard against large patents granted to individuals; they hoped, therefore, that no grants would be made except by townships 6 miles square (or multiples), to be subdivided by the proprietor associates themselves and administered after the pattern of a New England town. This township principle was also to apply to private purchasers of land in the region.

[21] John Armstrong to Horatio Gates, April 22, 1783, in *Letters*, VII, 150 n.
[22] *Cutler*, I, 159–160. This document has often been regarded as the first step leading to the founding of the New England Ohio Company.

Washington forwarded the petition and Putnam's letter to
Congress on June 17, 1783, and he himself urged the speedy adoption of the army plan, because its execution would connect the
government with the frontier, extend settlements progressively, and
plant in the new lands a brave, hardy, and respectable race of
people always willing to combat the savages. Despite this endorse-
ment, no action was taken on the proposal by Congress either then
or later. During the turbulent days of the insurrection of the
Pennsylvania troops, Congress referred the petition to a standing
committee, had it read in Congress a week later, and referred back
to another special committee which was discharged on October 15,
1783. Upon a pressing inquiry from Putnam, more than a year later,
Washington blamed the "want of cession of the land to act upon"
as the chief reason for the delay. He was vaguely hopeful that something might be done yet, because the Virginia cession had been
accepted, but the plan was never revived in its original form.[23]

Manifestly, it was futile to expect action from Congress in the
matter of the bounty lands as long as the squabble over the cessions
and their execution lasted. Moreover, Putnam and his comrades had
encumbered their plans with political aspirations of pronounced
character the open discussion of which would certainly upset the
delicate balance of a none-too-perfect union. However, they did
plant the proverbial mustard seed when they urged their fellow
officers and land claimants to form a voluntary association with the
characteristics of a corporate body. True, the idea of a pioneering
land corporation was neither new nor without precedent.[24] But
only the critical times of the 1780s had engendered strong enough
group sentiments to keep this basic feature of the army plan alive,
when all other proposals had to be given up. Eight years of war and
camp life had rendered many officers unfit for the old ways of life;
they were impoverished and despaired of ever again succeeding in
living up to the civilian Joneses. On the other hand, the long com-

[23] Correspondence in *Cutler*, I, 167–177. For the action in Congress, see
Journals, XXIV, 421 n. The Grand Committee mentioned had been appointed on
May 30, 1783, "to consider of the best manner of carrying into execution the
engagements of the United States for certain allowances of land to the Army at the
conclusion of the war." (*Journals*, XXIV, 376.)

[24] See introduction by Albert C. Bates, in *The Two Putnams, Israel and Rufus*
(Hartford, Conn., 1931); Livermore, *Early Land Companies*, pp. 97–102.

radeship in arms had imbued many officers with an esprit de corps which persisted and proved of great psychological value in the troubled times of war and peace alike.

Finally, many believed that the western lands were the destined proving ground for the political principles of independence, self-government, and personal liberty for which the war had been fought. Thus, the lands on the Ohio beckoned with the lure of still another Utopia. In these empty expanses would rise a new community from the seeds of a corporation of New England veterans who had forged their swords into plowshares.

These feelings and expectations, though seldom voiced by the tight-lipped backers of the original army plan, prevented the idea of a pioneering land corporation from vanishing. After 3 years of casting their weights about in various western enterprises, Rufus Putnam and Benjamin Tupper finally launched the Ohio Company of New England which included officers and men who were destined to play a vital part in the opening of Ohio. In the financial and corporate set-up of the company, military bounty claims again loomed conspicuously, and in the early life of Marietta, the first settlement on the Ohio River, some of the dreams of the army plan of 1783 came true.[25]

The very same routine procedure which buried the army plan in congressional committees obliterated yet another scheme designed to satisfy the soldiers' demands for their bounty lands. Introduced by Theodorick Bland and seconded by Alexander Hamilton, this scheme is of interest here chiefly because it seems to have been a counter-proposal to the army plan, though it foreshadows in some respects the system of land sales in Hamilton's famous public credit report of 1790. The plan as presented to Congress in 1783 proposed to merge the army's land claims with the commuted half pay and arrearages, every dollar of which was to be considered equal to a claim for 30 acres of land. The combined land grants were to be assigned within the vacant territory ceded by Great Britain, where

[25] For these special aspects of the beginnings of the Ohio Company, see *Cutler*, I, 178–197; A. B. Hulbert (ed.), *The Records of the Original Proceedings of the Ohio Company* (Marietta, Ohio, 1917); Joseph S. Davis, *Essays in the Earlier History of American Corporations* (Cambridge, 1917), I, 130–145; Livermore, *Early Land Companies*, pp. 134–136.

districts 2 degrees wide and 3 degrees long, subdivided into townships, were to be laid out. Finally, the United States was to reserve 10,000 acres out of every 100,000 granted as common and unalienable property, their revenues to be used for military and educational purposes. This plan represented one of the several attempts of the "financiers" to fund at least the army debt in toto. It also reflected the fear of the advocates of a strong central government that a new state might upset the delicate balance of the Thirteen Original States, and it combined both political and financial motives in the proposal that the Union keep a permanent interest in the western lands and their future development.[26]

The Bland proposals hinged directly upon the acceptance of the Virginia cession. Indeed, no move in the matter of the promised bounty lands was possible until the United States had acquired clear title to the western lands. As soon as this was accomplished, a gust of fresh air seemed to give new life to this and other questions concerning the future land policy of the United States. The Virginians took the lead, and among them Thomas Jefferson emerged as the leading spirit. True, he did not concern himself much with the bounty-land issue proper; nevertheless, his broad and general approach to the problems of the new west provided a principal solution for this question, albeit one which obliterated most of its political implications. Under his leadership, the legislative framework for the northwestern territory and its administration progressed so far that the lines for future action appeared securely drawn, even though many important changes might occur in carrying out his more detailed plans.

In this respect, one accomplishment stands out clearly before others. Congress agreed (and never deviated from this course) to deal with the problems of the northwest under two headings: the one relating to the form and powers of government, and the other relating to the disposal of land within the territory. This trend of affairs is clearly shown by the sequence of events after Virginia's deed of cession had been accepted on March 1, 1784. On the very

[26] Motion of Theodorick Bland, seconded by Alexander Hamilton, referred to Grand Committee, June 5, 1783, in *Journals*, XXIV, 384–386. *The Bland Papers*, ed. Charles Campbell (Petersburg, Va., 1840–1843), are silent on this subject; see, however, *ibid.*, II, 104–106; and *Letters*, VII, 143.

same day, Jefferson laid before Congress his proposals for the "Temporary Government of the Northwestern Territory" which had been under consideration by a committee for some time. They provided for the creation and administration of several western territories of rectangular shape and about equal size, established the procedure for their advancing to full statehood and membership in the Union, stipulated the republican form of government, forbade the admittance of citizens with hereditary titles, and abolished slavery after 1800. With the two last mentioned provisions stricken out, these proposals became law on April 23, 1784, but they were never put into effect. The unsettled conditions in the West prevented their early application, and in July 1787, the famous government ordinance for the Northwest Territory was passed which cast Jefferson's ideas, though with important alterations, in a new and permanent form.[27] On April 30, 1784, Jefferson laid before Congress "An Ordinance for ascertaining the mode of locating and disposing of lands in the western territory," the logical sequel and counterpart to the government ordinance just passed. In a measure, the land ordinance shared the fate of its twin; it was assigned to a committee, read in Congress again in the spring of 1785, referred to still another committee from which it emerged in the new and final dress of the renowned Land Ordinance of May 20, 1785.[28] As a matter of course and propriety, the military bounty lands are dealt with in both Jefferson's draft and the Land Ordinance of 1785. However, there seems reason to believe that the broader and political implications of the land-bounty issue were not entirely absent from Jefferson's mind when he drew up the Ordinance of 1784.

The disturbed conditions in the Northwest made it necessary that Congress decide on matters of government first and separately. The Indian claims had to be acquired by Congress, but it seemed

[27] On the cession, see *Journals*, XXVI, 112–117. For the Government Ordinance, see *ibid.*, 118–120, 247–252; and P. L. Ford (ed.), *The Writings of Thomas Jefferson* (10 vols.; New York, 1892–1899), III, 407–410, 429–432, 471. Hereafter cited as Jefferson, *Writings*. For the Ordinance of 1787, see *Territorial Papers*, II, 39–50.

[28] For the draft, see *Journals*, XXVI, 324–330, XXVII, 446–453; Jefferson, *Writings*, III, 475–483. For the Land Ordinance of 1785, see *Territorial Papers*, II, 12–18.

impossible that this body should also supervise and enforce the execution of the respective treaties with the Indian tribes. Consequently,
the delineation of the territory and its subdivisions as well as the
establishment of proper authorities there became more pressing.
Likewise, the eager settlers could not be allowed to move into a
political vacuum, as the troublesome squatters across the Ohio had
done. They had to be made responsible for law and order from the
very beginning, and this entailed the framing of governmental rules
in advance of their coming. In spite of the expediency of framing a
government ordinance first and leaving the land law until later,
there still remains the possibility, and even the probability, that
Jefferson's move was designed to serve his political ideas also. There
seems little doubt that the fight against the Society of the Cincinnati
raging at the time prompted him to insist on equal male suffrage in
the formation of truly democratic governments within the territory
and to insert in his ordinance a clause barring citizens with hereditary
titles from settling there.[29] In all probability, he was also aware of
the fact that the prime movers behind the army plan were all
prominent Cincinnati. Was the thunderer against the aristocracy of
wealth and privilege unaware of the possible danger that a landed
gentry might rise in the West whose wealth would be based upon
bounty lands and additional land grants from Congress and whose
privileges would be but a perpetuation of their military merits and
insignia ? The great civilian among the Founding Fathers was afraid
that there would "continue a distinction between the civil & military
which it would be for the good of the whole to obliterate as soon as
possible. . . ."[30] To attain this goal, he was resolved that the people
should be the sole source of democratic government in the East and
in the New West. The political realist would know that matters
pertaining to land holding might becloud the purity of this principle
when included in the same ordinance. Jefferson may have thought
it advisable, therefore, to deal with the modes for acquiring land in a
separate body of general rules and routine procedures.

That Jefferson was aware of the political implications of the

[29] Jefferson to Washington, April 16, 1784, to James Madison, April 25, 1784,
and to Francis Hopkinson, May 3, 1784, in *Letters*, VII, 493–495, 499–500, 511–
512; also, *ibid.*, preface, xxxviii–xli.

[30] Jefferson, *Writings*, IV, 170–175.

bounty question is shown by a peculiar clause in his land ordinance draft which prescribed that army warrants should pass as lands, by descent and device, but not by assignment or by survivorship. The prohibition of assignment had its precedent in a resolution passed by Congress on September 20, 1776. Both this resolution and Jefferson's clause were intended to prevent speculation in land warrants. In cases of land holding survivorship applied to joint tenancy under a grant and was regarded in Jefferson's time as a survival of feudalism and incompatible with democratic ideas.[31] Of course, this term must have slipped easily from the pen of the author of the laws against entail and primogeniture. The question here is, why just in the case of the bounty lands? True, these alone were grants whereas all other lands had to be acquired by purchase. But again, why should he be so careful if no possible danger threatened from this direction? However, none of Jefferson's provisions in these matters found a place in the Land Ordinance of 1785. On the contrary this law expressly recognized the right to assign bounty warrants. Nevertheless, his proviso that lands in the new territory should pass in dowry and descent according to gavelkind did become the basis of the first section of the Ordinance of 1787, as he had anticipated.

Pertinent features of Jefferson's two ordinances thus appear to reflect his running fight with military and Federalist circles of New England. By no means, however, did he leave this particular battlefield fully victorious. True, the Ordinance of 1787 upheld most of his cherished principles of democratic government. But his draft for the land ordinance underwent such drastic changes that it finally resembled the original draft in little more than name. Again, we are concerned with the land-bounty issue, this time wrapped up with the controversy about the proper way of promoting actual settlement in the West.

Jefferson's land ordinance plan combined the regular survey with a modified form of indiscriminate location. He wanted the new territory laid off in hundreds 10 geographical miles square, which in turn, were to be subdivided in lots 1 mile square; the hundreds were to be offered either entire or in lots.[32] However, the actual surveying

[31] Livermore, *Early Land Companies*, pp. 122 n., 225.

[32] See his humorous comments in letter to Hopkinson, May 3, 1784, in *Letters*, VII, 511–512.

was not to begin at a definite location but with the hundreds most in demand. This provision, of course, was closely tied up with the modes of acquiring title to land in the territory. Upon paying to the treasurer or loan officer an unspecified purchase price in specie, loan office, or debt certificates or handing over evidences of military rights to lands, the prospective settler would receive a warrant, go out himself to locate it, and describe to the surveyor the particular lot or hundred chosen. The surveyor would then proceed to lay off the land according to these requests and issue certificates of description which finally became the basis of deeds. Jefferson thus favored a rather liberal method of land allotment, albeit within the frame of regular surveys, and accorded no preferential treatment to soldier warrants; it was the idea of first come, first served applied generally.

In all these respects, the final land ordinance differed widely from Jefferson's scheme. First of all, it authorized the business of surveying and disposing of western lands in a definite and not too extensive area on the upper Ohio River where 7 parallel ranges of townships running due north and south were to be laid off completely before being opened to the location of warrants. The townships were to be 6 miles square and subdivided into lots of 640 acres each. The methods adopted for offering the townships either entire or in lots to prospective settlers and the procedures prescribed for securing warrant and title were rather complicated. Some of the features, especially those relating to the participation of the States in the scheme, were repealed in July, 1788, without having had much effect. Here it is sufficient to point out the special treatment accorded to the holders of army warrants. As soon as the Seven Ranges were surveyed, the Secretary of War was to withdraw by lot one-seventh of the townships for the use of the late Continental Army; henceforth, military bounty land claims had to be presented to the Secretary of War and be satisfied by him. The remainder of the townships were to be sold by auction at not less than $1 per acre to be paid in specie or in debt certificates.

In most of these stipulations, the New England viewpoint on the necessity of survey before sale and on more compact settlement and progressive advance into the West had prevailed. In the Seven Ranges it was thought that the United States would acquire a yardstick which would measure and delineate the westward movement in which the veterans would play their due part. In other respects, however, the ordinance clearly represented a compromise between the New England and Southern groups in Congress who had waged a hard battle in committees and on the floor before the measure was finally passed.[33]

To the holders of bounty claims and to prospective settlers in general, the results of the Ordinance of 1785 were disconcerting. Despite all caution, the Indians remained hostile, the chief geographer fell ill, and after 3 years not more than 4 ranges of townships had been laid off. It is not surprising, therefore, that the Secretary of War received incessant inquiries respecting the lands due the late army. In the spring of 1787, he addressed an urgent appeal to Congress. "Too many," he wrote, "have been compelled, by their necessities, to sell the evidences of their public debt, for a small proportion of the nominal sum. These unfortunate men now consider the lands promised them, as their only resource against poverty, in old age, and therefore are extremely solicitous to receive, immediately, their dues in this respect. . . . Assuming the surveys of the last year, as a data, or even supposing double the quantity will be surveyed annually in future, yet a very long period must elapse before the whole quantity due will be delivered. A period, at which very few of those entitled to the land will be living."[34]

Half a year later, when Congress was prodded into high gear by the proposed sale of land to the Ohio Company, an act was passed setting aside 1,000,000 acres north of the Ohio Company lands and west of the Seven Ranges and another tract at the mouth of the Ohio River for the exclusive purpose of satisfying the military bounties of the late army.[35] But only after 7 more years and after the Indian war had been terminated by the Treaty of Greenville was Congress able to stipulate the terms and modes under which these lands would

[33] See *Letters*, VIII, preface, vii–x; also, letters from Monroe to Jefferson, Grayson to Washington, King to Gerry, Howell to Green, Grayson to Madison, and others (*ibid.*, 90, 95–97, 104, 106, 129–130, *et passim*). For the influence of Timothy Pickering, see *Pickering*, I, 504–512; and Gerry to Pickering, King to Pickering, and Grayson to Pickering, in *Letters*, VIII, 55, 94, 105–106.

[34] Secretary of War Knox to President of Congress, April 26, 1787, in *Territorial Papers*, II, 27–28.

[35] *Ibid.*, 76.

be made available for the army, and then 3 more years elapsed before the first deeds were conveyed.

By an act of June 1, 1796, some of the cumbersome procedures of the Land Ordinance of 1785 were relaxed for the military districts. Townships 5 (instead of 6) miles square were divided into quarters of 4,000 acres each; these were assigned entire and by lot to either a single claimant or to groups of veterans who had pooled their warrants for the purpose, the actual locations of their lands to be left to their own care if they so desired.[36] The effect of these stipulations was that many of the quarter townships were carved up in rather irregular fashion and in about the same way as had been feared from the execution of Jefferson's original plan. On the other hand, the "unmilitary U.S. military district," as it has been called,[37] filled up more quickly than the rectangular sections in the Seven Ranges, thus testifying to the merits of Jefferson's plan as well.

Even this rapid survey shows how slowly and cautiously Congress was compelled to move in the matter of satisfying the land bounties of the Revolution. The first 4 ranges could not be opened to claimants before 1787, the Virginia Reserve remained closed till 1791, and the United States military districts did not welcome the first veteran settlers before 1800. Secretary of War Knox's dire prophecy that "few of those entitled to the land will be living" to see their expectations fulfilled did not come true literally, but the long delay had induced many of the veterans—soldiers and officers alike—to sell not only their certificates for half pay and arrearages but also their bounty warrants. The assignment of warrants, forbidden during the war, became legal in 1788, and this helped to hasten the sale of warrants by their original, and often destitute, holders. It is not necessary to reiterate here the well-known facts concerning the speculative mania which seized the moneyed parts of the Nation after the war and enabled a few persons and firms to reap profits from accumulated certificates and the sales of warrants for western lands. There is, however, need to point to the often forgotten circumstance that the existence of a market in debt certificates and land

[36] For the act of June 1, 1796, see *U. S. Statutes at Large,* Vol. I, chap. xlvi. This law supplemented the act of May 18, 1796. (*Territorial Papers,* II, 552–557.)

[37] Hutchinson, "The Bounty Lands," pp. 136–144, 151.

warrants could and did give to vigorous and enterprising men an opportunity and the means for concerted action of considerable public value and portent, even if they thereby advanced their own fortunes.

Reprinted from *Agricultural History*, XX (January, 1946), 8–18.

GEORGE ROGERS TAYLOR

2. *Agrarian Discontent in the Mississippi Valley Preceding the War of 1812*

AGRARIAN discontent has so often played an important part in our history that it is surprising that its importance in the Mississippi Valley preceding the War of 1812 has not been recognized. Western agriculture suffered, as this paper will show, a severe economic depression in the years just before the war, and this depression was an important factor in determining the support which the frontier gave first to the Embargo and Non-intercourse acts and finally to war. To understand western discontent, something of the situation in earlier years must be known. The examination of western economic conditions may well begin, therefore, with the period of prosperity which preceded the hard times of 1808–12.

In the first decade of the nineteenth century, the hunting and trapping frontier receded to the west and north, and, over wide areas, the valleys of the Ohio and lower Mississippi became definitely a farming country. For several years following the Louisiana Purchase this new agricultural West experienced a pronounced boom. The usual optimism and exaggerated anticipations of wealth which we have since learned to expect in such periods were abundantly present. The depression which accompanied the Peace of Amiens had been largely attributed by western farmers to Spanish interference with the Mississippi trade at New Orleans. When, therefore, news reached the West that the United States had purchased Louisiana, the frontiersmen believed that serious obstacles to western prosperity were a thing of the past.

Everywhere on the frontier people now believed that they saw the dawn of a new and prosperous day. A Kentucky editor declared that the undisturbed right to navigate the Mississippi insured in itself ". . . . a perpetual union of the states, and lasting prosperity to

28

the Western country."[1] And a contributor to the *Scioto Gazette* wrote: ".... No ruinous fluctuations in commerce need now be apprehended. Agriculture may depend upon those steady markets which trade shall open to industry."[2]

With this spirit abroad it is not surprising that settlers came crowding to the frontier in unprecedented numbers. Soon after the transfer of Louisiana to the United States, a great influx of pioneer farmers and adventurers began into the area bounded by New Orleans on the south and the frontier settlements in central Ohio on the north, and reached its crest in the boom years of 1805 and 1806.

One of the first parts of the West to feel the effect of this movement was New Orleans. Governor Claiborne reported, "Every boat from the western country and every vessel from the Atlantic States bring hither adventurers."[3] Tennessee was receiving more immigrants than ever before in her history, the influx being described by Governor Sevier as exceeding "anything of the kind that has heretofore taken place."[4]

But settlers migrated in greatest numbers in the years before the embargo to the region north of the Ohio River. They came not only from the Atlantic states but even from Kentucky and Tennessee. Opposition to slavery or inability to own slaves brought many from the upland regions of the South Atlantic states.[5] An Ohio editor reported in 1805 that the number of immigrants exceeded "all

[1] Frankfort (Ky.) *Guardian of Freedom*, July 20, 1803.

[2] October 1, 1803, issue. See also the Greensburg (Pa.) *Farmers Register*, July 16, 1803.

[3] Claiborne to Madison, New Orleans, February 13, 1804, in J. A. Robertson, *Louisiana under the Rule of Spain, France, and the United States, 1785–1807* (2 vols.; Cleveland, 1911), II, 251. Claiborne's letters show that many French fugitives from Santo Domingo sought asylum in New Orleans at this time.

[4] Tennessee, 7th Assembly, 1st Sess., *Senate Journal*, p. 13.

[5] Josiah Espy, *Memorandums of a Tour in Ohio and Kentucky in 1805* ("Ohio Valley Historical Series," No. 7 [Cincinnati, 1871]), pp. 22–23. A record which was kept at Kennedy's ferry opposite Cincinnati in Kentucky showed the following migration into Ohio from April 1 to December 31, 1805: South Carolina, 669; Kentucky, 568; Virginia, 465; North Carolina, 463; Georgia, 264; Tennessee, 200; Illinois, 10; total, 2,639. On the basis of these figures it was estimated that 30,000 people entered the state in 1805, in addition to those who came down the Ohio River. (Pittsburgh *Commonwea*

reasonable bounds of calculation."[6] Figures given by Cist show that
the population of Cincinnati increased 28 per cent from 1800 to
1805 and 142 per cent from 1805 to 1810. As there was but little
movement in 1808 and 1809, this Ohio town apparently more than
doubled its population in the three years—1805, 1806, and 1807.[7]

Not only was the westward migration in the period between the
Purchase and the embargo greater than ever before; but settlers,
and speculators as well, gave earnest of their faith in the new
country by purchasing, chiefly on credit, large tracts of western land.
In the decade before the war, the amount of public land sold in the
territory north of the Ohio River reached its highest point in 1805,
when 619,000 acres were purchased. In 1806 sales continued high
(473,000 acres), but in no other year for the period did they reach
the 400,000 mark.[8] State lands also in Kentucky and Tennessee were
bought on time, and debtors were to lament in the lean years to
come of obligations entered into at this boom period "when commerce was flattering hope."[9]

A wave of optimism once started by a propitious event—in this
case the removal of Spanish control over Mississippi River trade—
may, as subsequent crazes and booms have shown, go far on its own
momentum. Moreover, the ambitious hopes of the frontier farmers
had some solid basis. Good land was cheap; and, the land once
cleared, crops flourished and harvests were abundant. What could
be more encouraging to the farmers who had just left exhausted soils
on the eastern coast or the infertile lands of the Appalachian
Plateau?

And, for a time at least, the problem of marketing did not seem
over-serious. As long as immigration continued at full tide, those
producers living along the line of travel found a ready market by

---

[6] Chillicothe (Ohio) *Scioto Gazette*, November 7, 1805. See also *ibid.*, April 22,
1805; Rufus Putnam to John May, Marietta, January 17, 1806, in "The John May
Papers," ed. Elbert Jay Benton, *Western Reserve Historical Society Tracts*, No. 97
(1917), 191; Paris (Ky.) *Stewart's Kentucky Herald*, December 16, 1805, citing Gov.
Tiffin to Ohio state legislature; and Daniel Drake, *Natural and Statistical View . . . of
Cincinnati and the Miami Country* (Cincinnati, 1815), p. 131.

[7] Charles Cist, *Cincinnati in 1841* (Cincinnati, 1841), p. 38.

[8] *American State Papers: Documents, Legislative and Executive* (38 vols. in 10 classes;
Washington, 1832–1861), *Finance*, Vol. II, *passim*.

[9] Carthage (Tenn.) *Carthage Gazette*, December 15, 1809.

supplying the needs of the migrants. And farmers already established in the areas to which the new settlers came found the newcomers good customers for that season at least until their lands were cleared and their first crops harvested. Few, if any, worried about this metamorphosis, and everywhere new settlers were welcomed not only because they purchased the surplus produce but also because they brought money into the country.[10]

But especially stimulating to the high hopes of 1805 was the behavior of prices for western staples. The whole price situation has been dealt with in detail elsewhere.[11] Here it will suffice to point out that the extremely low prices of 1802 and 1803 had improved in 1804 and had reached in 1805 the highest level to be attained before the war. The year following saw slightly lower levels; and in 1807 the downward trend was clearly evident, though not to be compared with the precipitous decline of the embargo year which succeeded it.

From the vantage point of over one hundred years after the event, the fact is clear enough that the western agriculturist of 1805 was, despite elimination of Spanish interference on the Mississippi, abundant harvests, increased immigration, and high prices for western products, much more sanguine in his expectations of prosperity than fundamental conditions justified. Even without the embargo and non-intercourse of 1808 and 1809, it cannot be doubted that the bubble of 1805 would soon have burst. Time, it is true, was to iron out many of the obstacles to western prosperity; in the long run the West was in truth a land of promise. But underlying weaknesses existed in the immediate situation; and the most important of these must now be considered, although extended comment is not possible within the limits of this article.

Most serious was the problem of transportation. The physical obstacles to getting western products to market in the days before the steamboat and the railroad were even greater than is generally realized.[12] Some furs and peltries were being sent up the Ohio and

---

[10] See, for example, *Scioto Gazette*, October 1, 1803; Frankfort *Guardian of Freedom*, June 9, 1804; and Nashville (Tenn.) *Clarion*, February 16, 1808.

[11] See George Rogers Taylor, "Wholesale Prices in the Mississippi Valley Preceding the War of 1812," *Journal of Economic and Business History*, III (November, 1930), 148–163.

[12] Not until after the War of 1812 did the steamboat become a real factor in

over the mountains as late as 1811; but as the hunting and trapping areas moved westward, most of these products were exported by way of either the Mississippi or the St. Lawrence route.[13] When flax and hemp were bringing extremely high prices in 1809 and 1810, considerable quantities of rope, yarn, cordage, country linen, and twine were carried overland.[14] Cattle, horses, and even swine were sometimes driven literally hundreds of miles from Ohio, Kentucky, and Tennessee to Atlantic markets.[15] But the difficulties which attended this transmontane exportation are so patent that the small overland trade which did take place is chiefly a testimony to the obstacles by the Mississippi route. So great were the drawbacks to land transportation from western Pennsylvania, to say nothing of the vast region farther west, that the wagons which brought the needed imports from Philadelphia to Pittsburgh customarily returned empty.[16] Such frontier staples as hemp, flour, bacon, and even whiskey simply could not stand the cost of carriage over the mountain roads.

In consequence, Ohio Valley produce had to be sent a thousand miles or more down the Ohio-Mississippi river system to Natchez or New Orleans. This trip usually took about a month, and was beset with perils and hardships from beginning to end. To begin with, flatboats must be built at no little trouble or bought by the farmer

Mississippi River commerce. [EDITOR'S NOTE: See Louis C. Hunter, *Steamboats on the Western Rivers* (Cambridge, 1949) for a full history of steamboat technology and commerce in the West.]

[13] See, for example, New Orleans *Louisiana Gazette*, April 16, 1810; and Letter Book of Joseph Hertzog: Joseph Hertzog to Christian Wilt, May 2, 1811, in the Hertzog Collins Collection, Missouri Historical Society Library (St. Louis).

[14] Zadok Cramer, *Cramer's Pittsburgh Magazine Almanack for 1809*, p. 29; Raleigh (N. C.) *Star*, September 27, 1810; Chillicothe *Supporter*, February 2, 1811, from the *Commonwealth* of Pittsburgh. See also correspondence of James Wier, especially during 1808 and 1809, Letter Book of James Wier, in the Draper Collection, Wisconsin Historical Society (Madison).

[15] There are many contemporary references to this trade. For interesting statements regarding it, see *Carthage Gazette*, March 22, 1811; Frankfort *Palladium*, January 28, 1808; Lexington *Kentucky Gazette*, December 8, 1807; and Dayton (Ohio) *Ohio Centinel*, December 13, 1810. [EDITOR'S NOTE: Paul C. Henlein, *Cattle Kingdom in the Ohio Valley* (Lexington, 1959) treats fully of the early drives.]

[16] Lexington *Kentucky Gazette*, January 9, 1800; and F. A. Michaux, *Travels to the Westward of the Allegany Mountains* (London, 1805), p. 73.

who typically lived not far from some small tributary of the Ohio River.[17] Then the flats must be ready and loaded to take advantage of the first high water. This part of the journey, often several hundred miles down small tributaries to the Ohio, was full of hazards. If the waters were at flood, the boats often became unmanageable, and there was loss of boat and cargo. If the season was unusually dry, the flat might never even get started for market. If the rains were of too short duration or the trip delayed a few days too long, the river might go down before the Ohio was reached and flatboats be caught high and dry on sandbars, there to remain for months while their cargoes spoiled and their owners returned to their farms to raise more produce which must again run similar risks.

The perils of the trip down the Ohio and Mississippi can be hardly more than suggested. No river improvements had yet been made. Snags and bars were a constant menace. Travel at night, especially over the most dangerous sections, was extremely perilous; yet the river was liable to such sudden changes in the height of its water that tying up to the bank for the night might mean, at best, delay, at worst, loss of the entire cargo.

As the end of the journey approached, new dangers arose. The wideness of the river, combined with the frequency of storms accompanied by strong winds, was often fatal to the low-sided, wallowing flats. Every storm took its toll of these clumsy craft. If it was accompanied by rain, the cargo of flour or cotton, tobacco or cordage, might be ruined by water. If other hazards were avoided, the warm and humid climate of the south might cause the flour or pork to spoil before the market was reached.

But physical hazards were not all. From Cairo to Natchez the trip was made through a wild, unsettled region. Indians, and more especially renegade whites, preyed on the river trade. River pirates throve, and their exploits have become legendary.

The crew of each flat numbered from three to five men. They

[17] If the flatboat was bought, it cost from $50 to more than twice that figure. It was an operating expense, for at New Orleans flats were abandoned or broken up and sold for lumber. Frankfort *Palladium*, July 15, 1802; J. S. Bassett (ed.), *Correspondence of Andrew Jackson* (7 vols.; Washington, 1926–1935), I, 94; Christian Schultz, *Travels on an Inland Voyage* (New York, 1810), I, 132, 138; John Melish, *Travels in the United States . . . 1806 and 1807; and 1809, 1810 and 1811* (Philadelphia, 1812), II, 85; Michaux, *Travels*, 224.

must be paid for their services and supplied with food on the journey. If the farmer accompanied his own shipment, as was often the case, he must be absent for months from his farm. If he left home in December or January (most started even later), he was fortunate if he got to market, disposed of his cargo, and returned safely by land over the robber-infested Natchez trace in time to plant his crops for the next season. Many, indeed, never returned, for the Ohio Valley farmers were especially susceptible to the fevers common in the lower Mississippi. Each year as spring advanced into summer Natchez and New Orleans were full of flatboat men too sick to attempt the journey home and for whom no hospital facilities were available.[18]

The same difficulties of transportation which hindered western producers from getting their surplus to market made the bringing in of their imports very costly. Though self-sufficing to a considerable extent, the frontier was dependent upon the eastern states and foreign countries for a great variety of products, including most manufactured goods. For example, the letter books of James Wier, a leading merchant of Lexington, Kentucky, show that he imported coffee, tea, sugar, chocolate, prunes, spices, wines, needles, velvet ribbons, muslins and other kinds of cloth, men's slippers, crockery, lead, brimstone, glue, and a host of other commodities which even the unpretentious people of the frontier regarded as necessary to their happiness.

Except to ports on the lower Mississippi, such as Natchez and New Orleans, importations up-river remained relatively small until the advent of the steamboat. Forcing a barge up the Mississippi was a peculiarly difficult task. Not only was the current strong and treacherous, but the river bottom was often too soft for poling and the banks unsuited for towing. Every device then known for forcing

---

[18] A wealth of contemporary material exists on the condition of the early river trade. Many interesting descriptions are to be found not only in the correspondence of James Wier and Andrew Jackson referred to above (notes 14, 17) but also in the writings of early western travelers such as John Bradbury, Fortescue Cuming, H. B. Fearon, Timothy Flint, Henry Ker, John Melish, and Christian Schultz. Illuminating sidelights on the river trade are to be found in the following: Frankfort *Palladium*, April 8, 22, 1802, and March 17, 1808; Dayton *Ohio Centinel*, August 9, 1810, and May 15, 1811; *Scioto Gazette*, August 12, 1805; and the *Mississippi Herald and Natchez Gazette* (Natchez, Miss.), September 23, 1806. Most valuable of all perhaps are the New Orleans customs records in the Library of Congress.

a craft through water was attempted. Oars, sails, setting poles, treadmills operated by horses, "bush-whacking," and the cordelle, all were tried, and still the journey remained so slow, arduous, and uncertain that the passage from New Orleans to Louisville took three months and freight charges were from three to five times as high as down-river rates.[19]

Little wonder, then, that despite the inherent difficulties of land transportation most western imports were hauled three hundred miles by Conestoga wagon to Pittsburgh or Wheeling and then floated on the rivers often several hundred miles farther to local distributing centers. But the burden upon the frontier was great whichever route was used. The cost of carriage over the mountains is illustrated in the dealings of the Lexington merchant mentioned above. In 1808 he appears to have paid a little over two hundred dollars to have two wagon loads of goods brought from Philadelphia to Pittsburgh.[20]

The fact emerges from a survey of the physical conditions of the overland and river trade that the frontier suffered a severe handicap by reason of transportation difficulties. It has been insufficiently appreciated that, in point either of time or cost of carriage, Philadelphia was in the first decade of the nineteenth century nearer to Liverpool, Lisbon, or Havana than it was to Chillicothe, Lexington, or Nashville.[21]

[19] One of the best descriptions of the difficulties of this up-river trade is to be found in Timothy Flint, *Recollections of the Last Ten Years* (Boston, 1826), pp. 91–92. Down-river rates were usually given as a cent or a little more a pound. (See *Tennessee Gazette*, February 18, 1801; James Wier to Thomas Fitzpatrick, Lexington, Ky., February 23, 1805, Letter Book of James Wier; Christian Schultz, *Travels on Inland Voyage*, II, 186–187. Up-river rates from New Orleans to both Tennessee and Kentucky as quoted in the New Orleans *Louisiana Gazette* were ordinarily five cents a pound. [EDITOR'S NOTE: See Thomas Senior Barry, *Western Prices before 1861* (Cambridge, 1943) for the fullest analysis now available of transport rates and prices in the antebellum West.]

[20] James Wier to Abner Barker, Lexington, Ky., September 10, 1805, Letter Book of James Wier.

[21] Freight rates from Philadelphia and Baltimore to Pittsburgh were usually given as $5 per hundredweight, or even higher. Shipments to Lexington cost $7 or $8 and to Cumberland $9 or $10 per hundred pounds. See for example, *American State Papers: Miscellaneous*, II, 117; John Melish, *Travels*, II, 52; Greensburg (Pa.) *Farmers Register*, September 1, 1804; and Joseph Hertzog to Christian Wilt, Philadelphia, March 20, 1811, Letter Book of Joseph Hertzog.

Slow and unreliable communication of market information also added to frontier difficulties. This was due in part to the obstacles to travel emphasized above and in part also to the undeveloped trade organization of the frontier community. For news of market conditions the western merchant or farmer depended upon prices current either printed in the newspapers or communicated privately by letter. By 1810 the good-weather time for post riders from Philadelphia to Lexington was still at least two weeks. From New Orleans letters could, under favorable conditions, be delivered in Kentucky in twenty-five days.[22] Obviously the slow movement and frequent delays of the mails were of great disadvantage to those who shipped goods down the Ohio, for, as a result, they had to select their cargoes in the light of market information already nearly a month old, in addition to shipping goods which would, in all probability, be at least four or five weeks in getting to market.

This handicap was made all the more serious by the presence of eastern speculators. The editor of the *Kentucky Gazette* complained that because of the slowness of the mail:

> A speculator . . . . can hasten [from Philadelphia or New Orleans] . . . . purchase our production on his own terms, and lay the whole western country under contribution . . . . before we can have any information as to the change in price of produce in the markets of those places . . . . fortunes have often been made in this way . . . . when the loss of a battle, the death of a Bonaparte, or the fall of a minister of state, may change the course of business, and improve or depress markets.[23]

The undeveloped financial organization of the West can hardly be more than mentioned here as still another of those factors which contributed to the fundamental economic difficulties of the frontiersman. A scarcity of money often existed for the payment of taxes or to meet the ordinary needs of trade. Barter, everywhere common for small payments, was almost the only mode of exchange in the more remote settlements.[24] Public officers' receipts and land warrants

[22] Lexington *Kentucky Gazette*, October 9, 1810.

[23] *Ibid.*

[24] See, for example, *Scioto Gazette*, October 1, 1803; Dayton (Ohio) *Dayton Repertory*, December 14, 1809; *Natchez Gazette*, October 17, 1811; and Marshall to

were commonly issued by the frontier states; and, although helping somewhat to make up for the scarcity of other media, they were often unsatisfactory because subject to depreciation.[25]

Banking facilities developed beginning with the establishment of the Kentucky Insurance Company in 1802.[26] But, for most of the West, banks were just getting well started by 1812. Despite help from merchants who dealt in exchange and branches of the First Bank of the United States which were set up at Pittsburgh and New Orleans, payments at a distance were often costly and difficult to make.[27]

Probably more serious than the imperfect financial machinery was the scarcity of capital. The settlers did not bring much capital with them, nor had the country been settled long enough to develop its own surplus. As yet little eastern capital flowed westward except

---

Bosseron, Vincennes, June 7, 1800, Lasselle Collection, Indiana State Library. For an example of the almost complete absence of money in the more isolated regions, see Jonathan S. Findlay to James Findlay, Natchez, November 24, 1805, "Selections from the Torrence Papers," *Quarterly Publications of the HPSO*, IV (1910), 108–109. Major William Stanley, when he was about to start on a trip down the Ohio River, made this matter-of-fact notation in his diary: "sell my horse for 650 lbs. Bacon." ("The Diary of Major William Stanley, 1790–1810," *ibid.*, XIV [1920], 29.)

[25] Paris *Stewart's Kentucky Herald*, December 16, 1805; Lexington (Ky.) *Independent Gazetteer*, June 14, 1805; Steubenville (Ohio) *Western Herald*, December 27, 1806; and Bardstown (Ky.) *Western American*, April 5, 1805. See also C. C. Huntington, "A History of Banking and Currency in Ohio before the Civil War," *OAHQ*, XXIV (1915), 262; and R. T. Durrett, "Early Banking in Kentucky," Kentucky Bankers' Association, *Proceedings, 1892*, p. 37.

[26] The original act chartering the Kentucky Insurance Company may be found in the Lexington *Kentucky Gazette*, January 18, 1803, and in *Acts of Kentucky*, 11th Ass., 1st Sess., pp. 149–159. Although, as the name implies, this company wrote marine insurance, it does not appear that most western farmers insured their river shipments. (See Frankfort *Palladium*, April 10, 1806; and St. Louis *Louisiana Gazette*, August 16, 1810.)

[27] Notes on eastern banks often brought a premium on the frontier because of their superiority to specie in making distant payments. Western merchants found it necessary at times to assume the risk and expense of transporting the heavy silver specie over the mountains. (Frankfort *Palladium*, January 12, 1805 and March 6, 1806; F. A. Michaux, *Travels*, pp. 157 ff.; Charles Cist, *The Cincinnati Miscellany*, I, 6; Fortescue Cuming, "Sketches of a Tour to the Western Country . . . 1807–1809," in R. G. Thwaites (ed.), *Early Western Travels* [Cleveland, 1904–1907], IV, 183–184.)

as Atlantic merchants gave long credits to their frontier customers. The complaint of scarcity of money so frequently found in western newspapers no doubt often arose in reality from a scarcity of capital. Even in western Pennsylvania, one of the earliest settled portions of the West, the farmers did not, according to a newspaper account, have capital to invest even in such needed improvements as turnpikes.[28]

Finally, as a new, extensive, and sparsely settled region, the frontier suffered, as we should expect, from an imperfectly developed business and marketing organization. Importing was largely in the hands of small firms, usually partnerships, which were dependent upon Philadelphia or Baltimore merchants for long-term credits. As time went on, the function of receiving and forwarding goods was placed more and more in the hands of commission houses at such centers as Pittsburgh and Cincinnati. But for many years these small-scale western merchants commonly carried out the whole process, purchasing in Philadelphia, superintending transportation to the frontier, storing, retailing, and carrying back to the Atlantic Coast money, bills of exchange, or, more rarely, west-country produce.[29]

But especially in the disposal of his exportable surplus did the frontier agriculturist suffer from lack of adequate marketing machinery. In order to get his produce to market, the farmer had often to assume the risk of carrying his own produce to New Orleans and there disposing of it as best he could. In the words of a contributor to the Frankfort *Palladium* the producer became "a navigator, and a trader."[30]

Had this farmer-trader found a well-organized market at Natchez or New Orleans, he might not have fared so badly when he

[28] Pittsburgh *Commonwealth*, May 28, 1806; and Cincinnati *Western Spy*, November 10, 1802. A Kentuckian stated in 1805 that private lenders received from 10 to 50 per cent on loans. Lexington (Ky.) *Independent Gazetteer*, June 14, 1805.

[29] See the correspondence of James Wier and Andrew Jackson referred to above; also, Christian Schultz, *Travels*, II, 22; Morris Birkbeck, *Notes on America* (2d ed.; London, 1818), pp. 89–90; and Henry B. Fearon, *Sketches of America* (2d ed.; London, 1818), p. 231.

[30] April 10, 1806. See also Bardstown *Western American*, March 29, 1805.

arrived at the lower river port. But one who had probably engaged
in this trade himself wrote:

> He there meets with strangers—his time is precious—new expences
> ensue—the climate is unfriendly both to his own health, and the preser-
> vation of his cargo. The market may be dull—he cannot wait—he sells
> of necessity at what he can get, and he returns home after a long and
> fatiguing journey, with but little money, and less health. . . . .
>
> . . . . when the whole profit and loss is summed up, there are few I
> believe who do not find it a bad business. What is here said of the
> adventuring farmer, may be applied to all exporters on a small capital.[31]

Especially disadvantageous must have been what the writer
quoted above described as "the want of some established mode of
doing business between the citizens and traders." Is it surprising
that the farmer-adventurer often made hurried and bad bargains at
New Orleans? In a market glutted with produce, he was a stranger,
often unused to the forms of trade and ignorant as to the state of the
market. Fearful of the oncoming "sickly season" or even of "the
danger of robbery and assassination," he sold quickly for whatever
he could get and returned to Kentucky to tell of the "unprincipled
speculators" and "rapacious agents" at New Orleans or to attribute
the low prices to combination among the purchasers.[32]

Complaint that west-country merchants did not help the farmers
to market their produce was repeatedly voiced in western newspapers;
and when a merchant did engage in exporting farm produce down
the rivers, he was hailed in the press as a public benefactor.[33]
Numerous attempts were made to establish some agency which
would be primarily concerned in marketing the farmers' surplus
produce. In Ohio a number of attempts were made to set up stock
companies for this purpose.[34] And at Nashville (1810) a newspaper
published a long series of articles urging that the state take over the

[31] Frankfort *Palladium*, April 10, 1806.

[32] Lexington *Kentucky Gazette*, October 18, 1803, Aristides; and Frankfort
Palladium, April 15, 1802.

[33] See, for example, the Lexington (Ky.) *Reporter*, December 5, 1809; *Scioto
Gazette*, October 1, 1803; Nashville *Clarion*, February 16, 1808; and Nashville
Democratic Clarion and Tennessee Gazette, August 10, 1810.

[34] Cincinnati *Western Spy and Hamilton Gazette*, August 17, 1803; Cincinnati
Liberty Hall, August 29, September 26, October 3, 10, 17, 1810.

marketing function which, according to the writer, the farmer could not and the merchant would not assume.[35]

As a result, in part at least, of the absence of old, established firms and accepted ways of doing business, western products were usually poor in quality and bore a bad reputation.[36] Ohio River Valley flour usually sold at New Orleans for several dollars less than the Atlantic product. A New Orleans merchant declared, "There is . . . . a manifest repugnance shewn by the merchants, to ship it to foreign markets, where the quality is always found inferior to that of the Atlantic States, and almost invariably proves rotten at the end of two or three months."[37] Nor were other products much better. Kentucky producers were accused of putting up "everything that ever looked like tobacco."[38] Despite many attempts at state regulation, complaints were frequent of western corn and hemp and the "extreme bad quality" of Ohio Valley pork.[39] Baltimore merchants threatened to boycott Louisiana sugar producers unless their product was shipped in proper casks; and at Liverpool cotton

[35] Nashville *Democratic Clarion and Tennessee Gazette*, May 4–October 26, 1810, series signed "A Farmer." Of course, some down-river exportation was done by the west-country merchants, and even Philadelphia houses occasionally engaged in it. Insofar as the merchants did enter this trade, however, they confined their operations largely to cotton, tobacco, hemp products, and, in western Pennsylvania, to flour. Practically all exporting from New Orleans was done by local merchants and agents or factors for mercantile houses in Atlantic Coast cities or Great Britain. Natchez *Mississippi Herald and Natchez Gazette*, July 26, 1805; Frankfort *Palladium*, February 10, 1803; Bairdstown (Ky.) *Candid Review*, December 9, 1807; and New Orleans customs records, Library of Congress.

[36] Other factors, such as the crudeness of western flour mills and cotton gins, were of course important. Emphasis on quantity rather than fine quality is perhaps typical of frontier regions.

[37] New Orleans *Louisiana Gazette*, August 8, 1806. It was reported from New Orleans that "the reputation of Kentucky flour, formerly bad enough, is this year ten times worse than ever, so much Weavel eaten flour; and even *old flour with boles filled with fresh flour*, has been sold here. . . ." (Lexington *Kentucky Gazette*, June 21, 1803; italics in original.) For other references to the inferior grade of this frontier product, see for example, Frankfort *Palladium*, July 15, 1802, February 4 and March 17, 1808.

[38] *American State Papers: Miscellaneous*, I, 709.

[39] See the New Orleans *Orleans Gazette*, April 20, 1805; the New Orleans *Louisiana Gazette*, August 8, 1806; Cincinnati *Liberty Hall*, April 9, 1808; and the Lexington *Kentucky Gazette*, February 28, 1804.

importers deplored the presence of leaves, dirt, and considerable quantities of seed in bales of western cotton.[40]

No one of the drawbacks described above nor all of them together were necessarily fatal to western hopes, for, though difficulties are great and costs high, if prices are still higher, prosperity may yet be obtained. Still these difficulties surely tended to make the West of this period a sort of marginal area in relation to world-markets. When world-prices ruled high, Monongahela and Kentucky flour could be disposed of in competition with that from Virginia and Maryland. Likewise, when cotton and tobacco brought good prices, the Kentucky and Tennessee product could be sold along with that of the Atlantic states and still yield a profit to distant western farmers. But when markets were dull and prices falling, western producers not only saw the fading of their roseate hopes but often enough found themselves in desperate straits to secure necessary imported commodities or to meet obligations for land bought on credit when hopes ran high with prices.

Free navigation of the Mississippi, unprecedented immigration, and unusually high prices had brought a great wave of optimism to the West following 1803, despite the underlying difficulties just considered. The peak year proved to be 1805, but times were relatively good in 1806 and 1807 except for those parts of the West which were adversely affected by glutted markets and lower prices for west-country provisions. Acute depression did not come until 1808.[41] The price situation of that year speaks for itself. Since 1805

[40] See the following New Orleans newspapers: *Orleans Gazette*, August 3, September 18, 1805; *Union,* January 23, 1804; *Louisiana Gazette*, September 23, 1804.

[41] The building of seagoing ships at Ohio Valley river ports, which had generated tremendous enthusiasm earlier in the decade, had been proved an impractical venture several years before the embargo. This ship-building boom is one of the few *local* matters upon which the student may find very full comment in the western press. The authoritative study of this episode in Ohio Valley history is Archer B. Hulbert, "Western Ship-Building," *American Historical Review*, XXI (1915–1916), 720–733. Hulbert's suggestion that the failure of the experiment was due to the embargo is not acceptable. The insuring of the right of deposit at New Orleans by the Louisiana Purchase, combined with the repeated disasters experienced in getting seagoing ships down western rivers, had brought about a decline certainly before the embargo and probably as early as 1805. [EDITOR'S NOTE: See also Charles Ambler, *A History of Transportation in the Ohio Valley* (Glendale, Calif., 1932), pp. 81 ff.]

the index of wholesale prices of western products at New Orleans had fallen over 20 per cent. Except for hemp growers in Kentucky and infant manufacturing interests at Pittsburgh and Lexington, practically the whole West was prostrated.[42]

Immigration into Ohio seems virtually to have ceased, and land sales north of the Ohio River were greatly reduced.[43] Those who had previously purchased lands now found it impossible to meet their obligations. In a petition to Congress the legislature of Ohio stated:

> .... the unprovoked aggressions of both England and France, which could neither be foreseen or evaded, has so materially affected the whole commerce of the United States, that it has almost put a stop to our circulating medium, and rendered the payment of the installments of the purchase money for the .... lands almost impracticable; forfeitures of interest for two, three and four years, are daily accruing.[44]

Stay-laws and relief for debtors were the rule in Kentucky, Tennessee, and Mississippi Territory,[45] and depressed conditions were reported at New Orleans as early as April, 1807.[46]

Two main remedies for the situation received increasingly enthusiastic support from the frontiersmen in the period of falling prices and hard times, which began for parts of the West as early as 1806, became general by 1808, and continued down to the War of 1812 with but partial and temporary relief in 1809–10. One was the development of manufactures; the other was forcing the European powers to repeal their restrictions on our foreign commerce. Of

[42] Probably Kentucky suffered less from the embargo than other parts of the frontier. See Samuel G. Adams to Harry Innes (?), Richmond, July 15, 1809, Harry Innes Papers, Vol. XXI, Library of Congress; and Taylor, "Prices in the Mississippi Valley," cited note 11, *supra*.

[43] Jarvase Cutler, *A Topographical Description of the State of Ohio, Indiana Territory, and Louisiana, Etc.* (Boston, 1812), p. 11; Cincinnati *Liberty Hall*, July 11, 1810; Daniel Drake, *Natural and Statistical View*; and *American State Papers: Finance*, Vol. II, *passim*. On May 7, 1808, a resident of Marietta, Ohio, wrote that no land could be sold at that place "on account of the scarcity of money & the stoppage of business." (Rufus Putnam to John May, Marietta, "John May Papers," p. 202.)

[44] *Acts of Ohio*, 7th Ass., 1st Sess., pp. 222–223.

[45] Frankfort *Palladium*, February 16, 1809; Tennessee, 7th Ass., 2d Sess., *Senate Journal*, pp. 6–8; *Annals of Congress*, 10th Cong., 2d Sess., p. 1246; and Natchez *Weekly Chronicle*, October 12 and December 14, 1808.

[46] Frankfort *Palladium*, June 11, 1807, a copy of a letter from Sanderson and White, New Orleans commission merchants, dated April 6, 1807.

course, still other remedies were advocated from time to time. Occasionally, some one saw clearly enough that fundamental difficulties of marketing, of transportation, and of business and financial organization must be overcome.[47] Some violent partisans believed all would be well if only the Federalists might be returned to power and the national government thereby saved "from the incapacity .... of our own rulers, and the want of that pure patriotism" which distinguished the time of Washington.[48] Even the moralists were present to attribute economic ills to the laxity of the laws and the absence of a feeling of moral responsibility on the part of the people.[49] These, and other solutions were suggested, but the two most popular measures of relief were those intended to stimulate manufactures and those designed to force Great Britain to modify her commercial system.

The enthusiasm for manufacturing cannot be dwelt on here. The following statement from the *Western Spy and Miami Gazette* may be regarded as typical of this western attitude:

> Raise articles of produce, which can be manufactured, rather than such as require a foreign market; Rye to distill; Barley to brew; Flax and Wool to spin, rather than Wheat to ship.
>
> Above all *observe* the household manufactures of your neighbors. *Observe* the accounts of them in the newspapers. Immitate what you see manufactured. .... Shew our foreign spoliators we can live in comfort without their finery.[50]

Our attention in this paper is centered primarily upon western attempts to mend their failing fortunes through supporting commercial coercion and war. An understanding of the course of frontier opinion in respect to these measures involves, first, a realization of the degree of support which the West gave to the Embargo Act of December, 1807, and, second, an appreciation of the importance of economic motives in prompting the West to support a measure accompanied, as this one was, by widespread depression.

[47] See for example, Nashville *Democratic Clarion and Tennessee Gazette*, August 10, 1810, contribution signed "A Farmer"; and *Palladium*, April 10, 1806.

[48] *Natchez Gazette*, October 17, 1811.

[49] New Orleans *Louisiana Gazette*, March 7, 1811.

[50] August 13, 1808; italics in the original text. See also for similar statements: Lexington *Reporter*, September 8, 1810, February 23, 1811; and Carthage (Tenn.) *Carthage Gazette*, April 25, 1811.

An examination of the situation reveals that in his policy of commercial coercion President Jefferson received no more faithful
support than that which came from western congresmen. Almost to
a man, they voted for the original act of December, 1807, which
placed a general embargo on foreign trade; and they supported him
loyally in the numerous measures which followed to make its
operation effective. When, in November, 1808, the House of
Representatives by the very close count of fifty-six to fifty-eight voted
to continue the measure in effect, the western members were solidly
with the majority.[51] And the next spring, when others weakened,
western congressmen stood out for the continuance of the embargo,
or, failing that, for the adoption of a non-intercourse act. A westerner,
George W. Campbell, of Tennessee, was one of the Senate leaders
who held out most firmly against any loosening of commercial
restrictions.[52]

On the whole, the citizens of the western states were just as
enthusiastic for commercial restrictions as their representatives in
Congress. Yet some frontier opposition did appear. At Pittsburgh
and Presque Isle (Erie) in Pennsylvania, and in parts of Ohio where
some Federalism still survived (e.g., Dayton and Chillicothe), newspaper writers vigorously attacked the measure.[53] In Kentucky, the
Western World of Frankfort, a paper with an extremely small following, was the only one in the state antagonistic to the embargo.[54] As
might be expected from the presence of commercial and shipping
interests, some active disapproval appeared at New Orleans, where
at least two of the newspapers attacked the measure.[55] Even here

[51] *Annals of Congress*, 10th Cong., 2d Sess., p. 500.

[52] See for example, *ibid.*, pp. 1475–87, 1499, 1541. Matthew Lyon of Kentucky
was the only western representative in Congress who opposed the embargo and
deprecated talk of war with England. (*Annals of Congress*, 10th Cong., 1st Sess.,
p. 1222; and *ibid.*, 2d Sess., pp. 1504–1505.) In spite of his early services to his
party, his constituents were unwilling to have such a representative; and on
August 18, 1810, the Lexington *Reporter* announced that "the apostate Lyon" had
failed of re-election. See also the Lexington *Reporter* for July 1, 1809.

[53] On Federalism in Ohio before the War of 1812, see Homer C. Hockett,
Western Influences on Political Parties to 1825 (Columbus, 1917), pp. 54–62.

[54] The attack on the embargo which one finds most often in these opposition
papers is to the effect that the Democrats are ruining the country in an attempt to
help the French.

[55] *La lanterne magique* and the *Louisiana Gazette*.

probably the group opposed to the embargo formed but a small minority. Its size, however, may have been minimized by the intensely partisan Governor Claiborne, who wrote to Madison: "Two or three British Factors, and some violent Federalists censure the Embargo, but the better informed, and worthy part of Society, appears highly to approve the measure." [56]

Despite the opposition noted above, the frontier was, as a whole, no less favorable to the embargo than its representatives in Congress. The commercial boycott had been successfully used against England in our earlier struggles, and it now seemed to westerners a natural and powerful weapon. [57] State legislatures, local political leaders, and public meetings expressed their enthusiastic approval. [58] Most western newspapers printed articles which ardently championed the embargo. [59] Opinion was so united in its favor in Tennessee as to call forth the following statement: "We never witnessed a greater unanimity to prevail in any considerable district of country, and relative to any important question, than now prevails throughout

[56] Claiborne to Madison, New Orleans, June 8, 1808, in D. Rowland (ed.), *Official Letter Books of W. C. C. Claiborne* (6 vols.; Jackson, Miss.), IV, 176. The suggestion in a New Orleans paper that the people of Orleans Territory were opposed to the restrictions on trade brought a vigorous denial in the *Courrier de la Louisiane* for June 3, 1808.

[57] In what was perhaps the first book of a political character printed in the Trans-Appalachian region, Allen B. Magruder advocated the so-called "Chinese policy" and expressed the belief that foreign nations could best be coerced by depriving them of the benefits of commerce with us. (*Political, Commercial and Moral Reflections on the Late Cession of Louisiana to the United States* [Lexington, 1803], pp. 56–65.) The importance which the frontiersmen attached to our foreign relations may be illustrated by the assertion of a Kentucky farmer that "if our relations with foreign countries go on well, we are likely to have good markets at home, especially during the continuance of a European War." (Frankfort *American Republic*, June 21, 1811.)

[58] See, for example, Mann Butler, *A History of the Commonwealth of Kentucky* (Louisville, 1834), p. 330; *Acts of Ohio*, 7th Ass., 1st Sess., pp. 223–224; *Scioto Gazette*, February 13, 1809; *Acts of Kentucky*, 17th Ass., 1st Sess., p. 129; Washington (Pa.) *Reporter*, December 19, 1808; and Carthage (Tenn.) *Carthage Gazette*, February 6, 1809.

[59] Vincennes *Western Sun*, August 13, 1808; Natchez *Mississippi Messenger*, February 4 and March 24, 1808; Lancaster (Ky.) *Political Theatre*, December 10, 1808; Knoxville (Tenn.) *Wilson's Knoxville Gazette*, May 13, 1808; and Pittsburgh *Commonwealth*, March 16, 1808.

the state of Tennessee respecting the measures of the General Government. The voice of approbation is universal." [60] Two months after the measure had been superseded by the Non-Intercourse Act, they were still drinking toasts to it in Vincennes. [61] Perhaps at that distant frontier outpost they had not yet learned of its repeal.

Two American students, Professor L. M. Sears and Professor W. W. Jennings, have given special attention to the embargo of 1808. Both emphasize the traditional hatred for England, and the former specifically denies the significance of economic factors. Approval of the embargo, he tells us, was the result of the "simple trust" in Jefferson which filled the hearts of southern Democrats. As for the approval which was given the embargo in Mississippi Territory, Sears regards it as the pure flower of disinterested logic. [62]

It cannot be denied that traditional attitudes and party loyalty played some part in determining western support for the embargo. To some extent the westerner was playing the rôle of a good Democrat and supporting his president. In part he was acting as a good patriot and a high-spirited frontiersman who resented insults to the national honor either by France or England. The traditional friendship of Democrats for France doubtless made the westerner quick to resent untoward acts by Britain and slow to see evil in the French aggressions. But these explanations are, at most, not the whole story, for an examination of western opinion clearly indicates that the support which was given the embargo on the frontier had in it a considerable element of economic self-interest.

The western farmer was quite willing to admit his lack of interest in the carrying trade. Even impressment of seamen, though to be deplored, did not seem to him very important. [63] But he did want adequate markets and good prices for his produce, and these he believed impossible so long as Great Britain restricted the West Indian market, forbade direct trade with the Continent, and placed exceedingly burdensome duties upon American imports into Great

[60] Carthage (Tenn.) *Carthage Gazette*, February 6, 1809.

[61] Vincennes *Western Sun*, July 8, 1809.

[62] Louis Martin Sears, *Jefferson and the Embargo* (Durham, N. C., 1927), pp. 100, 126; and W. W. Jennings, *The American Embargo, 1807–1809* (Iowa City, 1921), pp. 201–202.

[63] *Annals of Congress*, 10th Cong., 2d Sess., pp. 204–206; Lexington *Reporter*, October 3, 1808, and Lexington *Kentucky Gazette*, August 30, 1808.

Britain. In the eyes of the western farmer, the depression of 1808 was primarily the result of the belligerents' decrees and orders in council, not of the embargo which he regarded as a highly desirable act, designed as a measure of retaliation to force the abandonment by foreign nations of their destructive interference with the marketing of our surplus products. "Who now blames the embargo?" demanded a Cincinnati editor. "Who considers it a matter of French interest or procurement? Who does not allow it to be a *saving measure?* .... The embargo was produced by the foreign belligerent powers. They made it wise, just and necessary. They made its continuance necessary."[64]

In Congress western representatives made no effort to conceal their economic interest in the embargo. Said Senator Pope of Kentucky, in stating the very core of the argument in defense of this measure:

> What, Mr. President, is our situation? .... The dispute between us and the belligerents is not about the carrying trade, but whether we shall be permitted to carry our surplus produce to foreign markets? The privilege of carrying our cotton to market, is one in which, not only the growers themselves are interested, but one which concerns every part of the nation.

He then went on to show that if the embargo were taken off while the orders in council remained in force, cotton would be confined alone to the British market and the price would fall to a ruinously low level. "The necessity," he continued, ".... of resisting the British orders and forcing our way to those markets where there is a demand for the article, must be evident to every one who will consider the subject." In conclusion he added that if England did not change her course war might be necessary.[65]

[64] Cincinnati *Western Spy and Miami Gazette*, August 13, 1808; italics in original text.

[65] *Annals of Congress*, 10th Cong., 2d Sess., pp. 1592–1593. The West was outraged not only that English restrictions should keep our goods from continental markets but also that heavy duties should be levied on the most important of our goods marketed in her ports. A contributor to a Kentucky newspaper declared: ".... the *tax* in '74 was imposed on the article of *tea* alone, & whilst we were colonies of that country—in 1808, it is imposed on *every article of our commerce*, and that too while we occupy the ground of an *independent nation*." (*Palladium*, November 3, 1808, from the *Western World*; italics in the original text.)

When the question of continuing the embargo was again debated in the spring of 1809, much was said of markets and prices by those favoring a continuance of restrictive measures. In arguing in the House of Representatives against the proposed repeal of the Embargo Act, George W. Campbell, of Tennessee, declared:

> . . . . though you relieve your enemy, you do not furnish any substantial relief to your own people. No, sir, I am convinced that, in less than three months from this day, should this measure succeed, produce will sink below the price which it now bears, or has borne for the last year. There are but few places to which you can go, and those will naturally become glutted for want of competition; and, in a short time, the prices will not pay the original cost. It will, therefore, afford no substantial relief. The relief, too, which it may afford will be partial, confined to certain portions of the Union, and not equally beneficial to the whole. Tobacco will find no market; cotton a temporary market only—for, although Great Britain will receive it, yet, as we have more on hand than she will immediately want, or can make use of, and as we cannot go to France, and our trade to the Continent will undoubtedly be interrupted by Great Britain, she has nothing to do but wait a few days, weeks, or months, and buy it at her own price.[66]

If the inhabitants of Mississippi Territory gave, as has been held, a completely disinterested support to the embargo, one must conclude that their delegate in Congress failed somehow to understand the position of his constituents. George Poindexter, the delegate in Congress from Mississippi Territory, wrote the editor of the *Natchez Chronicle* that nothing could be gained by removing the embargo, for British taxes and trade restrictions would so limit the market for cotton as greatly to depress the price.[67]

By the Non-Intercourse Act, which superseded the Embargo Act in the spring of 1809, direct trade with England and France and their colonies was prohibited. Although there was nothing now to stop an indirect trade with England, the British orders in council still kept American produce from reaching the Continent. On the whole the West did not like the change, and their representatives were right in predicting that such partial opening of trade would glut markets with our products and bring prices still lower. Poindexter denounced

---

[66] *Annals of Congress*, 10th Cong., 2d Sess., pp. 1481–1482. See also the Natchez *Mississippian*, February 2, 1809.

[67] Natchez *Weekly Chronicle*, December 14, 1808, letter dated Washington, November 12, 1808.

England's attempt to monopolize world-trade and "tax the product of our farms when exported to foreign markets." He even advocated war against her if necessary, and did not hesitate to recommend to his constituents that cotton be shipped immediately to England via a neutral port so as to get a fair price before markets were glutted.[68]

The course of events during the summer of 1809 was well calculated still further to inflame western hatred for Great Britain and convince the frontier farmers that their surplus could never be exported at a profit until England was somehow forced to permit free trade upon the seas. Prices, although somewhat improved, continued low as compared with pre-embargo years. The Spanish West Indies were now open to American trade; but as early as June 5, 1809, Havana, the most important Spanish port, was reported surfeited with exportations from New Orleans.[69] Erskine's treaty (April 19, 1809) by which direct trade was to be reopened with England was, at least in some quarters, regarded with suspicion. If it should not result in opening trade with the Continent, it was held that there would be loss for us and gain for England. The editor of the *Lexington Reporter* wrote:

> What will be the price of our produce confined and concentrated totally in British warehouses?
> Where will be our carrying trade? Why, British merchants and British manufacturers will purchase our productions for the mere expense of shipping and the duties and commissions to London and Liverpool merchants! *Our manufactures will be annihilated.* Britain will have gained a most glorious victory. . . . .
> What is become of the 100,000 hogsheads of Tobacco exported from the United States?
> Will Britain consume and manufacture all our cotton?
> No, not one tenth of our Tobacco—not one half of our Cotton; and our flour, our grain, our ashes, our staves, and every other property must center there, and be held as a *pledge for our allegiance.*[70]

In July news reached the West of the extension of the British continental blockade and of the new duties to be levied upon cotton. The *Reporter*, while bitterly attacking England, held that her insults

[68] Natchez *Mississippian*, May 1, 1809, Poindexter to his constituents, Washington, D. C., March 5, 1809.

[69] New Orleans *Louisiana Gazette*, June 27, 1809.

[70] May 13, 1809; italics in the original text.

were the results of our weak policy. "Submission only encourages oppression," wrote the editor, "and Britain will follow up her blow, 'till our chains are fully rivetted."[71] Probably this writer's attitude was extreme. Some westerners were inclined to look with considerable hope upon the Erskine arrangements.[72] But when, in the late summer of 1809, word was carried over the Appalachians that England had repudiated the acts of her minister, the frontier was thoroughly aroused. Public gatherings were called for the denunciation of British perfidy. Editors joined in the clamor, and state legislatures sent communications to the president denouncing England and declaring their willingness to resort to arms.[73]

The editor of the Lexington *Reporter* was not slow to drive home the moral. In a long analysis of the situation he said in part:

> The *Farmer* who is complaining of the low price of Cotton, of Tobacco, of any other produce cannot now be deceived of the real cause, he will not attribute it to embargo systems, or to French decrees, for French decrees were in full force when we so anxiously made the experiment of *confining* our trade to Britain, the farmers will see clearly that the orders in council prohibiting and interrupting all commerce to the continent is the only cause for his embarrassments.
>
> . . . . The farmer who wishes a market for his produce, must therefore charge his representative in Congress to cast off all temporising. . . . .[74]

The winter of 1809–10 found hard times on frontier farms and western sentiment more bitter than ever against the British as the chief cause of the farmers' troubles.[75] The attempt at commercial coercion had failed, but Congress was not yet ready to declare war.

[71] Lexington, Kentucky, July 1, 1809.

[72] Johnson of Kentucky, for example, was one of the chief supporters of the administration in its negotiations with Erskine. (*Annals of Congress*, 11th Cong., 1st Sess., pp. 156–161.) But most western representatives were not very enthusiastic. (See *ibid.*, pp. 187 ff.)

[73] Carthage (Tenn.) *Carthage Gazette*, August 17, September 1, November 17, 1809; Chillicothe (Ohio) *Independent Republican*, September 8, 1809; Tennessee, 8th Ass., 1st Sess., *House Journal*, pp. 147–149; *Acts of Ohio*, 8th Ass., 1st Sess., p. 347.

[74] October 24, 1809; italics in the original text. See also *Carthage Gazette*, December 15, 1809.

[75] *Ibid.*, December 15, 1809; Lexington *Reporter*, November 11 and December 30, 1809, and February 24, 1810; Chillicothe *Independent Republican*, February 8 and March 8, 1810; Cincinnati *Liberty Hall*, February 7, 1810. The plight of the settlers living west of the Great Miami River in Ohio may be regarded as typical. They could not, so they reported to Congress, make payments on lands which they

Beginning May 1, 1810, commerce was freed from the restrictive measures of our own government. On the whole, conditions seemed on the mend in the following summer, and western farmers were busy harvesting crops which they hoped might be floated down the river to good markets in 1811. Some thought they perceived a promise of better times, while others saw no assurance of prosperity until foreign restrictions should be withdrawn.[76]

But, instead of improving, conditions actually grew seriously worse during the next two years. Wholesale prices of western products were below even those of 1808 in the year before the war. In this new period of general depression on the frontier, the northern part of the Ohio River Valley appears to have suffered less than other parts of the West. Frequent newspaper notices of the building of flour mills in Ohio and increased advertising by those wishing to buy wheat and flour indicates at least some optimistic sentiment. Also, advantage must have resulted from a considerable increase which now took place in the number of cattle and hogs driven eastward over the mountains.[77] Although some settlers still came via Kentucky or by the river route, the fact which now called forth newspaper comment was the large number of wagons bringing immigrants to Ohio which were to be met on the Pennsylvania turnpikes and on the Zanesville Road in Ohio.[78] Along with this new wave of immigration, land sales rose, though not to their pre-embargo peak. So, at least a temporary market must have been afforded for considerable quantities of country produce.[79]

In so far as contemporary appraisals of the economic situation in this northern area are available, they show little or no reflection of the favorable factors just noted. Dulness of business, scarcity of

had bought because (1) specie could not be commanded, (2) laws for the relief of debtors made it impossible for them to collect payments which were due, (3) immigrants were no longer coming into the country and bringing money with them, and (4) there were no markets for their produce. (*Dayton Repertory*, December 14, 1809.)

[76] Dayton *Ohio Centinel*, May 31, 1810; Lexington *Kentucky Gazette*, July 31, 1810; Lexington *Reporter*, June 15, 30, and July 14, 21, 1810.

[77] Zanesville *Muskingum Messenger*, November 24, 1810; Dayton *Ohio Centinel*, December 13, 1810; Chillicothe *Supporter*, March 30, 1811.

[78] Dayton *Ohio Centinel*, December 13, 1810; Chillicothe *Supporter*, March 30, 1811; Zanesville *Muskingum Messenger*, November 13, December 18, 1811.

[79] *American State Papers: Finance*, Vol. II, *passim*.

money, "poverty, disappointment, embarrassment," "the present disasterous state of our affairs"—these are typical of contemporary statements. Taken along with what we know of the price situation, the disorganization of the Mississippi commerce in the winter of 1811–12, and the fact that settlers on public lands were still petitioning for relief, the indications are that, although there was some promise of better times, the region north of the Ohio River was certainly not enjoying general prosperity in the year or two immediately preceding the war.[80]

Judging from the extremely low prices brought by tobacco, hemp, and cotton, one might suppose that the frontier south of the Ohio River suffered from a more serious depression than that to the north. The records clearly show this to have been the case. The Kentucky farmers, who had turned so enthusiastically to hemp culture in 1809 and 1810 that hemp had become the most important staple of the state, now complained even more loudly than those who produced wheat, cotton, or tobacco. There is hardly an issue of the Frankfort and Lexington papers which does not give voice to the despair and resentment of these unfortunate frontiersmen. In spite of public resolutions and even co-operative action to keep up the price by refusing to sell (probably one of the first efforts of this kind among American farmers), ruin was not averted and prices continued their disastrous decline.[81]

In western Tennessee and Mississippi Territory where cotton was almost the only sale crop, the plight of the frontier farmers was most desperate of all. Tennessee cotton planters were reported in the fall of 1810 as so discouraged that to a considerable extent they had ceased the cultivation of their staple.[82] An able contributor to Nashville papers wrote:

[80] See William Rufus Putnam to John May, Marietta, Ohio, March 15, 1810, "The John May Papers," p. 211; Marietta *Commentator*, April 3, 1810; Cincinnati *Advertiser*, June 27, 1810; Dayton *Ohio Centinel*, March 7, May 15, 1811; Washington (Pa.) *Western Telegraph*, July 18, 1811; James McBride to Mary McRoberts, "Mississippi River, April 1, 1812," *Quarterly Publications of the HPSO*, V (1910), 27–28; and *Acts of Ohio*, 9th Ass., 1st Sess., pp. 90–91; *ibid.*, 10th Ass., 1st Sess., pp. 190–191.

[81] See files of the Lexington *Reporter* and the Frankfort *Palladium*, especially for January and February of 1811.

[82] Columbia (Tenn.) *Western Chronicle*, November 17, 1810.

> Ask a Tennessee planter why he does not raise some kind of crop besides corn! His answer is—if he were to do it he could get nothing for it—that he could not sell it for money, unless he carried it to Natchez or Orleans—and that was out of his power—therefore he was content to make just what would do him, (as the saying is.) Hence it is undeniable that the want of encouragement forms the principal cause of the indolence of our inhabitants.[83]

This was written in 1810. In the next year conditions were, if changed at all, worse; and "hardness of times and scarcity of money" continued to be the farmer's story.[84]

As for Mississippi Territory, conditions there were also "very dull."[85] Planters were heavily in debt for slaves as well as for land, and in the autumn of 1811 they petitioned Congress to permit them to defer payments due on public lands because of "the severe pressure of the times" and the "reduced price of cotton."[86]

In Orleans Territory the picture was much the same except that cattle raisers in the central and western part of the territory and sugar planters along the river received fair prices for their produce. But cotton growers were as hard pressed as elsewhere. And business at New Orleans experienced a severe crisis in 1811. The editor of the *Louisiana Gazette* declared:

> The numerous failures lately in this city, has not alone been distressing to the adventurous merchant, but it has in a great measure paralized commerce, by destroying that confidence which is the grand key stone that keeps the commercial world together. This city is young in business, we have but few capitalists in trade amongst us, and a shock of adversity is severely felt.[87]

Increased bitterness toward Great Britain and a renewed determination to force her to repeal her commercial restrictions accompanied the depression of 1811–12. But frontiersmen showed no desire to repeat the attempt at commercial coercion; past failures had shaken their faith in pacific measures. The new attitude is epitomized in the following toast offered at a Fourth of July celebration

[83] Nashville *Democratic Clarion and Tennessee Gazette*, September 21, 1810.

[84] Carthage (Tenn.) *Carthage Gazette*, August 21, 1811.

[85] Frankfort *Palladium*, November 8, 1811, from the *Baltimore Whig*.

[86] *Ibid.*; *Natchez Gazette*, October 17, 1811.

[87] March 7, 1811.

held at Frankfort in 1811: "Embargoes, non-intercourse, and negotiations, are but illy calculated to secure our rights. . . . . Let us now try old Roman policy, and maintain them with the sword."[88]

Although it cannot be questioned that this toast expressed the predominant feeling of the West, the existence of an opposition must not be overlooked. Two western senators, one from Ohio and the other from Kentucky, cast ballots against the declaration of war.[89] Letters to newspapers and editorial comments opposing a definite break with England are not uncommon in the Ohio and western Pennsylvania press. In Allegheny County, which included Pittsburgh, the peace party was actually in the majority.[90] Elsewhere in the Mississippi Valley, with the possible exception of New Orleans, where, as during the embargo, the *Louisiana Gazette* was outspoken in its attack on all administration policies, the opposition was of very little consequence.[91]

Taking the frontier as a whole, the predominance of the war spirit cannot be doubted. All of the congressmen from western states voted for war, and the delegate to Congress from Mississippi Territory repeatedly showed himself an enthusiastic advocate of hostile measures toward Great Britain. Both the governor and the state legislature of Ohio took occasion publicly to approve the aggressive stand taken by the Twelfth Congress.[92] In a vote regarded as a test of the peace sentiment the rural elements in Pennsylvania showed themselves strongly for war.[93]

In no part of the Union was the demand for war more clamorous

[88] Frankfort (Ky.) *American Republic*, July 5, 1811.

[89] The junior senator from Ohio was not present. His attitude toward the war is not known. See Zanesville *Muskingum Messenger*, July 1, 1812.

[90] *Pittsburgh Gazette*, October 23, 1812. See also *ibid.*, May 15, 27, and September 18, 1812.

[91] The *Natchez Gazette* of Natchez, Mississippi Territory, and the *American Republic* of Frankfort, Kentucky, were opposed to war, at least in the manner proposed by the party in power. [EDITOR'S NOTE: William T. Utter, *The Frontier State, 1803–1825* ("History of the State of Ohio," ed. Carl Wittke, Vol. II [Columbus, 1942]), chaps. iii–iv, treats fully of attitudes in Ohio toward the policies of the administration and the decision for war.]

[92] St. Clairsville (Ohio) *Belmont Repository*, December 21, 1811; and Zanesville *Muskingum Messenger*, July 1, 1812.

[93] *Pittsburgh Gazette*, October 23, 1812.

or determined than in Kentucky.[94] The *Reporter*, which had long called for war, now demanded it more insistently than ever, and the other papers of the state followed its lead.[95] Before Congress met in the autumn of 1811 the Georgetown *Telegraph* declared: "We have now but one course to pursue—a resort of arms. This is the only way to bring a tyranical people to a sense of justice."[96] And the next spring the editor of the *Kentucky Gazette* expressed the impatience of the frontier when he wrote: ". . . . we trust no further delay will now take place, in making vigorous preparations for War. Indeed those who believed Congress in earnest, expected a declaration of war long ago. . . . ."[97] The Kentucky state legislature, which had declared itself ready for war at least as early as December, 1808, now insisted upon a break with England and condemned further "temporising."[98]

To one familiar with the situation on the frontier in 1808–10 it can hardly come as a surprise that, in the same breath in which the farmers deplored their ruined agriculture, they urged war against England. Both on the frontier and in the halls of Congress westerners now demanded war as a necessary measure for economic relief.

When word of President Madison's warlike message to the Twelfth Congress reached western Pennsylvania, the editor of the Pittsburgh *Mercury* declared himself attached to peace but if necessary ready to fight for commerce.[99] And at the other end of the frontier, Governor W. C. C. Claiborne, in his inaugural address before the Louisiana state legislature, declared: "The wrongs of England have been long and seriously felt; they are visible in the

[94] John Pope, of Kentucky, who voted against war with England paid the penalty for acting contrary to the clearly expressed wishes of his constituents. He was defeated by an overwhelming majority when he came up for re-election in 1813. (John Bowman to Stephen F. Austin, August 5, 1813, in American Historical Association, *Annual Report, 1919*, II, 227–228.)

[95] See especially *Lexington Reporter*, November 2, 1811, and January 11 and April 14, 1812.

[96] Georgetown (Ky.) *Telegraph*, September 25, 1811.

[97] March 3, 1812.

[98] *Acts of Kentucky*, 17th Ass., 1st Sess., p. 129; *ibid.*, 20th Ass., 1st Sess., pp. 252–254. For other expressions of frontier demand for war, see: Pittsburgh *Mercury*, September 26, 1811; Pittsburgh *Commonwealth*, April 14, 1812; Zanesville *Muskingum Messenger*, July 1, 1812.

[99] November 12, 1811.

decline of our sea towns, in the ruin of our commerce and the languor of agriculture."[100] Perhaps the statements of the somewhat bombastic governor must not be taken too seriously. But the following by a Louisiana cotton planter seems to come directly, if not from the heart, at least from the pocketbook:

> Upon the subject of cotton we are not such fools, but we know that there is not competition in the European market for that article, and that the British are giving us what they please for it—and, if we are compelled to give it away, it matters not to us, who receives it. But we happen to know that we should get a much greater price for it, for we have some idea of the extent of the Continent, and the demand there for it; and we also know that the British navy is not so terrible as you would make us believe; and, therefore, upon the score of lucre, as well as national honor, we are ready.[101]

In Kentucky even the editor of the lone Federalist paper the *American Republic* denounced foreign restrictions as the cause for the depressed prices for western produce. He differed from the Democrats only in that he blamed not England but France, and also, of course, the Democratic administration for the hard times.[102] But this editor had almost no popular following. His paper, which went out of existence in the spring of 1812, represented little more than his own personal opinions.[103]

When aggressive action toward England seemed imminent late in 1811, the *Reporter*, which had advocated war to secure markets as early as 1809, printed an editorial saying: "It appears likely that our government will at last make war, to produce a market for our Tobacco, Flour and Cotton."[104] And as Congress hesitated over the fatal step, the *Reporter* continued to clamor for war. In April a communication printed in that paper violently attacked England as the

[100] Charles Gayarré, *History of Louisiana: The American Domination* (New York, 1866), p. 283.

[101] St. Francisville, West Florida (Louisiana) *Time Piece*, July 25, 1811.

[102] Frankfort *American Republic*, October 4, 1811. Also, *ibid.*, July 19, 1811.

[103] It is interesting to note that the frontier opposition to the war in western Pennsylvania and Louisiana emanated not from the farmers but apparently from the commercial interests in Pittsburgh and New Orleans, and that in Ohio it came from a part of the West in which economic conditions were least depressed and in which a similar Federalist opposition to the embargo has been noted.

[104] Lexington *Reporter*, December 10, 1811.

source of western difficulties and declared that western hemp raisers would be completely ruined by English measures.[105] And the editor himself wrote in similar vein:

> We are . . . . aware that many circumstances combined to reduce the price of produce. The *British Orders in Council*, which still prevent the exportation of cotton, tobacco, &c. to the continent of Europe, *are the chief*—(at the same time confining every thing to their own glutted market) whilst those continue, the carrying trade will be very limited, and bear down considerably the consumption and price of hemp, yarns, &c.[106]

In what was perhaps the most curious and at the same time most revealing article to appear in the West, this same editor wrote:

> Should those *quid* representatives and *quid* members of the administration support war measures after Britain has forced us into war, they support it only for *popularity*, and fear of *public* opinion. Not that their hearts are with their country—But with the British agents and U. States aristocracy.—But the scalping knife and tomahawk of *British savages, is now, again devastating our frontiers.*
>
> *Hemp* at three dollars.
>
> *Cotton* at twelve dollars.
>
> *Tobacco* at nine shillings.
>
> Thus will our farmers, and wives and children, continue to be *ruined* and *murdered*, whilst those half-way, *quid*, execrable measures and delays preponderate.
>
> Either *federal* or democratical energy would preserve all.[107]

When it is remembered that the streets of Lexington were safely distant from the nearest conceivable point of Indian depredation, the editor's reference to economic ruin and the depressed price of commodities appears somehow more sincere than his dramatic reference to danger of tomahawk and scalping knife.

Nor did the economic aspect of the situation fail to find emphasis in the debates at Washington. In the discussions there on declaring war, western congressmen repeatedly emphasized the economic argument. Said Felix Grundy, of Tennessee, a leader of the western War Hawks second only to Henry Clay: ". . . . inquire of the Western people why their crops are not equal to what they were in

---

[105] *Ibid.*, April 25, 1812.

[106] April 13, 1811; italics in the original text. Also, *ibid.*, February 23, 1811.

[107] Lexington *Reporter*, March 14, 1812; italics in the original text.

former years, they will answer that industry has no stimulus left, since their surplus products have no markets."[108] And Samuel McKee, of Kentucky, expressed frontier exasperation with those who counseled delay, in the following words:

> How long shall we live at this poor dying rate, before this non-importation law will effect the repeal of the Orders in Council? Will it be two years or twenty years? The answer is in the bosom of futurity. But, in the meantime, our prosperity is gone; our resources are wasting; and the present state of things is sapping the foundations of our political institutions by the demoralization of the people.[109]

So much has been made of the youthful enthusiasm of the War Hawks, of their national feeling and keen resentment of foreign insults, that it may possibly appear to some that these western leaders were great hypocrites who talked of national honor but acted secretly from economic motives. By way of extenuation it may be suggested that national honor and national interest seldom fail to coincide. Furthermore, the western leaders made no secret of their "interests" even though they did have much to say of "honor." Clay demanded vigorous measures against England, declaring that through failure to fight we lost both commerce and character. "If pecuniary considerations alone are to govern," he said, "there is sufficient motive for the war."[110] Three months later, when writing to the editor of the *Kentucky Gazette* assuring him that war would yet be declared, Clay did not hesitate to state in a letter which was probably intended for publication: "In the event of war, I am inclined to think that article [hemp] will command a better price than it now does."[111]

Confusion has sometimes arisen from the failure to realize that commercial privileges were as essential to those who produced goods for foreign exportation as for the merchants who gained by performing the middleman service. John Randolph did accuse the Democratic majority in Congress of being the dupes of eastern merchants. But one has only to read the words of the southern and western

---

[108] *Annals of Congress*, 12th Cong., 1st Sess., p. 426.

[109] *Ibid.*, p. 508.

[110] *Ibid.*, pp. 599–600.

[111] Clay to the editor of the *Kentucky Gazette*, March 14, 1812, printed in the Lexington *Kentucky Gazette*, March 24, 1812.

advocates of war to find that their position was clear and straight-forward enough. Said Felix Grundy:

> It is not the carrying trade, properly so called, about which this nation and Great Britain are at present contending. Were this the only question now under consideration, I should feel great unwillingness. . . . . to involve the nation in war, for the assertion of a right, in the enjoyment of which the community at large are not more deeply concerned. The true question in controversy, is of a very different character; it involves the interest of the whole nation. It is the right of exporting the productions of our own soil and industry to foreign markets.[112]

Repeatedly this matter came up, and as often western representatives clearly stated their position. Henry Clay left the speaker's chair to explain:

> We were but yesterday contending for the indirect trade—the right to export to Europe the coffee and sugar of the West Indies. Today we are asserting our claim to the direct trade—the right to export our cotton, tobacco, and other domestic produce to market.[113]

Too much has been made of Randolph's charge against the War Hawks that they sought the conquest of Canada, and not enough of his declarations that western representatives were much influenced by consideration of their own advantage.[114] It is true that pro-war Democrats of the coast states hurried to deny that their western colleagues were actuated by "selfish motives."[115] But Calhoun's reply to Randolph is worth quoting, for, although apparently intended as a denial, it is actually an admission of the charge. He is reported as saying:

> . . . . the gentleman from Virginia attributes preparation for war to everything but its true cause. He endeavored to find it in the probable rise of the price of hemp. He represents the people of the Western States as willing to plunge our country into war for such base and precarious motives. I will not reason on this point. I see the cause of their ardor, not in such base motives, but in their known patriotism and disinterestedness. No less mercenary is the reason which he attributes to the Southern States. He says, that the non-importation act has reduced cotton to

[112] *Annals of Congress*, 12th Cong., 1st Sess., p. 424. For the position of John Rhea, another Tennessee congressman, see *ibid.*, p. 637.

[113] *Ibid.*, p. 601.

[114] *Ibid.*, pp. 450, 533.

[115] *Ibid.*, pp. 467–475.

nothing, which has produced feverish impatience. Sir, I acknowledge the cotton of our farms is worth but little; but not for the cause assigned by the gentleman from Virginia. The people of that section do not reason as he does; they do not attribute it to the efforts of their Government to maintain peace and independence of their country; they see in the low price of the produce, the hand of foreign injustice; they know well, without the market to the Continent, the deep and steady current of supply will glut that of Great Britain; they are not prepared for the colonial state to which again that Power is endeavoring to reduce us.[116]

Not only were westerners accused of seeking war for their own economic advantage, but many held they were mistaken in believing that war with England would bring them the results they sought. Federalists and anti-war Democrats repeatedly declared in Congress that war would not open markets or restore the price of hemp, tobacco, or cotton.[117] These speeches, cogent as they often were, failed in their purpose of dissuading the frontiersmen from demanding war, but they are convincing evidence to us that the anti-war minority, no less than the majority which favored the conflict, recognized clearly enough the important relation of economic motives to the war spirit.

As noted at the outset, factors other than those emphasized in this study undoubtedly played a part in bringing on the war. The expansionist sentiment, which Professor Julius W. Pratt has emphasized, was surely present.[118] English incitement to Indian depredations and Spanish interference with American trade through Florida should be noted, as should also the fact that the frontiersmen sought every possible pretext to seize the coveted Indian lands. Restrictions on the carrying trade, even impressment of seamen, may

[116] *Ibid.*, p. 482.

[117] See, for example, *Annals of Congress*, 12th Cong., 1st Sess., pp. 626, 674, 676, and 710.

[118] *Expansionists of 1812* (New York, 1925); and "Western War Aims in the War of 1812," *MVHR*, XII (June, 1925), 36–50. [EDITOR's NOTE: Historians recently have devoted elaborate reconsideration to ideological, partisan, and sectionalist factors in Congressional behavior on the war question. See especially Reginald Horsman, "Who Were the War Hawks?" *IMH*, LX (June, 1964), 121–136; Horsman, "Western War Aims, 1811–1812," *IMH*, LIII (March, 1957), 1–18; Roger H. Brown, "The War Hawks of 1812: An Historical Myth," *IMH*, LX (June, 1964), 137–151, with commentary by Alexander DeConde and Norman K. Risjord, *ibid.*, 152–158; and Bradford Perkins, *Prologue to War: England and the United States, 1805–1812* (Berkeley, Calif., 1961).]

have had some effect in influencing western opinion. No doubt the traditional hostility of the Republican party toward England played a part. Many veterans of the Revolutionary War had settled upon western lands, and time had not failed to magnify the glory of their achievements or to add to the aggressive ardor of their patriotism.

But important as these factors may have been, the attitude of the western settler can hardly be evaluated without an understanding of his economic position. He was, after all, typically an ambitious farmer who moved to the Mississippi Valley in order to make a better living. In the boom times following the Louisiana Purchase he had regarded the western frontier as a veritable promised land. Moreover, the fertile river valleys rewarded his toil with luxuriant harvests. But somehow prosperity eluded him. When, in spite of tremendous difficulties, he brought his produce to market, prices were often so low as to make his venture a failure.

We know now that the farmers' troubles were, in no small degree, fundamentally matters of transportation, of communication, and of imperfect marketing and financial organization. But is it unexpected that in their disappointment (and not unlike their descendants of today who still are inclined to magnify political factors) they put the blame for their economic ills upon foreign restriction of their markets and supported the Embargo and Non-Intercourse acts as weapons to coerce the European belligerents to give them what they regarded as their rights? And when peaceful methods failed and prices fell to even lower levels, is it surprising that the hopeful settlers of earlier years became the War Hawks of 1812?

Reprinted from the *Journal of Political Economy*, Vol. XXXIX (1931), pp. 471–505; copyright 1931 by the University of Chicago Press.

TRAVAILS AND HOPES: SOCIAL LIFE

Part II
Travails and Hopes:
Social Life

The three essays that follow take strikingly different approaches to the subject of social life in the Old Northwest. In the first, Arthur Bestor, professor of history at the University of Washington, treats one feature of life in the region during 1805–55—the large number of communitarian settlements founded there—as a social phenomenon more intimately related to popular modes of thought in the nation than to anything inherent in the western environment itself. His central concern is contemporary perceptions of the westward movement, and particularly the possibilities for social experimentation that the West seemed to hold out to the society as a whole. As such, the essay makes an important contribution to the quickly growing historical literature on the "image" of the West in American thought.[1] Moreover, the article includes a brief but telling critique of Turner's view that the West and the frontier environment fostered "idealism," which in turn encouraged the founding of the many communitarian experiments in the region.

Merle Curti's subject is of entirely different dimensions. Together with a group of collaborators, Curti (who holds the Frederick Jackson Turner Professorship in History at the University of Wisconsin) has conducted an intensive study of one western community—Trempealeau County in Wisconsin—as it developed from 1850 to 1880. In the chapter reprinted here, he considers the wide range of contacts between "native" American groups and the outsiders who were absorbed into the Trempealeau community. His concern is to test current hypotheses regarding the impact of the

[1] See especially Henry Nash Smith, *Virgin Land: The American West as Symbol and Myth* (Cambridge, 1950); and Rush Welter, "The Frontier West as Image of American Society," *Mississippi Valley Historical Review*, Vol. XLVI (June, 1960).

frontier experience upon political and social behavior. He finds some evidence of tensions; he adduces data on marriage that imply considerable cohesiveness in ethnic-group identity; and he discusses the local elite of the county. On the whole, however, Professor Curti finds that ethnic and social "mingling" in this frontier society was marked by tolerance, and that assimilation was smooth though gradual.

It will not be a simple matter to duplicate the kind of study that Curti and his group undertook, for it is painstaking and time-consuming research. Yet Professor Curti himself made the first step toward comparison of Trempealeau County with other communities by offering data on a small Vermont community of the same period. In time, systematic comparison with other communities may provide a broader base for testing Curti's generalizations. Moreover, before we assign special importance to the frontier environment as a factor conditioning such processes as assimilation of immigrants, we must inquire whether the pattern differed substantially from one frontier to another—and also whether the pattern was different in older-settled areas.[2]

The essay by Peter T. Harstad considers a problem that was common in all frontier communities: disease.[3] Individually, pioneers in the Old Northwest sometimes expressed a fatalistic, almost laconic, view concerning the inevitability of epidemics and sudden death. But acting collectively, men in the Old Northwest mobilized their resources to combat epidemics and to handle the social problems that accompanied periods of serious and widespread disease. Here again is a social phenomenon which lends itself well to comparative community studies that may afford insight into the character of social institutions and attitudes in the Old Northwest: established urban centers in the East and seaboard South were also hit by epidemics, and it should be asked whether they responded in ways

[2] The comparative study of frontier development has usually taken the form of cross-national comparisons. See Dietrich Gerhard, "The Frontier in Comparative View," *Comparative Studies in History and Society*, Vol. I (March, 1959); and Marvin Mikesell, "Comparative Studies in Frontier History," *Annals of the Association of American Geographers*, Vol. L (March, 1960).

[3] When the essay reprinted below was first published, Mr. Harstad was a graduate student in history at the University of Wisconsin. He is now on the faculty of Idaho State University at Pocatello.

that differed materially from the responses in frontier areas of the West. Then too, Harstad's essay offers interesting data on the much-debated question of how prevailing technology interacted with environmental factors to influence development in frontier regions —for in this case, the author is concerned with how contemporary medical techniques and public-health technology were diffused in the West and applied in a series of social emergencies.[4]

[4] See also Charles E. Rosenberg, *The Cholera Years: The United States in 1832, 1849, and 1866* (Chicago, 1962); and, for comparative study, John Duffy (ed.), *The Rudolph Matas History of Medicine in Louisiana*, Vol. II (Baton Rouge, 1962). Pioneer ills and cures are a major subject treated in R. Carlyle Buley's classic study of *The Old Northwest: Pioneer Period, 1815–1840* (2 vols.; Bloomington, Ind., 1954).

ARTHUR E. BESTOR, JR.

3. Patent-Office Models of the Good Society: Some Relationships Between Social Reform and Westward Expansion

IN the mechanical realm, nineteenth-century American inventiveness left as its most characteristic record not a written description or a drawing but a working model, such as the Patent Office then required. In somewhat similar fashion, the societal inventiveness of the first half of the nineteenth century embodied itself in a hundred or so co-operative colonies, where various types of improved social machinery were hopefully demonstrated. Patent-office models of the good society we may call them.[1]

To build a working model is not the same thing as to draw a picture. Hence it is necessary, at the outset, to distinguish between communitarianism, or the impulse which constructed these hundred model communities, and utopianism, or the impulse to picture in literary form the characteristics of an ideal but imaginary society. The distinction is more than verbal. A piece of utopian writing pictures a social order superior to the present, and it does so, of course, in the hope of inspiring men to alter their institutions accordingly. But a utopian work (unless it happens also to be a communitarian one) does *not* suggest that the proper way of going about such a reform is to construct a small-scale model of the desired society. Edward Bellamy's *Looking Backward*, for example, was a utopian novel, but definitely *not* a piece of communitarian propaganda, because the social transformation that Bellamy was talking about could not possibly be inaugurated by a small-scale experiment; it could come about only through a great collective effort by all the citizens of the state.

[1] This paper was read before the Mississippi Valley Historical Association in Cincinnati, April 19, 1951.

The communitarian, on the other hand, was by definition the apostle of small-scale social experiment. He believed that the indispensable first step in reform was the construction of what the twentieth century would call a pilot plant. The communitarian was not necessarily a utopian; few of the religious communities, for example, attempted to visualize an ideal future society this side of heaven. When the communitarian did indulge in utopian visions, the characteristic fact about them was that they always pictured the future as something to be realized through a small-scale experiment indefinitely reduplicated. The communitarian conceived of his experimental community not as a mere blueprint of the future but as an actual, complete, functioning unit of the new social order. As the American communitarian Albert Brisbane wrote:

> The whole question of effecting a Social Reform may be reduced to the establishment of one Association, which will serve as a model for, and induce the rapid establishment of others. . . . Now if we can, with a knowledge of true architectural principles, build one house rightly, conveniently and elegantly, we can, by taking it for a model and building others like it, make a perfect and beautiful city: in the same manner, if we can, with a knowledge of true social principles, organize one township rightly, we can, by organizing others like it, and by spreading and rendering them universal, establish a true Social and Political Order.[2]

This is a fair summary of the communitarian program.

Historically speaking, the idea of undertaking social reform in this particular way—by constructing a patent-office model or a pilot plant—is not a common idea but a distinctly uncommon one. No other period comes close to matching the record of the first half of the nineteenth century, which saw a hundred communitarian experiments attempted in the United States alone. The vogue of communitarianism can be delimited even more sharply than this. During a period of precisely fifty years, beginning in 1805, when the first communitarian colony was planted in the Old Northwest, at least ninety-nine different experiments were actually commenced in the United States.[3] Nearly half of these—forty-five to be exact—

---

[2] Albert Brisbane, *A Concise Exposition of the Doctrine of Association* (2d ed.; New York, 1843), pp. 73–74.

[3] The statistical evidence incorporated in this and subsequent paragraphs is tabulated in a "Checklist of Communitarian Experiments Initiated in the United States before 1860," appended to Arthur E. Bestor, Jr., *Backwoods Utopias* (Philadelphia, 1950), pp. 231–243. Communities numbered 8–11, 24–30, 34–79, 82–109,

were located in the Old Northwest, strictly defined.[4] Another
twenty-eight were in areas which belonged to the same general
cultural region—that is, western New York, the parts of the Ohio
River valley outside the Old Northwest, and certain adjoining areas
on the other side of the upper Mississippi.[5] A total of seventy-three
communities—roughly three quarters of the total—thus belonged to
what can be described, without undue geographical laxness, as the
Middle West.

Such a clear-cut localization of communitarian ideas in time and
place can hardly be fortuitous. It is the kind of fact that cries aloud
for explanation in terms of historical relationships. What, then, were
the unique elements in the historical situation of the Old Northwest
that help to explain why communitarianism should have reached its
peak there during the first half of the nineteenth century?

Twenty years ago an answer would have been forthcoming at
once, and would probably have gone unchallenged: *the frontier.* If,
however, the frontier is given anything like a satisfactorily limited
definition—if, in other words, the term is taken to signify primarily
that "outer margin of the 'settled area'" which figured in Frederick
Jackson Turner's original essay—then a close relationship between
the frontier and communitarianism is hard to find.

In the first place, communitarian ideas cannot be said to have
arisen spontaneously among any groups living in actual frontier
zones. The leading communitarian philosophies, in point of fact,
were elaborated in Europe—not only those of Robert Owen, Charles
Fourier, and Etienne Cabet but also those of most of the religious
sects. The Moravians in the eighteenth century found their "general
economy" well adapted to new settlements, but its principles were
ones the sect had worked out and partially practiced before they
came to America. The Shakers faced frontier conditions when they

---

113–20, and 123–28 in the "Checklist" are the ones founded between 1805 and
1854, inclusive. Accounts of the individual communities established before 1829
will be found in the text of the work cited; later ones will be treated in a sequel
(nearing completion), tentatively entitled *Phalanxes of Social Reform: The Fourierist
Phase of Communitarian Socialism in America.*

[4] That is, twenty-one in Ohio, eleven in Indiana, eight in Wisconsin, four in
Illinois, and one in Michigan.

[5] That is, eleven in western New York, seven in western Pennsylvania, one in
what is now West Virginia, two in Kentucky, two in Missouri, and five in Iowa.

first arrived in America, but they worked out their communistic polity later. It was, in fact, their way of settling down after the frontier stage had passed. The nonreligious communitarianism of the nineteenth century drew its ideas from sources even more obviously unconnected with the frontier. Robert Owen's plan was a response to conditions which the factory system had created in Britain, and it made no significant impression in America until Owen himself brought it to this country. Americans did take the initiative in importing certain communitarian theories, but here again frontier motivation was absent. Albert Brisbane, though the son of a pioneer settler of western New York, became aware of social problems gradually, first in New York City, then in the ancient but impoverished realms of eastern Europe. He finally brought back from the Continent the most sophisticated social theory of the period, Fourierism, and made it the leading American communitarian system of the 1840's, by dint of propaganda directed largely from New York and Boston.[6]

If the ideas of the communitarians did not arise on the frontier, neither did the impulse to put them in practice. The handful of communities that were actually located in or near true frontier zones were all planted there by groups from farther east or from Europe.[7] They were not established there with the hope or expectation of gaining recruits from among the frontiersmen; on the contrary, communitarian leaders were often warned against accepting local settlers.[8] Finally, communitarians were misled if they

[6] See Arthur E. Bestor, Jr., "Albert Brisbane—Propagandist for Socialism in the 1840's," *New York History*, XXVIII (April, 1947), 128–158.

[7] The following communities of the period were closest to the actual western frontier: (1) communities of immigrants from Europe: Equality (No. 84 in Bestor, "Checklist"), Icaria, Tex. (No. 126); (2) communities founded close to the frontier by European theorists: New Harmony (No. 35), Nashoba (No. 49); (3) communities that migrated from the East: Harmonie, Ind. (No. 9), Iowa Pioneer Phalanx (No. 72); (4) frontier branches of eastern communities: West Union or Busro (No. 28), Union Grove (No. 111); (5) communities established on the frontier by groups from cities or settled areas of the West: Wisconsin Phalanx (No. 71).

[8] Just before the establishment of the New Harmony Community, for example, Robert Owen received the following advice from his son, who had been visiting the neighboring frontier settlements in Indiana and Illinois: "Although I do not perceive opposition to your plans in any quarter & although there is often an appearance of interest excited for a time, yet the character of the people is so little

expected greater toleration of their social nonconformity in the West than in the East. The mobs who attacked the Shakers in Ohio, at any rate, were indistinguishable from those who attacked them in Massachusetts.[9]

Nothing created by the frontier contributed positively to the growth of communitarianism. Only as a passive force—as an area of relatively cheap land or relatively few restrictions—could the frontier be said to have had anything to do with the communitarian movement. These passive advantages of the frontier were, as a matter of fact, almost wholly delusive. The Shakers afforded an excellent test case, for their villages were to be found in regions of various types. The most successful were in long-settled areas, reasonably close to cities. The one Shaker settlement on the actual frontier—at Busro on the Wabash River above Vincennes—had a dismal history of discontent, hostility, and failure, from the time of its founding in 1810, through its evacuation at the time of the War of 1812, until its abandonment in 1827.[10] The withdrawal of the Rappites from their westernmost outpost—in the very same region and at the very same time—may be taken as evidence that they too felt the frontier to be basically unfavorable to communitarianism. Thomas Hunt, a British Owenite who led a colony to Wisconsin in the 1840's, had to admit that whatever physical advantages the frontier might offer could "be secured, not only by bodies of men, but by private individuals." This fact was quickly discovered by members of co-operative communities which moved to the frontier. "On their arrival here," Hunt observed, "they . . . find many opportunities of employing their labour *out of the society they are con-*

----

enthusiastic & all parties have been so long accustomed to be dilatory in business & to be thinking only of overreaching others & acting an insincere part, that an entire change must be effected in order to make them valuable members. . . . I have seen only one or two persons, who *as they are*, I should consider desirable associates. I certainly look forward with more favorable expectations to those who come from Europe." William Owen, Vincennes, Ind., to Robert Owen, Washington, D.C., February 7, 1825, Ms in Robert Owen Papers, No. 58, in Co-operative Union, Manchester, England.

[9] Cf. Clara Endicott Sears, *Gleanings from Old Shaker Journals* (Boston, 1916), chaps. xi, xiv, xvii; and J. P. MacLean, "Mobbing the Shakers of Union Village," in his *Shakers of Ohio* (Columbus, 1907), pp. 362–387.

[10] See the vivid contemporary record in MacLean, pp. 281–346.

nected with." Though Hunt saw advantages for communitarianism in the cheaper lands of the frontier, he saw none in the state of mind which the frontier engendered. Among the factors prejudicial to success, he listed, with emphasizing italics, "the *influence which the circumstances of this country may exert over their minds, in drawing them again into the vortex of competition.*" [11]

Hunt was probably wrong in regarding even the cheap lands of the frontier as a real economic boon to communitarianism. They proved to be the exact opposite, according to the shrewdest of all the nineteenth-century historians of the movement. This was John Humphrey Noyes, himself founder of the successful Oneida Community (located, incidentally, far from the frontier), who reached the following conclusions after carefully analyzing the history— particularly the record of landholdings—of communitarian ventures contemporaneous with his own:

> Judging by our own experience we incline to think that this fondness for land, which has been the habit of Socialists, had much to do with their failures. Farming is . . . the kind of labor in which there is . . . the largest chance for disputes and discords in such complex bodies as Associations. Moreover the lust for land leads off into the wilderness, "out west," or into by-places, far away from railroads and markets; whereas Socialism, if it is really ahead of civilization, ought to keep near the centers of business, and at the front of the general march of improvement. . . . Almost any kind of a factory would be better than a farm for a Community nursery. . . . Considering how much they must have run in debt for land, and how little profit they got from it, we may say of them almost literally, that they were "wrecked by running aground." [12]

The frontier, then, did not generate communitarianism. It did not inspire its inhabitants to join communitarian ventures. It did not show itself particularly hospitable to communitarian ideas. It did not even offer conditions that could contribute substantially to communitarian success. Communitarianism, in other words, cannot be explained as an outgrowth of the conditions of frontier life.

In point of fact, communitarianism developed in a fairly normal

[11] Thomas Hunt, "The Past and Present of the Colony of 'Equality,'" *The New Moral World*, XIII (August 2, 1845), 472, a communication dated Equality, Spring Lake, Mukwonago [Wisconsin Territory], June 2, 1845.

[12] John Humphrey Noyes, *History of American Socialisms* (Philadelphia, 1870), pp. 19–20.

environment of settled agricultural and commercial life. The foreign-language sectarian communities, it is true, were not indigenous to the localities in which they were established. The Rappites, for example, were conducted as a body from Germany to Harmonie, Pennsylvania, then to Harmonie, Indiana, and finally back to Economy, Pennsylvania. None of the original members had any previous connection with these places, and the number of members recruited in the neighborhood was negligible. The same could be said of communities like Zoar, Ebenezer, and Amana. In the history of the communitarian movement as a whole, however, this pattern was the exception rather than the rule. The Shakers illustrated a more typical development. Each village of theirs was "gathered" (the phrase was a favorite one with them) from among the converts in a given locality, and was established upon a farm owned by one of the group or purchased with their combined resources. When communitarianism assumed a secular character, beginning in the 1820's, this local pattern became even more characteristic of the movement.

Of the thirty-six Owenite and Fourierist communities established in the United States during the half century under consideration,[13] only one—Hunt's colony in Wisconsin—represented an immigrant group comparable to the Rappites or Zoarites. Only ten others involved any substantial migration of members, and in many of these the recruits from the immediate vicinity clearly outnumbered those drawn from a distance.[14] At least two thirds of the Owenite and Fourierist communities were experiments indigenous to the

[13] The thirty-six are those named in Bestor, "Checklist," Nos. 35–41, 54–79, and 82–84. The Owenite and Fourierist experiments, rather than the entire group of communities, have been selected for analysis because their characteristics can be more accurately determined. They constituted the most important and representative group of secular experiments during the half century.

[14] Three communities only were clear-cut examples of migration to the western frontier: Wisconsin Phalanx (No. 71), Iowa Pioneer Phalanx (No. 72), and Hunt's colony (No. 84). Two communities migrated from the East to unite with an already existing western (but hardly frontier) experiment: Forestville Community (No. 38) and Integral Phalanx (No. 76). Though most of its population probably came from the surrounding neighborhood, New Harmony (No. 35) did include substantial groups of members who migrated from eastern centers. Five communities migrated from cities to unsettled mountainous areas in the East: Social Reform Unity (No. 55), Sylvania Phalanx (No. 57), Morehouse Union (No. 58), Society of One-Mentians (No. 82), and Goose Pond Community (No. 83).

neighborhood in which they were located. Sometimes groups in a small village or on adjoining farms threw their lands together or traded them for a larger tract nearby.[15] Sometimes groups in a larger town moved to a domain which they acquired a few miles out in the country.[16] It is difficult to distinguish between the two processes, and unnecessary. In neither case did the moving about of men and women constitute anything like a true migration to a new environment. Clearly enough, communitarianism as a secular doctrine of social reform made its impact in already settled areas and it inspired its adherents to act in their own neighborhoods far more frequently than it led them to seek the frontier.

Yet the fact remains that the great outburst of communitarian activity occurred during the period when the frontier of agricultural settlement was pushing ahead most rapidly, and it tended to concentrate in the area lying in the wake of that forward thrust. Some connection obviously existed between the idea and the situation. The true nature of that relationship must be explored.

In his original statement of the so-called frontier thesis, Frederick Jackson Turner enumerated certain ideas and habits of mind that he deemed characteristically American. "These," he exclaimed, "are traits of the frontier, or traits called out elsewhere because of the existence of the frontier."[17] The latter half of the sentence has a rather off-hand air about it, suggesting that Turner did not fully recognize how radically different were the two types of causation he was bracketing together.[18] Indeed, if the implications of the second

[15] For example, the Owenite communities of Kendal (No. 39) and Blue Spring (No. 41), and the Fourierist phalanxes of LaGrange (No. 60), Alphadelphia (No. 65), and Trumbull (No. 70).

[16] For example, the Owenite communities of Yellow Springs (No. 36), Franklin (No. 37), and Valley Forge (No. 40); Brook Farm (No. 54); the Clermont Phalanx (No. 69); and the various Fourierist communities that radiated from Rochester, N. Y.: Clarkson (No. 61), Bloomfield (No. 62), Sodus Bay (No. 66), Mixville (No. 67), and Ontario (No. 68).

[17] Frederick Jackson Turner, "The Significance of the Frontier in American History" (1893), as reprinted in his *The Frontier in American History* (New York, 1920), p. 37. Turner's most explicit discussion of communitarianism and its relation to the frontier is in his "Contributions of the West to American Democracy" (1903), *ibid.*, pp. 261–263.

[18] Turner's actual illustrations were such traits as the "practical, inventive turn of mind," the "masterful grasp of material things," and the "restless, nervous energy," which he believed were engendered by conditions of life on the actual

part of the statement had been followed out fully and carefully by Turner and his disciples, the frontier thesis itself might have been saved from much of the one-sidedness that present-day critics discover in it.[19] Be that as it may, the second part of the quoted sentence does describe the kind of relationship that existed between

---

frontier. If these traits were, as he believed, transmitted directly to other areas and to later generations, and if they constituted the dominant features of American thought as a whole, then no one could deny his thesis "that to the frontier the American intellect owes its striking characteristics." But then there would be no need for the saving clause, "traits called out elsewhere because of the existence of the frontier." This afterthought constitutes, in effect, a confession of weakness so far as the central thesis is concerned, for it introduces a totally different causal explanation. The traits that induced men to go to the frontier become, in this way of thinking, valid examples of frontier influence. To argue that the frontier was a creative force in such circumstances is a little like saying that the cheese created the mouse because it lured him into the trap.

[19] By failing to take seriously the ideas "called out elsewhere"—that is, by failing to reckon with these ideas as potent historical facts in their own right—the frontier school was trapped into its most notorious blunder: the acceptance of the "safety-valve" doctrine as an objective fact of economic history. The exposure of this error by recent scholarship has dealt a more serious blow to the frontier thesis than is sometimes realized. Turner shared very largely the nineteenth-century positivistic aim of explaining ideas as the products of external physical and material conditions of life. The frontier thesis must be understood partly in this light. By implication it denied (or at least played down) the importance not merely of ideas imported from Europe but of ideas generally, as creative, causative factors in history. The safety-valve doctrine served as a crucial test-case of the adequacy of this positivistic approach. If the frontier actually operated as a safety valve drawing off discontent from settled areas, then here was a clear-cut example of materialistic events or forces generating ideas directly and at a distance. But it turns out that the safety-valve doctrine was a preconception about the frontier, not a generalization from actual occurrences there. It was so powerful a preconception, moreover, that it actually generated action (in the form of homestead legislation, etc.) which directly affected the current of events in the West itself. By destroying the historicity of the safety-valve doctrine, scholarship did more than correct a mere detail of the frontier interpretation; it stood the whole theory on its head. Today the intellectual historian who would deal with "frontier" ideas is forced to take as a starting-point, not the conditions of life at the edge of settlement and the traits supposedly born out of that life, but rather the body of pre-existing ideas concerning the West and the significance thereof for mankind. One may even argue that the frontier thesis itself was less an induction from historical data than a restatement, with historical illustrations, of a time-honored set of intellectual assumptions concerning American westward expansion.

westward expansion and the vogue of such an idea as communitarianism. The latter was one of the "traits called out elsewhere because of the existence of the frontier."

This paper purposes to explore the process through which communitarianism—and, by extension, a variety of other social ideas—were "called out" by the mere existence of the frontier. The statement we are using is, in part, a figurative one. For the sake of precision it ought to be restated at the outset in completely literal terms. Three points require brief preliminary discussion. In the first place, ideas are not produced by the mere existence of something. They result from reflection upon that something, reflection induced either by direct observation or by knowledge derived at second hand. We are, by definition, interested in the reflections of men and women who did not participate in, and did not directly observe, the frontier process. In the second place, ideas rarely, if ever, spring into existence fresh and new. Reflection upon a new occurrence does not produce a set of new ideas. It exercises a selective influence upon old ones. It represses some of these. It encourages others. It promotes new combinations. And it may infuse the whole with deeper emotional feeling. The resulting complex of ideas and attitudes may be new, but the newness lies in the pattern, not in the separate elements. Finally, though we have adopted Turner's phrase, and with it his use of the word "frontier," we will find that it was really the westward movement as a whole, and not the events at its frontier fringe, that the men and women "elsewhere" were meditating upon.[20]

[20] Turner's central theme, likewise, was really not the frontier, but something larger: the westward movement, the West which it created, and the influence of both on American life. With something of the instinct of a poet, Turner seized upon one special aspect, the frontier, to serve as a symbol of the whole. But in the end, it seems to me, he was led astray by his own symbolism. The frontier was a picturesque part, but only a part, of the larger theme he was exploring. Instead of dropping the symbol, however, when it became obviously inapplicable to the other matters under discussion, he stuck to the word "frontier" until gradually its value as a denotative term was destroyed. Worst of all, vices of language are apt to become vices of thought. Having grown accustomed to speak of the influence or the significance of the frontier, rather than of the westward movement, Turner and his disciples tended to look for crucial factors solely among the events and ideas that occurred along the very margins of settlement, and then to assume that the intellectual life of the entire West (and, through it, the entire nation) derived from this pioneer thinking.

With these three considerations in mind, we are ready to restate the subject of our inquiry in distinct, if prosaic, terms. The rephrasing will be clearer if cast in the form of a series of questions, although these will not have to be taken up in order or answered separately in the discussion that follows. How, then, did the expansion of population into unsettled areas, and the planting of civilized institutions there, strike the imaginations of those who took no direct part in the process? What ideas of theirs about the nature of social institutions were confirmed and amplified by their reflections upon this continuing event? Which of their hopes were encouraged, which desires rendered more certain of fulfillment, by what they conceived to be taking place? And how did this new pattern of ideas and aspirations correspond to the pattern embodied in a doctrine of social reform like communitarianism?

Now, communitarianism involved, as we have seen, certain very definite convictions about the way social institutions are actually created. It assumed the possibility of shaping the whole society of the future by deliberately laying the appropriate foundations in the present. And it called upon men to take advantage of this possibility by starting at once to construct the first units of a new and better world.

In this set of beliefs can we not immediately detect certain of the ideas that took shape in the minds of men as they contemplated—from near or far—the upbuilding of a new society in the American West?

First among these ideas, certainly, was the sense of rapid growth and vast potentiality. No theme was so trite in American oratory and American writing; quotations of a general sort are not needed to prove the point. But one particular aspect of this belief in the future greatness of the United States requires special notice. The point in question was enshrined in a couplet which was composed in New England in 1791 and which quickly became one of the most hackneyed in the whole of American verse:

> Large streams from little fountains flow;
> Tall oaks from little acorns grow.[21]

[21] David Everett (1770–1813), lines beginning "You'd scarce expect one of my age," written in 1791 and first published in 1797. See Francis E. Blake, *David Everett* (n. p., n. d.), p. 7.

American civilization, to spell out the interpretation which hearers instinctively gave to these lines, was destined for greatness, but this greatness was growing, and would grow, out of beginnings that were small indeed.

The converse of this idea formed a second important element in the reflections which the westward movement induced. The habit of tracing greatness back to its tiny source, led easily to the conception that every beginning, however casual and small, held within it the germ of something vastly greater. In a stable society, small happenings might have no consequences. But to men who pondered the expansion going on in the West, there came a sense that no event was so insignificant that it might not affect the future character of an entire region—perhaps for evil (if men lacked vigilance), but more probably for good.

A third idea, closely linked to these others, provided the most distinctive element in the entire pattern. Human choice could play its part in determining the character of the small beginnings from which great institutions would in future infallibly grow. But—and this is the uniquely important point—an organized effort to shape them would be effective only during the limited period of time that institutions remained in embryo. This concept is not, of course, the obvious and quite unremarkable idea that what one does today will affect what happens tomorrow. On the contrary, it assumed that there was something extraordinary about the moment then present, that the opportunity of influencing the future which it proffered was a unique opportunity, never to be repeated so fully again.

The corollary to all this—the fourth element in the complex of ideas—was a moral imperative. Men and women were duty-bound to seize, while it still existed, the chance of building their highest ideals into the very structure of the future world. When men spoke of "the mission of America," it was this particular idea, more than any other, that imparted to their words a sense of urgency. This moral imperative applied to the transplanting of old institutions as well as the establishment of new. The link between reformer and conservative was their common belief that institutions required positively to be planted in the new areas. Naturally the *best* institutions were the ones that should be so planted. For most men and women this meant the most familiar institutions, or at least the most respected among the familiar ones. Consequently the greater part of the effort which this concept inspired went into reproducing old institutions in the new West. A few men and women, however, always sought these best institutions not among those that already existed but among those that might exist. Hence the concept gave scope for reform as well as conservation.

Even when it assumed a reformist character, however, this concept must not be equated with reform in general. That it is to say, it was not identical with the sense of duty that urges men to remedy social injustices and to remake faulty institutions wherever they find them. The present concept was much narrower. Without necessarily overlooking abuses hoary with age, those who thought in this particular way concentrated their attention upon institutions at the rudimentary stage, believing that the proper shaping of these offered the greatest promise of ultimate social reformation.

The group of four concepts we have been considering formed an altruistic counterpart to the idea of the West as a land of opportunity for the individual. The dreams of wealth, of higher social station, and of greater freedom were doubtless the most influential ideas which the West generated in the minds of those who reflected upon its growth. The action which such dreams inspired was participation in the westward movement. But all men who thought about the West did not move to it. There were also dreams which men who remained in the East might share, and there were actions appropriate to such dreams. Throughout the world, as men reflected upon the westward movement, they grew more confident that success would crown every well-intended effort to create a freer and better society for themselves and their fellows. And many of them felt that the proper way to create it was to copy the process of expansion itself, by planting the tiny seeds of new institutions in the wilderness.

What men thought about the West might or might not conform to reality. But in the fourfold concept we have analyzed, there was much that did correspond with developments actually taking place in America. At the beginning of the nineteenth century the vast area beyond the Appalachians was in process of active settlement, yet its future social pattern was still far from irrevocably determined. Different ways of living existed within its borders: aboriginal, French, English, Spanish, Southern, Yankee, the ways of the fur trader and the ways of the settled farmer. The pressures from outside that were reinforcing one or another of these patterns of life were vastly unequal in strength, and this fact portended ultimate victory to some tendencies and defeat to others. But the victory of no one of the contending social systems had yet been decisively won. And the modifications which any system would inevitably undergo as it spread across the region and encountered new conditions were beyond anyone's predicting. Half a century later this indeterminateness was no longer characteristic of the West. Many of the fundamental features of its society had been determined with such definiteness as to diminish drastically the range of future possibilities. Just as the surveyors had already laid down the township and section lines which fixed certain patterns irrevocably upon the land, so the men and women of the region, in subtler but no less certain fashion, had by the middle of the nineteenth century traced and fixed for the future many of the principal lines in the fundamental ground-plan of their emergent society.

The consciousness that they were doing this was stronger in the minds of Americans during the first fifty years of the nineteenth century than ever before or since. The idea had found expression earlier, of course, but never had it been validated by so vast a process of institutional construction as was taking place in the Mississippi Valley. The idea might linger on after the middle of the nineteenth century, but every year it corresponded less with the realities of the American scene, where social institutions were being elaborated or painfully reconstructed rather than created fresh and new. The first half of the nineteenth century was the period when it was most natural for Americans to assert and to act upon the belief that the new society of the West could and should be shaped in embryo by the deliberate, self-conscious efforts of individuals and groups.

This conviction received clearest expression in the pulpit and in the publications devoted to missions. An eastern clergyman, addressing the American Home Missionary Society in 1829, called upon the imagination of his hearers, asking that they place themselves "on the top of the Alleghany, survey the immense valley beyond it, and consider that the character of its eighty or one hundred million inhabitants, a century hence, will depend on the direction and impulse given it now, in its forming state." "The ruler of this country," he warned, "is growing up in the great valley: leave him without the gospel, and he will be a ruffian giant, who will regard neither the decencies of civilization, nor the charities of religion." [22]

The tone of urgency increased rather than diminished as the great valley filled up and men sensed the approaching end of the time during which its institutions might be expected to remain pliant. "The next census," wrote the editor of *The Home Missionary* in 1843, "may show, that the majority of votes in our national legislature will belong to the West." The myriads there, in other words, "are soon to give laws to us all." The conclusion was obvious: *"Now is the time when the West can be saved; soon it will be too late!"*

> Friends of our Country—followers of the Saviour—[the editor continued] . . . surely the TIME HAS COME . . . when the evangelical churches must occupy the West, or the enemy will. . . . The way is open—society in the West is in a plastic state, worldly enterprise is held in check, the people are ready to receive the Gospel. . . .
>
> When the present generation of American Christians have it in their power, instrumentally, to determine not only their own destiny and that of their children, but also to direct the future course of their country's history, and her influence on all mankind, they *must* not be—we hope they *will not be*—false to their trust! [23]

If one is tempted to regard this as the attitude only of easterners seeking to influence western society from outside, listen for a moment to a sermon preached before the legislature of Wisconsin Territory in 1843:

> It will not answer for you to fold your hands in indolence and say "Let the East take care of the West. . . ." The West must take care of itself —the West *must* and *will* form its own character—it must and will originate or perpetuate its own institutions, whatever be their nature. . . . Much as our brethren in the East have done, or can do for us, the principal part of the task of enlightening and evangelizing this land is *ours;* if good institutions and virtuous principles prevail, it must be mainly through our own instrumentality. . . . In the Providence of God, you have been sent to spy out and to take possession of this goodly land. To *you* God has committed the solemn responsibility of impressing

[22] J. Van Vecten, "Address," *The Home Missionary*, II (June 1, 1829), 21.

[23] "Important Position of Home Missionary Affairs," *ibid.*, XVI (September, 1843), 97–99, italics and capitals as in the original.

upon it your own image: the likeness of your own moral character—a likeness which . . . it will, in all probability, bear through all succeeding time. Am I not right then in saying that you . . . occupy a position, both in time and place, of an exceedingly important nature?[24]

The same evangelical fervor began to infuse the writings of educational reformers in the second quarter of the nineteenth century, and the same arguments appeared. When Horace Mann bade his "official Farewell" to the school system of Massachusetts, he too spoke in terms of "a futurity rapidly hastening upon us." For the moment this was "a futurity, now fluid,—ready, as clay in the hands of the potter, to be moulded into every form of beauty and excellence." But, he reminded his fellow citizens, "so soon as it receives the impress of our plastic touch, whether this touch be for good or for evil, it is to be struck into . . . adamant." "Into whose form and likeness," he asked, "shall we fashion this flowing futurity?" The West was explicitly in his mind. In settlements already planted, the lack of educational provision posed problems of peculiar exigency, for "a different mental and moral culture must come speedily, or it will come too late." Nor was this all.

> Beyond our western frontier [he continued], another and a wider realm spreads out, as yet unorganized into governments, and uninhabited by civilized man. . . . Yet soon will every rood of its surface be explored. . . . Shall this new empire . . . be reclaimed to humanity, to a Christian life, and a Christian history; or shall it be a receptacle where the avarice . . . of a corrupt civilization shall . . . breed its monsters? If it is ever to be saved from such a perdition, the Mother States of this Union,—those States where the institutions of learning and religion are now honored and cherished, must send out their hallowing influences to redeem it. And if . . . the tree of Paradise is ever to be planted and to flourish in this new realm; . . . will not the heart of every true son of Massachusetts palpitate with desire . . . that her name may be engraved upon its youthful trunk, there to deepen and expand with its immortal growth?[25]

Religious and educational ideals were not the only ones which Americans cherished and whose future they were unwilling to leave to chance. In establishing their political institutions, they were

[24] J. M. Clark, "The West Summoned to the Work," *ibid.*, XVI (August, 1843), 75–76.
[25] Horace Mann, "Twelfth Annual Report of the Secretary of the Board of Education," dated November 24, 1848, in Massachusetts, Board of Education, *Twelfth Annual Report* (Boston, 1849), pp. 141–144.

weighed down with thoughts of posterity, and of a posterity that would occupy lands as yet almost unexplored. At the Constitutional Convention James Wilson of Pennsylvania spoke to the following effect: "When he considered the amazing extent of country—the immense population which is to fill it, the influence which the Govt. we are to form will have, not only on the present generation of our people & their multiplied posterity, but on the whole Globe, he was lost in the magnitude of the object." [26]

Such ideas as these found embodiment in the great series of documents which provided for the extension of government into the American West. Usually the purpose was so self-evident as to require no explicit statement. The Northwest Ordinance of 1787, for example, was without a preamble. It proceeded directly to the task of providing frames of government for the Northwest Territory, through all the stages up to statehood, and it concluded by setting forth certain "articles of compact" which were to "forever remain unalterable" and whose manifest purpose was to determine irrevocably for the future certain institutional patterns of the region. The framers of this and similar constitutional documents were proclaiming, by actions rather than words, their adherence to the set of beliefs under discussion here, namely, that the shape of western society was being determined in their own day, and that they possessed both the opportunity and the responsibility of helping to direct the process. "I am truly Sensible of the Importance of the Trust," said General Arthur St. Clair in 1788 when he accepted the first governorship of the Northwest Territory. He was aware, he continued, of "how much depends upon the due Execution of it— to you Gentlemen, over whom it is to be immediately exercised—to your Posterity! perhaps to the whole Community of America!" [27]

Economic and social patterns, Americans believed, could also be determined for all future time during a few crucial years at the outset. Nothing was of greater concern to most inhabitants of the United

[26] Max Farrand (ed.), *Records of the Federal Convention of 1787* (New Haven, 1911), I, 405 (Mon., June 25, 1787, notes of James Madison). Robert Yates recorded in his notes of Wilson's speech the following additional sentence: "When we are laying the foundation of a building, which is to last for ages, and in which millions are interested, it ought to be well laid." *Ibid.*, p. 413.

[27] Address at Marietta, July 9, 1788, in Clarence E. Carter (ed.), *Territorial Papers of the United States*, III (Washington, 1934), 264.

States than the pattern of landownership which was likely to arise as a consequence of the disposal of the public domain. In this as in other matters, the present interests of the persons involved were naturally more compelling than the prospective interests of unborn generations. Nevertheless, concern for the latter was never pushed very far into the background. "Vote yourself a farm" was doubtless the most influential slogan of the land reformers. But not far behind in persuasiveness were arguments that dwelt upon the kind of future society which a particular present policy would inevitably produce. The argument was often put in negative form; propagandists warned of the evils that would inescapably follow from a wrong choice made during the crucial formative period.

> The evil of permitting speculators to monopolize the public lands [said a report of the land reformers in 1844], is already severely felt in the new states. . . . But what is this evil compared with the distress and misery that is in store for our children should we permit the evil of land monopoly to take firm root in this Republic? . . .
>
> Time rolls on—and in the lapse of a few ages all those boundless fields which now invite us to their bosom, become the settled property of individuals. Our descendants wish to raise themselves from the condition of hirelings, but they wish it in vain . . . and each succeeding age their condition becomes more and more hopeless. They read the history of their country; they learn that there was a time when their fathers could have preserved those domains, and transmitted them, free and unincumbered, to their children.

If once lost, the opportunity could never be regained. But if seized upon "by one bold step," the report continued, "our descendants will be in possession of an independence that cannot fail so long as God hangs his bow in the clouds."[28]

Certain aspects even of the slavery controversy grow clearer when examined in the light of this characteristic American belief. One central paradox, at least, becomes much more understandable. "The whole controversy over the Territories," so a contemporary put it, "related to an imaginary negro in an impossible place."[29] This was in large measure true. Even the admission of new slave

[28] *Working Man's Advocate* (New York), July 6, 1844, as printed in *A Documentary History of American Industrial Society*, ed. John R. Commons *et al.*, VII (Cleveland, 1910), 299, 302.

[29] James G. Blaine, *Twenty Years of Congress* (2 vols.; Norwich, Conn., 1884), I, 272, quoting an unnamed "representative from the South."

states or of new free ones—and such admissions were occurring regularly—aroused no such controversy as raged about the exclusion of slavery from, or its extension to, unsettled areas where no one could predict the possible economic utility of the institution or its ability to survive. The violence of this controversy becomes explicable only if one grasps how important in the climate of opinion of the day was the belief that the society of the future was being uniquely determined by the small-scale institutional beginnings of the present.

From the Missouri crisis of 1819–21 onwards, practically every major battle in the long-continued contest was fought over the question of whether slavery should go into, or be excluded from, territories whose social institutions had not yet crystallized. So long as both sides could rest assured that the existence or nonexistence of slavery was settled for every inch of territory in the United States, then the slavery controversy in politics merely smoldered. Such a salutary situation resulted from the Missouri Compromise, which drew a geographical dividing line across the territories. But when the Mexican War opened the prospect of new territorial acquisitions, the controversy burst into flame again with the Wilmot Proviso, which aimed to nip in the bud the possibility that slavery might ever become an institution in the new areas. The Compromise of 1850 composed the dispute with less definitiveness than had been achieved thirty years before, for the question of slavery in New Mexico and Utah was left open until those territories should be ripe for statehood. Though the Compromise was, for this reason, intrinsically less stable than the earlier one, the uncertainties that it left were in areas which settlement was hardly likely to reach in the near future. Comparative calm thus ensued until the Kansas-Nebraska Act of 1854. By opening to slavery the territories north of the old Missouri Compromise line, this measure threw back into uncertainty the character of the future social order of an area now on the verge of rapid settlement. Bleeding Kansas resulted from the effort to settle by force what could no longer be settled by law, namely, the kind of social institutions that should be allowed to take root in the new territory and thus determine its future for untold ages to come.

Abraham Lincoln in his speech at Peoria on October 16, 1854, made perfectly clear his reasons for opposing the doctrine of popular sovereignty embodied in the new act:

Another important objection to this application of the right of self-government, is that it enables the first FEW, to deprive the succeeding MANY, of a free exercise of the right of self-government. The first few may get slavery IN, and the subsequent many cannot easily get it OUT. How common is the remark now in the slave States—"If we were only clear of our slaves, how much better it would be for us." They are actually deprived of the privilege of governing themselves as they would, by the action of a very few, in the beginning.[30]

Four years later Lincoln restated the argument in a letter to an old-time Whig associate in Illinois. His point of departure was a statement of Henry Clay's. "If a state of nature existed, and we were about to lay the foundations of society, no man would be more strongly opposed than I should to incorporate the institution of slavery among it's elements," Clay was quoted as saying. "Exactly so," was Lincoln's comment.

In our new free ter[r]itories, a state of nature *does* exist. In them Congress lays the foundations of society; and, in laying those foundations, I say, with Mr. Clay, it is desireable that the declaration of the equality of all men shall be kept in view, as a great fundamental principle; and that Congress, which lays the foundations of society, should, like Mr. Clay, be strongly opposed to the incorporation of slavery among it's [*sic*] elements.[31]

These statements come as close as any to explaining the true nature of the issue which neither side was willing to compromise in 1860–61. In the midst of the crisis, it will be remembered, Congress passed and transmitted to the states for ratification a proposed constitutional amendment forever prohibiting any alteration of the Constitution that would permit Congress to interfere with slavery in the states.[32] This provision was acceptable to Lincoln and the Republicans even though they were refusing to concede a single inch to slavery in the territories. On the other hand, the complete guarantee of slavery where it actually existed was insufficient to satisfy the southern leaders, so long as permission to extend slavery into new areas was withheld. For both sides the issue was drawn over potentialities. But this does not mean that it involved unrealities.

[30] Roy P. Basler (ed.), *Abraham Lincoln: His Speeches and Writings* (Cleveland, 1946), p. 306.

[31] Lincoln to J. N. Brown, Springfield, October 18, 1858, *ibid.*, p. 479.

[32] It passed the House on February 28, 1861, by a vote of 133 to 65; the Senate on March 2, by 24 to 12.

In the mid-nineteenth-century climate of opinion, potentialities were among the most real of all things. The issue of slavery in the territories was an emotionally potent one because it involved a postulate concerning the creation and development of social institutions, and a corresponding ethical imperative, both of which were woven into the very texture of American thought.

How communitarianism fitted into this tradition should now be clear. The communitarian point of view, in simplest terms, was the idea of commencing a wholesale social reorganization by first establishing and demonstrating its principles completely on a small scale in an experimental community. Such an approach to social reform could command widespread support only if it seemed natural and plausible. And it was plausible only if one made certain definite assumptions about the nature of society and of social change. These assumptions turn out to be precisely the ones whose pervasive influence on American thought this paper has been examining.

A belief in the plasticity of social institutions was prerequisite, for communitarians never thought in terms of a revolutionary assault upon a stiffly defended established order. To men and women elsewhere, the West seemed living proof that institutions were indeed flexible. If they failed to find them so at home, their hopes turned westward. As Fourierism declined in the later 1840's, its leaders talked more and more of a "model phalanx" in the West. George Ripley, founder of Brook-Farm in Massachusetts, defended this shift, though it belied his earlier hopes for success in the East:

> There is so much more pliability of habits and customs in a new country, than in one long settled, that an impression could far more easily be produced and a new direction far more easily given in the one than in the other. An Association which would create but little sensation in the East, might produce an immense effect in the West.[33]

But it was more than pliancy which communitarians had to believe in. Their doctrine assumed that institutions of world-wide scope might grow from tiny seeds deliberately planted. Such an assumption would be hard to make in most periods of history. The great organism of society must usually be taken for granted—a growth of untold centuries, from origins wrapped in obscurity.

[33] [George Ripley], "Model Phalanx," *The Harbinger*, IV (January 16 1847), 94.

Rarely does experience suggest that the little projects of the present day are likely to develop into the controlling institutions of the morrow. Rarely has society been so open and free as to make plausible a belief that new institutions might be planted, might mature, and might reproduce themselves without being cramped and strangled by old ones. In America in the early nineteenth century, however, men and women believed that they could observe new institutions in the making, and they were confident that these would develop without check and almost without limit. Large numbers of Americans could be attracted to communitarianism because so many of its postulates were things they already believed.

Large numbers of Americans *were* attracted to communitarianism. If the experimental communities of the Middle West had been exclusively colonies of immigrants, attracted to vacant lands, then communitarianism would have had little significance for American intellectual history. But for the most part, as we have seen, communitarian colonies were made up of residents of the region. Though such experiments did not arise spontaneously on the frontier itself, they did arise with great frequency and spontaneity in the settled areas behind it. There men possessed a powerful sense of the plasticity of American institutions but were at the same time in contact with the social ideas circulating throughout the North Atlantic world. One strain of thought fertilized the other. In a typical communitarian experiment of the Middle West, men might pay lip service to Owen or Fourier, but their central idea was the conviction that a better society could grow out of the patent-office model they were intent on building.

On the whole, the fact that communitarianism stood in such a well-defined relationship to a central concept in American thought is perhaps the most important thing which the intellectual historian can seize upon in attempting to assess the significance of the communitarian movement. This movement has been looked at from many different points of view: as part of the history of socialism or communism, as a phase of religious history, as one manifestation of a somewhat vaguely defined "ferment" of democratic ideas. Communitarianism was relevant to these different categories, of course, but its true nature is hardly made clear by considering it within the limits of any one of these classifications. The only context broad

enough to reveal the true significance of the communitarian point of
view was the context provided by the early nineteenth-century
American way of thinking about social change.

This way of thinking was summed up and applied in the mani-
festo with which Victor Considerant launched his ambitious but ill-
fated colony of French Fourierites in Texas in 1854:

> If the nucleus of the new society be implanted upon these soils, to-day a
> wilderness, and which to-morrow will be flooded with population,
> thousands of analogous organizations will rapidly arise without obstacle
> and as if by enchantment around the first specimens. . . .
>
> It is not the desertion of society that is proposed to you, but the
> solution of the great social problem on which depends the actual
> salvation of the world.[34]

The last sentence stated an essential part of the true communitarian faith. A remaking of society, not an escape from its problems,
was the aim of communitarian social reform during the period when
it exerted a real influence upon American social thought. The
dwindling of the ideal into mere escapism was the surest symptom of
its decline. Such decline was unmistakable in the latter half of the
nineteenth century. By 1875 a genuinely sympathetic observer could
sum up in the following modest terms the role which he believed
communitarian colonies might usefully play in American life:

> That communistic societies will rapidly increase in this or any other
> country, I do not believe. . . . But that men and women can, if they *will*,
> live pleasantly and prosperously in a communal society is, I think,
> proved beyond a doubt; and thus we have a right to count this another
> way by which the dissatisfied laborer may, if he chooses, better his
> condition.[35]

In the late nineteenth century, it is true, numerous communitarian experiments were talked about and even commenced, and
their prospectuses echoed the brave old words about planting seeds
of a future universal social order. But such promises had ceased to

[34] Victor Considerant, *The Great West: A New Social and Industrial Life in Its
Fertile Regions* (New York, 1854), p. 58.

[35] Charles Nordhoff, *The Communistic Societies of the United States* (New York,
1875), p. 418. In his Introduction, Nordhoff expressed clearly his hope that through
communitarian colonies laboring men might escape from the growing sense of
economic dependence that was fostering "Trades-Unions and International Clubs,"
which wielded, he believed, "a power almost entirely for evil" (p. 13).

be credible to any large number of Americans. Industrialism had passed beyond the stage at which a community of twenty-five hundred persons could maintain, as Owen believed they could, a full-scale manufacturing establishment at current levels of technological complexity and efficiency. Before the end of the nineteenth century, even communitarian sects like the Rappites and Shakers were in visible decline. The impulse to reform had not grown less, but it had found what it believed were more promising methods of achieving its ends. Men and women who were seriously interested in reform now thought in terms of legislation, or collective bargaining, or organized effort for particular goals, or even revolutionary seizure of power. Rarely did they consider, as so many in the first half of the century instinctively did, the scheme of embodying their complete ideal in a small-scale experimental model. When they did so, it was almost always a temporary move, a way of carrying on in the face of some setback, or a way of organizing forces for a future effort of a quite different sort.[36] Such revivals of the communitarian program were apt to be sternly denounced as escapism by the majority of up-to-date socialists.[37] In America, as in the world at large, communitarianism had become a minor eddy in the stream of socialism, whose main channel had once been defined by the communitarian writings of Robert Owen, William Thompson, Charles Fourier, Albert Brisbane, Victor Considerant, and Etienne Cabet.

The decline of communitarian confidence and influence paralleled the decline of the cluster of beliefs or postulates which this paper has been exploring. These intellectual assumptions faded out, not because the so-called free land was exhausted nor because the

[36] On the episodic and tangential character of certain late nineteenth-century communitarian plans sponsored by individuals and groups whose main efforts took quite a different direction, see Morris Hillquit, *History of Socialism in the United States* (4th ed.; New York, 1906), pp. 331–332; and Howard H. Quint, "Julius A. Wayland, Pioneer Socialist Propagandist," *Mississippi Valley Historical Review*, XXXV (March, 1949), 585–606, especially pp. 592–593, 605.

[37] Thus Charles H. Kerr, head of the principal firm issuing socialist books, published a history of the Ruskin community written by one of the participants, but inserted his own cautionary preface explaining that the experiment was "a scheme which sought to build a new social order without regard to the essential facts familiar to all socialists . . . , an attempt on the part of a group of people to escape from capitalism and establish co-operation." Isaac Broome, *The Last Days of the Ruskin Co-operative Association* (Chicago, 1902), "Publisher's Preface," p. 4.

frontier line had disappeared from maps of population density but simply because social patterns had become so well defined over the whole area of the United States that the possibility no longer existed of affecting the character of the social order merely by planting the seeds of new institutions in the wilderness.[38]

How quickly and completely the old set of beliefs vanished from the American mind was revealed by certain observations of James Bryce in 1888. In a speech to a western legislature Bryce reminded his hearers of "the fact that they were the founders of new commonwealths, and responsible to posterity for the foundations they laid." To his immense surprise, he discovered that this point of view— "trite and obvious to a European visitor," so he believed—had not entered the minds of these American legislators.[39] In this instance it was not Bryce but his hearers who showed the greater perception. The idea he expressed had once been held with tenacity. In the end, however, it had grown not trite but anachronistic. No longer did it state a profound reality, as it might have done half a century before. By the 1880's there was no point in talking about laying the foundations of new commonwealths within the United States. The reforms in American life which Bryce thought necessary were not to be achieved that way. Serious social reformers in the later nineteenth century were faced with the task of altering institutions already firmly established. Henry George and Edward Bellamy recognized this in their writings; Grangers and trade unionists in their organizations; opponents of monopoly in the legislative approach they adopted. For most American reformers in an industrialized age, communitarianism was a tool that had lost its edge, probably for ever.

Reprinted from *The American Historical Review*, LVIII, No. 3 (April, 1953), 505–526.

[38] The most significant revival of communitarianism in recent times has been in Israel, precisely the spot in the modern world where the idea of planting a radically new society rather than transforming an old one has been most clearly put and most strongly supported. For a recent study of these cooperative colonies see C. W. Efroymson, "Collective Agriculture in Israel," *Journal of Political Economy*, LVIII (February, 1950), 30–46.

[39] James Bryce, *The American Commonwealth* (3d ed.; New York, 1894), II, 838.

4. Social Relationships in Trempealeau County

THE society of Trempealeau County, not only in the 1850's and early 1860's but in the later years of our period, was indeed simple. There were no cities or large population centers. Until 1873 no railroad ran through the county. Until several years later there were no telephones even in the villages. As we have seen, economic functions were not highly specialized. Farming and business were often combined. Professional men, ministers, lawyers, and doctors, often engaged in farming.

But it would be easy to exaggerate the simplicity of the social structure and of social relationships in Trempealeau even in the 1850's and 1860's. The first settlers and those that followed experienced, for instance, "the Indian problem," in at least a mild degree. The census of 1860 listed but one Negro, the servant girl of G. Y. Freeman, but a very few did drift in and out of the county in the later years, apparently failing to fit into the community. Much more important of course was the existence of many nativity groups, not only the native-born Americans from New England, New York, Pennsylvania, and Ohio, but the foreign-born, those today referred to as minority groups. These included Germans and Swiss, Scottish, English, Irish, Norwegians, Bohemians, and Poles. In any consideration of democracy in the society of Trempealeau in its formative years we must take account of the relative economic and social status of all these groups, of the amount of intermarriage between them, and of the ease and frequency of neighborly visits in each other's homes. We must ask how much joint participation there was in the voluntary associations, in civic festivals such as Fourth of July celebrations and the county fair, and in political activities and public office. Prejudice, friction, and litigation between these groups provide an indication of so-called social distance. We shall also inquire how much acculturation marked the passing of the years.

We must ask whether social classes existed and what manner of men were leaders in the county.

THE INDIAN

The Indian was never a serious problem in the period of the agricultural frontier, yet he did provide a test of the attitudes of the settlers toward a minority group. Trempealeau County had been the home of the friendly Winnebago, and Decorah [1] was known both to the trappers and to the first farmers as a "good Indian." Indeed, he was well on the way to becoming a legend when the county was still largely unsettled. This is the more interesting since actual social contacts with Decorah seem to have been few. Alex Crane Hart, who came to Trempealeau in 1859 at the age of 13, and two other boys visited the old chief in his tepee. "He seemed glad to see us," Hart recalled much later, "and got out his old pipe and passed it around, for each of us to take a whiff, a sign of peace. As we could only converse by signs, our visit was not a long one." [2] On another occasion the editor Samuel S. Luce visited the old Winnebago chief as he was camping with several of his tribe about three miles from Galesville. Antoine Grignon was on hand and acted as interpreter, and so Luce stayed longer than the Hart boy and his companions. Decorah gave his age as 130! "The expression on his countenance," wrote Luce with considerable respect and even a touch of veneration, "is mild and intelligent, and he speaks with animation, often smiling while relating incidents of his life, with a humor which we had deemed foreign to the Indian character." Decorah described the capture of Black Hawk; and then indicated that he himself had at last come back to die in his old stamping ground, in the home of his ancestors and his people. [3]

Such friendly contacts were not confined to the early days and to Decorah. In 1877, for example, the *Trempealeau County Republican* reported a visit on the part of "several of our distinguished citizens" to about 200 Winnebago gathered two miles from the village for a

---

[1] There were, actually, several chieftains named Decorah. This was One-Eyed Decorah (*ca.* 1772–1864).

[2] Alex Crane Hart, Ms, autobiography, Wisconsin State Historical Society.

[3] Galesville *Transcript*, June 6, 1862.

dog feast and for the corn and buffalo dances. The distinguished citizens, who went on invitation, expressed themselves as "well pleased with their entertainment."[4] And we have mention of a few stray Indians eager to earn a bit of cash and therefore turning up in harvest time to help get in the crops.[5]

But the record also contains many instances of tension and near tension. During the Sioux uprising in Minnesota in 1862, near panic seized many a settler. But even the casual appearance of Indians singly or in small encampments often occasioned alarm. Many early settlers recalled their uneasy feelings at the customary visitations by the Indians, who seldom knocked at the cabin door and who sometimes settled down in their blankets near the stove for the night but who often left, once food had been given them. Some of the pioneer mothers did not relish such intrusions, but there was little that could be done about it. On one occasion old Jim Reed, whose prestige with and authority over the Indians did not wane, told some Winnebago that they must not trouble the whites.[6] Years later, in 1869, a roving band raided the Olson farm in Hardie's Creek and carried off young Marius, a small lad. The grandfather, who was alone on the place, grabbed a rifle and followed the prowlers, forcing them to drop the child.[7] Even as late as the early 1870's the carousals, hard drinking, and thefts of Little Beaver and of a large number of Winnebago camped near the mouth of the Elk Creek occasioned considerable uneasiness if not outright fear.[8]

The record also contains accounts of particular episodes that point to uneasy relations. For example, in 1859 Jonathan Nash's son killed an Indian in a dispute over a game of cards, and this is evidence that members of the two races did engage in card games. The brother of the murdered Indian stabbed a brother of the Nash boy, and a feud resulted which, according to contemporary newspaper

---

[4] *Trempealeau County Republican*, May 18, 1877.

[5] Arcadia *Republican and Leader*, November 7, 1878.

[6] Hart, Ms, autobiography.

[7] Obituary of Marius Olson, January 16, 1936, House of Memories. [EDITOR'S NOTE: The House of Memories, located at Whitehall in Trempealeau County, is a repository of manuscripts, archives, interview reports, and other documentation of the county's early history.]

[8] Franklyn Curtiss-Wedge, *History of Trempealeau County, Wisconsin* (Chicago and Winona, 1917), pp. 207–208.

account, led to the murder of another Decorah, a chieftain who
had been asked to mediate the feud.[9] There was no mention, in
any of these accounts of murders, of any legal action. Again, a few
months later a band of Winnebago who had a grudge against Paul
Grignon descended on his Trempealeau house and drove him out at
midnight. Editor Newland of the *Representative* suggested that it might
be necessary to arm the village to prevent such outrages.[10]

The sale of liquor to Indians also caused friction. In 1876 some
Indians living in the county induced one Addison Garringer of West
Prairie to buy some whisky for them. This was an illegal but not
uncommon practice. He bought the whisky and they enjoyed a great
spree. One Indian, Black Thunder, entered a formal complaint
against Garringer. A warrant was issued and Garringer was lodged
in the Trempealeau jail. The case came before a justice of the peace;
a trial was set and a jury empaneled. Antoine Grignon acted as the
interpreter. Black Thunder testified that Garringer had made a
practice of selling whisky to Indians. The jury found him guilty, and
the court sentenced him to 30 days in the county jail. Editor Leith
believed that this was the first time in Wisconsin that an Indian
had secured judgment against a white man for selling liquor to
Indians.[11]

A dramatic and pathetic episode in Indian-white relations in
Trempealeau took place late in 1873 and in the early months of the
following year. In pursuance with the policy of confining the Winnebago to a Nebraska reservation Captain Hunt, and later Lieutenant
Stafford and six men, on December 26, 1876, stopped at the mouth
of the Trempealeau River and, deploying themselves on each side
of the stream, captured 26 Indians. Another camp of more than 30
Indians was discovered, and these were disarmed without resistance.
A few days later a detachment of six soldiers surrounded the Winnebago camp at Reedsburg and captured 38.[12] Captain Hunt on cap-
turing the Indians took away all their guns, traps, camp equipment,
and effects. Being deprived of the means of getting game, the Indians
not transported westward were forced to beg from farmers in the area.

[9] *Trempealeau Representative*, August 12, 1859.

[10] *Ibid.*, January 6, 1860.

[11] *Trempealeau County Republican*, May 26, 1876.

[12] *Trempealeau County Republican*, January 2, 1874.

Although Captain Hunt was notified of this, he refused to supply the Indians and advised Antoine Grignon, who on instruction had collected a party of 14 Indians on West Prairie, to let the Indians go until transportation could be supplied to take them to the reservation. But this would be an inhuman act, if such an order were obeyed, commented the editor of the *Republican*, "as it is evident that they would be likely to starve to death."[13]

In reporting the situation the *Republican* spoke of it as "A Case of Injustice" and clearly indicated the mixture of humanitarian and economic motives in so doing. The wretched remnant was at last shipped westward. One Indian, who had threatened to kill Captain Hunt, now tried to borrow five dollars from him, and when the officer refused, the Indian pulled out a navy revolver from his blanket. He was at once subdued, and the red men, to use the words of the local paper, "the last of the Indians in Trempealeau County," were headed on their westward way.[14]

Actually, wandering Indian bands continued to camp in various places in the county. Sometimes they staged dances in the public halls of the villages which they rented for the occasion. When a Trempealeau resident ventured to the dances, he inevitably reported the affair in such terms as "ludicrous," "strange," or "disgusting." The *Independence Weekly News*, for example, described a dance in German Hall. Drummers were squatted on the floor, the discordant drums and shrieking voices made tumult and confusion beyond words. The reds acted, the reporter concluded, "like an overjoyed idiot."[15] A different note was struck by the saucy Dan Camp of Whitehall who wandered out to visit a camp of Chippewa in the late summer of 1875. He professed to be quite intrigued with a bright-eyed maiden who had tried to beguile him on an earlier visit. But when he sought her out he had to confess that she was playing a game of cards with some greasy old squaws and "bless our eyes if she would speak to us."[16] Buckskin Joe Bear, a not unfamiliar figure on the streets of Blair, was, in local folklore, reputed to have made a remark

---

[13] *Ibid.*, February 20, 1874.

[14] *Ibid.*, February 27, 1874.

[15] *Independence Weekly News*, June 2, 1878.

[16] *Trempealeau County Record*, July 20, 1876; "Early Days in the Town of Preston," Ms, House of Memories.

which countless Indians in many parts of the West were also supposed to have made. One day at the post office—so the story went
—he demanded "any letcha?" (letter). The postmaster, not know-
ing him, asked "Who for?" Buckskin pompously gestured in a way
that would have shamed even Demosthenes and commanded, "Look
and see."

Only occasionally, except when reporting visiting Indian encampments or the weird dances in the public halls or squabbles over the
sale of liquor, did Trempealeau's spokesmen explicitly reveal their
feelings about the aborigines. The attitudes seem to have been mixed
and a bit contradictory. Perhaps this was natural in view of the fact
that most of the settlers had come from parts of the country long
without any direct experience in dealing with Indians and at the
same time subject to a considerable wave of humanitarian sentiment. On the one hand, many indications suggest that the whites
regarded the Indians with disdain. The Galesville *Transcript* in 1867,
calling the attention of the justices of the peace to the state law for-
bidding Indians (as well as whites) to shoot deer out of season,
expressed a kind of disgust for the well-known tendency of the
Indians to pay no attention to the white man's laws.[17] Three years
later the Galesville *Journal* reprinted an article from the *Clark County
Republican* in which sharp antagonism was expressed toward the
Indians as a horribly degenerate race without a spark of their
ancestral fire. "The timid cowardly remnant of a once powerful
race," the paper remarked, "have not the bloodthirstiness to kill the
lice on their own dirty hides."[18] Others too attributed to the Indian
indolence and lack of spirit.

But at least some attributed the degradation of the Indians to
the whites and spoke openly of the cruelty of the dominant race.[19]
Gale had noted with approval the actions of Senator Morrill in 1870
in defense of the rights of the Indian and had condemned the cheat-
ing of the aborigines.[20] If many did not share these humanitarian
views, there is little reason for doubting that Stephen Richmond, in
recalling the Trempealeau of 1870, was giving a reasonably accurate

[17] Galesville *Transcript*, July 26, 1867.
[18] Galesville *Journal*, December 16, 1870.
[19] *Galesville Independent*, April 24, 1879.
[20] Galesville *Journal*, June 17, 1870.

picture in saying that both half-breeds and Indians were kindly recognized in the simple society that then prevailed.[21]

THE NEGRO

Very few residents of Trempealeau County had probably had much direct contact with Negroes before their arrival. In 1860, only seven householders had been born in the South, in 1870 only 24, and many of these had no doubt long lived in the West. As we saw in the preceding chapter, the overwhelming majority of settlers in the first decades came from New England, the Middle States, and in smaller proportions the Old Northwest, where the number of Negroes was not large. Thus for the most part Trempealeau residents knew the Negro, if they knew him at all in person, in the places from which they had come.

It is true that in the early 1850's a Negro woman, Ada McCrarey, lived in the household of John Morey and Baptiste Collette, general laborers of Canadian origin. The 40-year-old Ada had been born in Virginia and had a 12-year-old mulatto daughter. It is also true that as early as 1859 a mulatto, Finley Casman, and his wife, with two white stepchildren and a big brood of light-colored ones, located on section 23 in Big Tamarack Valley. This holding Casman sold and moved out onto the prairie near Trempealeau village, where he broke land and built, only to sell out again and, as far as we know, to disappear from the county's records. Trempealeau village folk and those patronizing the river boats saw Negro hands working on the craft, and occasionally one of these may have drifted into the county. Or, possibly, the few that came may have come from Chicago or Milwaukee.

In view of the limited direct contacts Trempealeau residents had with Negroes, it is impossible to be very certain about attitudes toward Negroes during the Civil War and in the years that followed. It is certain, however, that the Galesville *Transcript,* under the editorship of Samuel S. Luce of Vermont and of his successors, C. A. Leith and R. H. Gale, took a firm, uncompromising abolitionist position, criticized race prejudice and tried to explain its base, and argued vigorously for Negro suffrage. The only letter published in

[21] Stephen Richmond, "Trempealeau in 1870," Ms, House of Memories.

the *Transcript* on the subject during the war was one upholding the paper's editorial position.

Luce regarded slavery as the cause of the Civil War. It was, he thought, "the foul stain which blackens the otherwise most perfect government on earth. Slavery," he continued in an editorial in the early summer of 1861, "is an element which if admitted into any human government will work its ruin. It is such a foul violation of moral law, such a wrong, that, if persisted in, will right itself though it should carry the destruction of a nation with it."[22] Luce himself would willingly have shared the expense of peaceful and gradual abolition; but since the South had rejected that course, he argued that there was nothing left for the federal government to do but to carry the war through and to make it the instrument of emancipation. In his mind at least, the only reason why the young men of Trempealeau County volunteered for the colors was to erase the stain of slavery. Nothing less, he wrote, would induce them to "so great and voluntary a sacrifice."[23]

Yet the Editor recognized that a great many Northerners did not share his view. He ascribed the ugly prejudice against Negroes which the draft riots revealed less to the ignorant mobs than to calculating demagogues "who would rather the government would go down to perdition than that the present administration would succeed in putting down the rebellion."[24] The kind of race prejudice that manifested itself in opposition to emancipation and to the enfranchisement of the Negro reflected, he thought, narrow and selfish views. Race prejudice, this Vermont printer and builder maintained, would disappear once the Negro was given the same status, privileges, and opportunities as the whites. He did not, however, share the view of his fellow citizen, Isaac Teller, who held that if the blacks and whites intermarried it would no doubt often be to improve the whites.[25] Nature, Luce felt, had, in endowing the races with different colors, endowed them with peculiar characteristics which "wisely made sexual intimacy between them repulsive." But this was no reason, he argued, for fanning the flames of hatred

[22] Galesville *Transcript*, June 7, 1861.

[23] *Ibid.*, August 22, 1862.

[24] *Ibid.*, May 24, 1863.

[25] *Ibid.*, May 27, 1861.

and prejudice. It was a moral duty to humanity to free and to extend the paternal hand to the Negro, to encourage him in his inalienable right to become a man.[26]

Even before emancipation, Luce had come out in favor of Negro suffrage. Brushing aside the argument that the Negroes were un-qualified, he maintained that they were as fit to vote as whites would be under the same circumstances. Indeed, Luce argued that in a republic justice could not accept color as the criterion for draw-ing a line between ignorance and intelligence. "The genius of a Republic is to make all of its citizens intelligent."[27] All were born, declared this Vermont Jeffersonian, with the same inalienable rights. "We have purchased their [the Negroes'] freedom at a fearful cost; let us make a clean record by admitting them to equal rights, and list not to the howlings of prostrate rebeldom and its sympathizers, or the fearful quaking of weak-kneed conservatism."[28]

No one, of course, can say what effect the fiery abolitionist editorials and the pleas for Negro suffrage had on Trempealeau people. It is worth noting, however, that in the autumn of 1865, when Wisconsin as a whole rejected a measure granting Negroes the suffrage, the editors of the Galesville *Transcript* rejoiced at the results in the county. The county voted 319 to 91 for Negro suffrage, and though the vote on the extension of the suffrage ran well behind the party vote for governor, still, the editors commented, Trempealeau could hold up its head with pride.[29]

The small number of Negroes in the post-Civil War period for whom records exist did little to support the friendly and favorable attitudes that Editor Luce had long cherished and publicized. In the spring of 1874 one Augustus Caesor was arrested for stealing from B. F. Wing. He was acquitted in circuit court since the evidence was "not strong enough to send him up."[30] This man apparently opened a barber shop in Galesville, and may even have been the very Augustus Warner who in the fall of 1884 was found guilty of

---

[26] *Ibid.*, May 28, 1864.

[27] *Ibid.*, August 4, 1865.

[28] *Ibid.*, August 25, 1865.

[29] *Ibid.*, November 17, 24, 1865. The vote was in pursuance of General Laws, chap. xxxxiv, approved April 10, 1865.

[30] Galesville *Journal and Record*, May 1, 1874.

manslaughter and sentenced to two years of hard labor at Waupun. In reporting Warner's almost successful attempt to escape, Leith, with perhaps some qualification of his well-known views, wrote: "Mr. Nig. will be watched more sharply hereafter."[31]

Nor were other colored men much better. Charles Miles was described in the press on arrival as "a No. 1 barber" and as having a mother who was ready to do washing, ironing, cooking, and general housework. But mother and son fought over the money the former earned when the son tried to possess it; and, in the editor's words, her unhappy hearthstone was strewn with ashes. The Mileses departed, separately, leaving behind unpaid bills.[32] In 1876 the county had four colored men, but little is known about them. We catch a fleeting reference to one whom the sheriff had to take from Blair to the asylum in Madison.

Although in 1865 pioneer Trempealeau favored Negro suffrage and could hold up its head with pride, 20 years later an incident occurred which caused Editor Luce to bow his own head in shame. He admitted that Charles Jones, a colored barber, was "by no means a desirable citizen," but he condemned as "a disgrace to the village" the behavior of citizens, following the Negro's remark in a saloon that he could whip anybody in town. Jones was insulted in the street, and a fracas ensued in the course of which a window was broken. Someone called for a rope to hang him. Better counsel prevailed. Although color prejudice was not the only factor in the case, it was obviously present. The episode was described in the paper under the heading "A Shameful Affair."[33]

IMMIGRANT GROUPS

The rapid influx of immigrants coming from many different countries inevitably posed important problems of relationship between nationality groups. These problems can be approached more understandingly when the general characteristics of the foreign-born immigrants and their cultures, as understood in the county, are at least broadly outlined. It is possible to do this, thanks to the auto-

[31] *Trempealeau County Republican*, October 16, 1884.

[32] *Trempealeau County Messenger*, November 14, 1877.

[33] *Galesville Independent*, March 6, 1884.

biographies, biographical sketches, and sketches of national groups in the typescript collections of the House of Memories, and to some of the material in existing county histories, as well as to newspaper references.

The Scots [34] were among the earliest settlers in the southern part of the county, coming in closely knit groups in the early 1850's. William Dick, David Cook, Duncan Grant, Robert Grant, Collins Irving, Robert Sommerville, Robert Oliver, James Sampson, John Davidson, Thomas Hunter, and others came to the fertile Decorah Prairie. To a settlement to be known as Glasgow came James Hardie, Richard Bibby, John Bibby, Joshua Bibby, Peter Faulds, Andrew Gaitherer, and John McMillan. In 1859 the south-eastern part of the township of Trempealeau became the town of Caledonia. Most of the early Scottish settlers came from the mining regions of the homeland, though the McMillans were Highlanders. These groups did not come directly to Wisconsin, but rather accumulated savings by working in the mines of Maryland, Pennsylvania, Kentucky, and other states. Then, hearing of the opportunities for acquiring homesteads in the West, and learning somehow of Trempealeau County, they headed for Judge Gale's new county. None of them, it was said, knew much about agriculture, and at first the farming methods they employed were crude. For years they endured the hardships incident to pioneer life. But hard-working, tenacious, and frugal as they were generally said to be, they almost invariably made a go of it and in time established comfortable homes and made a good living from the soil.

Individualistic, freedom-loving, and proud of their homeland, the Scottish settlers maintained their Old World loyalty to the idea of schooling and to Presbyterianism. The Sabbath was strictly kept. Sometimes the Presbyterian preacher from Galesville took charge of the services in the school-house; on other occasions, one of the local group led the meeting. But piety and Presbyterianism did not interfere with their love of games, dances, and songs. Not everyone in the settlements interested himself in or even took part in the Burns festivals which came to be more or less annual occasions in Galesville and elsewhere; but many, notably Joshua Bibby, did. Bibby could recite Burns by the hour. An occasional Scottish settler, such as

[34] See Curtiss-Wedge, *History of Trempealeau County*, 205–207.

Alexander Vallens, was too much a nonconformist to get along well in the new home;[35] but nearly all the Scots took seriously their public obligations and fitted well into the general life of the community. Alex Flemington, for example, when once introduced as a Scotsman, exclaimed, "No sir! I am not a Scotsman. I am an American."[36]

In any case, the reputation of the Scottish settlers for hard work, frugality, and conscientiousness was quickly established. In later years Alex Arnold, himself the leading spokesman of the native American settlers, described them as a frugal, contented, and thrifty people who "never made trouble in the community, always keeping the Sabbath and about everything else they could lay their hands on."[37] Which was to say that when these hardy, frugal folk earned a dollar or accumulated property, no one euchred them out of it.

It is hard to speak of the English settlers as a group, for, in contrast with the Scottish and Irish, they did not tend to perpetuate a national tradition and did not figure in the contemporary records as a separate group, except in the census. In general there are only fleeting and fragmentary glimpses of these men and women as transplanted Englishmen and Englishwomen. On the one hand there was the Trempealeau fellow who was so arrogant and condescending that his neighbors called a special school election to oust him as clerk. Then there was Sarah Vernon, a former barmaid whose profanity shocked some who heard her in the public house over which she presided with admitted competence and kindness. And there was George Bonner, reputed to be a careful worker, a good neighbor, and a minder of his own business, although completely illiterate.

On the other hand there were the Markhams, a family of the gentry with a tradition of public service in the British armed forces, and with sufficient means to bring as tutors and retainers a graduate

[35] Vallens, a dour and queer fellow, for some reason refused to pay his taxes. But his conscience troubled him and figured in his decision to return to Scotland. "Recollection of Jemima Bibby," 1929, Ms, House of Memories.

[36] Ms, House of Memories.

[37] Letter of Alex Arnold to R. S. Cowie, quoted in a paper that Cowie read on November 12, 1912, at the Trempealeau County Historical Society, now in the House of Memories. We are indebted to this paper and to the Jemima Bibby recollections for the treatment of the Scots.

of Oxford and one from Cambridge and to build fairly soon after settlement in Burnside in 1856 an impressive stone octagonal house. This family, however, identified itself with the community, provided important leadership, and apparently made no conscious effort to keep alive the Old World traditions which might have marked them off from their humbler neighbors.

Many of the Canadians who came to Trempealeau were in fact only transplanted Englishmen and Scotsmen—Canadian nationalism had not yet markedly developed. This group also included men and women with marital and social connections with Americans. And it was a group that contributed considerable ability and leadership and included well-known figures.

The Irish were like the Scots in being thought of as having definite characteristics. They began to come in the early 1850's, settling in the township of Trempealeau. The Irish were also in the 1860's and 1870's to be found, in small numbers, in Hale, Preston, and Arcadia, and in much larger numbers in Ettrick, where they were able in 1872 to establish St. Bridget's parish. Some Irish were Protestants from northern Ireland, and others were Catholics from the southern part of the island. The census does not make clear from what part of the country Irish-born residents came.

Accounts of the time would have us believe that the Irish fell into two distinct groups. One was made up of men and women of no book learning, of extremely limited means, and of no great drive or ambition. Such were the firstcomers who took up small farms in Trempealeau in the 1850's and were content to play little part in community life. The separateness of this group was emphasized by reports of much fighting and contention among them and by the relatively low social and economic status of those who came in the early 1870's to work on the railroad construction.

But Trempealeau highly approved of "another group" including men of some education and culture. J. H. Pierson, for example, came to Trempealeau from Dublin in 1861, having been in the constabulary service and having been trained as a druggist in Canada. Pierson, the only real pharmacist in the county, after having worked for a time in the drugstore in Trempealeau, set up a store of his own. Known as a refined gentleman, he left, by report, a deep impression on all who came in contact with him. Then there were

Robert Warner, Protestant, who settled in Hale in 1863, and his brother, M. J. Warner, who after Civil War service succeeded in farming, as did his brother, and who served the town of Hale on the county board and was ultimately elected, Democrat though he was, to the legislature. And there was David Maloney, who had not enjoyed formal education, but who had a good deal to do with the development of Hale.

Other Irishmen, like Charles Donnely, came with practically nothing at all in the way of worldly possessions and succeeded in becoming prosperous farmers. We could add to this list many more, such as James Gaveney who came to Arcadia in 1856, or James McKivergan, who after working for a time in the lead mines and in milling, took up land in Preston in 1862; or Daniel English, who, again, had no formal education but who made the most out of life and raised a family that did credit to him and to their mother. One is tempted to describe also the Gleasons, the O'Briens, the Binghams, and various others, but it may be well to stop with Dennis Lawler, Dublin-born, Civil War veteran, squatter in the northern end of the county, and, like so many of the other Irish, a man of positive, marked character.

Whether the Irish-born in Trempealeau actually did fall into two distinct groups, one shiftless and improvident, the other industrious and successful, is a question which of course cannot be settled by the talk of neighbors or even of newspapers. Some of our objective studies of certain occupational groups will furnish evidence bearing on this point.

The evidence at hand suggests that the alleged Irish traits of buoyancy, optimism, and a certain improvidence and impulsiveness did characterize a great many of Trempealeau's Irish-born settlers. Foremost in a fight, in a frolic, at a funeral, these men and women were later remembered as, on the whole, sound citizens, good-natured, and everybody's friends. This is not to say that prejudices were never manifested against them, or that their relations with other groups were free from tension. We do not now recall seeing the phrase "shanty Irish" in the accounts of the time. But the attitude implied in these words was clearly present, along with admiration for the Gaveneys and the McKivergans.

Among those of German birth the census records included the

Prussian Poles except for the very few who explicitly stated that they were born in Poland or Prussian Poland. It was only in the later part of our study that we isolated for separate analysis all those with Polish names. Now in all three census years the great majority of "Germans" gave Prussia as birthplace—61 percent in 1860, and 67 percent in both 1870 and 1880. And there were many Poles in Prussia. Hence some of the Germans we speak about in this chapter, as for instance in discussing intermarriage, were really Polish, and some did not even speak German.

The people of Trempealeau, however, knew who was Polish and who was not, except that there was some natural confusion of Bohemians with Poles. And the people of Trempealeau liked the Germans better. Scattered fairly widely in the southern and western portions of the county, and always a minority among the foreign-born, the German-born settlers were chiefly farmers. A few achieved positions of local leadership in terms of election to town offices. The German Swiss also met with approval. In general the Germans, as distinct from the Poles, were respected as industrious and reliable. They were no problem.

During the winter of 1862–63, several Polish families came from Winona and settled at Pine Creek in the northern part of Trempealeau Township. According to earlier local historians of Trempealeau, these included Paul and Mike Lessman, Paul Livera, Frank Meyer, Joseph Lubinski, and Joseph Wunk (or Winook). With the heads of these families also came Math Brom and his family, Bohemians. The Poles had originated chiefly in the provinces of Posen and Pomerania and formed a closely knit community. By 1868, they had established a parish, for they were generous supporters of the Roman Catholic Church. By the mid-1870's, the group dominated the area, and the newly established town of Dodge was virtually a Polish township. According to accounts preserved in the House of Memories, which represent local tradition, the original settlement was the second Polish settlement in the state and one of the oldest in the country.[38]

At about the same time that the settlers from Winona made their first rude homes at Pine Creek, Albert and Lawrence Bautch and

[38] House of Memories; Curtiss-Wedge, *History of Trempealeau County*, 88–89 150–152.

Peter Sura with their families, coming from New Lisbon, Wisconsin, settled at North Creek in Arcadia. Silesia had been their home in the Old World, and their Polish vernacular differed considerably from that of their countrymen in Trempealeau. The Bohemians, numbering perhaps ten or twelve families, tended to become identified with the Poles, since the children learned Polish, and the two groups intermarried.

Whatever the differences among the Polish and the Bohemians who merged with them, accounts of the time would lead one to suppose that all were farmers and all were poor. Whether this opinion is justified by the facts is one of the things that can be settled by objective counts of numbers in occupational groups and by census data on total property. [EDITOR'S NOTE: Curti's data show that in 1870, of 1,418 foreign-born from Continental Europe, 1,168 were farmers; most Poles owned 150 acres or less.]

Devoted Catholics, Poles could be counted on to establish parishes, which they did in Pine Creek in 1868 and in Arcadia somewhat later. Decades later, John F. Kulig characterized the Poles as generous church-givers, hard losers, and given to cherishing grudges and animosities. This reluctance to forget when some harm had been done them, together with their taste for heavy drinking, explained in good part the brawls which frequently broke out among them. On the other hand, they were gifted with a capacity for pleasure and took great joy in dancing. Gradually a few engaged in business and established a kind of leadership in the group, but for the most part they farmed, lived in isolation from other settlers, and only gradually became assimilated into the larger life of the community.[39]

The Norwegian settlers in Trempealeau were by far the largest immigrant group, almost equaling the native-born American group in 1870, and considerably surpassing it ten years later. Some of these Norwegians came to Trempealeau from other American communities, notably from Coon Valley in nearby Jackson County, Wisconsin. But many came directly from Norway. As in the case of immigrants from other countries, the new Norwegian settlers tended to go where some of their fellow countrymen were already established.

[39] Paper of John Kulig, dated Independence, November 12, 1912, Ms, House of Memories.

Thus we have certain communities thought of as Norwegian. Of the 298 farm operators who arrived in the county during the 1860's, 104 settled in Ettrick, already the home of a number of Norwegian families; 64 came to Preston township, 47 to Arcadia, and 30 to Gale. None came to Caledonia, a Scottish stronghold, and only one to Burnside; but Hale, Lincoln, Sumner, and Trempealeau each received from six to 20 of them.

The first Norwegian community to take shape, dating from the arrival in 1854 of Gulick Olson, was in the Trempealeau Valley near Blair, and it was chiefly made up of migrants from Solor. The North Branch Beaver Creek settlement, originating with the coming of Iver Knudtson in 1857, was comprised largely of immigrants from Hardanger. Hardie's Creek Valley in the town of Gale dated from 1860, and was made up in good part of men and women originally from Biri, a parish in south central Norway. Other settlements included the one begun in 1859, in French Creek Valley, and the very important one in the large and beautiful valley of the Pigeon Creek, which dated from 1867. There were also settlements in Sumner, in Plum Creek, in Eleva, and elsewhere.

Many Norwegians were poor, and some were extremely poor, as [Curti's] data on total property and farm value [of ethnic groups] show. Norwegian immigrants tended to seek the hills rather than the prairies or the sandy soils of the southeastern part of the county. Some homesteaded; some settled on land claimed by the West Wisconsin Railroad Company; a smaller number were able to buy land, which in some instances was improved, in more instances, unimproved. In the census of 1860, 12 Norwegians were reported as agricultural laborers; in 1870, 348 were so reported; in 1880, 541. The first homes were often dugouts with walls of sod, roofs of thatch, and floors of dirt; but some put up log huts at the start. Farming implements, according to Judge Anderson's recollection, included the wood beam plow, "A" drag, Morgan cradle, swath and scythe, hand rake, and crudely constructed wagon. Although Judge Anderson, himself an immigrant from Norway and a conscientious historian of the county, believed that virtually all Norwegian immigrants could read their own language, literacy figures as reported in the census indicated that he was wrong.[40]

[40] See chapter xiv. [Curti, *Making of an American Community.*]

It seems likely, however, that Judge Anderson was correct in holding that almost all Norwegians were religious. In any case, they quickly set about establishing churches. Although a few leaders emerged, as we shall see, in both the larger business and political life, the number that did, especially in the early years, was far below that to which their proportion in the whole population would have entitled them. By and large, the Norwegians tended to maintain their own life—as is evidenced not only by their churches, schools, and stores, but also by the establishment in 1877, under the leadership of N. L. Tolvstad and Iver P. Enghagen, of a Scandinavian Insurance Company. The Norwegian communities were not free from quarrels among themselves; but by and large this group established its reputation fairly early as a hard-working, frugal, and law-abiding folk.[41]

NATIVE AMERICAN ATTITUDES TOWARD EUROPEAN NEWCOMERS

What was the attitude of the old American stock, the New Englanders, New Yorkers, and other Middle States men, and the smaller numbers of people from the Old Northwest, toward the newcomers from Ireland, Germany, Poland, and Norway? The question cannot be answered in any complete way. But the evidence available indicates that on the whole the spokesmen of the older American group welcomed the newcomers. Editor Luce of the Galesville *Transcript* described appreciatively a Norwegian settlement in the eastern part of Preston which he visited in 1864. "The evidences of thrift are unmistakable," he noted. "Broad fields have been cultivated, good dwellings built, and the farm yards are well filled with stock." He was pleased to see that Syvert Johnson had the best barn in the county, and he looked forward to the day when the children of these intelligent newcomers would fill important positions in the county; he was sure they would if English-speaking schools were made available to them.[42] The perseverance, thrift, and industry of the Norwegians were frequently noted in his newspaper.

[41] Paper of P. H. Johnson, "Pioneer Scandinavian Settlers in Trempealeau County," Ms, House of Memories.

[42] Galesville *Transcript*, March 22, 1864.

Four years later, the *Trempealeau County Record* in calling attention to the large number of Scandinavians that had been settling in the county spoke of them as "an honest, hardworking, industrious class." [43] From time to time leaders of the county urged that efforts be made to secure even more of the large number of immigrants flooding into America. [44] The vigor of the Norwegians was much admired. These were just the sort of people, remarked the editor of the *Trempealeau County Record*, that were needed to develop the fields of Wisconsin. "Trempealeau County wants more of them." [45]

As the numbers increased, there were no signs of any change in the welcome that spokesmen of the older residents extended. The *Arcadia Leader* in 1877 reported that about 200 Norwegians from Biri parish in the town of Mjosen, traveling together and neatly dressed in homespun, were on their way to settle in Blair. "They are just the class of which the Northwest needs thousands more." [46] The hard-working character of the Norwegians continued to impress the editor of the *Trempealeau County Record*, who wrote in 1878 that these new-comers made "the best citizens." [47]

The press had less to say explicitly about the Polish immigrants. But Luce, in reporting "assault and battery cases" among the Poles of the town of Trempealeau in 1870, good-naturedly took pains to speak highly of these people who had come to "assist in cultivating our hills and valleys." [48] The Whitehall *Times* in describing a Fourth of July celebration wrote of the "husky Polack from his sod hut, the sturdy German, the honest, hard-working Norsk" and rejoiced that they joined hands and hearts with the native Yankees in doing honor to the great national holiday. [49]

Editor Luce was probably exceptional in holding that the country could profitably absorb even the Chinese immigrants. [50] But there seems little reason to doubt the general accuracy of the impressions reported by a newcomer of American background,

[43] *Trempealeau County Record*, September 18, 1868.
[44] Galesville *Transcript*, March 19, 1867.
[45] *Trempealeau County Record*, August 13, 1869.
[46] *Arcadia Leader*, June 28, 1877.
[47] *Trempealeau County Record*, June 12, 1878.
[48] Galesville *Journal*, July 22, 1870.
[49] Whitehall *Times*, July 6, 1882.
[50] *Galesville Independent*, February 27, 1879.

Stephen Richmond, when he took stock of the village of Trempealeau in 1870. He heard many people speaking German, Polish, Bohemian, and Scandinavian, and even other languages which he did not recognize; he was struck by the oddity of dress of these folk; but he was even more impressed by "the general inter-social manner of the people and their truly democratic manners and customs," with the fact that "no notice appeared to be taken of difference in nationality."[51]

Henry A. Rhodes, who was a young man in the later 1870's, in reply to a question about the degree of social democracy in the Trempealeau of his youth, wrote: "As to the question of frontier democracy I can report from firsthand observation and experience that no social barriers existed between the various population groups, nor was there any lack of cordiality on the part of the older families toward newcomers, whether foreign-born or native Americans. Picnics and other social gatherings brought most elements of the population together on an equal and entirely democratic basis. The atmosphere was neighborly and friendly."[52] Even when old-stock Americans criticized the drinking habits of the newcomers, they could add that these people were welcome to "the higher birth-right of freedom and manhood" that America offered—a heritage to be won more surely and readily if a sound view were taken on the issue of temperance![53]

The verbal hospitality thus extended in general terms was sometimes spelled out in newspaper reports of specific incidents in the immigrant communities or in other expressions of concrete interest. Thus in 1867, the Galesville *Transcript* invited "our German friends" to call weekly at the office to read copies of the *Nord Stern*, "the best German paper in Wisconsin."[54] O. E. Stearns sent to the *Galesville Journal* the information that a Mr. Rezab, a Bohemian "over the pass," had raised 220 bushels of oats from three and a half bushels of seed, and wondered whether anybody could beat that record.[55]

[51] Curtiss-Wedge, *History of Trempealeau County*, p. 78.

[52] Henry Rhodes to Merle Curti, April 3, 1953.

[53] Letter from Gilfillan, Gray, and Smith to the *Trempealeau County Republican*, March 13, 1874.

[54] Galesville *Transcript*, July 12, 1867.

[55] *Galesville Journal*, November 11, 1870.

Merle Curti

The talk among the Scandinavians of building a church edifice led to the announcement that they would "meet with general encouragement" from the citizens of Galesville.[56] In 1872, the *Galesville Journal* noted that the Reverend Svenngsen had called on the editor to give a list of the marriages at which he had officiated. The list was printed.[57] "There was a wedding among our Norsk friends last Saturday night," reported the *Trempealeau County Messenger* a few years later, "and we do hereby extend our heartfelt sympathies, just the same as if they had been the childmates of our playhood (*sic*)."[58] The *Independence Weekly News* wrote in the spring of 1879 that the Norwegians had held a dance the night before in Walters Hall and that presumably everyone had a pleasant time though the editor himself had been unable to be on hand.[59]

Doings among the Polish also found their way into print. "Our Polander friends had a wedding and dance at J. K. Cysewieski's on Monday evening, and all appeared to enjoy themselves well," reported the *Arcadia Leader*.[60] And the same journal gave the names of the heads of the five Polish families that arrived one week in the spring of 1876.[61] Early in 1876, the *Trempealeau County Republican*, noting that the number of its Irish subscribers had increased, published a column of Irish news.[62]

These are only a few examples of many evidences in the press of interest in the immigrants and their day-by-day lives. But even these friendly notices often betrayed a considerable degree of social distance between the old stock American group and the newer arrivals. The references in the press to Germans, Bohemians, Norwegians, Poles, and Irish take it for granted that these are separate groups with their own interests. It was even common in the earlier years of settlement for the press in reporting events relating to the immigrants to speak only of their nationality, not using their names. For instance, it was said that the pastor of the Norsk Lutheran

[56] *Galesville Journal and Record*, August 1, 1873.
[57] *Galesville Journal*, November 21, 1872.
[58] *Trempealeau County Messenger*, May 24, 1876.
[59] *Independence Weekly News*, March 22, 1879.
[60] *Arcadia Leader*, January 26, 1877.
[61] *Ibid.*, May 26, 1876.
[62] *Trempealeau County Republican*, February 18, 1876.

church had arrived direct from Norway, without giving his name
—though he was wished well in his new field of labor.[63] Even as late
as 1879, the *Galesville Independent's* correspondent in reporting some
incident used the term "a couple of Germans."[64] Long before this,
however, it had become usual to refer to the Germans by name, and
this was increasingly true also of the Norwegians in the later 1870's.
In some instances, the names of Poles were also given; though
perhaps because of the difficulty of the names themselves or because
the social distance between these immigrants and the old Americans
was greater, it remained usual much later to refer merely to "a
Pole" or a "Polander."

Although the increasing use of individuals' proper names and
the growing tendency to give more specific and fuller accounts of
news stories about immigrants from German lands and from Norway
indicate progress in acculturation, the 1870's continued to furnish, as
had the 1860's, some evidences of prejudice against the newcomers.
It is noteworthy that almost all of the examples of prejudice against
the Norwegians and Polish come from the newspapers of the 1870's
rather than of the 1860's—which suggests that perhaps tensions were
less evident in the early frontier period. Only a few examples can be
cited, but they give the tone. Sometimes the reference is sarcastic or
disapproving. Thus an unnamed "Polander" was badly cut with a
reaper, and the family thought they did not need a doctor. When
the man died, the paper in referring to the incident commented:
"They certainly don't now."[65]

Or take an item like this: "Several Polanders resisted constable
Alex Lintz, while securing a cow, by virtue of a chattel mortgage,
Wednesday. The result was, the Polanders were badly handled.
Thinking to have revenge, they had the constable arrested, but
found, after a trial before an Arcadia justice, that the constable was
in the right and they were in the wrong. Now Mr. Lintz proposes to
pick them up for interfering with his duties as an officer."[66] One
more: "A Polander residing near the village went home drunk the
other night, beat his wife and children, turned them out into the

---

[63] *Trempealeau County Messenger*, May 31, 1876.

[64] *Galesville Independent*, April 17, 1879.

[65] Independence *Weekly News Bulletin*, August 16, 1879.

[66] *Ibid.*, July 19, 1879.

road, locked the doors and went to sleep. The bruised and bleeding wife and children passed the remainder of the night in the barn."[67]

Drunkenness, scraps, and carryings on at dances often shocked the old American residents. In commenting on one Polish dance the Independence paper remarked that such disgraceful scenes should not be permitted on Sunday.[68] Indeed, the conflict between the old American views of Sabbath observance and those of the newcomers from the Continent was often in evidence. When a boatload of Germans from Winona came to Trempealeau for a Sunday picnic and were joined by local fellow countrymen, the correspondent who reported the affair called it a bacchanalian carousal, most demoralizing to a Christian community.[69] Marked disapproval was also expressed of the reported drunkenness, fighting, yelling, and rowdyism, with pistol shots on occasion, at the Ettrick wedding of Knudt Baur and Anna Thompson.[70] In view of the incidence of drunkenness and rowdyism among some immigrant groups it is understandable that when two haystacks on James Gaveney's farm were burned, the affair was laid at the door of "drunken Polanders returning from a mid-night pow-wow." Actually in this case the Arcadia *Republican and Leader* had been misinformed. The paper subsequently noted that Joe Cysewieski discovered the fire and gave the alarm, and that Mr. Gaveney concluded that the fire had been set, not by Polanders, but by some miserable scamp who did the deed purposely. The *Republican and Leader* was pleased to make the correction.[71]

Now and again something happened which brought out latent suspicions and prejudice on the part of the older Americans. Such an instance was the affair in which a "Polander" refused to aid four boys who called to him for help from the railway bridge near New City, with the result that the boys' legs were amputated. Feeling ran so high that the Pole was hidden by his friends.[72]

Another much publicized incident causing tension occurred at Fugina's tavern at New City, the gathering place for the drinking crowd and for many Polish farmers near Independence. Some of the

[67] *Trempealeau County Republican*, October 10, 1877.
[68] Independence *Weekly News Bulletin*, November 23, 1878.
[69] *Galesville Independent*, July 24, 1879.
[70] Galesville *Journal*, February 23, 1871.
[71] Arcadia *Republican and Leader*, October 21, 28, 1880.
[72] *Galesville Independent*, March 30, 1876, comment from the Whitehall *Messenger*.

non-Polish drinkers decided upon some mischief and one day stole some clothing hanging on a line in Mr. Fugina's store, which adjoined the tavern. Some Polish residents informed Mr. Fugina of the theft and, in the words of John Hunter who preserved the record of the affair for posterity, "a race riot ensued." One of the men fired shots into the crowd from outside the window, injuring one of the participants. Order was restored, arrests were made. A hearing was held one winter night at the Cripps schoolhouse before Justice of the Peace George Parsons. The prisoners were defended by G. Y. Freeman of Galesville, and Mr. Fugina was represented by Edward Lees of Buffalo County. A number of prisoners were bound over, but the Circuit Court later acquitted them.[73]

The affair indicates that the Poles were not only thought of as a distinct group but that they were ready to act in defense of one of their number. Further, leadership was stimulated by the need the Poles obviously felt for having their side fairly presented. Peter Eichman of New City called on the editor of the Galesville *Journal and Record*, and Mr. Luce, in describing the call, spoke of his visitor as an influential man among the Poles who expressed concern with the way in which the "shooting affray" had been handled in the press. Eichman alluded to certain remarks in the *Trempealeau Republican* which he regarded as libels on his countrymen as a class. Luce reported to his readers that Eichman spoke in a sensible way, and added that though Polish conduct might be different from American, "Polish hospitality, good will and industry recommend them as a people worthy of consideration far above the level of brute, an epithet that had been applied to them in no very charitable way."[74]

If the Fugina affair revealed the latent hostility present in some American circles toward the Poles and evoked a defense on the part of its own leaders and in Luce's paper, it also showed that, however great the tensions, legal processes and institutions were respected as a mode of adjusting differences and conflicts. Participants looked to the law, not to further violence. Clearly, conflict could be settled by

[73] Curtiss-Wedge, *History of Trempealeau County*, p. 208, giving the narrative of John Hunter of Independence.

[74] Galesville *Journal and Record*, October 17, 1873. Luce's position may in part be explained by the rivalry between him and Mr. Leith of the *Trempealeau Republican*.

resort to available institutions and by the mediation of leaders on both sides.

It would be pointless to multiply instances of friction between the old American residents and the newcomers from continental Europe and, in lesser degree, from Ireland. But it is of some consequence to ask what evidence is available to illuminate the feelings of the newer immigrants toward the native Americans and the long-resident British. The only foreign language newspaper in the county was the short-lived and ill-fated *Nordstjernen,* copies of which we have not discovered. Letters written by the Norse and the Poles to friends and kin in the Old World might throw some light on the question, but these, too, are unavailable to us. Only now and again is there anything in the English language press that suggests how the newer arrivals from Norway, Ireland, and Poland actually felt about things. One correspondent reported that in the northern part of the county he observed a man sitting on a cask who looked half Indian, half German. John Dettinger at once wrote to protest against this slur on the Germans—his letter expressed indignation and resentment.[75] An Irish resident publicly criticized the district attorney, Mr. Robinson, for giving Americans the right to sell liquor and beer in the brewery and saloon during court session while denying it to the Irish. Neither the district attorney nor the editor commented on the charge of prejudice: the former merely stated that if the law was being broken it should be reported to the justice of the peace who might recommend prosecution.[76]

On the other hand foreign-born often expressed appreciation of native Americans. Many turned to Charles J. Cleveland, a farmer who had once been a lumberman on the Black River and a sailor on Lake Michigan, for help in ironing out their business and political differences.[77] We also have the record of John Lee's remark about the interest among his Norwegian-born neighbors in having children learn the mother tongue: "They don't need to learn Norwegian. Dis is Amerika. Teach dem English."[78] And Michael Konkel was famous for his wonted remark which revealed an exceptional

[75] *Galesville Independent,* March 6, 1879.
[76] *Galesville Journal,* October 19, 1871.
[77] "Big Tamarack," House of Memories.
[78] *Ibid.*

attitude, "Dis is one hell of a free country."[79] But perhaps the best available evidence of the desire of many foreign-born to identify themselves with their new home comes from H. A. Anderson, himself Norwegian-born, and subsequently both county judge and local historian. Judge Anderson's writings, which exist in manuscript in the form of his own autobiography and the biographies of many others based on interviews, indicate that there was a fairly widespread appreciation of the kindliness of the American-born residents and of their hospitality to immigrant newcomers.

There is other evidence of efforts to bridge the gap of social distance, the motives and methods varying with the situation. Judge Anderson's notebooks indicate that the sons of Lars Larson Haugen, who came to Hale in 1871, changed their names to Lewis and that one of the boys took an interest in politics and became ambitious for political honors.[80] How many other foreign-born residents changed their names, whether for personal, business, or political reasons, is not known. Perhaps a study of the records of the county clerk would throw light on the question. It is unlikely, however, that many did so, for the newspaper press makes little if indeed any reference to such a practice.

There are also examples of native-born Americans endeavoring to bring the foreign-born into closer association with the community life. Thus Alex Arnold, aware of the slender participation of Norwegians in the competitive exhibitions at the county fair, bestirred himself to interest more of this group in the annual show.[81]

It was in the political sphere, however, that the leaders of the older American stock made particular efforts to win the support of the newcomers. The *Trempealeau County Record* in 1868 included in its praise of the Norwegians the statement that they showed their "good sense of law and order by voting the Republican ticket."[82] But it was not until the election of 1872, apparently, when the party was somewhat split by factional contests affecting even local areas, that concerted efforts were made to win the Norwegian vote. The press

[79] *Ibid.*

[80] See also Curtiss-Wedge, *History of Trempealeau County*, biography of Simon Lee.

[81] *Galesville Independent*, October 10, 1878.

[82] *Trempealeau County Record*, September 18, 1868.

and Norwegian language posters, put up in various villages, announced a series of meetings at which out-of-county Norwegian Americans were to address their fellow countrymen.[83] This suggests that the language barrier had been partly responsible for the hitherto relatively slight interest of the Norwegians in politics. Now the Norwegians were to experience the sense of being wanted and, at the same time, to have the opportunity of learning more about American political customs.

In the later 1870's Norwegians were increasingly recognized in political nominations. In September 1877 a Republican caucus chose S. E. Listoe and Mathias Anderson as members of the convention in Ettrick. The *Trempealeau County Messenger* remarked that it was glad to see the town represented by at least two Norwegians, and that it hoped the state convention might receive at least one Norwegian delegate from Trempealeau County.[84] The growing interest and political ambition of a few Norwegians could cause embarrassment, too. Thus a petition was circulated in 1877 among the Norwegians asking to have Hall Steensland a candidate for the office of Secretary of State. Noah Comstock, the editor of the Arcadia *Leader*, wise in the way of politics, commented that it would have been better procedure to wait until the state convention acted, lest the Republican ticket be jeopardized.[85]

There is less evidence of Republican interest in winning German-American votes, but the party convention in 1876 did nominate Paul Heyse who had acted as deputy county surveyor for two years.[86] While this, as well as the nomination at the same time of John Melby of Galesville as register of deeds, indicated an increasing participation of the foreign-born in county politics, our analysis of the national backgrounds of local and county offices in this period suggests that in relation to the place these groups had in the total population, their participation in officeholding in the period of our study was negligible.[87] [Of all county board members to 1870, 85 per cent were native-born; in 1875–79, 53 per cent.]

[83] *Galesville Journal*, October 17, 31, 1872; also November 7, 1872.

[84] *Trempealeau County Messenger*, September 5, 1877.

[85] Arcadia *Leader*, June 14, 1877.

[86] *Trempealeau County Messenger*, October 18, 1876.

[87] See chapter ix. (Curti, *Making of an American Community*.)

INTERMARRIAGE

An even more reliable index of acculturation than participation in politics was the amount of intermarriage between the old American stock and the newer arrivals from Europe. Naturally language barriers and other factors for some time inhibited intermarriage.

If intermarriage can be taken as a chief criterion, the melting pot in Trempealeau worked slowly in the early years, as Table 4–1 shows.

TABLE 4–1

INTERMARRIAGES, CHIEF NATIVITY GROUPS

Birthplace of Husband	Birthplace of Wife								No. of Hus-bands
	U.S.	Can.	Eng.	Scot.	Ire.	Nor.	Ger.	Other	
				1860					
U.S.	269	2	3				2		276
Can.	6	6	2						14
Eng.	10	1	20	2				1	34
Scot.	3	1	1	35					40
Ire.	4	1			32				37
Nor.	3	1			1	36			41
Ger.	1						33	1	35
Other			1					1	2
No. of wives	296	12	27	37	33	36	35	3	479
				1880					
U.S.	709	30	22	11	8	221	14	10	1,025
Can.	35	23		1	2	2		2	65
Eng.	51	7	25	2	3		2	1	91
Scot.	11		1	35				1	48
Ire.	19	2	3		80	1		2	107
Nor.	58	1	1			1,117	2	12	1,191
Ger.	19	1	1			3	387	26	437
Other	40	1	1						42
No. of wives	942	65	54	49	93	1,344	405	54	3,006

We note that there were only four instances in 1860 in which a man from a non-English-speaking country had married the daughter of his American neighbor. Of a total of 479 married couples reported in the 1860 census, there were but 46, or 10 percent, in which the wife reported a country of birth different from the husband's. Twenty years later there were still few "inter-national" marriages reported, but they were more common. In the 1880 census, of a total of 3,006 married couples, we count 630 or 29 percent in which husband and wife were of different national origin. We should keep in mind that these percentages do not represent the marriages which actually occurred either in 1860 or in 1880, but rather represent all the married couples then living in the county. The heaviest foreign immigration did not get under way until the 1860's and many immigrants were married when they came.

Many of the intermarriages, the table shows, were between foreign-born males and American-born women. Even after a score of years the foreign-born woman was less likely to marry an "American" than was her brother. The greater freedom of the male not only gave him opportunity to seek an American mate, but it permitted him a greater chance to become Americanized and so acceptable to an American.

Not all the foreign-born were equally likely to marry persons of other nationalities. Between Lutheran Norwegians and Catholic Germans there was little intermarriage. (Some "Germans," we recall, were actually Poles who gave Prussia as birthplace.) Of the 1,873 marriages in 1880 in which Norwegians or Germans were partners, only five were between Norwegians and Germans. Despite a common tongue there was relatively little intermarriage, we note, between different groups of British settlers, although this occurred on a wider scale than did intermarriage between Norwegians and Germans. Still more of the intermarriages were between American-born and the foreign-born.

It seems probable that about one-half of the native-born Americans involved in these marriages were themselves children of immigrants. For the husbands we have data not only on their birthplace but on birthplaces of both their parents. And of 117 American-born husbands whose wives were foreign-born, there were only 59 both of whose parents were American-born. In 47 of these marriages both parents of the husbands were foreign-born. It seems probable that perhaps half the American-born wives with foreign-born husbands also had foreign-born parents, although since nearly all our subjects were men we do not have, for these women, data on birthplace of parents. We do however have a record of the place of birth of each spouse, and so we know that in 75 out of 97 such marriages the American wives were born in Wisconsin or in one of the states of the Old Northwest, the area most sought out by immigrants at this time.

What are the implications of these figures for social democracy in Trempealeau? One condition favoring equality of social opportunity is the freedom for persons of differing cultures and values to meet frequently in order that the differences may be understood, if not appreciated. The tendency of the various nativity groups to cluster together was a deterrent to this—as was the state of technology which deprived these people of quick, inexpensive transportation and communication facilities. Intermarriage, of course, is both a measure of acculturation and an instrument of it. As seen in Trempealeau the mixing of nationalities to produce that new man, the American, had begun on a small scale in 1860 and had increased moderately during the score of years that followed. The traditional role which society assigned to women deprived them of the opportunity to become Americanized as quickly as the male. Finally, the non-English-speaking foreign-born, who stood most remote from the culture of the Americans, were least inclined to marry native Americans—an important factor in Americanization.[88]

THE SOCIAL ELITE

It may be fairly assumed that among the foreign language groups few of the Old World class distinctions operated with any great strength since most of these newcomers belonged to the agricultural or laboring classes. The number of skilled craftsmen was small, and the number of men with capital derived from the sale of holdings in the Old World was negligible. Moreover, many of the Norwegians and Poles who settled in a given neighborhood had lived together in the old country. It is true that an Iver Pederson and a Peter Ekern did soon establish themselves as men of substance, thanks to what they brought of worldly goods and to what they managed to acquire by unusual talent for business. But if such men became recognized leaders, there is no evidence to suggest that they regarded themselves or were regarded by their fellow countrymen as of substantially different social status.

[88] In this connection it would be useful to know whether the Polish Catholic Church or the Norwegian Lutheran Church, by the use of the foreign tongue, by the substance of sermons, or by admonition from the clergy, tended to perpetuate these nativity groups and thus to delay acculturation.

And with some exceptions, the same thing was at least initially the case with the native-born Americans. It is indeed true that from the start a few were well enough off to build houses that contrasted markedly with the humble dugouts and with the log cabins that fairly soon replaced these first shelters. Skilled workmen were on hand in Galesville in 1855 building a substantial house for Judge Gale. Reference has been made to the stone octagonal "castle" that the Markhams quickly erected on their holdings near what was to be Independence. We know that in 1856 Benjamin F. Healy was having built near Trempealeau a costly ten-room house. In 1862 W. S. Johnston was building a handsome home in Galesville. And in the early 1870's the press frequently called attention to the new impressive houses the Field family in Osseo or the Clarks and other leading Galesville families were building, or to roomy additions to already constructed residences.

Even more impressive is another type of evidence concerning the large number of people in Trempealeau who started with a dugout or a pole shanty, replaced it in a year or two with a log cabin, and then, in time, constructed a larger and more permanent frame dwelling. This is the testimony of innumerable biographical sketches in the Curtiss-Wedge county history and in the biographies that were inspired by Judge Anderson, and in obituary notices. It may be said, then, that with a few notable exceptions, most people started out with very simple dwellings in the earlier years of settlement, and that as householders became more firmly established, the tendency was to build more permanent and larger houses. This was true of the immigrants from the Old World as well as the native-born. But the relatively small number of really impressive houses that were built in the early years or in the later 1860's and early 1870's was evidence of a social elite. The more substantial residents also sometimes displayed fancy rigs and cutters.

One might think that the number of domestic servants reported would be a good index of social status. Only a small minority reports any at all. In 1860, there were 27 in the whole county. Three percent of the 144 U.S.-born farm operators reported servants (one to a family) and 8 percent of the British-born farm operators had servants. None were reported by other nativity groups among the farmers. In 1870, of the "first census" or new settlers, 6 percent of the

U.S.-born farmers reported a servant, and the same percentage of British-born did so, with 4 percent for the German-born farm operators and 9 percent for the Norwegian-born.

These percentages seem large, but a hundred years ago it was much more common than it is today to have household help at least occasionally or at some seasons of the year, even in modest homes. When we consider the amount of hard work to be done on a pioneer farm with few of the conveniences so common today, not even running water, we realize that help was often badly needed. And it could be obtained cheaply at that time, for not much more than board and room. A family with older girls could easily spare one to help out a neighbor. And reports are that the "domestic servant" was often a neighbor's daughter, or sometimes a relative.

"Domestic servant" was the term used in the census records, but it is doubtful if the term was used at all in common Trempealeau talk. "Hired girl" and "hired help" were the terms used. Often the hired girl would work only a few weeks or months in a household. She played with the children and ate with the family as a matter of course. We find no evidence that hired girls were considered to be of particularly low social status.

One farm household in which one "domestic servant" was reported in 1860 is that of John Burns, Irish-born farmer, age 35, who had a wife and five children and one servant, Martha Smith, age 20, also Irish-born. Burns is credited in the census with only $200 worth of real property and $60 personal property. We can imagine that this was a frugal household. On the other hand the farmer Benjamin Healy, with a reported $8,000 in total property, could easily afford the servant he reported. Healy was one of the leading men of the county. So was Charles Utter, a well-to-do printer of Montoville. Though he had only a wife and a six-year-old daughter, he reported two servants.

One questions, on thinking over the situation, the notion that the employment of servants in Trempealeau was a reliable indication of high social status or of more than average income. It is significant that in 1870 the highest percentage of farm operators reporting servants was found in the group with the lowest rank in value of total property, the Norwegians. This suggests the persisting influence of a European custom.

It is clear from the frequent reappearance of the names of substantial families in various undertakings that something like a social elite existed at least as early as the Civil War period, and became better defined in the 1870's. Whether the occasion was the assembling of ladies to make a regimental flag, to collect for the Sanitary Commission, to provide for a monument to Trempealeau, to solicit funds for the Freedman's Aid Commission, to sponsor a donation for the minister, to raise funds for St. Paul's Sunday school, or to make some needed improvement in the village cemetery, the same names appear again and again, and are those, no doubt, of the social leaders in the villages and their hinterlands.[89] In Trempealeau village one finds the names, for example, of Mr. and Mrs. Newman, Dr. and Mrs. Atwood, Mr. and Mrs. A. H. Kneeland, Mr. and Mrs. George Batchelder, Mr. and Mrs. F. H. Kribs, Mr. and Mrs. Leith, Mr. and Mrs. C. F. Holmes, Mr. and Mrs. J. C. Utter. In Galesville the most frequently recurring names are those of Mr. and Mrs. Isaac Clark, Mr. and Mrs. Charles E. Perkins, Mr. and Mrs. John C. French, Mr. and Mrs. Odell, Mr. and Mrs. J. C. Button, Mr. and Mrs. George Y. Freeman, Mr. and Mrs. Samuel S. Luce, Mr. and Mrs. W. A. Johnston, Mr. and Mrs. Wilson Davis, Mr. and Mrs. Delavan Bunn, and Mr. and Mrs. Alex Arnold. In the northern villages the Comstocks, the Lindermans, the Fields, and other families played the same role.

Also, in reading accounts of New Year's celebrations, anniversaries, sleigh rides to Winona, and other social events, one gets used to seeing the same familiar names of people who enjoyed prominence in business, politics, the professions, and farming, and who, in general, were relatively well-to-do. It was also these people who went on pleasure trips to the Twin Cities, to Chicago, and, in 1876, to Philadelphia to take in the World's Fair. Thus among those to make the trip to the Centennial City were J. C. Utter, A. W. Newman and daughter, W. A. Johnston, B. F. Healy and family, Mr. and Mrs. Charles Nettleton, G. W. Gale, Isaac Clark and family, J. M. Garrett, D. W. Gilfillan, Dr. Atwood, and D. O. Van Slyke. It

[89] See, for example, accounts in the Galesville *Transcript*, May 16, 1862, December 2, 1864, October 12, 1866, January 25, 1867; *Trempealeau County Record*, May 15, 1868, February 7, 1868; *Galesville Independent*, October 4, 1877, February 28, 1878; *Arcadia Republican and Leader*, January 20, 1881.

should be noted that one misses in these lists the names of a few families who were among the most well-to-do in the county. Further, one does not in general find the names of Norwegians, Germans, and Poles attending social events outside their own group, even when some among these had established themselves as substantial property holders and as leaders among their own people.

This is not to say that these groups were closed to newcomers, or that their members did not mingle in a neighborly way in everyday casual relationships as well as at church and civic functions with those less in the public eye. But it is to say that there was in each community a more or less well-defined group of close friends and acquaintances whose common interests and tastes tied them together, and that this group in general constituted the better-to-do and the leadership of the community. At the same time it should be said that in describing the functions in which these people took part the press seldom went beyond referring to them as "leading" or "respectable" or "prominent." Indeed, it was somewhat exceptional for the Whitehall paper, in narrating the gossip and even scandal attached to the simultaneous disappearance of the station agent and Mrs. G. D. Olds, in whose house he boarded, to refer to the lady as belonging to "the highest social circles of the community."[90]

The picture would not be a fair one without reference to occasional explicit items in the press which disparaged snobbishness or which contrasted the democratic society of Trempealeau with the "more aristocratic and money-conscious" communities in the older sections of the country. Luce of the *Transcript* retold in 1864 in his paper the story of the girl who "wouldn't marry a mechanic" and who through bitter experience learned her lesson. "In this country," Luce commented, "no man or woman, in our way of thinking, should be respected who will not work bodily and mentally, and who curl their lips contemptuously if they are introduced to a man who is obliged to work for a living."[91]

Writing from the East where he had gone on a visit, Charles White, formerly of Galesville and in 1866 of Ettrick, contrasted the situation in the older part of the country with that in Trempealeau. In the Eastern community, White wrote, a man would not be

[90] *Trempealeau County Messenger*, August 30, 1876; September 6, 20, 1876.
[91] Galesville *Transcript*, June 3, 1864.

considered as politically sound in running for even the humblest office unless he had money and would use it for buying up floating votes. "A town supervisor can be purchased in this beautiful, moral, rich, and intelligent part of the country for about $400. A man is judged by his amount of 'stocks' and not by his stock of common sense. A young man that works out by the month and gets his living monthly would no more be noticed as a suitor by one of the Dam-sels of the Aristocracy than would a cheese skipper be by a full grown alligator." But White added a bit ruefully that it was only a matter of time when the same situation would prevail in the new states.[92] Whatever the substance or lack of it in his comparison, it is significant that he could feel this way, and that no one contradicted him by writing contrariwise to the local paper.

Editor Luce's paper consistently stressed the democratic nature of Trempealeau life, and the fact that he and others had such an attitude is significant. For what a man thinks has some relation to his conduct, and people who constantly hold up before themselves an ideal of democracy are in one way or another contributing to its growth, however short they may fall of achieving it in actual practice. Luce himself was consistent. In 1870 he advised his readers to beware of "those men whose hands are polluted with political trickery, though they may stand high in the scale of social respectability."[93] On another occasion he expressed himself as opposed to any recreation, such as archery, if it were available only to the well-to-do.[94]

ATTITUDES TOWARD PAUPERS

Reference at least as early as the 1860's to the presence of paupers suggests that if the frontier offered equality of economic opportunity, not everyone could or would take advantage of it. The references also imply the existence of a group at the bottom of the social scale. Ways of dealing with this group may reflect contemporary social attitudes toward poverty.

As early as 1865 the editor of the Galesville *Transcript* felt that the problem of pauperism in the county warranted the establishment of

[92] Galesville *Transcript*, May 18, 1866.
[93] *Galesville Journal*, July 22, 1870.
[94] *Galesville Independent*, June 12, 1879.

a poorhouse. "This is what we have wanted for a long time," he added.[95] The prevailing system was that of New England—town responsibility. This sometimes resulted in quarrels between two towns as to which had responsibility for a given indigent. On one occasion in 1866 the town of Gale appealed a decision from a local justice to the circuit court at La Crosse, only to have the higher court rule that the pauper was not at the time a resident of that town.[96] A decade later the town of Trempealeau was bearing the annual cost of $920.36 for the maintenance of its poor. Itemized, the account indicated that $131.71 had been spent for the sickness and burial of J. W. Long; $12.34 for wood for B. H. Stewart; $14.80 for wood and groceries for F. Hollenbeck; $251.55 for the care of Mrs. Wheelock and girl; and $475.76 for the support of P. Decker and family. In addition there were minor items, chiefly fares of indigents to other places.[97]

The next year, 1877, Preston paid $336 for the support of the town's poor.[98] In the same year Arcadia's town board audited the expenses of three coffins for paupers, and shortly thereafter buried Joseph Sanders, who had been on the town for five or six years.[99] Apparently the town fathers in Arcadia as elsewhere made contracts with residents for boarding an indigent—they paid Thomas Olson, for example, $6 a month for keeping a 92-year-old woman.[100] Sometimes these cases, usually tragic, carried humorous overtones. Thus for example one H. P. Hanson solicited the town board of Arcadia for aid but was refused on the ground that he was abundantly able to take care of himself. According to the report, he informed them that he simply had to have help as his wife had just had a baby born to her. But they found that his age was 62, his wife's 71![101]

We have little evidence about the attitudes taken toward paupers, but such as there is suggests that the problem was regarded as burdensome. One citizen protested that his town, Trempealeau, was spending too much on its paupers and demanded that something be

[95] Galesville *Transcript*, December 8, 1865.
[96] *Ibid.*, May 25, 1866.
[97] *Trempealeau County Republican*, April 14, 1876.
[98] *Trempealeau County Messenger*, April 11, 1877.
[99] *Republican and Leader*, December 13, 1877; January 21, 1878.
[100] *Ibid.*, April 11, 1878.
[101] *Ibid.*, December 12, 1878.

done about it.[102] The *Galesville Independent* seemed considerably relieved when Joseph Dusso, Mexican War veteran, "well known here as a pauper," was after several futile efforts finally placed in the Soldiers' Home in Milwaukee.[103]

That paupers were regarded as somehow at fault for their situation was implied in the reporting of sundry incidents in connection with them. For example, some point was made of the fact that a Galesville pauper, the widow of the veteran Dusso, was having a fit of rage when she fell from a chair and broke a leg.[104] Certainly the county people found the nuisance of the wandering tramps hard to put up with and when possible made short shrift of them by hastening them on their way.[105] But in point of fact there is little evidence about the attitudes taken toward Trempealeau's indigents. The fact that they existed is an illustration of the point that the general economic structure of Trempealeau society was essentially like that of most other Western societies, using both the terms "society" and "Western" in the broad general sense.

We have not in this chapter presented evidence which would prove that social relationships in Trempealeau were more democratic than in Europe or on the Eastern seaboard. But as a result of long living with the materials we have gained the impression that in this pioneer county there was indeed, especially in the 1850's and 1860's, a high degree of social democracy. The facts we have reported on will in any case help form a useful background for general understanding of life in Trempealeau. In seeking such understanding it is important to keep in mind certain considerations that must qualify any conclusions about the degree of democracy prevailing on this frontier.

In the first place, the great growth in number of non-English-speaking foreign-born residents after the Civil War made the society of the county far less homogeneous than it had been when the native-born American pioneer stock predominated. The newcomers from the Old World were, on the whole, welcomed, for almost

---

[102] *Trempealeau County Republican*, April 28, 1876.

[103] *Galesville Independent*, December 7, 1882.

[104] *Ibid.*, January 25, 1883.

[105] *Ibid.*, June 5, 1879.

everyone already on the ground was eager to have unoccupied land taken up, to see the value of his own real property increase, and to experience the growth of the towns and villages. Little evidence of intolerance toward the increasingly important Catholic element in the population found articulate expression. But varying degrees of tension did exist between the groups of different national origins, particularly between the old American and the British-born, on the one hand, and, on the other, the Norwegians, Germans, and, particularly, the Poles. With very few exceptions, it is true, the tensions leading to overt conflicts were resolved within the frame of democratic processes. Varying degrees of social distance between groups of different national origin continued, however, to exist, if intermarriage and participation by the non-English-speaking immigrants in civic enterprises can be taken as criteria.

Second, with the growth in maturity of the towns and villages, something like a little social elite had emerged by the 1870's. But lines were not tightly drawn. Nor could they be in view of the fact that with few exceptions there were no really wealthy families in the county, and particularly in view of the fact that men, women, and children, native-born and foreign-born alike, were constantly coming into the county and leaving it.

Thus, in terms of social structure and relationships, the life of Trempealeau continued throughout the period to be highly fluid. Geographical mobility, we shall see, existed along with a striking tendency toward occupational mobility. Trempealeau County was certainly not a pure democracy in the sense of a population of social equals who participated equally in all social enterprises. But the high degree of social equality in the early period of settlement proved, in the face of new challenges to it as the years went by, to possess a great deal of vitality.

Reprinted from *The Making of an American Community: A Case Study of Democracy in a Frontier County*, by Merle Curti (with the assistance of Robert Daniel, Shaw Livermore, Jr., Joseph Van Hise, and Margaret W. Curti), pp. 85–113, with the permission of the publishers, Stanford University Press, © 1959 by the Board of Trustees of the Leland Stanford Junior University.

PETER T. HARSTAD

5. Disease and Sickness on the Wisconsin Frontier: Cholera

AMONG the many maladies afflicting the settlers of early Wisconsin, the two most troublesome and generally feared were malaria and cholera. Both produced disturbing effects on a populace ignorant of their causes; yet each disease was peculiar in its inception and duration. On the one hand, all that was needed for malaria to spread was that an anopholes mosquito carry a minute organism from one human to another, a process as easily accomplished in an isolated cabin as in a military garrison or a frontier town. Although malaria seldom brought a high mortality rate, it often left its victims ill for months or even years.

On the other hand, cholera, which was spread mainly through the consumption of infected food or water, thrived in a dense population and left a high mortality in its wake even though a victim, if he survived the first few days of an attack, could usually expect a full recovery. What made cholera so terrifying was the swiftness and decisiveness with which it struck. One evening in July, 1852, the editor of a Madison newspaper saw Edward Fisher, one of the town's leading citizens, walking down the street in his usual robust health; the next day he reported Fisher's death in his paper. In Milwaukee, two gentlemen stood on a street corner discussing the progress of cholera in the city. Within two hours one was dead and his body on the way to the cemetery. In Galena, during August of 1850, fifty persons who were in complete health on a Sunday morning were in their graves Tuesday evening.[1] The unlimited stories of horrid death that circulated during the cholera years caused frightening thoughts in the minds of everyone.

[1] Madison *Daily Argus and Democrat*, July 28, 1852; Frank A. Flower, *History of Milwaukee, Wisconsin* (Chicago, 1881), p. 400; Prairie du Chien *Patriot*, September 4, 1850. For a general account of the cholera epidemics of the United States see J. S. Chambers, *The Conquest of Cholera* (New York, 1938).

Throughout the centuries cholera has been regarded as a mysterious and dangerous disease—an attitude shared by the pioneer residents of Wisconsin who generally attributed its indirect cause to "Providence," a word which appeared often in the newspapers when the plague approached. An Indian agent during the Black Hawk War called it "The Scourging hand of an Almighty Providence." Reverend John H. Ragatz, a circuit-riding minister in the western part of the state, prayed God during the epidemic of 1849 to have mercy on the nation "although we have deserved punishment, for one must fear that thousands die as a result of the plague without being prepared for it. When we see the godlessness which is in vogue everywhere, we must not be surprised if God manifests his judgment and destroys whole nations through war, hunger, and pestilence."[2]

The symptoms of the disease were graphically described in a pamphlet, *The Cholera Beacon*, written by Dr. Elam Stimson, a Dartmouth graduate, and circulated in America after the epidemic of 1832. In it Stimson stated that prior to the outbreak of an epidemic in any particular community "unusual morbid sensations are experienced by many persons . . . which have commonly been called 'premonitory symptoms.'"

More tangible symptoms, as Stimson explained them, were a faint fluttering sensation in the heart, dizziness, headaches, cramps in the legs, indigestion, a sense of creeping coldness over the surface of the body, and sometimes hot flashes of fever. As the disease progressed, "cholic-like pains" wandered through the body, vomiting became severe, and the bowels uncontrollable. The inside of the mouth was of a darker hue than natural and the patient commonly had an insatiable thirst. Stimson believed that these symptoms varied greatly in different patients, "some cases terminate fatally within two or three days after they are thought to be seriously ill—others linger eight or ten days and often recover."

Stimson went on to describe the last or "bilious attack" phase of cholera. "As this stage approaches, all the symptoms become greatly

[2] "Papers of Indian Agent Boyd—1832," *WHC*, XII (1892), 278; "A Circuit Rider in the Old Northwest: Letters of the Rev. John H. Ragatz," *WMH*, VII (1923), 98.

aggravated and still greater uniformity exists in different cases. The pulse grow small, thready and tremulous, and are soon imperceptible. Spasms are more severe, attacking the legs, thighs and body. The fingers and toes are reduced in size, being shrivelled and purple or black. The veins in the arm are only flat and black lines—a cold, clammy sweat covers the whole surface, and to the feel the skin is like a cold, wet hide. The spasms increase and some patients utter the most piercing cries—the thirst is more and more intense, and of a peculiar kind, the patient often supplicates his friends and physician with the most pitiful tones for 'cold drink' as the last, greatest and only favor in their power to bestow. The eyes are sunken in their sockets and surrounded by a blue or black circle. The voice fails, is dry, hoarse, or only a whisper. . . . After having suffered more than horrible martyrdom, the patient has commonly a great alleviation of suffering before death, being less purging, vomiting and spasms, and he often expresses himself better—or lies in a sort of apopleptic stertor . . . indifferent and unconscious of his fate, and expires with but little additional suffering."[3] Such was the death of several thousand Wisconsin residents during the epidemic years 1832, 1834 and 1849–1854.

The cause of cholera was indeed baffling to people of the first half of the nineteenth century. The theory commonly accepted by the medical profession—the one found in the *Cholera Beacon*—was an attempt at a scientific explanation: "We believe the remote cause of Cholera to be some *atmospheric* impurity, and the *proximate cause an imperfection of* the lungs." The *Beacon* went on to explain this proximate cause. "The lungs performing the double function of decomposing atmospheric air, and robbing it of its impure and noxious matter—hydrogen and carbon—but the blood not being fully decarbonized in the lungs, has an adjuvent or supplementary organ in the liver, which extracts another portion of this impurity in the form of bile—to be like the manure of the farmer, converted to a useful and important purpose. And last, the kidneys, like a wasteweir to the system, clear the blood of such superfluous matter as is of no further use. . . . In whatever the atmosphere impurity consists, the

[3] Elam Stimson, M.D., *The Cholera Beacon* (Dundas, 1835), reprinted in *Transactions of the London and Middlesex Historical Society*, Part XV (1937), 13–21.

effect of it when inhaled is to incapacitate the lungs from fully performing their excretory function." [4]

This theory, carried over from the 1832 epidemic, was generally accepted during the epidemic years from 1849 to 1854. Moreover, there were further attempts to justify it. In June 13, 1849, a column appeared in the Milwaukee *Sentinel*, reporting that a Cincinnati chemist had difficulty making sulphuric acid for a number of days. He blamed the unusual atmospheric conditions, claiming that "the air underwent a change a few weeks ago, (about the time Cholera commenced,) . . . There was less oxygen than common, and more carbonic acid gas, which produced the effect referred to [his inability to make sulphuric acid] but that, within a day or two, the proportions have again changed, (the Cholera has sensibly abated) and a healthy condition now exists." The inference was that the same atmospheric abnormalities that made it impossible to produce the acid, also caused the cholera. Thus, with the sanction of the medical profession, backed in this case by a chemist, this theory was widely proclaimed through Wisconsin and the nation.

Since the medical profession accepted this theory of causation, it followed logically that cholera was not contagious. The *Cholera Beacon* proclaimed it noncontagious, but added that excretions and filth in the sick room rendered the air more unfit for respiration and thus aided cholera's spread. Newspapers which represented the commercial interests repeated this doctrine often, since cholera had the effect of keeping the country people away from the larger trading centers such as Milwaukee when an epidemic raged. Therefore the Milwaukee *Sentinel* printed many authoritative claims that cholera was not contagious. [5] Apparently the medical profession sincerely believed in the noncommunicable nature of the disease. The St. Louis Medical Society debated the question and in good democratic manner put the question to a vote, twenty-six doctors voting that it was not contagious and ten that it was. [6]

But on this point the general public did not agree with the

---

[4] *Ibid.*, 24–25.

[5] One such claim appeared in the Milwaukee *Sentinel*, July 25, 1850.

[6] Prairie du Chien *Patriot*, August 13, 1851. It is significant, however, that this same group of physicians also voted to continue the quarantine of cholera patients in St. Louis.

medical profession. There is much evidence to show that people tended to flee cholera-infested places, as was the case in the village of Wingville. When fifteen cases of cholera broke out there in the summer of 1850, the "greatest consternation prevailed," and the village, containing 100 inhabitants, was entirely deserted.[7]

The very fact that people fled from cholera helped in its spread, and Wisconsin pioneers have left a number of anecdotes concerning the outbreak of the disease in traveling vehicles. Isaac Stephenson of lumbering renown and "Grandmother" Gratiot of lead region fame, to cite examples, were both stricken while traveling; the former recovered but the latter did not. Brought into close contact in boats, trains, and stage coaches, and undoubtedly using a common source of contaminated drinking water, travelers did much to spread the disease from one locality to another. There is a record of seventy-five cholera fatalities on a Mississippi steamer carrying 600 passengers, and it is very likely that the survivors carried the disease elsewhere.[8] Perhaps a group of Mineral Point residents hit upon the best solution when, instead of fleeing the locality altogether, they left their homes to camp upon a hillside during the worst cholera days.

For a time Milwaukee, Racine, and Kenosha served as havens of refuge for the wealthier Chicago citizens escaping the plague. In July of 1854 Racine reportedly received a hundred such refugees in a single day. Because the early 1850's were years of intense rivalry between Milwaukee and Chicago for supremacy in the West, the fleeing Chicagoans took considerable ribbing from their neighbors to the north. In defending his move one man said, "I like Chicago, generally speaking. I enjoy living there, but it is not just pleasant to see black crape on seventeen doors within a block from your home."[9]

Pitiful are the stories of sick and dead being abandoned by panic-stricken friends and relatives. As Frank Flower put it, "Life, happiness, and self-preservation were the motive powers. And though happiness was left behind, self-preservation held sway. Families even locked up the dead in their houses and fled." Flower

[7] *Ibid.*, July 10, 1850.

[8] Ragatz, "Letters," p. 99.

[9] Racine *Advocate*, quoted in Milwaukee *Sentinel*, July 13, 1854; Flower, *Milwaukee*, p. 398.

cited an instance of a sickening odor emanating from a closely shut house on the south side of Milwaukee. "The authorities were notified. An officer was sent to break into the house. He did so. In the middle of the room lay the body of an old man, badly decomposed, his cramped body covered with fat, eager, Summer flies." One early Milwaukee resident recalled seeing seven bodies in a single house on Lisbon Avenue when he stopped to water his horse.[10]

In addition to the orthodox medical theory of the cause of cholera, there were several others. Daniel Drake, one of the leading physicians of the West, believed that a quarantine was useless "as well as embarrassing to commerce." Drake, however, differed from his contemporaries by accepting the animalculae hypothesis, which is a rather close approach to the later germ theory of the origin of cholera and other diseases.[11]

Increase A. Lapham, an early Wisconsin geologist and scientist, took an entirely different view. In his correspondence with Charles T. Jackson, a prominent Boston scientist, Lapham wrote in August of 1849, "Your suggestion that there is a greater amount of cholera in limestone districts, than in those based on granite and other primary rocks, is now receiving melancholy proof and confirmation at Sandusky City, Ohio." Jackson wrote back that he had tested his hypothesis by studying the 1832–1833 epidemic in Europe. "I collected maps giving the track of the cholera from India to Vienna while in Europe, and I collected also all the works I could find published on the subject in Austria, Russia, Poland, Bosnia and France. It was obvious that the disease followed the river valleys but it did not follow the current of the water, but came up the Danube and it took its abode chiefly in the basins of Vienna and Paris— both of which are calcareous and in both these cities the waters of the wells and rivers are almost saturated with carbonate of lime." Jackson's studies convinced him that his theory was also confirmed in America during the epidemic of 1832–1833. Jackson and Lapham were certain that they had founded a new discipline, "Medical

[10] *Ibid.*, pp. 400–401; Louis F. Frank, *Medical History of Milwaukee* (Milwaukee, 1915), p. 181.

[11] Madge E. Pickard and R. Carlyle Buley, *The Midwest Pioneer: His Ills, Cures, and Doctors* (Crawfordsville, Ind., 1945), p. 28.

Geology," which would attract future scientific investigations.[12]

Still another theory concerning the cause of cholera was that it was brought on primarily by fear. During the Black Hawk War, William Beaumont, medical officer at Fort Crawford, contended that "The greater proportional numbers of deaths in the cholera epidemics are . . . caused more by fright and presentiment of death than from the fatal tendency or violence of the disease." During the 1849 to 1854 epidemics, local newspapers often printed something on this subject, though not usually in as extreme form as the advice given by a Madison paper in 1849: "Don't Be Alarmed.—Keep cool, take it easy, beware of excitement, and keep the spirits up, not by pouring spirits down, but by being lively, cheerful, and friendly. Don't put on that long face every time a funeral meets your eye, or the tho't of the dread scourge comes over you, but 'away with dull care;' send drooping melancholly about her business, jump, laugh, shout, play, dance and sing; any thing in fact, but downheartedness in cholera times."[13]

In attempting to determine the cause of cholera mid-nineteenth century investigators were frequently confronted with baffling evidence. Sometimes cholera appeared simultaneously at widely distant points with no apparent connection, as, for example, near the end of 1848, when it broke out in New York and New Orleans at practically the same time. Since within the time limitation there was no possibility that the disease could have been carried from one city to the other, people were convinced, as their forebears had been for centuries, that an epidemic was due to some atmospheric or terrestrial influence far beyond the control of man.

It has since been determined, however, that the outbreak which occurred in these two geographically separated cities actually had the same source—two immigrant ships both of which sailed from the European port of Le Havre, one bound for New York, the other for New Orleans. Especially baffling in this case was the fact that there was no cholera at Le Havre at the time of departure, and that cases

[12] H. H. Voje, M. D., "Two Letters Concerning the Cause of Cholera as Understood in 1849," *Wisconsin Medical Journal*, XIII (1915), 365–367.

[13] Deborah R. Martin, "Doctor William Beaumont: His Life in Mackinac and Wisconsin, 1820–1834," *WMH*, IV (1920–21), 278; Madison *Wisconsin Express*, July 24, 1849.

developed simultaneously in both ships when they were a thousand miles apart on the open sea. The explanation is that the passengers were from a cholera-infected district of Germany, and that the cholera germ can live for at least a week in a water or food supply.[14]

In studying the cholera epidemics of the first half of the nineteenth century, it must be kept in mind that bacteriology was then an unborn science. Sanitation, if it could be said that it existed at all, was rudimentary. Shallow wells from which water was raised by bucket and rope were easily polluted, and open streams from which soldiers obtained their water during the Black Hawk War were even more easily contaminated.

Characteristics of the disease were conducive to its dissemination, and made sanitation difficult. The fact that cholera victims suffered extreme thirst was an important factor in the spread of the disease. Since few homes in mid-nineteenth century Wisconsin had indoor piping, the bucket and dipper method was used, making it almost inevitable that if one member of a household came down with cholera the others would also be exposed to the germ. Add to this the fact that victims suffered from acute diarrhea, and that during one stage of the disease vomiting was almost incessant. Furthermore, methods of disposing of human wastes were of the crudest; some of the newly settled communities did not even have privies. Cholera struck during the hot summer months of July and August when it was necessary to keep windows and doors open. Since there was no screening, flies and other insects could easily find their way from infected human waste in one house to the dinner table in another. Even in the larger cities hogs roamed the streets freely and performed the service of disposing of garbage.

Cholera first reached America in the spring of 1832, brought here according to the best accounts, by immigrants to Quebec and Montreal. It spread to the shores of Lake Ontario and Lake Erie, and thence to Lake Champlain and Albany. In July it arrived at New York; from there it spread south and west over the continent. In all likelihood the disease would never have become serious in

[14] Knut Gjerset and Ludvig Hektoen, "Health Conditions Among Early Norwegian Settlers," *Publications of the Norwegian-American Historical Association: Studies and Records*, I (1926), 14.

Wisconsin had not a group of Sauk and Fox Indians under the leadership of one of their minor chiefs, Black Hawk, returned to the lands of their fathers in the Rock River Valley to grow corn. By the middle of July, 1832, the frontiersmen, fearing a general invasion, raised a force of almost 4,500 to push the Indians back across the Mississippi. More than once Black Hawk and his "host" of 1,000 tribesmen (numbering in their ranks 600 women and children), tried to surrender but the army pursued them until only 150 remained alive, and these were taken prisoners. The War Department, apparently fearing a general uprising of the frontier Indians, sent General Winfield Scott west, by way of the Great Lakes, with nine companies of federal troops. By the time Scott reached Detroit cholera broke out on the troop transports. The close quarters and central water supply of the ships were evidently conducive to the spread of cholera, for by the time the convoy reached Chicago in the second week of July, scores of men were ill and many died. Fort Dearborn at Chicago became a hospital and the main body of Scott's men were not dispatched to the scene of action until the heaviest fighting was over.[15]

Indian Agent Boyd at Prairie du Chien protested on July 21 that it would be unwise for Scott's diseased troops to be brought into contact with General Atkinson's healthy volunteers for it would not only encourage desertion, but what was more serious, might also lead to greater trouble with the Indians. "Is it not within human probability," Boyd asked, "that Indian Tribes, at present luke warm & indifferent as to the fate of this War (such as the Pottawattamies & Winnebagoes,) both partially allied to the hostile Indians by inter-marriage—may not, by Witnessing the ravages made by disease among our troops—at once, and to a man, join the Sacs & Foxes, and raise the Tomahawk against us?"[16]

General Scott, hastening to take part in the campaign, proceeded with a few men to Prairie du Chien where, as Boyd had feared,

[15] Chambers, *Conquest of Cholera*, 85–102, gives a detailed account of the introduction of cholera to Scott's troops on their way to Chicago and the progress of the disease after their arrival. *Niles' Weekly Register*, July 28, 1832, contains a contemporary account of the havoc and confusion which cholera generated among these men.

[16] "Papers of Indian Agent Boyd," pp. 278–279.

cholera broke out among the volunteers and also among the federal troops garrisoned at Fort Crawford. According to a soldier, John H. Fonda, a hundred men died at Prairie du Chien within two weeks and were buried in a common grave south of the dragoon stable at Fort Crawford. The healthy portion of the army then proceeded to Rock Island where they arrived on August 9. About the 20th of August more of Scott's men arrived from Chicago and a week later there was another outbreak of cholera. Captain Henry Smith recalled that cholera raged for several days among the troops at Rock Island. Even though General Scott enforced the "Strictest sanitary regulations . . . four officers and upwards of fifty rank and file, out of about three hundred infantry, became its victims." Cholera also broke out in other detachments; men were buried in the wilderness in unmarked graves. Moses Strong estimated that by the close of the "Cholera Campaign" 400 of Scott's men had fallen victim to the disease. In addition to these must be numbered the inestimable fatalities among the volunteers. It is probably a safe estimate that cholera fatalities among the troops at least equalled the approximately 850 Indian fatalities in the Battle of Bad Axe and elsewhere.[17] At any rate, in the course of the Black Hawk War cholera proved more fatal to the whites than did the scalping knife.

Cholera also affected the civilians in the river towns of Wisconsin and Illinois. At Galena and Prairie du Chien there were several fatalities. In her reminiscences, Mrs. Elizabeth Baird stated that each day when her husband rode off to Menomineeville to attend his law practice she wondered if she would ever see him again, "the cholera threatening on one hand, the Indians on the other."

There is some indication that cholera also visited Wisconsin two years later. Mrs. Baird mentioned the "fearful cholera visitation in 1834." At Menomineeville, according to another source, hardly a

[17] John H. Fonda, "Early Wisconsin," *WHC*, V (1868 reprint), 259; Henry Smith, "Indian Campaign of 1832," *ibid.*, X (1888 reprint), 165; Moses M. Strong, "The Indian Wars of Wisconsin," *ibid.*, VIII (1879 reprint), 285; Paul F. Crane-field, in his article "Cholera in Wisconsin, 1832–1834," *Wisconsin Medical Journal*, XLIX (1950), 509, quotes one estimate that the epidemic cost "thousands of lives" among the soldiers. Still another estimate, that of Edmund Wendt in *A Treatise on Asiatic Cholera* (New York, 1885), p. 72, is that seven of Scott's companies (probably containing about 125 men each) were reduced by cholera and desertion to a total of but 68 men.

household was spared from the scourge. Father VandenBroek, in charge of the mission there, reported that "It often happened that while I was attending the sick, sometimes even while confessing them, they died at my side, so that we could not get enough people to dig the graves. We had to bury four or five in one grave. We could not even find people enough to prepare the bodies for burial and I had to bury them myself, assisted by two Sisters of the Order of St. Clare." Another reference to cholera in 1834 appears in the *Memoirs* of Father Mazzuchelli, missionary to the settlers and Indians of western Wisconsin. He reported that when some superstitious Winnebagoes heard that cholera had caused deaths at Prairie du Chien, a hundred miles west of their encampment, they shot off their guns towards the west at sunset in order to "kill the cholera." "Their warlike fusillade against the setting sun was kept up for more than half an hour."[18]

Cholera did not reach Wisconsin again until 1849, by which time the former territory was a rapidly growing state of nearly 300,000 inhabitants, with new immigrants flocking in by the thousands. Some conception of the rate of immigration can be gotten from the passenger lists of steamboats arriving in Milwaukee. During the week ending June 18, 1849, six steamers brought a total of 1,240 English, German, and American passengers.[19] With such an influx of new arrivals, Milwaukee had by 1849 surpassed in population the mining towns of southwestern Wisconsin and also its rivals on Lake Michigan. With its 18,000 inhabitants Milwaukee was the largest town in the young state, and it is not surprising that during the epidemic years 1849 to 1854, a period of continuing growth, cholera presented a serious problem. And since Milwaukee's health problems were on a larger scale than elsewhere in the state, attempts were made to handle them in a systematic manner.

In 1840, nine years before cholera entered the community, the Milwaukee County Medical Society was founded. Concerning the practice of medicine the Society's charter read: "No person shall be

[18] Elizabeth T. Baird, "Reminiscences of Life in Territorial Wisconsin," *WHC*, XV (1900), 238; VandenBroek is quoted in T. J. Oliver, "History of Medicine in Brown County," Ms, Wisconsin State Historical Society, pp. 3–4; Father Mazzuchelli, *Memoirs* (Chicago, 1915), p. 136.

[19] Milwaukee *Sentinel*, June 18, 1849.

permitted to be examined as a candidate for a diploma, and membership of this Society, unless he shall have arrived at the age of twenty
one years, has at least a good English education, has studied
medicine at least three years with some respectable practitioner, and
can produce satisfactory evidence of good moral character." Thus,
to practice medicine in the state's largest town, one did not have to
attend a medical school, though many did. In 1852 the standards
were raised, so that in addition to the existing requirements "the
applicant shall produce evidence that his preliminary education is at
least sufficient to entitle him to admission to the sophomore class in
the academical department of our State University."[20] With the
payment of a $10 fee any man who qualified under these provisions
could receive a license to minister to the sick in Milwaukee. During
the years 1849 to 1854 the epidemic that plagued the city was not
once mentioned in the records of the Society; the main concern was
the collection of dues and $3 fines for not attending annual meetings.
Several of the leading doctors seemed to be more interested in land,
timber, and politics than in their profession. It can be concluded that
the doctors of Milwaukee and elsewhere in the state were of little
help in efforts to control the disease and to treat cholera patients.
But even had they been well versed in the medical knowledge of their
time, it is doubtful if they would have been of much more assistance.

Late in 1848 the cholera which had been brought from Germany
aboard the two previously described immigrant ships, appeared
simultaneously in New York and New Orleans. The next spring it
spread steadily to the interior of the country. From New York it
spread to Philadelphia and other places on the Atlantic coast; from
New Orleans it spread through the Mississippi Valley and was
carried to California by the forty-niners. Soon it reached St. Louis,
then Cincinnati, and by the beginning of July, Chicago. The
Milwaukee *Sentinel*, under the exciting title, "Telegraphic Sparks,"
carefully reported the disease's progress. City officials, vainly hoping

[20] Milwaukee County Medical Society Minute Book, Ms, Wisconsin State
Historical Society, entries for December 2, 1840, November 9, 1852. William S.
Middleton reports that only twelve of sixty physicians in the western part of the
state (Iowa, Grant, and Lafayette Counties) were graduates of medical schools at
this time. See Middleton, "Cholera Epidemics of Iowa County, Wisconsin,"
Wisconsin Medical Journal, XXXVII (1938), 894.

to escape an epidemic, took measures to reduce the amount of cholera-producing "miasma" in the air by giving the city a much-needed cleaning. One thousand loads of dirt and filth were carted away, and it was estimated that there were 4,000 more loads in plain sight which would cost $3,000 to remove. Streets were cleaned, dirty lots were declared nuisances, and legal action was taken if nothing was done to bring about abatement. Concerning the mass clean-up Frank Flower wrote that "A luckless cat or dog could not breathe his last and be at rest five minutes ere twenty citizens would rush breathless to the flying Board of Health and street inspectors. A slimy puddle, a rotting stick, were pounced upon as the children of the terrible pestilence." Aldermen were authorized to purchase lime and use it in "noxious" places.[21]

The Board of Health which Flower mentioned was organized June 30, 1849, and was made up of physicians. The legislative body of Milwaukee, together with this Board, set up several strict rules to avert the plague. The mayor was to charge circuses a license of not less than $500 a day, and theatres $150. A strict quarantine of immigrants was enacted and physicians were ordered under penalty of $50 or thirty days in jail to report every case of cholera to the Board of Health. The Board had absolute authority to abate all nuisances.

During June, the Milwaukee papers found that they had a new type of public relations on their hands. Notices in the *Sentinel* appeared frequently under the title "No Cholera Yet!" The object was to assure the country folk that "we have as yet had no cases of Cholera in Milwaukee; and it is necessary to make that assertion, for reports are rife in the country, of the ravages of the fell disease, and if the press are silent, it is said at once that there is some concealment."[22]

By the beginning of July the public was uneasy. Scores of people fled cholera-infected Chicago for Milwaukee, and immigrants continued to pour in. The Council passed an ordinance to erect a

[21] Flower, *Milwaukee*, p. 397. Many Wisconsin newspapers carried advertisements of lime for sale during the cholera years. In both Madison and Milwaukee, lime was available to the public free of charge for sprinkling on bad parts of streets, lots, or filthy cellars. The following notice appeared in the Madison *Daily Argus and Democrat*, July 29, 1852: "The Village Board has ordered a large quantity of lime which will be distributed on application, for purifying the streets."

[22] Milwaukee *Sentinel*, July 16, 1849.

bathing house on the lake shore so that arriving immigrants could cleanse themselves. While there had been some sickness in the city, the press insisted it was not cholera. Conceding that the law requiring cases of cholera to be reported to the Board of Health was necessary, the *Sentinel* nevertheless hoped that none of the city physicians would be guilty of "such contemptible conduct, as to report an aggravated case of diarrhoea, or something else of that sort, *as Cholera*, in order that they may gain a fictitious notoriety for successful treatment of the disease," a trick which was not above the morality of the profession at the time. The main point that the editor of the *Sentinel* wished to make was that "nothing should be done to create needless alarm and injure our trade with the country." The *Sentinel* advised, "Let our citizens continue to use lime freely, our street inspectors to attend faithfully to their duties, and the same sanitary measures be practiced as heretofore, and we shall probably be spared from a visitation of this dreaded scourge."[23]

The records of the Board of Health show that it took cognizance of the first case of cholera on July 1. However, its first public report came on July 17. In good journalistic form, the editor of the *Sentinel* chose this day to launch an attack on the Board. His charge that it was "inoperative and inefficient" reveals a rift in the medical profession of the time. The charge proceeded in a milder tone: "Now we are not alarmists, and do not desire to do anything that would have an injurious effect upon the business of the city. But we cannot disguise the fact that the cholera exists here, and that many people endeavor to suppress its extent. For every case thus kept from the public, rumor will make ten, if our neighbors find that we do not give full and truthful reports." Then the editor arrived at the crux of the matter. "Now, gentlemen, we propose to tell you the reason why cholera cases are suppressed. Our city physicians, as you know are Homeopaths; hence the Allopaths[24] feel a reluctance to report

[23] Frank, *Medical History*, p. 180; Milwaukee *Sentinel*, July 10, 1849.

[24] The former believed that diseases were cured by administering very small doses of drugs which, if given in large doses to a healthy person, would produce symptoms similar to those of the diseased patient; the latter believed the exact opposite, and used remedies which produced symptoms different from those of the disease under treatment.

to what they call 'quacks'—if the case was reversed; and the city physicians were Allopaths, the Homeopaths would probably pursue a similar course and assign a similar reason. . . ." The editor believed that the solution was to remove all physicians from the Board of Health and make it a citizens' body.[25]

For the next two months cholera raged in Milwaukee. Even the anecdotes and short stories in the newspapers had cholera as their themes. On August 3rd the Milwaukee *Sentinel* summarized the progress of the epidemic to that date. The number of cases up until noon of August 2 was 104, with forty-five deaths. "The great majority of the cases, four-fifths, we should think, have been among new comers; though a few residents have been attacked." In comparison, Chicago had 434 cholera fatalities, but the epidemic had begun earlier there.[26]

By the beginning of August it was evident that the rules adopted earlier in the season were inoperative. The *Sentinel* charged that neither the circus that visited the city nor the theatres had paid the required fees. A Dr. Hoard was brought into police court for not reporting a case of cholera as the law demanded. Hoard was able to escape the fine or imprisonment by resting his defense on the technicality that his patient was afflicted with "Cholera Morbus," and not "Asiatic Cholera." Justice Walworth claimed that the rule requiring physicians to report every case of cholera to the Board of Health would have to be reworded if it was to be enforced. According to Frank Flower, the system of handling immigrants also broke down. If cholera broke out in the quarantine buildings, which held as many as 125 at a time, there was no other choice but to release the healthy immigrants or they would perish. There was neither adequate housing nor personnel to make the quarantine work. By this time there was a provision that the indigent sick should have medical care at public expense. An ordinance was passed "providing that any regular physician in the city should be paid by the city for attendance on the poor, including those in the Alms House, but not

[25] Milwaukee *Sentinel*, July 17, 1849.
[26] *Ibid.*, August 3, 1849.

more than $150 could be allowed these physicians for each quarter of the fiscal year." [27]

Because of the nation-wide plague, President Taylor set aside the first Friday in August as a day of "fasting, humiliation and prayer," during a season when the "PROVIDENCE OF GOD has manifested in the visitation of a fearful pestilence" which spread its ravages throughout the land. The *Sentinel* reported after the "National Fast" that it was generally observed in Milwaukee. "The Churches were all opened for service, morning, noon and evening, and the attendance was large. Our merchants and business men, with scarce an exception, closed their stores and offices, and abstained from secular occupations. Our citizens of all denominations united cordially, and, we doubt not, sincerely, in the due observance of the day." [28] It is entirely possible that the very bringing of these people together contributed to the violent outbreak that was soon to come.

By August 14 fatalities became more numerous. A summary for the previous four days revealed that there were twenty-nine cases and eighteen deaths, "*half* of these in one party of German emigrants who landed here last week, and were crowded into one or two small rooms in a building on West Water Street." The City Marshal cleared the house and separated the inmates but "the poison had already seized upon them, and nine of the party died."

In general the Milwaukee papers used the immigrants as scapegoats. Quarters in which immigrants often crowded were viewed with suspicion. The Board of Health strongly condemned "the practice of certain persons, in filling their houses to their utmost

[27] *Ibid.*, July 25, 1849; Flower, *Milwaukee*, pp. 397–398. Rules established early in the summer of 1849 stipulated that a health officer inspect all immigrants landing at the Milwaukee piers. The city had a quarantine building, but in July of 1854 the authorities took over the government buildings at the harbor to be used as additional space to house sick immigrants. (See Milwaukee *Sentinel*, July 13, 1854.) All in all, the attempts to inspect immigrants and to quarantine those suspected of carrying cholera were not successful. The regulations were simply not enforced. Except for the fears which kept people from cholera-infected homes, there seems to have been no attempt to quarantine cholera patients in Wisconsin other than at Milwaukee.

[28] The text of the proclamation appeared in the Milwaukee *Sentinel*, August 1, 1849; also, *ibid.*, August 6, 1849.

capacity with newly arrived immigrants and their baggage, before their clothing has been washed and ventilated—especially at such a time as this—as the Cholera is . . . sure to commence its ravages." When the Board learned of overcrowded hotels or homes it proceeded to disperse the inhabitants. Even crowded boarding houses were invaded and the tenants dispersed, "the proprietors themselves being ready to admit that in such an emergency the most extreme measures were justifiable." [29]

Describing the immigrants Flower wrote that they "came up in boats by scores, landing at the Huron, Detroit and Erie street piers. Reduced in bodily strength and often sadly scant of means, they were fit subjects for the ravages of the disease. Wandering around, as they did, in search of lodging and food, these poor unfortunates became dangerous bearers of the plague, and were looked upon with loathing." [30] Without a doubt the immigrants were often carriers of the disease, but in all fairness the refugeeing Chicagoans should also have been suspected.

Throughout the remainder of August cholera continued to rage. Reminiscent of the plagues of the middle ages, rough carts, sometimes containing four or five corpses at once, rumbled through the streets to the Poor House burying grounds "while the remains of many in better circumstances were borne along to other resting places more gently in appropriate vehicles." [31]

In this, as in all of the epidemics between 1849 and 1855, disposal of the bodies of cholera victims presented a real problem. In Milwaukee a group of men working under the City Marshal was hired expressly for the purpose. One of the Sisters of Charity recalled that they were rough men who reeked with the smell of alcohol and who prided themselves on their strength to resist cholera. Their job was to pick up bodies, put them in rude carts, and haul them to the cemetery where on one morning the City Marshal counted eighteen bodies awaiting burial. Often there were no church funerals. At Muskego, where whole families sometimes succumbed to the disease, funerals were not possible. "The dead were wrapped in white garments, put in ordinary boxes, driven at night by ox teams to the

[29] *Ibid.*, August 14, 1849; Flower, *Milwaukee*, p. 401.
[30] *Ibid.*, p. 398.
[31] *Ibid.*, p. 399.

churchyard and buried in sand trenches." John L. Dyer, a Methodist Episcopal itinerant, wrote that the people thought bodies could not be disposed of soon enough after death, "and it was doubtful if some were not buried alive." He reported that when an entire family died of cholera at Wiota, the neighbors got together and "burnt the house with the bodies in it." [32]

Milwaukee papers carried accounts of travelers who died while visiting the city. Notices of their deaths were accompanied by orders for the appropriate exchanges to reprint them so that relatives and friends could be informed. One such account, from the Milwaukee *Sentinel* of July 30, 1849, reads, "The death reported yesterday proves to be a man by the name of Charles Campbell, late from Canada, a Scotchman by birth, about 50 years of age. He stated, before his death, that he had a wife in Canada, a son at Toronto; also one in St. Louis, and one or two more in Cincinnati. Toronto, Cincinnati, and St. Louis papers, please copy." In the confusion it inevitably happened that persons who were very much alive were reported to be dead. The *Galena Jeffersonian* carried a story to the effect that "John Kenedy, (known in the Mines as 'Kentuck,') died of Cholera, in Galena, a few days since." Several days later the *Grant County Herald* carried this notice: "Kentuck says he isn't dead nor ha'nt been." [33]

On August 31, 1849, the Milwaukee *Sentinel* printed the statistics of mortality for the past season. Actually, cholera claimed a few victims after this date, but it is likely that the editor wished to create an illusion of finality so that the country folk would think it safe to come into the city to do their trading. The published report enumerated 209 cases of cholera, of which 105 proved fatal. The week of the greatest number was that ending August 15 in which there were 41 cases and 23 fatalities. The *Sentinel* concluded its report with the refrain, "The disease has been confined mostly to certain localities, and almost exclusively to the newly arrived emigrants. Nearly one-half of the fatal cases were among newly arrived emigrants or unacclimated persons, and many of the other cases are traced

[32] Albert O. Barton, "Muskego: The Most Historical Norwegian Colony," *WMH*, XXI (1937), 132; John L. Dyer, *The Snow-Shoe Itinerant* (Cincinnati, 1890), p. 53.

[33] Quoted in Milwaukee *Sentinel*, July 27, 1849.

directly to some gross imprudence in article of diet, drink, &c."
However, the day-by-day reports of the Board of Health do not bear
this out. There were cholera fatalities in all wards of the city, and
in the reports that give names and addresses of victims, many more
natives than immigrants are listed.

The epidemic of 1850 closed in on Milwaukee in much the same
manner as that of the previous year, but it came earlier, lasted
longer, and was more severe. The wish of the *Sentinel* became reality,
and the Board of Health was reconstituted as a salaried body whose
four lay members received an aggregate compensation of $500.
The reasoning behind this rearrangement was probably that it was
easier to color the reports of the Board if it was made up of citizens,
especially if they were business men. At any rate the reports issued
during 1850 are not as complete as those of 1849. Many of the 1849
reports reveal the identity of the victims, whether they were immigrants or natives, and often gave their age, but reports of 1850 give
only statistics. Later in the season the *Sentinel* was forced to admit
that the reports were inaccurate.

Concerning the epidemic of 1850, Louis Frank in his *Medical
History of Milwaukee* wrote: "The first case broke out in the beginning of July, on Broadway. For three months similar scenes as
the year previous were enacted, men, women and children falling
and dying in the streets, patients deserted by family and friends,
corpses piled into rough wagons and buried in ditches in pauper
ground. Spectators of these sights one day would fall victims the
next."[34]

It was not until late August that the epidemic reached its peak.
The August 26 report of the Board of Health listed more deaths in a
short period than either of the last two seasons. "The Board of
Health met at the Council Room at the usual hour to-day, and
report 20 deaths from Cholera within the last 48 hours, to wit:—1
in the 1st Ward, 4 in the 2nd Ward, 6 in the 3d Ward, 2 in the 4th
Ward, and 7 in the 5th Ward."[35] The fact that the fatalities were
spread over the city indicates that they did not occur solely among
closely cramped, "loathsome" immigrants.

[34] Frank, *Medical History*, p. 181.
[35] Milwaukee *Sentinel*, August 27, 1850.

During the same month the Chicago journalists charged Milwaukee with falsifying its cholera reports so as not to disturb the commerce of the city. From August 15 to the month's end Milwaukee suffered more severely than ever before, the Board of Health reporting an average of seven deaths a day. Meanwhile the Chicago press became suspicious because the reports stopped carrying the number of new cases and simply stated the daily mortality. Under the heading, "Dreadful Mortality in Milwaukee, the *Chicago Democrat* of Monday, August 27, informed its readers that "several despatches" from Milwaukee of the previous Saturday reported 109 burials in the city on Friday and Saturday. The *Chicago Tribune* carried the same report under the heading, "Terrible Mortality." The dispatches attributed the startling mortality to "bilious dysentry," but both the *Democrat* and the *Tribune* suspected that the real cause was cholera.[36] This led to a series of charges and countercharges between the Milwaukee and Chicago papers which seem irrelevant and unimportant today but which in their setting were very important. The early 1850's were years of railroad construction, canal building, and laying of plank roads. Any factor that might serve to tip the balance to Chicago in the race to become the "Queen City of the West" was viewed with alarm by Milwaukeeans. Therefore it was all important that Milwaukee defend herself against reports of "Dreadful Mortality."

The *Sentinel* countercharged, "Had we followed the course taken by our Chicago friends, and published the 'rumors' that reached us from day to day in relation to sickness there, instead of simply copying the official reports of their Board of Health, we should have treated our readers to a daily dish of very much such stories as the Democrat and Tribune served up to their readers on Monday." The *Sentinel* gave ground, however, and admitted that "in addition to the deaths reported by the Board of Health, there have undoubtedly been many others, from cholera, and others from the disease incident to the season. . . ." By the latter the *Sentinel* more than likely meant malaria; however it would not admit that mortality reached anything like the numbers reported by the Chicago press. According to Frank Flower, Timothy O'Brien who was City Marshal and also chairman of the Board of Health during 1850, told tales years later,

[36] Quoted in *ibid.*, August 28, 1850.

that "really over-step the 'fabrications' of any press." The *Chicago Argus* joined the attack by stating that on Thursday, August 22, the sexton of Milwaukee recorded 59 interments; "on Friday, 23d, 47; on Saturday, 24, 62. Total for three days, 168." The *Sentinel* sloughed this off as "another specimen of this Chicago Bogus."[37] Very likely the mortality was not as high as claimed by the Chicago press nor as low as reported by the Board of Health and the Milwaukee *Sentinel.*

The 1850 epidemic spent its force in Milwaukee by the middle of September, having lasted fully two weeks longer than that of the previous year and having taken more lives. The Milwaukee papers learned from the experience of the previous year that it was not wise to print a recapitulation of cholera mortality, for it would be picked up by the exchange papers throughout the country. Frank Flower stated that the Board of Health "took cognizance of fully 300 deaths . . . and it is doubtless true that nearly as many more escaped the record, the bodies being buried secretly."[38]

During the years 1851, 1852, and 1853 cholera was severe elsewhere in the state but does not seem to have been serious in Milwaukee. No Board of Health reports were issued but from time to time the *Sentinel* had to defend Milwaukee against "false reports." "Travelers from the north say that reports are prevalent there that the cholera is raging terribly in this city, and deaths occurring at the rate of 40 or 50 a day. They are all lies, without the shadow of a foundation, Milwaukee has never been healthier. We know of but one case of Cholera this season, and that was the case of a man landed here from a boat, sick, a month since, and who died at the Hospital. Flower reported that there were only a few cases in Milwaukee in 1851, 1852, and 1853.[39]

In 1854 there were several violent outbreaks of cholera in Milwaukee, but since the Board of Health published no reports it is difficult to know just how serious the epidemic was. The *Sentinel* of August 23, 1854, reported an outbreak of cholera in the city jail.

[37] *Ibid.*, August 28, 1850; Flower, *Milwaukee*, p. 399; Milwaukee *Sentinel*, August 31, 1850.

[38] Flower, *Milwaukee*, p. 401. If this mortality rate is projected on a yearly basis it gives the startling rate of 1,440 deaths in a city of 18,000.

[39] Milwaukee *Sentinel*, August 21, 1851; Flower, *Milwaukee*, p. 401.

Forty-two men were crowded into a space where there was only room for twenty. Sickness broke out and two men died, a larcenist and a man named Steffinger who was serving time for robbing a body at the poor house. The jailer turned loose fifteen men before their terms expired and took some of the sick men to the jury rooms of the court house. Later, several others of the inmates died. Another record of a violent outbreak in 1854 is found in a letter from a German doctor, Carl Feld. "I was called to treat a young child in a loghouse . . . [near Milwaukee] in which there was also a cholera patient. The following morning instead of one cholera case there were four, all vigorous men; these four were followed by three men, so that within a few days seven persons died in the house of the plague." According to Dr. Louis Frank, 1854 was the last year in which a cholera epidemic occurred in Milwaukee.[40]

There will be no attempt here to give a year-by-year account of cholera in other Wisconsin towns and villages during the epidemic years 1849 to 1854, though for many this would be possible. However, a few of the more striking incidents, and a number of the different ways of handling the problem of cholera will be brought into focus.

In the towns and villages along Lake Michigan and in those in the eastern part of the state the progress of cholera was quite similar to what it was in Milwaukee and brought with it the same problems, but on a smaller scale. In Kenosha, Michael Frank who served as Poormaster and chief of the Board of Health during the summer of 1850, recorded the cholera fatalities of that city in his diary.[41] His entry of August 26, reads, "Cholera seems to have disappeared. The actual number of cases . . . this season has been about 32 fatal."[42]

Among the Norwegian settlers of Muskego, cholera was parti-

[40] Dr. Feld's letter is found in Frank, *Medical History*, p. 30; *ibid.*, pp. 181–182. There were cholera epidemics elsewhere in the United States in 1866, 1867, and 1873.

[41] The larger Wisconsin towns including Milwaukee, Madison, Mineral Point, Racine, and Kenosha, had boards of health; very likely, some of the other towns and villages had them also. Some communities held mass meetings to consider health problems. See *Wisconsin Tribune*, July 12, 1850.

[42] Frank, "Diary," August 26, 1850. See also "Autobiography of Michael Frank," *WMH*, XXX (1947), 470.

cularly devastating. John Molee stated that 1849 was the worst summer he experienced in his life: "By this time there were a great number of our people in Muskego. When the epidemic cholera struck our settlement, there were at one time, only seven families, all well, so that they could get away to help their neighbors. From three to four persons died every day. Hans Tveito and myself had all we could do, to carry the dead out of the houses and haul them to the grave with our oxen, while others dug the graves. No ceremony took place, and there were no glittering coffins with silver knobs and handles. We simply rolled a white sheet around the dead, unwashed and unshaved; and then we placed him or her into a rough board box, unplaned and unpainted, and hauled them to a spot selected for a graveyard, called 'the Indian hill' (Indiehaugen); there we laid them to rest. It was the best we could do, God knows. We cared for them best we could, while living, but when dead, they did not need more care." Because of the severe malaria and cholera epidemics at Muskego it became known as the "region of death," and those that were spared generally went to other settlements.[43]

No doubt most of the physicians of south-eastern Wisconsin were as busy as Thomas Steel, an Englishman who lived on a small farm near Waukesha. Dr. Steel wrote his father back in London in the fall of 1850: "There has been a good deal of sickness this last six weeks, in fact a great deal more business than I could attend to, though had it not been for the great distances between the parties I could easily have attended to all—probably after riding 30 miles, no bad days work, I had only been able to visit five or six patients." Steel hoped he would get paid for some of his trouble, "but we have now in this locality at least had three years of bad harvests so that the means of paying doctors or any one else is of course very small."[44]

Cholera also prevailed north of Milwaukee. In the village of Twin Rivers, for example, during the first weeks of August, 1850, there were thirteen deaths from cholera. "One American, one

---

[43] Rasmus B. Anderson, *The First Chapter of Norwegian Immigration* (Madison, 1906), p. 231. For an account of the severity of malaria at Muskego, see Peter T. Harstad, "Sickness and Disease on the Wisconsin Frontier: Malaria, 1820–1850," *WMH*, XLIII (1959–60), 89–90.

[44] Dr. Thomas Steel to Father, October 8, 1850, Ms, State Historical Society of Wisconsin. Steel often took goods or services as payment.

Frenchman, three Germans, and eight Indians. It first broke out among the latter," according to a correspondent of the *Sheboygan Democrat*.[45]

The Wisconsin pineries seem to have escaped the disease. In the first place there were few men in the pineries during the cholera months, and in the second place those who were there were fairly well isolated. Isaac Stephenson, who acted as doctor to the men in his lumber camps, reported that sickness was rare among the lumbermen; the most serious problem was wounds inflicted from glancing axes as the men worked with frozen timber.[46]

In northeastern Wisconsin cholera was ravenous among the Belgian immigrants of Brown, Kewaunee, and Door counties. In addition to economic hardship, according to Xavier Martin, the Belgians met a worse fate: cholera attacked nearly every family. "Not a few families lost as many as five of their members in a single week; most of them were buried on their own land, and in great haste." There were 15,000 Belgians in these three counties by 1855, but when the cholera news reached the Fatherland, according to Martin, immigration was checked, "and for the next five years very few families came over."[47]

Nor did the inhabitants of central Wisconsin escape cholera. The newspapers of Watertown, Madison, Beloit, and the smaller villages all carried cholera reports, especially in the years 1849, 1850, and 1854. Since there was a steady stream of German immigrants to Watertown, it was rarely free from the malady during July and August of these years.

Sanitary conditions in the mining communities of western Wisconsin made them susceptible to cholera. In a letter dated September 17, 1849, a resident of Mineral Point revealed that although his own family was healthy "We have had the cholera in this village for the last two or three months and perhaps some thirty or more have died with it. There were four or five deaths from it, I think, last week. We have had it here so long that it has almost ceased to be a subject of

---

[45] Milwaukee *Sentinel*, August 24, 1850.

[46] Isaac Stephenson, *Recollections of a Long Life, 1829–1915* (Chicago, 1915), p. 130.

[47] Xavier Martin, "The Belgians of Northeast Wisconsin," *WHC*, XIII (1895), 379–380.

conversation or alarm."[48] In 1849 several public meetings were held in Mineral Point on the subject of cleaning the town to make it less susceptible to cholera, and in 1850 a Board of Health was formed.

In the lead region, the epidemic of 1850 was more devastating than that of 1849. It was in July, 1850, that the plague-ridden village of Wingville was abandoned by its surviving inhabitants who fled to Franklin and Dodgeville where subsequently the cholera broke out dreadfully. The *Wisconsin Tribune* of July 26 reported the deaths at Franklin to number about fifty, "a great mortality for a place the size of Franklin." Later estimates ran as high as sixty-nine. Victims in Galena on two days, the 19th and 20th of August, numbered fifty persons. "Out of a population of 7,000, one in every hundred has been followed to his grave within a week," reported the *Galena Jeffersonian*.[49] There were many cholera deaths in the lead region in both July and August. The *Green County Union*, for example, furnished a list of twenty-two persons who died of cholera at the "New Diggings."[50]

During 1851 and 1852 Mineral Point was troubled with "false rumors" of cholera; actually the disease was present in the village, but its toll did not reach the proportions of 1850 there or elsewhere in the lead region. In 1854 there were a few violent outbreaks of cholera in places other than Milwaukee, such as at Lamar's Stage Station, a few miles west of Shullsburg, where "Mrs. Lamar and four children, two servant girls, two stage drivers, the bar keeper, and a man employed in making coffins," all died of cholera within four days.[51]

It would be impossible to estimate the number of deaths from cholera in Wisconsin during the years 1849 to 1854. In many cases newspapers reported the fatalities, but there is good reason to believe that scores of deaths were not reported. At this time, the state had no system of vital statistics; in fact, one of the main objectives of the Medical Society in the mid-1850's was provision for the registration of births, marriages, and deaths. It is certain however, that cholera deaths numbered in the thousands.

[48] Quoted in Middleton, "Cholera Epidemics," p. 895.
[49] Quoted in Prairie Du Chien *Patriot*, September 4, 1850.
[50] Milwaukee *Sentinel*, August 24, 1850.
[51] Mineral Point *Tribune*, August 2, 1854.

Although the cholera years were a period of much immigration to Wisconsin, they were also a period of emigration, especially from the southwestern counties. After 1849 the "California fever" exerted a strong pull on the lead miners whose labors were becoming increasingly unprofitable while their skills—or so they believed— would make them rich in the gold fields of California. Among the adventurers who treked their way across the continent there was considerable mortality, with cholera being the main killer. The deaths of many Wisconsin men, including that of William S. Hamilton (son of Alexander Hamilton), were announced in Wisconsin newspapers. A Plattville doctor, James Claibourne Campbell, augmented his income by putting up little packages of "California Medicine." [52]

Medical knowledge of the mid-nineteenth century was of little value in the prevention and treatment of cholera. Preventive advice usually consisted of the admonition: eat moderately, don't over work, and don't become frightened. "Cholera Advice" appeared in all Wisconsin newspapers prior to the arrival of the disease. [53]

Dietary care was deemed especially important. Fresh vegetables were frequently believed to be the cause of cholera. One contemporary doctor was suspicious of "indigestible vegetables, ardent spirits, beer, ale, and wine; pork, lobsters, and crabs; green corn, clams, and oysters; watermelons, cucumbers, strawberries, peaches, and pears; cabbage and greens; cheese . . ." and a few other foods. Occasionally the Milwaukee Board of Health cautioned people against the consumption of specific foods. On August 20, 1849, the Board warned against the use of green vegetables, "especially green corn, cabbage and cucumbers, as some of the recent cases are directly traceable to such imprudence." Some dietary measures were reportedly beneficial even after a person contracted a case of cholera. For the "Best Cholera Medicine Known," one paper instructed its readers to "Parch half a pint of rice until it is brown;

[52] Dr. James C. Campbell, "Journal," Ms, State Historical Society of Wisconsin, entry for April 13, 1852.

[53] For examples of "Cholera Advice," see Milwaukee *Sentinel*, July 17, July 28, 1849.

then boil it as rice is usually done. Eat slowly, and it will stop the most alarming case of diarrhoea."[54]

Alcohol was viewed as both a preventive and a cure, though in an age of strong temperance movement there were divergent views on the matter. *A Helping Hand*, a curious volume by Lyman C. Draper and William A. Croffut, includes about a dozen remedies for cholera, the main ingredients of most being "Best French brandy, one pint," "Old cognac," rum, and the like. The concluding directions for one such cure are, "If the medicine thus administered promote signs of intoxication, this is to be regarded as a favorable sign of recovery. . . ." Apparently, according to the local press, some of the boys in Lancaster, Grant County, carried their medications to extremes. "Thus far we have escaped the Cholera, but how much longer can we hope to if men are allowed to lay around our streets, perfectly saturated with whiskey [?] If men who do not live in town believe whiskey to be a preventive, we do not object, but let them get their medicine and go home and use it. One intoxicated man, by exposure, might bring disease upon a whole community." An exchange item in the Milwaukee *Sentinel* estimated that "the practice of drinking brandy, during the past seasons of Cholera, made more drunkards than would have been produced in ten years of health. . . ." Undoubtedly the epidemics raised havoc among the converts of Father Matthew, a popular leader of the temperance movement.[55]

Perhaps the following popular verse reflected the spirit of the cholera years:

> Now fill your glasses to the brim,
> And drink with steady eyes.
> Here's to those already dead
> And here's to the next who dies!

Patent medicines quickly adjusted to cholera and so added another disease to the list of ailments which they "infallibly cured." Dr. Townsend's Sarsaparilla was perhaps the most thoroughly

[54] Pickard and Buley, *Midwest Pioneer*, 28; Milwaukee *Sentinel*, August 21, 1849; Madison *Daily Argus and Democrat*, July 31, 1852.

[55] L. C. Draper and William A. Croffut, *A Helping Hand* (Cincinnati, 1870), p. 727; *Grant County Herald*, quoted in Milwaukee *Sentinel*, July 25, 1850; *ibid.*, July 20, 1854.

advertised patent medicine during the late forties and early fifties, but there was a furious war raging between the "Old Doctor" and the "Young Doctor" as to which was the genuine Townsend's Sarsaparilla. New medicines also sprang into existence to take advantage of a new situation. There was an "Anti Cholera Syrup" agent in Milwaukee before the disease arrived. A newspaper advertisement stated that a Chicago doctor used the syrup and lost only three cases out of a hundred. "This remedy may be had at one dollar per bottle at the United States hotel. . . . Those who are not able to procure the remedy will be treated gratuitous."[56]

There was a more ingenious way of making money off the cholera scare. Prompted by "pure philanthropy," an agent appeared in Milwaukee in 1854 selling "cholera conductors." This gimmick was based on the conventional theory that cholera was caused by "impurities in the air, which affect the human frame." The agent appealed to the authority of a Prussian physician who "proved the possibility of attracting these impurities by chemically prepared metal, (which if worn about the person, acts against them in a similar manner as a lightning conductor does against lightning,) by receiving the impurities of the atmosphere, and thereby protecting the human body from their injurious influence." The agent backed up his product with highly successful claims of its use in Europe, charged 50c for each conductor, and accepted country orders accompanied by payment.[57]

A farmer in Iowa County advocated steaming cholera patients, his reason probably being the fact that a cholera sufferer's skin felt like "a cold, wet hide." According to one authority, this method gained some local repute.[58]

Drugs believed by the medical profession to have value in the treatment of cholera were: calomel (mercury), laudanum (opium), morphine, turpentine, and sulphur. The object of their use was "to restore the vital functions of the body," as the doctors often said. In 1849 there was much excitement about the use of sulphur as a cholera cure. It was supposedly determined that "cholera never prevailed in the vicinity of sulphur springs, or in situations where this substance abounds, hence the conclusion that sulphur might be and

[56] *Ibid.*, July 31, 1849.
[57] *Ibid.*, July 13, 1854.
[58] Middleton, "Cholera Epidemics," p. 896.

properly was the antidote for cholera." The editor of the *North Western Medical and Surgical Journal* was convinced of its value. It was suggested that "a combination of powdered charcoal, one part to four of sulphur," made the remedy more efficient. However, the editor of the *Wisconsin Herald* warned against the use of such powerful medicines as preventives, saying that it was as absurd as to "blow your nose with gunpowder, for fear of a general conflagration."[59]

Orthodox doctors resorted to bleeding as the primary treatment of cholera patients. Even Daniel Drake, despite the modernity of his views regarding the animalculae theory of cholera's origin, resorted to this old standby. Writing in the *Western Journal* he said, "To bleed a patient who cannot be raised from his pillow without fainting, whose pulse is nearly imperceptible, whose skin is cold, and extremities shrunk up to half their ordinary size, would at first view, seem rash and unwarrantable," he wrote in the *Western Journal*. "But experience, which in medicine can grant warrants for any procedure, has sanctioned the use of the lancet even when all other symptoms of extreme prostration, are present. . . ."[60]

Bleeding was justified by the *Cholera Beacon* on the grounds that cholera was caused by polluted air. The object then, was to diminish the circulating blood so that the heart could with greater facility move a blood supply to the cleansing organs—lungs, liver, and kidneys. "The principle is plain," explained the *Beacon*. "By diminishing the body to be moved the relative power of the mover is increased. It is apparent, then that bleeding is necessary. . . . It is true the aged and infirm, the debilitated emigrant will not bear— neither do they require so large bleedings as patients of an opposite description. But the principle . . . is the same, which should be borne in mind and abstract such a quantity as will enable us to excite a more vigorous action of the heart . . . and thus the congested vessels will be unloaded."[61] One wonders if this entire theory was rationalized in order to justify "scientifically" the time-honored practice of bleeding.

[59] Milwaukee *Sentinel*, May 31, 1849; Lancaster Wisconsin *Herald*, September 26, 1846. In contrast to other Wisconsin newspapers, advertisements for patent medicines were conspicuously absent from the *Herald*.

[60] *Western Journal*, V (1832), 612, quoted in Pickard and Buley, *Midwest Pioneer*, p. 29. Drake's letters reveal that he had not changed his ideas by 1849.

[61] Stimson, *Cholera Beacon*, p. 32.

Since the middle of the last century rapid advances in sanitation have made cholera relatively easy to control. Nowadays when the modern doctor is called upon to treat a case of the disease he advocates the administration of large amounts of hypertonic salt solutions in order to counteract the extreme dehydration, and "it should be emphasized that large amounts means quarts and gallons, not pints." This is in sharp contrast to the practices of early physicians who too often were inclined to believe with *The Helping Hand* that "in this disease the thirst is often uncontrollable, *but if the patient drink water he will die.*" However, not all cholera sufferers abided by this theory. Dr. Middleton, in his study of cholera in Iowa County, cites several incidents in which patients took water in spite of their doctor's orders and therefore recovered. Joseph Schafer, former superintendent of the State Historical Society, recalled that his mother, stricken with cholera in Mineral Point, was ordered by her doctor not to drink water. One day when the lady who cared for her left the room, Mrs. Schafer noticed a large dipper of water on a chair, "sprang out of bed, seized the dipper, and drained it to the last drop. Then she got well." [62]

From incidents such as these it can be concluded that the cures offered cholera victims by mid-nineteenth century physicians were of little or no benefit. Rather, by denying the patient water or depleting him through bleeding, the physician was robbing the patient of the very fluids necessary to the restoration of health.

At least one Wisconsin physician exhibited a wholesome attitude towards his profession's ignorance of the cause of cholera and inability to give adequate care to its victims. In a speech before the Wisconsin State Medical Society in early January of 1855, Dr. Alfred L. Castleman stated that the pestilence of the last seasons "presented to us so pointedly the fact of our inability in many instances to wrestle successfully with the mysteries of disease. . . . We have seen the pestilence seize upon our friends—we have in many instances found ourselves wholly incapable of arresting the progress of the disease—we have seen Death snatch his victim from us as uninterruptedly in his progress as though we had not been

[62] Harold W. Jones, M. D., "Cholera," *Encyclopedia Americana* (New York, 1954), VI, 586; Draper and Croffut, *Helping Hand*, p. 727; Middleton, "Cholera Epidemics," p. 896.

there to interpose. I hope that no member of this Society in such cases allowed himself to be satisfied with the reflection that the result was one of God's providences, but that he more properly attributed it to his own ignorance of the nature and character of the pestilence, and that he determined not to be satisfied till he had fully unravelled the mystery." [63]

Castleman did not realize it, but at the very time he spoke a way had been discovered to check the spread of cholera, though the mystery was not as yet "fully unravelled." It was a simple remedy discovered by John Snow, a successful and fashionable London anesthetist. Using the process of elimination, Snow concluded that the disease was spread by drinking water. After his famous order to remove the handle from the Broad Street pump, cholera practically disappeared from London and a means was known for controlling cholera epidemics in the civilized world. [64]

At the outbreak of the 1849 epidemic there was only one hospital in the state, St. John's Infirmary in Milwaukee (later known as St. Mary's Hospital), which opened its doors November 12, 1848. When residents of Wisconsin were stricken with cholera they generally remained in their homes, but immigrants often had no place to go. During the 1849–1854 epidemics there were three havens of refuge for immigrants and indigent sick in Milwaukee, the alms house, the pest house, and St. Mary's Hospital. [65]

Some of the smaller communities improvised to take care of the sick and dying. In Muskego, for example, where there were many newly arrived immigrants, a large barn on the shores of Big Muskego Lake was used as a hospital in 1849. Two years later when the plague raged with frightful violence and fatality, "a log house near the town line in Norway was then an improvised hospital, and graves

[63] Wisconsin State Medical Society, *Proceedings, 1855,* p. 34. At this time there were fifty-one members in the Society.

[64] Although Snow was convinced that cholera was water-borne, recognition of his theory came slowly. The epidemics which occurred in the United States in 1866, 1867 and 1873 do not seem to have reached Wisconsin. With Kock's identification of the cholera bacillus in 1884, the miasmatic theory gave way to the germ theory, and medical scientists had the knowledge they needed to eliminate cholera.

[65] In the Milwaukee *Sentinel*, August 4, 1854, St. John's Infirmary was charged with spreading disease by accepting cholera patients.

were dug and kept open for expected corpses." In Luther Valley, near Beloit, the home of Gullik Springen was used to care for the sick. "One can well understand the conditions," wrote Springen, "when 18 corpses were carried from our house that summer [1854] my parents and one brother included." It is probable that many family homes served as local hospitals during the cholera years.[66]

Cholera left in its wake scores of orphaned children. In Milwaukee the problem was especially acute because of the influx of immigrants. Before the cholera epidemics there was apparently no need for an organization to care for orphans, but in January of 1850 the Milwaukee Orphan Association, supported mainly by the Protestant churches, was founded. Its aim was to place the unfortunate children in private homes as soon as possible. By 1853, sixty-nine children were received by the Asylum; four years later 201 had entered, though all but thirty-nine had been placed in homes. The Asylum was supported by gifts of food, boxes of clothing, cords of wood, and occasionally cash from the citizens of Milwaukee.[67] In rural areas and small communities orphans were no doubt taken into the homes of relatives and friends.

Thus it is seen that despite the cost in lives and human suffering, the cholera epidemics which swept Wisconsin in the first half of the last century brought about certain social benefits. Because of cholera public sanitation became a matter of communal action and concern; hospitals sprang up in communities where none had previously existed; and orphanages were established.

Reprinted from the *Wisconsin Magazine of History*, Vol. XLIII (Spring, 1960), pp. 203–220.

[66] Anderson, *Norwegian Immigration*, pp. 275–276; Blaine Hansen, "The Norwegians of Luther Valley," *WMH*, XXVIII (1945), 429.

[67] Milwaukee Orphan Association, *Annual Reports*, 1850–1857 (Milwaukee). In his budgetary request to his superior in Vienna for the year 1851, the Catholic Bishop of Milwaukee wrote of the need for orphanages in Milwaukee. "To all this must be added the building of two orphan asylums—one for boys and the other for girls—which I must build, since even now 53 orphans were left homeless by the cholera last summer; and I must not expose the little ones to dangers of being drawn away by Protestants. Besides, I fear much from the epidemic mentioned above, and also dysentery, which has robbed several children of their parents—especially at Westpoint, the most unsanitary ward of the city. "Letters of the Right Reverend John Martin Henni and the Reverend Anthony Urbank," *WMH*, X (1926), 81–82.

III

THE LAND AND ITS PLENTY

Part III
The Land and Its Plenty

Agriculture, in the Old Northwest as in most of the United States, was still the mainstay of economic life as late as the 1870's. And so any effort to treat the region's life in the nineteenth century must take account of the land and its plenty—and men's efforts to wrest from nature its bounty—as a principal part of the context of social development. It was not a simple story of unilinear evolution from one kind of agriculture to a more developed kind, affecting the entire five-state area. For in the first place, certain areas of southern Ohio and Indiana were already in cash-crop production before 1810, whereas other parts of the Old Northwest were not first settled until the 1850's.[1] Even in the older-settled states, settlement was staggered: certain portions of Ohio, for instance, were still undeveloped and sparsely populated nearly half a century after the first centers of agriculture in the state went into production.[2] The article by Allan Bogue, professor of history at the University of Wisconsin, makes clear that settlement and the commencement of agriculture in the pre-1820 period took place under different— indeed, vastly different—conditions than comparable activity in the

[1] See the essay by George Rogers Taylor, reprinted in this volume, for a discussion of pre-1810 production; and also the chapters on economic life in R. Carlyle Buley, *The Old Northwest: Pioneer Period*, already cited; and the excellent discussion in William T. Utter, *The Frontier State, 1803–1825* ("History of the State of Ohio," ed. Carl Wittke, Vol. II [Columbus, 1942]). Western agricultural development is treated in a national context, with especially full attention to land policy as it affected settlement and landownership patterns, and with a chapter on prairie farming, in Paul W. Gates, *The Farmer's Age, 1815–1860* ("Economic History of the United States," ed. Henry David *et al.*, Vol. III [New York, 1960]).

[2] Northwestern Ohio did not undergo rapid settlement until the 1850's. See Harry N. Scheiber, "State Policy and the Public Domain: The Ohio Canal Lands," *Journal of Economic History*, Vol. XXV (March, 1965); and Francis P. Weisenburger, *The Passing of the Frontier, 1825–1850* ("History of the State of Ohio," Vol. III [Columbus, 1941]), chaps. i–iii.

1850's or 1860's.[3] Discussion of agricultural development in the Old Northwest therefore must be based on keen awareness of regional differences: in the timing of the initial settlements, in the degree to which specific subregions were tied into the national economy by improved transportation, in the technology that was brought to bear on problems of production and marketing, in the soil and terrain that men had to work, and so on. Moreover, the development of agricultural regions spilled easily over political boundaries; and so, as Professor Bogue indicates, the common natural conditions of the "prairie triangle," which embraced the state of Iowa, became compelling historical determinants of economic structure, blending with the mix of social, political, and cultural factors that gave the Old Northwest its larger common identity.

Within the Old Northwest, moreover, there were many specialties practiced in agriculture. Often, as in the Western Reserve subregion of northeastern Ohio, production of a specialty crop or product became heavily concentrated within a relatively small spatial area. Professor Robert Leslie Jones of Marietta College has written on many of the issues that make Ohio's agriculture especially interesting to economic historians.[4] Ohio stood first or second in the 1840's and 1850's, among the states of the federal Union, in many of the major crops and farm products systematically covered by the dicennial Census. Indeed, so developed was Ohio's agriculture by the fifties that the painful signs of maturity and post-maturity were already evident: many counties underwent an absolute decline in population; soil exhaustion had become a problem in some of the oldest-settled counties; and the production of the old staples, wheat and small grains, fell off as the farmers of Ohio found themselves faring badly under pressure of competition from farming areas located farther west, now linked to eastern markets by railroad lines.[5]

[3] Professor Bogue has written a full-length study of changing technology and other factors affecting development in the prairie triangle, in *From Prairie to Corn Belt* (Chicago, 1963).

[4] See especially Jones, "The Beef Cattle Industry in Ohio Prior to the Civil War," *OHQ*, LXIV (April, 1955), 168–194, and *ibid.* (July, 1955), 287–319; "The Horse and Mule Industry in Ohio to 1865," *MVHR*, Vol. XXXIII (June, 1946); and "Special Crops in Ohio before 1850," *OAHQ*, Vol. LIV (1945).

[5] In this sense, Ohio underwent the same kind of agricultural readjustment that had been forced on the eastern states when the Erie Canal first opened western

And yet extraordinary viability and strength were exhibited by some of the crop specialists in Ohio, among them the dairy producers that Professor Jones treats in the article below. The manner in which dairying arose as a specialty, and the continuing responses of the dairymen to new market constraints and opportunities, are a microcosm of "readjustment" as it marked the Old Northwest's agricultural subregions throughout the nineteenth century.[6]

New York and Ohio to commercial agricultural production. See Percy W. Bidwell, "The Agricultural Revolution in New England," *American Historical Review*, Vol. XXVI (July, 1921). On Indiana in the 1850's see Harvey L. Carter, "Rural Indiana in Transition, 1850–1860," *Agricultural History*, Vol. XX (April, 1946).

[6] An original and incisive account of agricultural readjustment in Wisconsin, as the state's farmers shifted from wheat to dairying, is in Eric E. Lampard, *The Rise of the Dairy Industry in Wisconsin* (Madison, 1963). For Illinois readjustment, see Roy V. Scott, *The Agrarian Movement in Illinois, 1880–1896* (Urbana, 1962).

ALLAN G. BOGUE

6. Farming in the Prairie Peninsula, 1830–1890

FLARING westward from the upper valley of the Wabash lies the prairie triangle, embracing most of central and northern Illinois and almost all of Iowa. Much of this region today lies in the heart of the corn belt. Its economic history is a story of practical experimentation, adaptation, and change as its restless settlers endeavored after 1820 to unlock its wealth. To do so, the prairie pioneers had to adapt techniques and crops to the novel environment of an almost treeless grassland at a time when both technology and markets were undergoing revolutionary change. In 1830 the farm-makers had hardly begun their task; by the 1890's the land was tamed, the corn belt a fact, its farmers on the threshold of a golden age.

I

"The soil is as black as your hat and as mellow as a[n] ash heap. . . ," wrote Oliver Ellsworth to his brother from Bloomington, Illinois, in 1837, "If you, John, will come on, we can live like pigs in the clover. . . ."[1] Particularly, the prairie farm-makers were the

[1] "Ninety-Eight Years Ago in Bloomington," *Journal of the Illinois State Historical Society*, XXVIII (April, 1935—January, 1936), 209. Iowa settlement is described in: Cardinal Goodwin, "The American Occupation of Iowa, 1833 to 1860," *Iowa Journal of History and Politics*, XVII (January, 1919), 83–102; William L. Harter and R. E. Stewart, *The Population of Iowa: Its Composition and Changes: A Brief Sociological Study of Iowa's Human Assets* (Iowa State College of Agriculture and Mechanic Arts, *Bulletin* No. 275 [Ames, 1930]). There is a series of excellent population maps based on the township population figures given in the state censuses of 1856, 1867, and 1875 in G. B. Schilz, "Rural Population Trends of Iowa as Affected by Soils" (Unpublished Ph.D. thesis, Clark University, 1948), pp. 67, 68, 69. See also Clare C. Cooper, "The Role of Railroads in the Settlement of Iowa: A Study of Historical Geography" (Unpublished M.A. thesis, University of Nebraska, 1958).

The basic accounts of settlement in Illinois are: Arthur C. Boggess, *The Settle-*

children of New York, Pennsylvania, the Ohio valley states, the British Isles, the German states, and, to a lesser extent, the Scandinavian countries. A sampling of the manuscript Federal censuses indicates that the typical farm-maker was a man in his thirties, married, and the father of several children who had accompanied him from his previous place of residence. Among the native-born, older residents were found generally farther from their birthplace. For some twenty or thirty years after first settlement, the average age of the farm operators in new communities increased. The frontier population was not a cross section, therefore, of that in older settlements. The typical pioneer was younger and possibly better prepared to cope with farm-making problems than the average operator of the older settlements.[2]

Taken as a group, the farm-makers were mobile. No matter the age of the community, between 50 and 80 per cent of any new group

---

ment of Illinois, 1778–1830 (Chicago Historical Society's *Collection*, Vol. V [Chicago, 1908]) ; William V. Pooley, *The Settlement of Illinois from 1830 to 1850* (University of Wisconsin, *Bulletin* No. 220, "History Series," Vol. I [Madison, 1908]). The appropriate volumes of the *Centennial History of Illinois* include useful summaries of the settlement process; see particularly the maps in Solon J. Buck, *Illinois in 1818* (Springfield, 1918), pp. 4, 174, 384; Arthur C. Cole, *The Era of the Civil War, 1848–1870* (Springfield, 1919), pp. 16, 330.

The various accounts of the immigrant groups are also helpful, as are the materials of the Federal censuses.

[2] The discussion of pioneer demography in this and the following paragraph is based on Harter and Stewart, *Population of Iowa*, pp. 16–17; Mildred Throne, "A Population Study of an Iowa County in 1850," *Iowa Journal of History*, LVII (October, 1959), 305–330; William Bowers, "Crawford Township, 1850–1870: A Population Study of a Pioneer Community," *ibid.*, LVIII (January, 1960), 1–30; and my own unpublished studies of farmers in Bureau County, Illinois, in 1850 and 1860, and farmer turnover in townships in Bremer, Davis, Hamilton, and Washington Counties, Iowa. The method in these studies stems mainly from James C. Malin's article, "The Turnover of Farm Population in Kansas," *Kansas Historical Quarterly*, IV (November, 1935), 339–372. Miss Throne utilized both population and agricultural manuscript censuses, as I did in my township studies. In the Bureau study of farmer households, I made use primarily of the population censuses. The work of Throne, Bowers, and myself revealed patterns of turnover in Illinois and Iowa similar to those discovered by Malin, but to some degree I interpret them differently than did Malin. For similar research, see Merle Curti *et al.*, *The Making of an American Community: A Case Study of Democracy in a Frontier County* (Stanford, Calif., 1959), pp. 55–83.

of farmers were gone ten years later. The prosperous were most likely to stay, but some of these too might leave after very short periods of residence. Undoubtedly, ethnic and cultural origins were linked at times to persistence patterns, but facile generalizations on this point cannot yet be made. In Bureau County, Illinois, some 46 per cent of the British-born farmer householders of 1850 remained in 1860; only 28 per cent of the German-born farmers stayed. Of the New England-born farmers of 1850, 45 per cent remained in 1860, but only 24 per cent of those who claimed Kentucky and Tennessee as their birthplaces remained. As Table 6–1 shows, persistence among the members of such groups rose over time, and 10 to 15 per cent of groups that had lost 60 to 70 per cent of their numbers between 1850 and 1860 remained in 1880. These residuals were important; they formed the continuing core of the western communities.

TABLE 6–1

FARM OPERATOR TURNOVER IN FOUR IOWA TOWNSHIPS BY DATE OF ARRIVAL

	1850		1860		1870		1880	
	No.	Per Cent	No.	Per Cent	No.	Per Cent	No.	Per Cent
Crawford Township[a]								
Group 1	66	100.0	21	31.8	11	16.6	7	10.6
Group 2	—	—	94	100.0	35	37.2	23	24.5
Group 3	—	—	—	—	141	100.0	36	25.5
Union Township								
Group 1	81	100.0	35	43.2	22	27.2	11	13.6
Group 2	—	—	84	100.0	41	48.8	25	29.8
Group 3	—	—	—	—	149	100.0	44	29.5
Hamilton Township								
Group 1	—	—	50	100.0	28	56.0	14	28.0
Group 2	—	—	—	—	64	100.0	30	46.9
Warren Township								
Group 1	—	—	28	100.0	12	42.9	7	25.0
Group 2	—	—	—	—	163	100.0	72	44.2
Continental-born[b]	—	—	—	—	102	100.0	47	46.1

  [a] The counties were Washington, Davis, Hamilton, and Bremer.
  [b] The continental-born group consisted mainly of natives of the German states, with a few Frenchmen and Swiss as well. This group was included in Warren township, Group 2, as well as being placed in a separate category.

Census-derived turnover patterns suggest a number of conclusions. Original land disposal policies could hardly have been a direct controlling influence on the farming operations of the majority of midwestern pioneers. They bought their land at second, third, or even fourth hand, rather than from the government. The turnover rates suggest also that new communities lost much valuable agricultural experience soon after farmers had accumulated it.[3] They force us to qualify the stage formula of agricultural settlement which appeared in the travel and guide literature of the early national period and ultimately in Frederick Jackson Turner's famous essay.[4]

II

If the American pioneers had once believed that the prairies were infertile because trees did not grow there, they were rejecting this misconception by the 1820's. The smaller prairies of Ohio and the barrens of Kentucky had already demonstrated that treeless lands could grow abundant crops. As late as the early 1850's, however, some Iowa settlers maintained that the lack of timber on the larger prairies of the state rendered them useless for intensive husbandry.[5] But other farm-makers were already adjusting to this limiting factor.

Adjustments to the timber shortage took various forms. In part,

[3] Malin, "Turnover of Farm Population," p. 356.

[4] Elias Pym Fordham, *Personal Narrative of Travels in Virginia, Maryland, Pennsylvania, Ohio, Indiana, Kentucky; and of a Residence in the Illinois Territory: 1817–1818*, ed. Frederick Austin Ogg (Cleveland, 1906), pp. 125–127; John Mason Peck, *A New Guide for Emigrants to the West containing sketches of Ohio, Indiana, Illinois, Missouri, Michigan, with the Territories of Wisconsin and Arkansas, and the Adjacent Parts* (Boston, 1836), pp. 114–116. In citing Peck, Turner also called attention to a number of similar analyses. See *The Frontier in American History* (New York, 1920), p. 21, fn. 36.

[5] Western Historical Company, *The History of Cedar County, Iowa, Containing a History of the County, its Cities, Towns, &c.* . . . (Chicago, 1878), pp. 600, 605. A number of accounts of nineteenth-century agriculture give attention to the particular problems of the prairies, but are not cited specifically by the writer in later notes. Percy W. Bidwell and John I. Falconer, *History of Agriculture in the Northern United States, 1620–1860* (Washington: The Carnegie Institution, 1925); Theodore L. Carlson, *The Illinois Military Tract: A Study of Land Occupation, Utilization and Tenure* (Illinois Studies in the Social Sciences, Vol. XXXII, No. 2, Urbana, 1951); Paul W. Gates, *The Farmer's Age: Agriculture, 1815–1860* ("*The Economic History of the United States*," ed. Henry David *et al.*, Vol. III [New York, 1960]); Earle D. Ross, *Iowa Agriculture: An Historical Survey* (Iowa City, 1951); Fred A. Shannon, *The Farmer's Last Frontier: Agriculture, 1860–1897* ("*The Economic History of the United States*," ed. David *et al.*, Vol. V [New York, 1945]). See also Mildred Throne, "A History of Agriculture in Southern Iowa, 1833–1890" (Unpublished Ph.D. thesis, State University of Iowa, 1946).

the claim club reflected the unique features of the prairie landscape. Where timber and prairie alternated, locations in or near wooded areas were relatively much more attractive. This set the stage for associations, which the early comers used to engross the best locations in their own hands for resale to later arrivals or large land speculators.[6] If the Midwest had been all prairie or all timber, the clubs would have been less common. More important, as the land passed into private hands, there developed a landholding pattern of which the timber lot was an integral part. Settlers on the prairie purchased five or ten acres along the stream bottoms or in the prairie groves and drove five, ten or fifteen miles to cut building timber or to split rails during the winter months.[7] Broken in surface and relatively deficient in organic content, the timber soils were often much less productive than the prairie soils, but the price of timber land remained above prairie land prices for thirty or forty years after the arrival of the first settlers.[8]

When he sought to fence his crops against marauding livestock, the prairie farmer faced the timber problem at its most acute.[9] The Virginia worm-rail fence with stakes and riders was an efficient, although somewhat untidy fence. But it demanded timber in large

[6] Allan G. Bogue, "The Iowa Claim Clubs: Symbol and Substance," *MVHR*, XLV (September, 1958), 231–253.

[7] Leslie Hewes, "Some Features of Early Woodland and Prairie Settlement in a Central Iowa County," *Annals of the Association of American Geographers*, XL (March, 1950), 51, 53. This pattern first came to my attention while working in the county records of Hamilton and Bremer Counties, Iowa.

[8] Adrian H. Lindsey, "The Nature and Cause of the Growth of Iowa Land Values" (Unpublished Ph.D. thesis, Iowa State College, 1929), p. 144.

[9] The following account is based mainly on: Clarence H. Danhof, "The Fencing Problem in the Eighteen Fifties," *Agricultural History*, XVIII (October, 1944), 168–186; Earl W. Hayter, "Barbed Wire Fencing—A Prairie Invention: Its Rise and Influence in the Western States," *Agricultural History*, XIII (October, 1939), 189–207; Mary Louise Rice, "The Role of the Osage Orange Hedge in the Occupation of the Great Plains" (Unpublished M.A. thesis, University of Illinois, 1937); Margaret Beattie Bogue, *Patterns from the Sod: Land Use and Tenure in the Grand Prairie, 1850–1900* (Springfield, 1959), pp. 117–121, 133–136; U. S. Commissioner of Agriculture, *Report*, 1871 (Washington, 1872), pp. 504–505; as well as numerous references in *The Prairie Farmer, 1841–1889* (began publication as *The Union Agriculturist and Western Prairie Farmer*); *The Iowa Homestead and Western Farm Journal*, 1858–1883; and the annual *Reports* of the Iowa State Agricultural Society, 1856–1890.

amounts, and the rails might last no more than ten to twenty years. The willow and cottonwood groves of the pioneers were of no immediate help. Some farmers tried to conserve resources by moving the division fences on their cropland as needed and by resorting, where possible, to the Shanghai rail fence in which several of the lower rails were omitted; such solutions were mere stopgaps.

Farmers suggested a variety of substitutes for rail fences. Early settlers had high hopes for ditch and earthen bank fence, capped perhaps by rail or hedge, but the prairie herds had discredited sod fence, on the Illinois prairies at least, by the early 1830's. Smooth iron wire fencing was popular briefly during the 1840's, but the strands stretched and sagged, inspiring only friendly contempt among western livestock. By the 1850's, farmers close to major water routes or to Chicago-based rail lines could use board fencing, although its cost was a deterrent.

By the 1850's, Osage orange had emerged from a host of competing hedge plants as a practicable living hedge. Initially it was inexpensive, but it started slowly and demanded continuing attention. Over time, hedging involved a considerable labor cost. Despite problems in its culture and a shortage of seed during the Civil War, Osage orange hedge gained in popularity and made up a significant percentage of the fencing in prairie counties during the early 1870's. Meanwhile, many prairie farmers had supported an institutional solution to the fencing problem. This was the herd law, which held the owners of livestock responsible for their confinement. In herd-law contests in the 1860's and 1870's, there was sometimes a clear split in sentiment between timbered and prairie regions of the same county. The invention of a practicable and cheap barbed wire solved the fencing problem. The cost of a four-strand barbed wire fence in the mid 1870's, as shown in Table 6-2, was less than half that of a board fence and a third less than the cost of rail fencing, where rails were available.

Prairie farm-makers argued both about the method of breaking prairie sod and about the nature and capabilities of the soils which lay beneath it.[10] Over time, the breakers learned that the proper time for breaking prairie extended from early May to late July. They also changed the approved technique of breaking from one in which

[10] *Prairie Farmer*, May, 1843, p. 118.

TABLE 6–2

AVERAGE FENCING COSTS PER ROD, 1840–1874

	Board	Wire	Picket	Sod	Worm	Post and Rail	Four-Strand Barbed Wire
1840–1860[a]	$1.75	$.83	$.43	$.40	$.55–.75		
1871 Illinois[b]	1.31				.99	$1.27	
Iowa	1.31						
1874 Iowa[c]					.91	.94	
							$.60

[a] *Prarie Farmer*, March 1846, pp. 90–91; July 1846, pp. 204–5; Feb. 1847, pp. 67–68; April 1848, p. 113; May 1848, p. 144; Oct. 1848, p. 302; July 1848, p. 211; March 1850, p. 76; April 1850, pp, 117–18; April 2, 1864, p. 226; *Union Agriculturist and Western Prairie Farmer*, Oct. 1841, p. 77; Nov. 1841, p. 43; *Northwestern Farmer*, April 1856, p. 104; *Iowa Homestead and Western Farm Journal*, Jan. 3, 1873, p. 1; Frederick Gerhard, *Illinois As It Is:* . . . (Chicago, 1857), pp. 311–12. The estimate for seven-rail worm is mine, based on a rail cost of two cents per rail.
[b] United States Commissioner of Agriculture, *Report*, 1871, p. 509
[c] Iowa State Agricultural Society, *Report*, 1875, p. 43. By 1885, barbed-wire fencing costs were probably well down below thirty cents per rod, depending upon the local cost of labor and posts. The wire for a rod of four-strand fence cost ten cents at that time. *Prairie Farmer*, April 4, 1885, p. 209. Three-strand fencing was probably always much more common than four.

the furrows were as deep as five inches and the overturned furrow slices lay in neatly flat, tight rows to one in which the plow pared off a thin rind of grass and roots, leaving the furrow slice broken and riffled. The pioneers of northwestern Iowa believed that they hastened the decomposition process by planting a sod crop of flax.[11]

The farm-makers assumed that there were important differences in the soils of the prairie regions. A writer in the *Prairie Farmer* of 1851 presented an analysis of western soils based on their suitability for wheat culture. On the uplands where the white oaks grew was a pure wheat soil; that supporting yellow and red oaks differed somewhat; and where the burr oaks and hazels grew was "perhaps the richest soil." Least adapted to wheat culture, he maintained, was the soil of the open prairie.[12] Others suggested that wheat grew best on the soil of the timbered tracts or on the soil of the barrens, those stretches of alternating timber, hazel brush and prairie. Some believed that newly broken prairie was superior for wheat-growing to old prairie fields.[13] By the mid-1840's there had emerged the idea that much of northern Illinois constituted an "infected district," in which tame

[11] L. S. Coffin, "Breaking Prairie," *Annals of Iowa*, 3d series, V (July, 1902), 447–452; *Prairie Farmer*, May, 1841, pp. 34–35; October, 1841, p. 76; April, 1842, p. 34; Iowa State Agricultural Society, *Report, 1879* (Des Moines, 1880), 35. Hereafter the latter series will be cited as I. S. A. S. R.

[12] "W" in *Prairie* Farmer, April, 1851, pp. 166–167.

[13] *Prairie Farmer*, February, 1854, p. 56; June 1854, p. 205; *Northwestern Farmer*, January, 1857, p. 7; I. S. A. S. R., 1857, pp. 256, 434; 1863, p. 481; 1866, p. 186.

grasses and clovers would not grow.[14] As late as 1866, the editor of the *Prairie Farmer* mentioned that "the generally conceived ideas that prairie land is not well adapted to the production of tame grasses" were being disproved.[15]

If the prairie environment perplexed the pioneer on occasion, it also rewarded his efforts. Whatever their regional variations, the prairie soils were usually highly productive, with considerable staying power. Nor was there need here for the farmer to invest a generation of family labor in removing a heavy mantle of forest. It is hard to exaggerate the importance of this fact in explaining the rapid development of mechanized agriculture in Illinois and Iowa after 1850.

III

A variety of factors may have influenced the pioneer farmer of the prairie triangle when he made his production plans. Markets, transportation facilities, the general price level, changes in the prices of farm products relative to each other, his cultural heritage, and his understanding of prairie soils all probably affected the farmer's calculations. On the other hand, it is sometimes suggested that pioneer agriculture was essentially subsistence agriculture or that there were typical frontier cropping sequences through which the farmers moved as their communities developed. The data of the Federal agricultural censuses from 1850 to 1890 give us considerable information about such matters. Maps based upon average county production per improved acre of the field crops, and upon numbers of farm animals per farm, show areas of high and low production on a subregional basis in Illinois and Iowa as early as 1850.[16]

---

[14] *Prairie Farmer*, October, 1848, p. 324.

[15] *Ibid.*, November 3, 1866, p. 281.

[16] Prior to 1880, the Federal census does not show acreages planted to the various field crops, giving only total yield per county and improved acreages. Maps based on production figures, of course, must be used with caution. Unusual seasons and regional differences in soil productivity could both distort production maps in comparison to maps based on acreage. However, comparison of maps based on acreages in 1880 with those based on production in the same year does reveal very similar patterns. Some of the Iowa state censuses do give acreages planted to specific crops, and maps based on these figures suggest that the maps based on Federal production figures give a fairly accurate picture of production patterns.

Had the farmers in newly settled areas been subsistence farmers, their counties would not ordinarily have appeared among the leading producers of wheat or corn per improved acre in Iowa or Illinois in a particular census year. Yet this was the case. Nor apparently was there any one crop-production or farm-management sequence through which most pioneer farmers of Illinois and Iowa moved. The farm-makers of northern Illinois and Iowa placed considerable emphasis upon wheat production in early years and later moved to heavier dependence on other combinations of crops and livestock; the farmers of central Illinois and southern Iowa gave a much more important place in their plans to corn and livestock from the very beginning. If one must have a yardstick for measuring the basic difference between the agriculture of older and more recently settled communities, most satisfactory would be the relative amounts of improved land. Better still, but impossible to calculate, would be the percentage of labor used in farm-making tasks in contrast to that used directly in the production of food, feed, and fiber.

The farmers of the prairie triangle were never monoculturists. Even when they described themselves as wheat farmers or corn-hog farmers, their farming operations were really combinations of wheat, corn, oats, barley, hay, cattle, sheep, hogs, and other minor enterprises. Enough farmers in any particular area reacted similarly to the economic and physical environments to produce subregional production patterns. Many of these patterns, however, were unstable. Between 1849 and 1879 the area of high wheat production in Illinois shifted from northern Illinois to the southwestern region of the state. The area of highest hog production per farm unit moved northward from its position in southern Illinois in 1850 to lie particularly in the Military Tract in 1880. In 1850 central Illinois below the Sangamon reported the largest numbers of other cattle per farm unit, reflecting the stocker and feeder operations of that region. By the 1880's the upper Military Tract and adjacent counties to the north had become the major feeding area in Illinois. On the other hand, there were elements of stability in the production patterns of these prairie states. The counties of southeastern Iowa, for instance, were always the leading sheep producers in that state. Hay was always much more important to the farmers of northern Iowa than to those farther to the south.

By the 1870's and 1880's, the subregional patterns of crop and livestock production in Illinois and Iowa were beginning to resemble those which prevailed in the early twentieth century. The increasing concentration of milk cows in extreme northern Illinois during this period stamped the agriculture of that region as closer to the agriculture of southern Wisconsin than to the corn and livestock farming of central Illinois. During the 1880's the milk cow was coming to dominate the agriculture of northeastern Iowa. In the same decade oats assumed a more significant role in the agriculture of central and northern Illinois and Iowa. Barley emerged as a crop of considerable importance in northwestern Iowa. By 1880 the farmers of the Grand Prairie had concluded that it was to their advantage to concentrate on cash grain production; the farmers of the northern Military Tract had already linked their destinies to the feeder steer and the hog. Although the outlines of the eastern livestock area of Iowa were becoming clear by 1880 and a western livestock area was present, the cash grain section ultimately found in north central Iowa was still in flux. Some of the counties there, of course, were still raw frontier. Wheat production was still important in northwestern Iowa, and farmers there were experiencing difficulty in finding strains of corn which would ripen early enough for their needs.

Comparison of the production maps based on the censuses from 1850 to 1890 does in general reveal that the farmers of the various subregions in Illinois and Iowa specialized increasingly in particular crops or farm enterprises. If the census statistics of 1850 are to be trusted, however—and there are grounds for skepticism—one must qualify the generalization somewhat. The average production of corn per improved acre and the holdings of hogs and other cattle per farm unit in the leading counties of both Iowa and Illinois during the census year 1850 were actually greater than those reported from the leading counties in some subsequent censuses. The farmers of McLean County, Illinois, for instance, reported seventeen other cattle per farm unit in 1850; not until 1890 did Warren County farmers surpass this with a figure of eighteen other cattle per farm unit.

Crop and livestock enterprises were related to each other in a variety of ways. Not surprisingly, corn and hogs were strikingly complementary. Frequency tables based on the production returns of ninety-eight Illinois counties in the agricultural census of 1850 show, for instance, that forty-eight counties appeared in the same quintile as corn producers which they occupied as hog producers. Tables illustrating the relationship between corn production and other cattle and corn production and milk cows show much weaker relationships. Only twenty-seven counties ranked in the same quintiles as producers of both corn and other cattle; in the case of corn and milk cows the number was only sixteen. The census returns of 1890 showed the same rank order of correlation, but the relationship between corn production and hog raising had weakened, while that between other cattle and corn raising had strengthened somewhat; with 102 counties reporting, the quintile correlation of corn to hogs was thirty-nine and that of corn to other cattle was thirty-four. On the other hand, some farm enterprises in the prairie triangle were notably antipathetic to each other. High wheat-producing counties were almost never high corn-producing counties, for instance.

IV

The agricultural production maps reflect a variety of geographic factors. As early as 1849, some of the Shelbyville Moraine counties of Illinois seemed to mark a transition in farming patterns. In the crop-production maps of 1869, if not earlier, one can see reflected the contrasting topography and soil conditions of the northern and southern portions of the Illinois Military Tract. During the 1880's the farmers of northwestern Iowa turned to barley, in part because the loessial soils and relatively lower humidity of that area were highly congenial to the crop.

Transportation facilities played their part in shaping subregional production patterns. Every one of the Mississippi River counties of Iowa fell in the top quartile of wheat producers in the state during 1849. As soon as the Illinois and Michigan canal was completed, farmers of north central Illinois discovered that they could now sell part of their corn production as a cash crop for shipment to other regions. The railroads which girded Illinois and Iowa after 1850 produced comparable changes on a broader scale. In interior areas where herds had formerly been driven to feed on surplus corn, the farmers had now the option of letting their corn be shipped to feed cattle and hogs elsewhere. If the farmers of northwestern Iowa found barley a profitable crop during the 1880's, it was in part because railroad construction in that section guaranteed a market for a small-grain specialty.

Underlying the production responses of prairie farmers, of course, was the fact that they were producing for an expanding domestic and foreign market. We cannot here recount the developments, innovations and inventions which allowed midwestern producers to enter these markets on competitive terms: lard oil, dressed beef, refrigeration, and futures trading, to mention a few of them. The meaning of some of these developments was unclear to most prairie farmers. What many of them did understand, however, was that the relationship between corn and hog prices made it almost always profitable to feed hogs. In Iowa, one hundred pounds of pork was worth less than ten bushels of corn in only three years between 1861 and 1900. Iowa price indices show also that beef prices were relatively stable through the whole period from 1864 to 1896. On the other hand, the declining significance of wheat in the economy of many districts in Illinois and Iowa undoubtedly reflected the very striking decline in the index of wheat prices between 1866 and 1896, relative to the indices of other major farm products.[17]

Students of agricultural development in the Midwest of the nineteenth century have often suggested that cultural or ethnic influences affected the decisions of farmers. With the contention that particular cultural or ethnic groups drew upon their unique heritages to help in solving the problems of adaptation to the midwestern environment, there can be little quarrel. Quite possibly, English settlers did bring improved drainage techniques to the Illinois prairies.[18] Englishmen may well also have solved a major problem in the development of Osage orange hedging by introducing the plashing technique.[19] Hungarian refugees evidently did introduce Hungarian

[17] The price indices referred to here are based on data presented by Norman V. Strand in *Prices of Farm Products in Iowa, 1851–1940* (Iowa State College of Agriculture and Mechanic Arts, *Research Bulletin* No. 303 [Ames, 1942]), pp. 934, 938–942.

[18] George Flower, *History of the English Settlement in Edwards County, Illinois, Founded in 1817 and 1818 by Morris Birkbeck and George Flower* (Chicago, 1882), pp. 165–166.

[19] *Prairie Farmer*, August 12, 1862, p. 111.

grass or millet in Iowa, although the experiment was of little long-range significance.[20] Undoubtedly the Yankees, those "shrewd, selfish, enterprising, cow-milking" men spread the skills of dairying in many western communities.[21] And John M. Peck argued that even the southerners most wedded to dog and gun better appreciated the need of keeping a clean cornfield in the crucial June weeks than did some of their tidier Yankee neighbors.[22] It would have been strange had western farm-makers not brought their fund of previous experience to bear on the unique problems of midwestern agriculture.

Writers on occasion, however, have suggested that the members of particular cultural groups consistently followed farming practices which were significantly different from those of neighbors who drew upon other cultural heritages. The Norwegians and Danes, one writer hints, may have had a particular affinity for the wet prairie in central Iowa.[23] Contemporaries wrote that the Yankees were more apt to be orchardists than were farmers of other backgrounds.[24] Both contemporaries and later writers have suggested that the Germans, and to a lesser extent the Scandinavians, farmed differently from their neighbors. The Germans were pre-eminently wheat growers in south-western Illinois. In Iowa, they grew more barley than did their neighbors and preferred mules for draft stock.[25] Two eminent agricultural historians wrote:

[20] *Northwestern Farmer*, December, 1857, p. 457; June, 1858, p. 191.

[21] H. C. M. Case and K. H. Myers, *Types of Farming in Illinois: An Analysis of Differences by Areas* (University of Illinois Agricultural Experiment Station, *Bulletin* No. 403 [Urbana, 1934]), p. 123. The quotation is from Pooley, *The Settlement of Illinois from 1830 to 1850*, p. 385, quoting Chicago *Weekly American*, February 4, 1837.

[22] John M. Peck, *A Guide for Emigrants, Containing Sketches of Illinois, Missouri, and the Adjacent Parts* (Boston, 1831), pp. 153–154.

[23] Leslie Hewes and Philip E. Frandson, "Occupying the West Prairie: The Role of Artificial Drainage in Story County, Iowa," *Annals of the Association of American Geographers*, XLII (March, 1952), 33.

[24] I. S. A. S. R., 1859, p. 246.

[25] John C. Weaver, "Changing Patterns of Cropland Use in the Middle West," *Economic Geography*, XXX (January, 1954), 19; Herbert Quick, *One Man's Life* (Indianapolis, 1925), p. 194; U. S. Commissioner of Patents, *Report, 1850* (Washington, 1851), p. 242; I. S. A. S. R., 1863, p. 378; 1865, p. 400; 1870, pp. 483, 490, 527.

> . . . what pulled most of the debt-ridden out of the red was the com-
> bination of pluck, perspicacity, and pigs. This was particularly so in the
> case of the German and Swedish immigrants. Less skilled in the manage-
> ment of horses, sheep, and beef cattle than the English and native
> Americans, they concentrated with dogged tenacity on their hogs. . . .
> The chief economy practiced by the German farmer that made him
> competitively efficient was fattening his hogs behind beef steers, . . .[26]

Where there is so much smoke there certainly ought to be fire.
But it is quite possible that the Norwegians and Danes of Story
County, Iowa, moved to the wet prairie because that was the only
land which they believed they could afford. The area of Illinois
which became pre-eminently a fruit region was settled for the most
part by southerners, not Yankees. I selected 10 per cent samples of
the continental-born farmers, mostly Germans and Scandinavians,
in Bremer and Hamilton Counties, Iowa, from the manuscript
census of 1880 and compared their farming operations with those
of like samples of the native-born. One of the few common patterns
in the agriculture of the former group in the two counties was that
these farmers kept fewer hogs than the native-born. Obviously, we
must make many more detailed comparisons of this sort before we
can put cultural influences in their proper perspective. When local
conditions reinforced cultural bias, the members of a particular
cultural group may have farmed somewhat differently for a time.
Greater difficulty in obtaining access to capital may have accounted
for differences also. Perhaps, however, cultural differences were more
clearly apparent in diet, minor farm practices, and socio-economic
behavior such as the use of wives in the fields, than in significantly
different combinations of enterprises, maintained over a considerable
period of time.

None of the foregoing means, of course, that all farmers in an
agricultural subregion of Illinois or Iowa farmed in exactly the same
way. It is true that there were considerable numbers of so-called
general farmers in most western communities. They kept up to six
or seven cows and young stock of varying ages.[27] Through the 1840's

[26] Charles W. Towne and Edward N. Wentworth, *Pigs: from Cave to Corn Belt*
(Norman, Okla., 1950), 208–209, 210–211.

[27] Here I generalize on my examination of the agricultural census rolls of some
ten counties scattered through Iowa and Illinois for the years 1850 and 1880 as well
as a study of the rolls of all Iowa counties in the latter year.

they might own a yoke or two of oxen. By the 1850's they usually owned at least one horse and perhaps two or three. If one of these was a brood mare, such farmers raised the occasional colt. They ordinarily tended several sows and their litters. In their fields the general farmers grew corn and the small grains. They derived their cash income each year from the sale of a few steers or perhaps a fat cow; they might sell a horse or a colt. Fat hogs, however, frequently brought them their largest increment of cash income. Generally they sold some grain, wheat or oats, and corn on occasion. Depending on the time and location, they might also have some barley, buckwheat, or even timothy seed for sale. They, or more likely their wives, made butter and traded the excess, along with a few eggs perhaps, at the local store. But even the general farmers differed in the scale of their operations, and other differences stemmed from the varying speeds with which they adapted to new developments in crop and livestock management and in agricultural technology.

If the general farmers provided a kind of matrix of farm operators in the western community, there were also specialists living side by side with them. Usually operating larger farms than average, such men might concentrate on growing cash grain or raising hogs or on cattle feeding. Occasionally, and more commonly by the 1870's, one finds the fine stock man who sought to sell breeding stock to his neighbors, or by the late 1870's looked also to the western ranges for his market. In a sense, the operations of these specialists were complementary to those of the general farmer. This was particularly true in the case of the cattle feeder. Cattle feeders never constituted a majority of the farmers in any particular community. In Clarion township, Bureau County, lying in the heaviest feeding area of Illinois for instance, only 21 per cent of the farmers bought or sold as many as twenty cattle during the year 1879.[28] But from the general farmer the cattle feeder might purchase surplus corn, two or three

[28] This figure is derived from a farm-by-farm count in the Illinois manuscript agricultural census of 1880, in the possession of the Illinois State Archives, Springfield. The columns showing cattle bought and sold in the previous year were evidently not totaled for publication in the printed census of 1880. Comparable county percentages in Iowa ranged from 15.1 per cent to 1.4 per cent. Manuscript copies of the Federal agricultural census for Iowa are available at both the State Historical Society, Iowa City, and the Department of History and Archives, Des Moines.

steers, weanling pigs or stocker hogs.[29] He might rent the stalk fields after the general farmer had picked his corn crop in order to provide a month or so of forage for stocker steers.[30] He might even work out a feeding contract with the general farmer so that the latter could in effect sell a portion of his labor along with surplus corn and hay. The unique characteristics of a particular agricultural subregion perhaps derived particularly from the activities of the specialists plus minor differences in emphasis in the farming operations of the general farmers as compared with those in other areas.

V

While changes in production patterns went on, the prairie farmers worked a considerable change in the fundamental elements of production—plant strains, breeds, and techniques. In so far as they grew wheat, they changed from heavy emphasis on winter wheat in the 1840's to considerable dependence on spring wheat and by the late 1870's back, in many cases, to winter wheat. Within the broader pattern, the popularity of specific strains or varieties rose and fell with great suddenness. In the corn field, the northern flints, supposedly dominant in much of Illinois during the 1840's, yielded to the dent corns, so that one writer could use "western" as a synonym for "dent" in 1866.[31] But the dents that came to rule the fields of the prairie triangle were themselves the products of hybridization with the northern flints—some of it accidental, some of it purposeful. Some western farmers understood simple hybridization techniques by the early 1840's.[32] Delay in the development of varieties suited

[29] The diaries of George F. Green of Miles, Jackson County, Iowa, present a particularly fine picture of the operation of a cattle feeder and dealer during the early 1870's. These were made available to me through the kindness of Mrs. Curtis Frymoyer of Wilton Junction, Iowa, a great-granddaughter of Mr. Green.

[30] A common price in Putnam County, Illinois, about 1850 for wintering two- and three-year-old cattle was $2.00 to $2.50 per head. U. S. Commissioner of Patents, *Report, 1850* (Washington, 1851), p. 404.

[31] *Prairie Farmer*, June 23, 1866, p. 429.

[32] Edgar Anderson and William L. Brown, "The History of the Common Maize Varieties of the United States Corn Belt," *Agricultural History*, XXVI (January, 1952), 2.

to the growing season of north central Iowa, however, did slow down the development of corn-belt patterns of farming in that area.[33]

Under the ministrations of midwestern farmers, the American lard hog emerged in its most impressive form. For the lean, stump-sucking, mast-fed rangers of the 1830's and early 1840's, swine-raisers by the early 1870's had substituted fat hogs of gargantuan size.[34] The farmers of the Neponset area in Illinois particularly prided themselves on their hogs, and one of them reported that in a month and a half of the winter of 1870–1871, nineteen farmers there shipped 932 hogs weighing well above four hundred pounds each.[35] Typifying the development, in a sense, was the rise of the Poland China, an Ohio contribution originally, but so popular and known by so many names in the Midwest of the early 1870's that the editor of the *Western Live Stock Journal* tried to resolve the conflict by suggesting the name "Great Western," only to withdraw it in favor of "Polyonomous."[36] By the end of this decade, however, changes in consumer demand were making themselves felt and packers and butchers were turning increasingly to hogs sold at earlier ages and at weights in the vicinity of two hundred pounds.

The nondescript prairie steer of the 1830's that might attain a top weight of 850 pounds at the age of five or six years had yielded place to animals that could reach weights in excess of 1,300 pounds in their third or fourth years by the late 1860's and early 1870's.[37] Some zealots or publicity-conscious feeders indeed, brought the midwestern steers of this era to weights of a ton or more. Exhibited before the Chicago Board of Trade in 1867, "Bob Burns," "Abe Lincoln," and "John Williams" averaged almost 3,200 pounds in

---

[33] See the conclusions in Clare C. Cooper, "The Role of Railroads in the Settlement of Iowa: A Study in Historical Geography," pp. 136–138.

[34] For early descriptions of western hogs see: John Woods, *Two Years' Residence in the Settlement on the English Prairie, in the Illinois Country, United States* . . . (London, 1822, reprinted in Vol. VIII of Reuben Gold Thwaites (ed.), *Early Western Travels, 1748–1846* [Cleveland, 1906]), p. 285; William Oliver, *Eight Months in Illinois, with Information to Emigrants* (Newcastle-upon-Tyne, 1843; reprinted Chicago, 1924), pp. 80–81; John M. Peck, *New Guide for Emigrants to the West*, p. 284.

[35] *Prairie Farmer*, June 4, 1870, p. 169.

[36] *National Live Stock Journal*, March 1871, p. 223.

[37] For early descriptions of Illinois cattle see: Oliver, *Eight Months in Illinois*, p. 104; Peck, *A Guide for Emigrants*, p. 168.

weight.[38] John Dean Gillett's mammoth steers of the next decade gained international fame.[39] Undoubtedly there were still many very scrubby native steers in prairie feed lots during the 1870's, but short-horn blood had worked a marvelous improvement.

At first glance the invasion of midwestern pastures and feed lots by Texas steers during the late 1860's and early 1870's may seem to represent a retreat from the rising standards of quality found among the domestic steers. In reality the Texas interlude emphasized the fact that the stockmen of Illinois and Iowa were businessmen, alert for profit. Although critics stigmatized the invaders as mere "vitalized rawhide," the prices of the lean rangers were low enough so that they repaid a period of fattening on prairie corn or blue grass as generously as did local steers, despite the superior fattening qualities and choicer meat of most domestic animals.[40] One Illinois stock firm estimated that to feed the Texans required only half the capital necessary to handle prairie steers.[41] To the stockmen of central Illinois the Texas era drove home the lesson that local agricultural resources were most profitably used for feeding rather than rearing cattle. Other regions could supply the stocker and feeder beasts.

Although Illinois stockmen continued to obtain considerable numbers of steers from local general farmers, particularly in the more broken areas of the state, such cattle represented a declining percentage of those fed. Similar developments took place in Iowa, although at a somewhat slower pace.[42] The farmers who raised young cattle for sale as breeding stock provided an exception to the rule that, relatively speaking, it did not pay to maintain breeding herds in the prairie states. But the fine stockmen of Sangamon County, Illinois, or the West Liberty area in Iowa found the ranchers of the plains country to be increasingly important among their customers.

[38] *Prairie Farmer*, January 4, 1868, p. 9.

[39] Paul W. Gates has described Gillett's stock interests in "Cattle Kings in the Prairies," *MVHR*, XXXV (December, 1948), 391–396.

[40] *Iowa Homestead*, February 23, 1877, p. 60.

[41] James N. Brown's Sons in *National Live Stock Journal*, April, 1874, pp. 123–124.

[42] John A. Hopkins, Jr., *Economic History of the Production of Beef Cattle in Iowa* (Iowa City, 1928), is a standard and very useful account of the development of the cattle industry in Iowa.

In the thirty years between 1850 and 1880 there occurred a
veritable revolution in agricultural technology. In part the prairie
farmer was simply the beneficiary of industrial achievements which
were being applied to agriculture throughout the country. A portion
of the new agricultural technology, however, bore directly on the
peculiar problems of prairie agriculture. The stories of the steel
plow, barbed wire and harvesting machinery are well known. Less
emphasized, however, are the changes in the technology of corn
culture. Here the important developments of the period were the
horse-drawn corn planter and the riding and walking straddle row
cultivators. A variety of practicable models of both were available
by the early 1860's.[43] Together with the steel plow, these implements
increased by at least twice and perhaps three times the twenty acreas
of corn which a single worker could bring through satisfactorily to
harvest in earlier years.[44]

Superficially at least, the agricultural-machinery inventors failed
the prairie farmer most flagrantly in the corn harvest. Although a
corn harvester useful for cutting and bundling fodder, or ensilage
corn had appeared by the end of the century, no satisfactory corn
picker was available. But there was little of the urgency in corn-
picking time that characterized the harvest of the small grains.
Although October and November were the most pleasant months for
corn picking, the ears could remain on the stalk until the following
April or March with little damage to the grain. The prairie farmer
had almost six months available for the task, when other farm duties
were not of an urgent nature. Even so, the character of the corn
harvest changed drastically between the 1830's and the 1880's. At
the earlier date, western farmers cut great quantities of corn fodder
and piled or cribbed the ears in shuck to wait the husking frolic.

[43] R. L. Ardrey, *American Agricultural Implements: A Review of Invention and
Development in the Agricultural Implement Industry of the United States* (Chicago, 1894),
pp. 30–35, 36–39. George W. Brown's two-row planter was the first to win a considerable reputation, but there were at least three other two-horse corn planters on
exhibit at the Illinois State Fair in 1854. *Prairie Farmer*, November, 1854, pp. 405–
406.

[44] Peck, *Guide* (1831), 150; *Prairie Farmer*, January 6, 1866, p. 2. In *ibid.*, March
14, 1863, p. 163, "Small Farmer" struck a more conservative note, arguing for
thirty to thirty-five acres. Estimates of 1885 give forty to fifty acres, *Prairie Farmer*,
February 7, 1885, p. 82; February 28, 1885, p. 130.

Farmers still cut some corn fodder in the 1880's, but as Herbert Quick so ably pictured in *The Hawkeye*, they more commonly exploited the fact that one man armed with husking peg and aided by a driverless team pulling a wagon equipped with a throw board could pick as much as one hundred bushels of corn per day from the stalk.[45] No doubt this was several times the average product of the laborer of the 1830's and, doubtless too, the work was much less fun than a husking frolic. In the meantime the Virginia or Kentucky system of feeding cattle their corn on the cured stalk had yielded generally to a regime of ear corn and hay fed in bunkers, although under certain conditions farmers might resort to the so-called Illinois system of turning cattle or hogs into the corn fields to pick their own feed.[46]

In part mechanization accounted for the changes which occurred in the draft animals of the prairie triangle between the 1840's and 1880's. As long as plowing was the major machine task in grain culture, oxen held an honored place on many farms. Although horses admittedly, under good conditions, could plow two acres per day to the one and one half expected of oxen, the greater strength of mature oxen and the smaller investment involved in them appealed to farmers.[47] Mechanical harvesting equipment, however, changed the picture drastically. If the reciprocating cutting bars were to operate effectively, the machines must move at a faster clip than oxen displayed. At the same time, however, the weight of such machinery emphasized the need of larger and stronger horses than the Morgan or other roadster strains that farmers had preferred until this time. The light horses, also, as one journalist put it, "were too weak in the poop" for farm-to-market hauling over heavy prairie roads or to

[45] Herbert Quick, *The Hawkeye* (Indianapolis, 1923), 263–264. The one hundred-bushel-per-day man was never common. Two wagonloads or seventy bushels per day was a day's work. A good team, a heavy crop, a strong youthful back, a short haul to the granary and an immediate change of wagons were all essential for a one hundred-bushel day. I am indebted to my colleague John Clifford on this point.

[46] For use of these terms in primary source material see: U. S. Commissioner of Patents, *Report, 1845* (Washington, 1846), p. 384; *Prairie Farmer*, March 14, 1868, p. 163; April 11, 1868, p. 236; among secondary works, Hopkins, *Beef Production*, has a particularly useful section on feeding methods, pp. 122–142.

[47] John Savage Diary, May 6, 1862. Department of History and Archives, Des Moines, Iowa.

fill the needs of the prairie towns and cities for heavy dray horses.[48] The importation of Norman or Percheron breeding stock was a response to this situation.[49]

Between the 1830's and the late 1870's, machinery increased the productivity of the worker in the small-grain fields by perhaps four to six times, in the hay meadow by certainly as much, and in the corn field by perhaps twice.[50] Farmers, of course, did not spend all of their time in work on those crops or tasks which had yielded to machinery. Yet it would not be too rash probably to suggest that, over-all, the potential productivity of the individual agricultural laborer doubled during this period, most of the increase coming after 1855. Wage data are both difficult to find and hard to interpret. Apparently, however, the increased productivity of agricultural labor was not reflected in agricultural wages.[51] At the same time, the

[48] *Prairie Farmer*, July 27, 1872, p. 237.

[49] The standard work on the Percheron is Alvin H. Sanders, *History of the Percheron Horse* (Chicago, 1917).

[50] Despite its importance, we lack satisfactory work on the subject of labor productivity in nineteenth-century agriculture, although at least one scholar is now working on it. The most frequently used secondary works are: Fred A. Shannon, *The Farmer's Last Frontier*, pp. 140–146, and Leo Rogin, *The Introduction of Farm Machinery in Its Relation to the Productivity of Labor in the Agriculture of the United States During the Nineteenth Century* (Berkeley, 1931). The tendency has been to give too much emphasis to the relatively few examples given in U. S. Commissioner of Labor, *Report*, 1898, *Hand and Machine Labor* (2 vols.; Washington, 1899). Rogin pointed out (pp. 227–229) that in the case of wheat-growing, these examples suggested labor input requirements under machine methods which were considerably less than those prevailing in many parts of the country in the 1920's as given by C. D. Kinsman in an *Appraisal of Power Used on Farms in the United States* (U. S. Department of Agriculture, *Bulletin* No. 1348 [Washington, 1925]), p. 59. It seems clear that wheat culture under hand methods required more than sixty hours of human labor per acre, although seeding in standing corn might reduce the amount; the Kinsman estimate under machine methods in the mid-1920's was fifteen hours in both Indiana and Illinois. Students have been less interested in the labor savings effected in the hay meadows, but see U.S. Commissioner of Agriculture, *Report*, 1872 (Washington, 1873), pp. 289–290. See my references for corn culture, note 44.

[51] U.S. Department of Agriculture, *Wages of Farm Labor in the United States* (Division of Statistics, Misc. Series 4, [Washington, 1892]), pp. 16–17, 65–66; U.S. Commissioner of Patents, *Report*, 1845 (Washington, 1846), p. 1152; John Goodell (ed.), *Diary of William Sewall, 1797–1846, Formerly of Augusta, Maine, Maryland, Virginia, and Pioneer in Illinois* (Beardstown, 1930); Benjamin F. Harris, Ledger and Daybook, First National Bank, Champaign, Illinois. See also U.S. Industrial Commission, *Report*, XI (Washington, 1901), 140–141.

percentage of nonfamily labor was increasing in farm family households. Table 6–3 suggests that it probably rose by some 5 per cent between 1850 and 1880 in central Illinois and eastern Iowa. Evidently some farmers by the 1870's were either farming more intensively or increasing the size of their farm units. The latter suggestion is not confirmed by state averages until the next decade.

TABLE 6–3

MALE WORK FORCE SAMPLE
FOUR CORN-BELT COUNTIES
1850–1880[a]

| | 300 Farm Households Iowa and Illinois | | | | 240 Farm Households Jones County, Iowa | | | |
| | 1850 | | 1880 | | 1850 | | 1880 | |
	Num- ber	Per Cent	Num- ber	Per Cent	Num- ber	Per Cent	Num- ber	Per Cent
Owner-Operator	242	45.1	226	36.8	198	51.8	193	43.3
Tenant House- holders	14	2.6	42	6.8	45	11.8	34	7.6
Laborer House- holders	36	6.7	33	5.4			17	3.8
Additional Males 15 Years and Over (family)	187	34.9	200	32.5	98	25.7	134	30.1
Additional Males 15 Years and Over (nonfamily)	57	10.7	115	18.5	41	10.7	68	15.2
Total	536	100.0	616	100.0	382	100.0	446	100.0

a This table is based on data from the manuscript agricultural and population censuses of 1850 and 1880. The three hundred households include one hundred in Clarion township, Bureau County, one hundred in Center township, Cedar County, Iowa, and one hundred in Dutch Creek township, Washington County, taken in order from the census enumerator's rolls. In Washington County in 1850, it was actually necessary to follow the enumerator through several townships to obtain one hundred families. I made no effort to obtain the same households in 1880; because of turnover this would have been a hopeless task. These selections of "neighbors" of course were not random samples. To check the work a 10 per cent random sample was taken from Jones County, Iowa, in 1880 and the same number of households, 240, was taken at random from the 1850 Jones County census, amounting in that year to almost half of the rural households. I used a standard set of random number tables in this process. I did not exclude households which were headed by women, but I did not include the ladies in my final table. Among the 240 farm households of Jones County there were seven women householders in 1850 and six in 1880; among the three hundred households there were eight in 1850 and nine in 1880. Census enumerators did not list tenants in 1850, but by comparing the property returns in the population census with the farm returns of the same year, it was possible to designate men who listed no real property, but reported a farm business as tenants. Since farm returns were in part based on the previous year's production, some new tenants may have been missed. Evidently a number of the Jones County enumerator's return sheets were not included in the final agricultural census compilation of 1850; I did not, therefore, attempt to separate tenants and householders who were simply farm laborers in that year. The number of householders designated as laborers may be too large. I placed them in this category if they designated themselves as farmers or farm laborers, and reported neither real property nor farm production. Some farmers who had just arrived in the community but had not yet purchased a farm may therefore have fallen into this group, as well as the occasional tenant farmer.

VI

The changes in prairie agriculture sketched above did not take place with equal speed or thoroughness on every farm. In general, the operators of the larger units first adopted the cropping patterns and combinations of enterprises best adapted to the peculiar economic and physical environments of the agricultural subregions in Illinois and Iowa or led in the introduction of improved livestock.[52] A few owners of average-sized or small farms, however, were as innovation-minded as the larger operators and gentlemen farmers were notorious experimenters. Occasionally, no doubt, landlords also assisted in the innovation process either through specific leasing terms or by retaining a larger share in management decisions than ordinary. There is reason to suspect that the innovators were somewhat better educated than the average farmer and certainly no older than the average age of farm operators in their communities. Almost certainly, too, the innovator was found among those who provided leadership in farm clubs, Grange chapters and agricultural societies. He was also apt to be a community leader in the broader sense, a township or county officeholder.

Although the Illinois Industrial University was conducting cattle-feeding experiments in the 1870's and 1880's and testing varieties of corn in the 1880's, the agricultural colleges of Illinois and Iowa made only minor contributions to the agricultural adjustments of the farmers in those states prior to 1890. The adjustments stemmed rather from the ideas, successes and failures of the farmers themselves and of the mechanics and businessmen who served them. Few, if any, inventions or adaptations were the work of isolated geniuses who sensed an important need and met it by the application of principles hitherto unapplied to the problem. The early files of the *Prairie Farmer* confirm Jonathan B. Turner's role as the most articulate of the promoters of Osage orange hedge, but he was certainly not the first midwesterner to suggest the possibilities of Bois d'Arc in print.[53] John Deere received no mention in an article on the development of

[52] For a discussion of these matters and a case study see Allan G. Bogue, "Pioneer Farmers and Innovation," *Iowa Journal of History*, LVI (January, 1958), 1–36.

[53] *Prairie Farmer*, September, 1841, p. 65; March, 1842, p. 26; September, 1844, p. 217.

the steel plow in northern Illinois which appeared during the mid-1840's.[54]

"The power of capital in this newly settled or *settling* region," wrote Morris Birkbeck in 1818, "is not thoroughly understood. . . ."[55] A shortage of capital and credit retarded economic change in the prairie triangle through much of the period of our interest. Historians generally agree that farm-making on the prairies called for more capital than had been the case in older timbered regions. Scarcity of capital, of course, was a relative matter and generally typical of new settlements. The rate of return on loans backed by farm property in Illinois and Iowa rode above 10 per cent for the most part during the 1850's, 1860's, and early 1870's, a more handsome yield than that from funds invested in a variety of enterprises elsewhere. During the 1840's the rate may have been still higher, and certainly was in areas where Federal land sales were scheduled to take place shortly.

Easier access to credit would no doubt have speeded changes in farm practices and affected the combination of enterprises on many prairie farms. Complaints of plows that would not scour long after the development of the steel plow reflected the reluctance of western farmers to pay the added cost of the steel implement—almost double that of iron plows. Horses no doubt would have replaced oxen much more rapidly than they did if credit had been easier. Although

[54] *Ibid.*, February, 1846, p. 42.

[55] Morris Birkbeck, *Notes on a Journey in America, from the Coast of Virginia to the Territory of Illinois* (London, 1818), p. 144. We need more studies of farm credit in the nineteenth-century Midwest, particularly of lending at the local level. At this point the major dependence must be on William G. Murray, *An Economic Analysis of Farm Mortgages in Story County, Iowa, 1854–1931* (Iowa State College of Agriculture and Mechanic Arts, Agricultural Experiment Station, *Research Bulletin* No. 146 [Ames, 1933]); David Rozman, "Land Credit in Walnut Grove Township, Knox County, Illinois," *Journal of Land and Public Utility Economics,* IV (August, 1928), 305–312; Margaret Beattie Bogue, *Patterns from the Sod,* 156–175; Allan G. Bogue, *Money at Interest: The Farm Mortgage on the Middle Border* (Ithaca, 1955), pp. 1–43. For interest rates in other lines of enterprise in the same period, see Frederick R. Macaulay, *Some Theoretical Problems Suggested by the Movements of Interest Rates, Bond Yields, and Stock Prices in the United States Since 1856* (New York: National Bureau of Economic Research, 1938), A3–A176; and Lance E. Davis, "The New England Textile Mills and the Capital Markets: A Study of Industrial Borrowing, 1840–1860," *The Journal of Economic History,* XX (March, 1960), 1–30.

available markets and transportation facilities modified the pattern, the pioneer farmer was under economic pressure to find the farming system which required the smallest capital outlay. This in many cases was cash grain farming. No doubt easier credit would have allowed some farmers to introduce livestock into their production programs to a greater extent at an earlier period than they were able to do. It would doubtless also have more rapidly eliminated from the prairie scene the Sucker and Iowa barns, those hay-topped draughty stables which sheltered many of the prairie farm animals in the early years of farm-making.

Western interest rates were related to the age of the community as well as to broader factors in the American economy as a whole. But, if rates tended to fall during the settling-in process, the farmer of our period discovered that he must increase his investment in farm machinery and add to the size of his farm if he were to use his labor most effectively in the new era of horsepower technology. And from the time that the first settler ran his claim lines in most prairie settlements, the direction of land values was steadily upward, except in years of acute depression. Although there are other ways of viewing them both, land speculation and tenancy are properly considered in the perspective of capital deficiency.[56]

The land speculator was prepared to sell land on credit, a service which the Federal Government refused to offer after 1820. Speculation was a mechanism, in other words, which allowed the impecunious settler to capitalize his sweat and muscle. The taxes which speculators paid on their lands prior to sale to resident farmers assisted pioneer communities, hard up for public revenues, in providing community services for the early settlers.[57] Perhaps the fees which they exacted for their service were greater than need be. But given the institutional framework and the capital resources of the settler class in general, the speculators may actually have speeded the development of some areas, instead of retarding it as is often suggested.

[56] Of American agricultural historians, Paul W. Gates has devoted the most attention to land speculation and tenancy in the Midwest. Typical of his work is "The Role of the Land Speculator in Western Development," *The Pennsylvania Magazine of History and Biography*, LXVI (July, 1942), 314–333; and *Frontier Landlords and Pioneer Tenants* (Ithaca, N.Y., 1945).

[57] Margaret B. Bogue and Allan G. Bogue, "Profits and the Frontier Land Speculator," *The Journal of Economic History*, XVII (March, 1957), 2–3 fn. 7.

The Federal census takers did not collect data on tenancy prior to the enumeration of 1880, and part of the literature on prairie tenancy is devoted simply to proving that it existed at an early date. The manuscript censuses of 1850, 1860, and 1870 do provide information from which we can calculate fairly precise maximum and minimum estimates of tenancy. Thus between 7 and 11 per cent of the farm operators in Clarion township, Bureau County, Illinois were tenants in 1850, as were between 10 and 22 per cent in Union township, Davis County, Iowa.[58] In those sections of Illinois and Iowa which settlers occupied between 1830 and 1890, probably between 5 and 15 per cent of the farm operators were tenants at a very early stage of settlement. They became so because they did not have the funds with which to purchase a farm for themselves, or in some cases the means to develop their own small holdings rapidly enough to insure an income in their first years' residence in a new community.

We can never know the exact composition of the landlord class. Some lessors were land speculators or large holders who rented land in order to improve it or to defray the cost of taxes and supervision prior to sale. Some few planned long-term tenant operations. Others were moneylenders who met the costs of upkeep on foreclosed land by renting. The greatest number of prairie landlords, however, was probably made up of the owners of only one farm or at the most several—farm widows, local businessmen, county officers and especially farmers, both active and retired.[59] These latter types of landlords became more common as communities aged, but they were present in numbers soon after the first settlers had arrived.

[58] The procedure here is to extract from the manuscript population census the names of all those heads of households listing themselves as farmers, but owning no real estate. This group comprises the maximum number of possible tenants. By checking these names against the agricultural census rolls, one can find those who reported a farm business. This group represents the minimum number of possible tenants, and probably all of those who were farming on any considerable scale. Since, however, the agricultural census in part involved reports on the crops harvested in the previous year, some new tenants may not have given a farm return. This method of course disregards bachelor tenants who did not maintain their own households, but the number of these was probably quite small. The Federal census of 1880 did, of course, show tenancy present in the frontier region of northwestern Iowa.

[59] I hazard this suggestion on the basis of much reading in the biographical sketches in the county histories. Such information defies quantification for various reasons, but certainly does show a wide distribution of the ownership of tenant farms.

By 1900, just under 50 per cent of the farmers in one Iowa county were tenants; the maximum in Illinois was over 60 per cent. The rates of tenancy were much higher in some districts of the two states than in others. Why so? The areas of highest tenancy lay mainly on highly productive soils. The wet prairies of east central Illinois and central and northwestern Iowa supported a high percentage of tenant operators.[60] Drainage was necessary to make the wet prairies fully tillable, in effect raising the price of the land for the farmer. On the other hand, the high productivity of these soils, once brought to tilth, encouraged businessmen to buy farms as investments. Prosperous farmers invested their savings in tenant farms as well. Some owner-operators of these areas amassed competences rapidly and retired to live on their savings and rents. Instead of liquidating estates by cash sale, nonresident heirs preferred to retain or divide the family holdings in the belief that they could find no safer investment. In limited districts long-term tenant estates which dated from the settlement period may have increased the rate of tenancy. Finally, topography and marketing facilities encouraged cash grain farming in the wet prairie region, a type of farming operation which was somewhat more adapted to tenancy than those in which greater emphasis is placed on livestock. But, in 1900, there was a high rate of tenancy in eight of the nine westernmost counties of Iowa, which lie on the well-drained Missouri loess of the western slope. Here drainage was no great problem, but most of the other factors inducing high tenancy rates were apparently present.

It is clear that the farmers of the prairie triangle in Illinois and Iowa experienced their greatest difficulties during the mid- and late 1870's. Depressed prices, bad seasons, and, in Iowa, even grasshoppers bedeviled them. We need to know much more about the behavior of taxes at the community level in the nineteenth century, but local commitments for railraod building especially may have made tax rates relatively high and sticky in many counties during the 1870's.[61] In many cases, too, farm units were too small to allow

[60] For a discussion of the northern wet prairie with maps see, Leslie Hewes, "The Northern Wet Prairie of the United States: Nature, Sources of Information, and Extent," *Annals of the Association of American Geographers*, XLI (December, 1951), 307–323.

[61] The works bearing most particularly on this subject are Kathleen Bessie Jacklin, "Local Aid to Railroads in Illinois, 1848–1870" (Unpublished Master's

the operator and his family to utilize the enhanced labor productivity which machinery had given them—they were underemployed. In three widely scattered Iowa townships the percentage of real estate mortgages which went to foreclosure proceedings between 1852 and 1896 was 3.2.[62] But of the mortgages filed between 1870 and 1874, inclusive, and between 1875 and 1879, inclusive, the average number going to court was 5.2 per cent in both cases. By contrast the failure rate in the years 1885–1889 and 1890–1896 was 1.7 and 1.8 per cent. Somewhat less precise evidence reveals a similar picture in Illinois. Contrast these percentages with the failure rates of 40 and 50 per cent which occurred in parts of Kansas during the late 1880's and early 1890's. Here, no doubt, is one reason why the farmers of Illinois and Iowa had little interest in Populism. Perhaps, too, the time-hallowed notion of a thirty-year agricultural depression following the Civil War does not fit the facts for all parts of the Middle West.

The more progressive farmers of the prairie triangle evidently entered the 1880's aware that their best future lay in increasing the size of their farm units to take advantage of the new technology. They had learned, too, that profit lay in judicious combinations of corn, hogs, and cattle while not discarding the small grains, particularly oats, nor ignoring tame grasses and clovers—a necessity as the prairie-grass commons disappeared. Corn-root worms and smut convinced farmers who cast their lot unreservedly with the corn crop that some rotation paid. The need to utilize labor supplies effectively worked to the same end. Prairie farmers now found that tiling rewarded the investment. The farmers of the black-earth countries

---

thesis, Cornell University, 1958); Earl S. Beard, "Railroads in Iowa, 1865–1875: a Study of Attitudes" (Unpublished Master's thesis, State University of Iowa, 1950); Robert M. Haig, *A History of the General Property Tax in Illinois* (University of Illinois *Studies in the Social Sciences*, III [Urbana, 1914]), 1; John E. Brindley, *History of Taxation in Iowa* (Iowa City, 1911). My own research on the taxation of agricultural land in Muscatine County, Iowa, showed that taxes there were probably higher relative to the value of agricultural land during the 1870's than in the later years of the century.

[62] These were Warren township, Bremer County, Union township, Davis County, and Hamilton township, Hamilton County, data taken from the Mortgage Indexes and Registers and analyzed by me. The findings are in accord with the works cited in note 55.

in Illinois took up this task seriously in the 1880's, although there had of course been much ditch drainage earlier. The farmers of the wet prairies in Iowa followed suit in a few years. Cheap labor and falling interest rates helped speed the tasks of adjustment. Ten per cent was the usual rate on farm mortgages in 1878 in central Illinois and much of Iowa; it had fallen to 6 per cent by 1896.

If owner-operators were apparently solving their problems with considerable success during the 1880's and 1890's, the same was hardly true of the tenants or farm laborers who aspired to ownership. During the last half of the nineteenth century, the increased productivity of agricultural labor benefited the farm operator considerably more than it did the laborer. At the same time, the land equivalent of the monthly agricultural wage fell drastically. Land obtained for $1.25 per acre in central Illinois or eastern Iowa in the 1830's or 1840's now commanded prices of $40 to $60 and, in many cases, even more. The cost of drainage alone could add from $5 to $20 to the farmer's investment in his acres. The cost of necessary machinery had also increased during the same period, but in the face of rising land values it had become proportionately less important in the total investment of the owner-operator. According to the Federal censuses, land and buildings accounted for 76 per cent ($1,261) of total investment in land, machinery, and livestock on the "average farm" of 1850 in Illinois and 77 per cent ($1,125) in Iowa; the corresponding 1900 figures were 89 per cent ($7,586) and 84 per cent ($8,023) in these two states. Tenancy rates, therefore, edged upward in Illinois and Iowa during the last years of the nineteenth century. We should remember, however, that no agricultural area in the national history of this country has been able to absorb all of its would-be farmers.

So the virgin land of central Illinois and Iowa gave way to farms, to feed lots and above all, to corn fields. A recent writer has maintained: "By 1879 there existed a well defined, although unnamed corn belt. . . ."[63] At his date the northwestern and western boundaries of the corn belt as we know it were, of course, still quite fluid. But in Illinois and the older areas of Iowa, regional allegiance to the corn plant had been pledged somewhat earlier. In 1870 the

[63] William Warntz, "An Historical Consideration of the Terms 'Corn' and 'Corn Belt' in the United States," *Agricultural History*, XXXI (January, 1957), 40.

National Live Stock Journal used the phrase "corn belt" in its columns.[64] It would be years yet before it became a part of national or official parlance. But out in Illinois and Iowa the farmers already knew that productive soils and the recurring miracle of broad-leafed fields of green, growing in rain and summer heat, had set their land apart.

Reprinted from *The Journal of Economic History*, XXIII, 1 (March, 1963), 3–29.

[64] *National Live Stock Journal*, November, 1870, p. 78.

ROBERT LESLIE JONES

7. The Dairy Industry in Ohio Prior to the Civil War

THE beginnings of the dairy industry in what is now Ohio date from the third quarter of the eighteenth century. By the period of the French and Indian War, Indians like the Shawnee, the Wyandots, and the Mingoes had cattle, which they came into possession of in some cases perhaps by purchase or gift in the Detroit settlement, but which they ordinarily obtained through raiding the frontier clearances of Pennsylvania and Virginia.[1] Certainly by the early 1770's most of the Indians of Ohio had cattle. At that time the Reverend David Jones noticed that the Shawnee near Paint Creek were well supplied with them, as were the Shawnee and Delaware of the upper Muskingum Valley.[2] In 1772 there was an important addition, for in that year the Moravian missionaries brought into the Christian Delaware settlement at Schoenbrunn 71 cattle. These were of the distinctive breed introduced into New Amsterdam by the Dutch more than a century earlier, and were to transmit to their descendants in Tuscarawas County their proclivity to be spotted brown and black.[3] By 1781, when they were forced to move to Upper Sandusky, the Moravian Delawares had more than 100 cattle, chiefly milch cows.[4] They and the other Indians kept milch cows because they were very fond of milk and butter. However, they did not provide any store of winter fodder for their cattle, but

[1] Beverley W. Bond, Jr. (ed.), "The Captivity of Charles Stuart, 1755–57," *MVHR*, XIII (1926–27), 59 ff., 81; Franklin B. Hough (ed.), *The Journals of Major Robert Rogers* (Albany, 1883), p. 200; Robert Rogers, *A Concise Account of North America; Containing a Description of the Several British Colonies on That Continent* (London, 1765), p. 169.

[2] David Jones, *A Journal of Two Visits Made to Some Nations of Indians on the West Side of the River Ohio, in the Years 1772 and 1773* (New York, 1865), pp. 57, 87.

[3] J. B. Mansfield, *History of Tuscarawas County, Ohio* (Chicago, 1884), p. 400.

[4] John Heckewelder, *A Narrative of the Missions of the United Brethren Among the Delaware and Mohegan Indians* (Philadelphia, 1820), p. 281.

left them to range through the woods, where, fortunately, there was usually enough grass to enable the animals, or at least the hardier ones among them, to maintain a starving existence till spring.[5]

For a while dairying among the first white settlers of the future Ohio was not much more significant than it had been among the Indians. The pioneers at Marietta began with a very limited supply of cattle. In June 1788 there were only three yoke of oxen in the settlement,[6] but that there was even this many was really a considerable achievement for the days when cattle had to be brought down the Ohio in flatboats. It was difficult to get cattle into the boats, and, when they were let ashore, as was necessary sometimes, they often became ungovernable, and led their owners a wild chase before they could be rounded up and once again put on board.[7] When they arrived, and were turned out to pasture, they were liable to be killed or stolen by the Indians. The scarcity which resulted from these factors meant that for many years there was a fairly continuous demand for cattle, especially milch cows. This demand, like that of the garrisons for fresh beef, was satisfied, beginning in 1790, by importations of droves from the vicinity of Clarksburg, Virginia, 80 miles away.[8] In the Miami Valley cattle were obtained mostly from Kentucky.[9] At a later date many of the cattle of the pioneer Western Reserve were purchased in the Finger Lake country of New York and driven along the shores of Lake Ontario and Lake Erie to their destination, each animal carrying pork, flour, blankets, or

---

[5] A. B. Hulbert and W. N. Schwarze (eds.), "David Zeisberger's History of the Northern American Indians," *OAHQ*, XIX (1910), 14, 45.

[6] R. S. Edes and W. M. Darlington (eds.), *Journal and Letters of Col. John May, of Boston, Relative to Two Journeys to the Ohio Country in 1788 and '89* (Cincinnati, 1873), p. 69.

[7] See the experiences described in "Journal of General Butler," in Neville B. Craig (ed.), *The Olden Time*, II (1847), 438, 454, 458, 460.

[8] Samuel P. Hildreth, *Contributions to the Early History of the North-West, Including the Moravian Missions in Ohio*, (Cincinnati, 1864), pp. 199–200; Samuel P. Hildreth, *Pioneer History; Being an Account of the First Examinations of the Ohio Valley, and the Early Settlement of the Northwest Territory* (Cincinnati, 1848), p. 300.

[9] Beverley W. Bond, Jr. (ed.), "Memoirs of Benjamin Van Cleve," in *HPSO, Quarterly Publications*, XVII (1922), 52–53; Randolph C. Downes, "Trade in Frontier Ohio," in *MVHR*, XVI (1929–30), 474–475.

implements on its back.[10] Subsequent settlers coming in from the east or the south continually reinforced the existing stock in the west with the cattle they drove with them to their new homes.[11] However, even when the number of cattle became adequate, dairying in most of the new settlements languished. The frontiersmen found it burdensome to hunt their cows in order to milk them, and accordingly did so only once a day or even only four or five times a week.[12] Moreover, especially in the autumn, it was dangerous to use the milk of cows pastured in wood lots or uncultivated pastures, because the cows might acquire the "trembles" from eating a poisonous plant since identified as the white snakeroot, and transmit the poison in their milk to humans, who thereupon suffered from "milk sickness." This ailment in cows was particularly characteristic of the Virginia Military District and the region watered by the tributaries of the Miami and the Little Miami.[13]

Despite the tendency throughout the new west to neglect dairying and emphasize other branches of farming, cheese making early developed as a specialized industry in parts of the Ohio country. This was to be attributed to the influence of New England immigrants. Shortly after 1796 A. W. Putnam, one of the pioneers of Belpre, had "a thriving dairy . . . composed of the cows raised from his father's famous Harlem breed, and celebrated for their rich milk."[14] This was but the first of many in that section of Washington County. At the beginning of the new century, Hildreth stated, "Belpre furnished more cheese for the down river trade than any

[10] Henry Howe, *Historical Collections of Ohio* (2 vols.; Norwalk, O., 1896), II, 627; Charles Whittlesey, *Early History of Cleveland, Ohio, Including Original Papers and Other Matter Relating to the Adjacent Country* (Cleveland, 1867), 227–229, 270, 296–297.

[11] Cf. Fortesque Cuming, *Sketches of a Tour to the Western Country, Through the States of Ohio and Kentucky* (Pittsburgh, 1810), reprinted in R. G. Thwaites (ed.), *Early Western Travels* (Cleveland, 1904–07), IV, 62.

[12] Henry B. Fearon, *Sketches of America: A Narrative of a Journey of Five Thousand Miles Through the Eastern and Western States of America* (2d ed.; London, 1818), p. 223.

[13] *Mad River Courant*, quoted in *Farmer's Reporter and United States Agriculturist* (Cincinnati), I (1830–31), 55; *Western Farmer and Gardener* (Cincinnati), II (1840–41), 167; "Diary of Aaron Miller," in *OAHQ*, XXXIII (1924), 72.

[14] Samuel P. Hildreth, *Biographical and Historical Memoirs of the Early Pioneer Settlers of Ohio, with Narratives of Incidents and Occurrences in 1775* (Cincinnati, 1852), p. 378.

other district west of the mountains," the trading boats picking up the cheese at the doors of the dairies, and paying over a period of years sixteen cents a pound.[15] The size of the dairies in this region may be taken as typified in an advertisement offering for rent "a good dairy farm" near Marietta, with a stock of from sixteen to twenty cows.[16] The cheesemaking industry of the Western Reserve soon attained much greater importance and reputation than that of Washington County. Apparently the first Western Reserve cheese exported was a lot of 800 pounds sold by George Stillson of Boardman, a community south of Youngstown, at Pittsburgh in 1803. His product was evidently so much superior to that previously offered there that buyers bid up to $37\frac{1}{2}$ cents a pound for the last of it, whereas he had commenced selling for less than seventeen cents.[17] Other "Connecticut" farmers of the Western Reserve followed Stillson to the new market, and soon (1807) established a reputation at Pittsburgh for supplying "cheese not inferior to English."[18] On the eve of the War of 1812 Hudson, Summit County, had dairymen whose cheese was specially quoted in the Cleveland market and who were exporting small quantities down the Ohio and Mississippi to New Orleans.[19]

After 1815 the Western Reserve became more and more the distinctive "cheesedom" of Ohio and, for that matter, of the entire western country. Though the cheese of Washington County remained in demand for the down river trade till the 1830's, its manufacture gradually became a sideline rather than a main industry for most of the farmers, who found fruit growing, tobacco growing, or wool growing more profitable. By 1849 much more cheese was being imported into the county than was being exported therefrom.[20] In

[15] Hildreth, *Pioneer History*, p. 418.

[16] *American Friend* (Marietta), June 30, 1815.

[17] Ohio State Board of Agriculture, *Annual Report for the Year 1860* (Columbus, 1861), Part II, p. 446. Hereafter this authority is cited as *Ohio Agricultural Report*.

[18] Cuming, *Sketches of a Tour*, p. 91.

[19] John Melish, *Travels through the United States of America in the Years 1806 & 1807, and 1809, 1810 & 1811* (Philadelphia, 1818), pp. 449, 455.

[20] John Delafield, *A Brief Topographical Description of the County of Washington, in the State of Ohio* (New York, 1834), p. 34; Frederick Hall, *Letters from the East and from the West* (Washington and Baltimore, c. 1840), p. 101; *Marietta Gazette*, November 8, 1834; *Ohio Agricultural Report for 1849*, p. 216.

other parts of Ohio a great deal of cheese was produced in the aggregate, but usually only because the farmers had a surplus of milk after the calves were weaned. Wheat-growing farmers, such as those in Richland County and Stark County, imported most of what they consumed from the Western Reserve.[21] One merchant in the village of Shelby, Richland County, sold forty tons of Western Reserve cheese at retail in a single year.[22] The only competition which at any time threatened the predominance of the Western Reserve dairymen came, beginning about 1834, from some "Yankees" on the Darby Plains west of Columbus. Though the cheese made in this small section of Franklin, Madison, and Pickaway counties had the advantage of propinquity to market at Cincinnati and was admitted by Western Reserve dairymen to be the equal of their own in quality, it never became a real menace to the Western Reserve. The farmers of the upper Scioto Valley made such large profits from cattle grazing and cattle fattening that few among them paid much attention to dairying, and so only a relatively small amount of cheese was manufactured.[23]

The progress of the cheese industry in the Western Reserve after 1815 was steady rather than spectacular. Though by 1816 the farmers of the Western Reserve had practically a monopoly of the cheese market at Pittsburgh,[24] they were forced by their own increased production to look farther afield. In 1820 Harvey Baldwin took a wagon load—less than a ton—of cheese from Aurora, Portage County, to Beaver Point, Pennsylvania, transferred it to a small boat, peddled it at the towns along the Ohio as far down as Louisville, and made a satisfactory profit. His imitators found that the river market was somewhat disappointing, presumably on account of the depression then prevailing throughout the West. Two of them in consequence started overland from Louisville in 1826 with about

[21] *Ohio Agricultural Report for 1850* (Scott ed.), p. 362; Patent Office Report for 1851, *Senate Executive Document*, 32nd Cong., 1st Sess., No. 118, p. 381.

[22] *Ohio Agricultural Report for 1853*, p. 652.

[23] *Cincinnati Chronicle*, quoted in *Ohio Cultivator* (Columbus), IV (1848), 77; *Ohio Agricultural Report for 1847*, p. 75; *Ohio Agricultural Report for 1859*, p. 194; *Pioneer and General History of Geauga County, with Sketches of Some of the Pioneers and Prominent Men* (n.p., 1880), p. 30.

[24] David Thomas, *Travels Through the Western Country in the Summer of 1816* (Auburn, N.Y., 1819), p. 63.

thirty tons of Geauga County cheese. One of the pair ultimately disposed of his share in Alabama, and the other of his in Tennessee and North Carolina. By 1830 the Ohio Valley had sufficiently recovered from the depression so that one of these men had no difficulty in selling thirty tons of cheese in Cincinnati, Louisville, and Nashville. The result of the activities of these and other dealers was that, even before the Ohio Canal was completed in 1832, Cincinnati became the chief outlet for Western Reserve cheese.[25] With an assured ultimate market at every river town along the Ohio, the Mississippi, and their tributaries, and with nothing to fear from the cheese makers of New England and New York, the dairymen of the Western Reserve felt justified in expanding their production. In 1836 a single township in Trumbull County manufactured 150 tons of cheese, and in 1837 a single township in Portage County, 500 tons. About this time, too, a single farm in Cuyahoga County had the reputation of curing approximately five tons annually.[26]

The period beginning in the early 1840's and continuing to the outbreak of the Civil War was afterwards looked back upon as a golden age for the Western Reserve dairymen.[27] The most important factor contributing to the expansion which then took place was the development of new markets and the continued growth of old ones. One new market, which for a time promised greater success than it finally achieved, was in the British Isles. According to returns made to the House of Commons, there were 15,154 hundredweight of American cheese imported into the United Kingdom in 1841, 14,098 hundredweight in 1842, 42,312 hundredweight in 1843, and 53,115 hundredweight in 1844.[28] The amount of this cheese which

---

[25] *Pioneer and General History of Geauga County*, p. 29.

[26] *The Hesperian: Or Western Monthly Magazine* (Columbus), I (1838), 189.

[27] "Between 1840 and 1863 thousands of farms on the Western Reserve were purchased by young men on credit, and were paid for, in many instances, by purchasers who were not remarkable either for energy or economy. During those years families engaged in dairy husbandry could, without practicing painful economy, and with only ordinary industry, pursue the even tenor of their ways, content with old methods, with a practical certainty that each year would show at least a moderate balance of income over expenditure." *Ohio Agricultural Report for 1890*, p. 115.

[28] Patent Office Report for 1845, *Senate Executive Document*, 29th Cong., 1st Sess., No. 307, p. 325.

was the product of Ohio is not known. However, for reasons which will be pointed out hereinafter, Ohio cheese met British standards in neither style nor quality.[29] During the 1840's and 1850's Ohio cheese had an important share of the market in Upper Canada on account of the emphasis most of the farmers there put on wheat growing.[30] For a few years, beginning in 1849, large shipments of Western Reserve cheese were made to California and even to China.[31] On the whole, however, most Western Reserve cheese sought outlets in either the west or the east throughout the period. In Boston, New York, and other eastern centers it had to be sold in competition with the cheese of Connecticut and upstate New York. Even when Western Reserve cheese was being sold in New York City, superior ("Hamburgh") New York cheese was being imported into Ohio to satisfy consumers who did not favor the local variety.[32]

The steady expansion of cheese dairying in the Western Reserve, especially the northeastern part of it, was the subject of frequent comment in the 1840's and 1850's. According to the records of the cheese dealers, in 1846 the dairymen of Portage County brought to market 800 tons, worth about $76,000, and in 1847, over 1,000 tons, worth about $100,000, a 25 per cent increase in production. In 1848, 1,450 tons of cheese were exported from this county, an increase of about 45 per cent over 1847. In 1850 the county exported 2,000 tons.[33] Other counties reported similar increases, and attributed them to better prices for cheese. "Cheese the great staple of the county," wrote a Trumbull County correspondent in 1848, "has been made in greater quantities than in any former year."[34] "The amount of cheese produced in Ashtabula County the present season,"

[29] *Ohio Cultivator*, VII (1851), 201.

[30] *Journal and Transactions of the Board of Agriculture of Upper Canada for 1855-6* (Toronto, 1856), pp. 56, 263. Cf. also: "The demand for American cheese in Canada causes its production in such large amounts in Ohio." *Census of Canada 1851-2* (Toronto, 1852), I, xxxvii.

[31] *Conneaut Reporter*, quoted in *Ohio Cultivator*, V (1849), 198; *Ashtabula Telegraph*, quoted in *Ohio Cultivator*, VI (1850), 297; *Cultivator* (Albany, N.Y.), n.s., VII (1850), 315; *Western Reserve Chronicle*, quoted in *Ohio Cultivator*, VII (1851), 291.

[32] *Cleveland Herald*, quoted in *Ohio Cultivator*, III (1847), 126.

[33] *Ohio Agricultural Report for 1846*, p. 59; *Ohio Agricultural Report for 1847*, p. 81; *Ohio Agricultural Report for 1848*, p. 96; *Ohio Agricultural Report for 1850* (Scott ed.), p. 340.

[34] *Ohio Agricultural Report for 1848*, p. 107.

according to a correspondent in an adjacent county at the same time, "will greatly exceed the amount of any former year. Many of our farmers, who have heretofore been engaged in other modes of Agriculture, have turned their attention wholly to the dairy business."[35] The next year witnessed an expansion of cheese dairying in Ashtabula County estimated at fifty per cent over the level attained in 1848, and brought forth the comment that in Geauga County mixed farming was giving way entirely to dairying.[36] It was stated in 1856 that the number of dairymen had doubled in eastern Cuyahoga County within the space of two years on account of the great profits to be made in dairying.[37] The only interruption came with the Panic of 1857. It was then reported from Ashtabula County that "the production of cheese has been equal to the average of good seasons, but the 'times are out of joint' so as to derange the market for this staple, and seriously lessen its value."[38] According to the federal census, the Western Reserve counties of Ashtabula, Cuyahoga, Geauga, Lorain, Portage, and Trumbull produced respectively 2,375,705, 1,433,727, 4,519,998, 1,177,293, 4,064,351, and 5,201,951 pounds of cheese in 1860, while Ohio as a whole produced 21,618,893 pounds. It might be pointed out that no other western state had anything near the amount of cheese reported produced in the Western Reserve. Illinois, with 1,848,557 pounds, was the second largest producer.[39]

Several aspects of the cheese-making industry, especially during its years of rapid expansion on the Western Reserve, are worthy of particular consideration. There was no uniformity in the size of dairy farms, though there was a tendency for them to be larger in the 1840's and 1850's than they had been earlier. However, even at an early date, some were quite large. Thus, in Trumbull County in 1835, most of the dairy farms had from forty to 100 cows.[40] At the

[35] *Ibid.*, p. 32.

[36] *Conneaut Reporter*, quoted in *Ohio Cultivator*, V (1849), 198; *Ohio Agricultural Report for 1849*, p. 102.

[37] *Ohio Farmer* (Cleveland), December 20, 1856, p. 201.

[38] *Ohio Agricultural Report for 1857*, p. 237.

[39] *The Agriculture of the United States in 1860; Compiled from the Original Returns of the Eighth Census* (Washington, 1864), pp. lxxxiii, 114, 118.

[40] Samuel P. Hildreth, "Miscellaneous Observations Made during a Tour in May, 1835, to the Falls of the Cuyahoga, near Lake Erie," in *American Journal of Science and Arts* (New Haven, Conn.), XXXI (1837), 24.

end of the 1840's the increased demand for Western Reserve cheese brought about an increase in the size of the dairies. In Ashtabula County, for instance, it was stated in 1849 that "where a few years ago two or three cows only were kept, the same occupants now number their 40, 50 and 60 cows." [41] Though dairies of from forty to sixty cows seem to have been quite common in Ashtabula and Geauga counties, and parts of Portage County, there were few that were much larger. However, in parts of Trumbull County there were at this time "dairies of more than 200 to 300 cows, and embracing every convenience and improvement that modern ingenuity has devised." [42]

Western Reserve dairymen (like most others at the time) were of the opinion that it was cheaper to buy their cows than to raise them. Accordingly every spring many of them would travel into such near-by counties as Stark and Richland to buy cows. The "Yankees" considered themselves sharp bargainers, but apparently they were often taken in by the Pennsylvania farmers of the Backbone Counties. [43] Sometimes the dairymen of the Western Reserve even visited the Scioto Valley and the Miami Valley, purchasing "much on the plan which has been pursued in hiring the schoolmaster, that is, in regard to cheapness." [44] If the Western Reserve farmers were too busy to go on a cattle-buying expedition, they were ordinarily able to purchase cows out of droves brought into their communities by cattlemen from the more southerly and westerly parts of the State. [45] The practice of buying dairy cows from outside the Western Reserve continued beyond the period of the Civil War. [46]

As the dairymen typically considered that calves would not be worth the expense of raising to maturity, they "deaconed" them when they were a few days old, saving the skins and rennet, [47] and

[41] *Conneaut Reporter*, quoted in *Ohio Cultivator*, V (1849), 198.

[42] *Ohio Cultivator*, IV (1848), 109.

[43] *Ibid.*, VII (1851), 163; *Ohio Agricultural Report for 1870*, p. 490; *Ohio Agricultural Report for 1893*, p. 311.

[44] *Ohio Cultivator*, VIII (1852), 170.

[45] *Ohio Farmer*, February 6, 1858, p. 44.

[46] *Ohio Agricultural Report for 1866*, Part II, p. 174; *Ohio Agricultural Report for 1870*, p. 490; *Ohio Agricultural Report for 1874*, p. 467.

[47] For a method of preparing rennet, as used in Ashtabula County, see *Ohio Agricultural Report for 1857*, p. 157.

either feeding the carcasses to the hogs or throwing them behind the fence for the crows. This slaughtering of calves was regarded as the most unpleasant part of the labor of the dairymen.[48] Tender-hearted individuals therefore no doubt felt themselves fortunate when they were able to sell some of the young calves for vealing.[49] As dairying operations in the Western Reserve were extended in the 1840's and 1850's, many of the calves of the dairymen were, however, kept till autumn, when they were bought up by dealers, who ultimately transferred them to the beef-cattle raisers or fatteners of the Scioto Valley.[50] Some of the calves, too, were raised to maturity on the farms where they were born, or on others in the vicinity, and, with the discarded dairy cows, therefore contributed to the maintenance of a sizable beef-cattle industry in the Western Reserve itself.[51]

In the dairies of the Western Reserve the "native" cattle were long given preference over improved breeds, because it was felt that they were better milkers, as well as being cheaper. A herd of native cows, bought at from $12 to $30 a head in the spring, would, it was believed, furnish several animals of superior milking qualities. These could be retained, while the inferior ones could be sold to drovers. Yet, in the absence of modern recording and testing, few farmers were really able to tell which of their cows were most profitable, and still less were they able to show any justification for their belief that improved cattle might prove second-rate milkers. It was therefore

---

[48] *Ohio Cultivator*, VI (1850), 116.

[49] A letter written from Twinsburg, Summit County, in 1858, says: "Most of the calves are disposed of as soon as possible after they are three days old, (the cow's milk then being good,) and fortunately for dairy-men, but unfortunately (I would think) for those who eat them, there is a ready market. Men, who are called Jews, go from house to house with horse and wagon every week, during the calf season, and buy all they can find, paying from one to three dollars a piece, according to size and the number of hours they are old. These wagons, when loaded, leave town on the road that leads to Cleveland. Who eats the tender meat, or whether it has anything to do with city sausages, [I] can't say." *Ohio Farmer*, February 6, 1858, p. 44.

[50] *Agriculture of the United States in 1860*, pp. cxxxiii-cxxxiv; *Ohio Agricultural Report for 1866*, Part II, p. 152.

[51] [James H. Perkins], "Fifty Years of Ohio," in *North American Review*, XLVII (1838), 40; *Ohio Agricultural Report for 1847*, p. 23; *Ohio Agricultural Report for 1848*, p. 96; *Ohio Agricultural Report for 1849*, pp. 52, 204; *Ohio Agricultural Report for 1850* (Scott ed.), p. 165; *Ohio Agricultural Report for 1853*, pp. 559, 598.

not till mid-century that Devon and Shorthorn grades began to be used to any extent in the dairies.[52] In any case the production of milk per cow was excessively small by modern standards. Typical estimates as to the amount of cheese made per cow in the late 1840's and early 1850's ranged from 350 to 500 pounds, with 400 pounds being regarded as more or less average, and being stated moreover as the minimum amount necessary to assure profitable operation of a dairy.[53]

Cheese dairying has been notoriously a branch of agriculture which involves long hours of labor through the season. Unfortunately, even in the Western Reserve, the various operations were frequently performed by those least fitted for their drudgery. In the large dairies men usually did the cheese making, but in the smaller ones, it was stated, "as a general rule cheese making and severe female labor are combined. Indeed the condition of women in dairies is frequently little better than servitude; and in too many instances this is the lot of the mistress of the family." [54] "When we take a look at the daily life of a dairy farm," Anson Bartlett wrote at the end of the Civil War, "all wonder that the dairy farmer's wife should become prematurely wrinkled, decrepit and old, ceases; and the wonder arises that any woman could be found who can endure so much as she actually does, even for a single season, to say nothing of a term of years, and retain even the semblance of health and strength." [55] The only alleviation seems to have been that in the Western Reserve, as in other parts of Ohio where the family was of New England extraction, the milking was done by the men and

[52] *Ohio Agricultural Report for 1848*, p. 32; *Ohio Agricultural Report for 1849*, pp. 79–80; *Ohio Agricultural Report for 1851*, p. 223; *Western Reserve Farmer and Dairyman* (Jefferson), I (1852), 65.

[53] *Ohio Agricultural Report for 1847*, p. 89; *Ohio Agricultural Report for 1850* (Scott ed.), p. 267; *Documents, Including Messages and Other Communications Made to the General Assembly of the State of Ohio*, XVII, Part II (Columbus, 1853), No. 5, 255–256. Hereafter this authority is cited as *Ohio Legislative Documents*.

[54] *Ohio Cultivator*, IV (1848), 111. This condition was largely owing to the great difficulty which western farmers had in hiring girls to work in the dairy in what was regarded as a menial employment. Cf. James Flint, *Letters from America, Containing Observations on the Climate and Agriculture of the Western States, the Manners of the People, the Prospects of Emigrants, &c.* (Edinburgh, 1822), in Thwaites, *Early Western Travels*, IX, 122.

[55] *Ohio Agricultural Report for 1865*, Part II, p. 173.

boys. However, even on the Western Reserve there were households in which young women milked eight or ten cows morning and night.[56]

The cheese-making technique of the pioneers was an inheritance of literally centuries. Most cheese makers, male or female, were content to follow traditional procedure without attempting to improve on it. Yet there were a few dairymen who found it profitable to manufacture something better than "white-oak" cheese. Such a one was Elias Follett of Granville, who, while he obtained from eight to twelve cents for his ordinary cheese, was able to sell his "Pineapple" and his "Brandied" cheese for over eighteen cents.[57] Pineapple cheese was a variety, it might be noted, which was first manufactured in the United States at Goshen, Connecticut, in 1808.[58] Evidently most Ohio cheese makers who attempted to manufacture it were less successful than Follett, for the Pineapple cheese of the State enjoyed none too good a reputation. "Heretofore," according to one authority, "they have been made more to grace the table than to please the palate."[59] The "Brandied" cheese of the average dairymen appears to have been often enough simply spoiled cheese liberally saturated with brandy.[60] Some Swiss cheese was being made in Ohio prior to the Civil War, but its manufacture was confined to "German" settlers in Monroe and Tuscarawas counties and so was quantitatively insignificant till the 1880's.[61]

The method of manufacturing ordinary cheese in the Western Reserve varied slightly with every dairy, but the common or "Yankee" method was more or less as follows: In the evening the milk was strained and "set" in clean tin pans over night. In the

---

[56] *Ohio Cultivator*, IV (1848), 111; *Ohio Agricultural Report for 1858*, p. 304; Martin Welker, *Farm Life in Central Ohio Sixty Years Ago* (Cleveland, 1895), p. 51.

[57] *Western Farmer and Gardener*, III (1841–42), 116.

[58] *Cultivator*, quoted in Patent Office Report for 1845, *Senate Executive Document*, 29th Cong., 1st Sess., No. 307, p. 989.

[59] *Western Reserve Chronicle*, quoted in *Ohio Cultivator*, VII (1851), 291. Occasionally, however, it met every expectation. For example three hundred boxes sold at Boston in 1849 were highly approved. *New England Farmer*, quoted in *Ohio Cultivator*, V (18–49), 55.

[60] Ihna T. Frary, *Ohio in Homespun and Calico* (Richmond, Va., 1942), p. 129.

[61] *Ohio Agricultural Report for 1881*, p. 256; *Ohio Agricultural Report for 1886*, p. 356.

morning the cream was removed for use in butter making or cooking. The morning milk was then mixed with the skim milk, which had already been heated to about the same temperature as the fresh. Then rennet was added, with the result that in twenty or thirty minutes the milk was curdled. After the curd had stood a few minutes, it was cut, or rather broken, into cubes with a long wooden knife, and the whey allowed to separate. The next steps were cutting the curd again, dipping off a considerable part of the whey, ladling the curd into a cheese-basket with a strainer in it, and permitting or forcing the curd to drain. The next day the curd was chopped fine, permitted to harden somewhat, and scalded with hot whey. It was now ready for its final draining, its salting, and its pressing. The cheese was pressed for an hour, then turned over and pressed again, this time overnight. Now a fine cheesecloth band was wrapped around it, and it might be pressed for another day or even longer. Then it was placed on a shelf, where it was turned every day and rubbed all over with melted butter, till such time as it was considered sufficiently cured for market.[62]

In the late 1840's there was a craze for making large cheeses, that is, in excess of sixty pounds. The largest then produced in the State was manufactured by Elias Follett in 1847. It weighed 1,000 pounds, and sold at Cincinnati for $250.[63] Most of these large cheeses were only partially cured at the time they left the dairies, so that many of them decomposed even before they reached New York, and all but a few of the rest in the warehouses of either New York or Liverpool.[64] During 1849 and 1850 the big cheeses were difficult to dispose of at five and a half cents a pound, whereas the small ones, of from ten to twenty pounds, were readily salable at nine cents and nine and a half cents.[65] In the 1850's the largest cheeses manufactured appear to have weighed about 30 to 35 pounds. These went to the "cut trade," that is, the eastern and

---

[62] This was a method used in Summit County. *Ohio Cultivator*, II (1846), 29. It is practically the same as the prevailing method in Connecticut about 1800. Cf. Charles S. Phelps, *Rural Life in Litchfield County* (Norfolk, Conn., 1917), pp. 76–77.

[63] *Cincinnati Chronicle*, quoted in *Ohio Cultivator*, III (1847), 181.

[64] *Ashtabula Telegraph*, quoted in *Ohio Cultivator*, VIII (1852), 193.

[65] *Ashtabula Telegraph*, quoted in *Cultivator*, n.s., VII (1850), 105; *Ashtabula Telegraph*, quoted in *Ohio Cultivator*, VI (1850), 297.

southern groceries. The smaller cheeses were shipped either abroad or to the remoter parts of the United States.[66]

Pioneer cheese making in the Western Reserve was carried on with makeshift accommodations for the cattle and a minimum of equipment. "As soon as a log-cabin was up," writes the historian of Geauga County, "might often be seen a rail or pole, with one end under the lower log of the cabin, and lying across a rudely constructed cheese-hoop, with a weight attached to the outer end, sufficient to press the cheese."[67] In the early days cheese was made in such small quantities that a tub sufficed for a vat and a woodshed or loft was considered an adequate—if invariably foul smelling— place for curing.[68] During the late 1840's the dairymen of the eastern Western Reserve began to make important improvements in their working facilities. They began to build "milking barns," which were long, narrow structures with a feeding aisle down the center. The cattle were fastened in stanchions, and faced one another across the aisle. Overhead there was a small loft. Though these buildings were cold and drafty, they were an advance on the sheds which had preceded them.[69] Beginning about the same time, the cows were better fed, for in addition to the grass of the pasture, they were now given whey and meal or shorts.[70] Notable among the new contrivances which came into use in the dairies during this period was the thermometer.[71] About a decade earlier, that is, even before 1840, patented cheese presses were fairly common in the Western Reserve. A popular kind, "Whipple's Press," was the same as that ordinarily sold in New England. Though it was priced at only seven dollars, it

[66] *Ohio Agricultural Report for 1850* (Scott ed.), p. 62; *Western Reserve Chronicle*, quoted in *Ohio Cultivator*, VII (1851), 291; *Ohio Cultivator*, XIII (1857), 233; *Cleveland Herald*, cited in *Country Gentleman* (Albany, N.Y.), XIV (1859), 255.

[67] *Pioneer and General History of Geauga County*, p. 29.

[68] *Ohio Agricultural Report for 1866*, Part II, p. 171.

[69] *Ohio Agricultural Report for 1849*, p. 51; *Ohio Agricultural Report for 1893*, p. 312.

[70] *Ohio Agricultural Report for 1847*, p. 25. However, at their best the dairymen of the Western Reserve were years behind the Germans in the community at Zoar in the manner of caring for dairy cattle. For dairying among the Zoarites, see James S. Buckingham, *The Eastern and Western States of America* (3 vols.; London, ca. 1841), II, 293, and *The Silk Culturist*, quoted in *Maine Farmer and Journal of the Useful Arts* (Hallowell, Me.), V (1837–38), 187.

[71] *Ohio Agricultural Report for 1849*, p. 51.

was infrequently encountered in other parts of Ohio.[72] Another improvement was introduced into Geauga County in 1849, and into other parts of the Western Reserve then or shortly thereafter. This was a cheese vat or steamer, the essential principle of which was that the milk in the container was heated by a steam-pipe which could be moved back and forth through it.[73] In spite of the introduction of all these improvements, the dairy cheese of the Western Reserve never quite kept pace in quality with the best New York cheese.[74]

There was another innovation, however, which seemed for a time to be the most important change of all. This was the coming into operation, beginning in 1847, of cheese factories, or rather, of curd factories.[75] The first of these, an establishment at Hartford, Trumbull County, may possibly have been modeled on a curd factory which was mentioned in 1845 as being in operation at Goshen, Connecticut.[76] By purchasing curds from the neighboring farmers, the Hartford factory was able in 1847 to produce an average of 1,000 pounds of cheese a day. In 1849 other factories were opened at Richmond Center and Wayne, both in Ashtabula County. During 1850 and 1851 several others appeared in these two counties, as well as a few in Geauga and Portage counties. All of them made what was called "English Dairy" cheese, which for a time was more popular than the ordinary dairy cheese, as is attested by the fact that in 1850 the cheese manufactured in the factories of Geauga County sold at seven cents a pound, while dairy cheese from the near-by farms brought only four and a half cents.[77]

The system operated in this fashion: Some individual or firm

[72] *Western Farmer and Gardener*, II (1840–41), 91.

[73] *Ohio Agricultural Report for 1850* (Scott ed.), p. 62; *Ohio Agricultural Report for 1865*, Part II, p. 171.

[74] *Ibid.*, p. 171.

[75] The Census of 1820 lists among the manufacturing establishments of Champaign County a "factory" producing cheese. It employed six persons, used 12,500 gallons of milk, and had an output estimated as worth $1,190. *Digest of Accounts of Manufacturing Establishments in the United States, and of Their Manufactures* (Washington, 1823), n.p. This was in all probability an ordinary dairy.

[76] For the Goshen factory, see *Cultivator*, quoted in Patent Office Report for 1845, *Senate Executive Document*, 29th Cong., 1st Sess., No. 307, p. 989.

[77] *Ohio Agricultural Report for 1847*, p. 92; *Ohio Agricultural Report for 1850* (Scott ed.), p. 165; *Ohio Agricultural Report for 1865*, Part II, p. 171; *Conneaut Reporter*, quoted in *Ohio Cultivator*, V (1849), 198.

erected a building and equipped it with the necessary machinery. Then, in the spring, the owner contracted with the farmers within a radius of six or seven miles to furnish curd, which was to be prepared in accordance with specific instructions. Every weekday morning the farmers placed their unsalted curd in sacks, which were gathered by covered wagons, each of which had a route of from five to ten miles. One factory, that at Gustavus, Trumbull County, employed eight teams in thus collecting curd.[78] As soon as the curd reached the factory, the workmen commenced the manufacturing process. A visitor to the factory at Gustavus in 1850 thus described the procedure:

> The building in which the business is carried on is frame, and contains some two or three large rooms. The first one you enter contains the machines for cutting curd, presses and other utensils, (the common screw press is the one used here,) and in one end of this room is a furnace, over which is a large tank of water for various purposes, and a kettle, in which is fixed a large pan, which is kept hot by the steam in the kettle. In this pan or vessel the grease is placed, from which the cheese, when taken from the press, are rubbed before being placed upon the shelves. Two men were engaged in this operation, while another marked them before undergoing the process. Several girls I was informed, were engaged in making sacks, in which all the cheese are encased. There were two large rooms where the cheese are placed upon shelves reaching from the bottom to the top of the building or room, and a richer sight I have seldom seen than was here presented. One of them contains as my informant told me, 6,000 cheese, while in the other there were between three and four thousand. In these rooms men are employed who turn the cheese every other day, to keep off mould, etc. until they are ready to be shipped. . . . One hundred per day is the average manufacture of this mammoth cheesery, being the product from the milk of 500 cows.[79]

It was stated in 1851 that the same factory made a daily average of 300 small cheeses, weighing in all 5,000 pounds, and depended on the milk of 2,500 cows.[80]

[78] *Conneaut Reporter*, quoted in *Ohio Cultivator*, V (1849), 198; *Western Reserve Chronicle*, quoted in *Ohio Cultivator*, VII (1851), 291; *Ohio Farmer*, December 5, 1856, p. 193.

[79] *Ohio Cultivator*, VI (1850), 243–244. Another account of the same time states that this factory was then making from 100 to 120 cheeses a day, from the milk of 1,000 cows. *Cultivator*, n.s., VII (1850), 315.

[80] *Western Reserve Chronicle*, quoted in *Ohio Cultivator*, VII (1851), 291.

The system had obvious advantages. Though the farmers received only between three and four and a half or five cents a pound for the curd,[81] they had none of the labor and responsibility of curing it or of marketing the final product. Theoretically, too, the large manufacturer should have been able to introduce economies into the process of curing, and to have a more uniform quality of cheese than could be expected in the individual dairies. Unfortunately there was one defect which he could not overcome. There were almost as many different grades of curd as there were farmers contracting to furnish it, and mismanagement in the early stages rendered impossible the making of good cheese later. Added to this defect was the fact that the demand for "English Dairy" cheese shortly fell off. By the end of 1851 the factories found that the market for it was glutted and that they could not get as much for it as ordinary dairy cheese was bringing.[82] In the spring of 1852 most of the factories either closed or were about to close, and the sellers of curd were being forced to go back to the making of dairy cheese. In 1857 there was left apparently only a chain of four factories in the north-eastern corner of Trumbull County which made in all about 250 tons of cheese.[83] In the autumn of 1859 it was reported that the curd factories "have all gone down, most of them ruining their owners."[84] The consequence was that when the modern cheese-factory system was introduced into Ohio from New York in 1862, it was handicapped less by its novelty than by the remembrance on the part of many dairymen of the failure of a few years before.

As was the case with other staple products of Ohio, there developed from an early date a somewhat specialized marketing organization for cheese, though for many years after Ohio had a respectable output, it was not unusual for cheese to be transported to a consuming center by its maker and there sold by him. As late as 1842 Elias Follett of Granville took a boat load of his own cheese and

[81] *Conneaut Reporter*, quoted in *Ohio Cultivator*, V (1849), 198; *Ohio Farmer*, December 5, 1856, p. 193; *Ohio Cultivator*, XIII (1857), 233.

[82] *Cultivator*, n.s., VIII (1851), 325–326; *Ohio Agricultural Report for 1850* (Scott ed.), p. 62; *Ohio Agricultural Report for 1851*, p. 222; *Ohio Agricultural Report for 1865*, Part II, p. 171.

[83] *Ashtabula Telegraph*, quoted in *Ohio Cultivator*, VIII (1852), 164; *Ohio Cultivator*, XIII (1857), 233.

[84] *Cleveland Herald*, cited in *Country Gentleman*, XIV (1859), 255.

pork down the Ohio and the Mississippi.[85] Sometimes, as was true of most other commodities, the country storekeeper accepted small lots in trade. Between 1827 and 1842 much Western Reserve cheese was taken in by country merchants in satisfaction of their store bills and shipped to New York. As late as 1850 the storekeepers were still commonly buying Western Reserve cheese for export, though probably in smaller quantities than earlier.[86] However, even during the 1820's, there appeared in the Western Reserve specialized dealers in cheese. These men, as has already been noticed, gathered cheese from the storekeepers and dairymen, and took it to the southern and eastern markets. Around Youngstown in 1835 such traders were said to "contract with the farmers for their cheese before it is made, stipulating a certain price to be paid on delivery, generally from six to seven cents per pound, at the door of the dairy, or at some adjacent store."[87] Till about 1843 cheese sent to the eastern states, especially that forwarded by the country storekeepers, was often handled by ordinary commission agents as part of their general trade. After this date new commission houses came into existence to deal exclusively in cheese or in cheese and other dairy products. By 1848 there were several of these in both Boston and New York. A single Boston commission firm sold 1,000 ordinary cheeses from Ohio in 1849, as well as 300 boxes of Pineapple cheese.[88]

The local dealers did not introduce as much system into the trade as might have been expected. The practice, almost universal among them, of paying a uniform price for cheese regardless of quality made it difficult for careful dairymen to profit from their extra pains, and tended to bring the cheese, even of the Western Reserve, into disrepute in the east. It was not till about 1850 that the dealers began to discriminate in their offers, and then they did so only because they found that they were losing money on the poorer grades of cheese they obtained and that the better farmers were marketing directly through commission men.[89] Another difficulty

---

[85] *Western Farmer and Gardener*, III (1841–42), 116.

[86] *Pioneer and General History of Geauga County*, p. 29; *Ashtabula Telegraph*, quoted in *Cultivator*, n.s., VII (1850), 105.

[87] Hildreth, "Miscellaneous Observations Made During a Tour," p. 24.

[88] *Detroit Free Pass*, quoted in *Ohio Cultivator*, IV (1848), 78; *New England Farmer*, quoted in *Ohio Cultivator*, V (1849), 55.

[89] *Ohio Agricultural Report for 1851*, p. 221.

arose in connection with a practice which became fairly widespread about 1850—that of making contracts whereby the dealer agreed to take from the farmer, at specified times throughout the season, all the cheese he had on his shelves which had been curing two weeks or more. If the dealer took the cheeses and continued the curing process, there were advantages in this plan, for he got a more uniform product, and the workers in the dairy were relieved of much heavy labor. Often, however, the dealer shipped the partially cured cheese to market immediately. Much of it spoiled in transit, with the result that the commission houses of Cincinnati sometimes refused to trade in cheese during the hot months.[90]

The second great branch of the dairy industry, butter making, though found on every farm from the days of earliest settlement, and being in the aggregate of more value than the cheese industry,[91] attracted much less attention than the latter. This was doubtless partly because there was little about butter making in Ohio to distinguish it from butter making in any of the adjacent states and partly because there was not much concentration of production in special areas. While it is true that the leading butter counties were in the Western Reserve, owing to the fact that butter was made in the dairies there as a by-product of cheese making throughout the summer as well as after the cheese season ended in the autumn, their predominance over other counties was not marked. Thus, in 1860, of the five counties in Ohio which had a production exceeding 1,000,000 pounds of butter—Cuyahoga with 1,162,665, Lorain with 1,243,992, Portage with 1,437,556, Stark with 1,091,923, and Wayne

[90] *Ashtabula Sentinel*, quoted in *Western Agriculturist* (Columbus), I (1851), 156; *Western Reserve Chronicle*, quoted in *Ohio Cultivator*, VII (1851), 291; *Ohio Cultivator*, XI (1855), 217.

[91] In 1850 Ohio was credited with producing 34,449,379 pounds of butter and 20,819,542 pounds of cheese, and in 1860 with 48,543,162 pounds of butter and 21,618,893 pounds of cheese. Cf. *Agriculture of the United States in 1860*, p. lxxxiii. In the early 1850's butter ordinarily sold by the pound for about twice the price of cheese. Butter marketed in Mahoning County in 1850 brought from ten cents to twelve cents a pound as compared with five cents for cheese, and in Ashtabula County in 1852 and 1853 from twelve and a half cents to twenty cents as compared with from five cents to nine cents. Cf. *Ohio Agricultural Report for 1850* (Scott ed.), 267: *Ohio Legislative Documents*, XVII, Part II (1853), No. 5, 255; *ibid.*, XVIII, Part II (1854), No. 21, 517.

with 1,169,581 [92]—only the first three were in the Western Reserve. It is worth pointing out, however, that Ohio made more butter in 1860 than any other state west of New York and Pennsylvania. Illinois, its nearest rival, produced 28,052,551 pounds. Only two western counties outside Ohio at that time produced as much as 1,000,000 pounds; they were Cook County, Illinois, and Oakland County, Michigan.[93]

As butter was an article of small bulk and weight in proportion to its value, it formed part of the cargo ordinarily carried down river on the flatboats to New Orleans at the beginning of the nineteenth century.[94] The same quality made it one of the few products of the farm which would bring cash in out-of-the-way communities during the 1820's and 1830's.[95] By the 1840's butter became the chief medium of barter between the farmers' wives and the traveling hucksters. Such men went through the country with a load of groceries, dry goods, and odds and ends, and took butter in exchange, usually allowing a cent or so more per pound than the storekeepers. They then sold it to the steamboats on the Ohio, or at river towns such as Portsmouth or Cincinnati.[96]

Some of the butter made in Ohio was first class. This was true especially of that brought to market by the Amish people in Tuscarawas[97] and other counties. However, the farmers of Pennsylvania origin had in general a good reputation as butter makers. Those in Stark County, and doubtless most of the others, proceeded in this manner:

> Our best butter-makers have what we call a "spring-house"—a small building of stone or brick, with large shallow troughs, through which run streams of spring-water. After milking and straining, the pans or crocks of new milk are placed in these water-troughs, and the cream

[92] *Agriculture of the United States in 1860*, pp. 114, 118.

[93] *Ibid.*, pp. 32, 78, 186.

[94] F. A. Michaux, *Travels to the West of the Alleghany Mountains, in the States of Ohio, Kentucky, and Tennesea, and Back to Charleston by the Upper Carolines* (London, 1805), in Thwaites, *Early Western Travels*, III, 191.

[95] D. Griffiths, *Two Years' Residence in the New Settlements of Ohio, North America: With Directions to Emigrants* (London, 1835), p. 74.

[96] *Ohio Agricultural Report for 1850* (Scott ed.), pp. 109, 234, 397; *Ohio Agricultural Report for 1853*, p. 554.

[97] *Ohio Agricultural Report for 1855*, p. 213.

soon rises to the top. The barrel churn is the kind in general use here. To preserve butter in warm weather for a week, it must be worked over until the milk is all expelled; to preserve it for winter use, it may be packed in stone jars, containing about 20 pounds each, with 1 pound pulverized rock salt, ½ pound loaf sugar, and ½ ounce saltpetre. The crock or jar should then be covered, first, with a clean white cloth, and then with drilling or heavy muslin, dipped into a preparation of melted tallow and beeswax, and bound round tight with wire, to exclude the air, and then deposited in the spring-house for winter use.[98]

Butter manufactured in this careful fashion never lacked a market. Thus there were farmers in Muskingum County about 1850 who had come originally from Bucks County, Pennsylvania, whose butter went to supply a private clientele in Philadelphia.[99]

Ohio butter in general was, however, very poor. One dealer wrote in 1845: "I have had occasion to examine a good deal of Ohio butter, in that State, and at various points out of it. I am sorry to say that I have found it uniform in only one particular, and that was bad."[100] Again, of something over 6,000,000 pounds of butter from Ohio received at Buffalo during 1849, it was stated that "a very small proportion . . . ranked as prime; far the greater proportion only as *grease butter*."[101] One reason for the inferiority was the small-scale and slovenly method of manufacture. On the typical wheat, wool, livestock, or general farm, butter was commonly made from the milk of a few cows, partly to satisfy the needs of the family and partly to provide pin money. The farm wives knew nothing of the chemical and mechanical principles involved in butter making, and if they had, would have been indifferent to applying them, for the peddlers and storekeepers seldom discriminated in price between good and poor samples. Ohio farmers were, of course, reluctant to admit that the prevailing methods of working butter were defective, so they claimed that the reason their butter was inferior to that of Orange County, New York, was that the grass of Ohio was different

[98] Patent Office Report for 1852, *Senate Executive Document*, 32nd Cong., 2d Sess., No. 55, Part II, p. 257. In the late 1840's there was a great rage for patent churns, most of which were inferior even to the old dash variety. Cf. *Ohio Cultivator*, V (1849), 17.

[99] Patent Office Report for 1851, *Senate Executive Document*, 32nd Cong., 1st Sess., No. 118, p. 400.

[100] *Ohio Cultivator*, I (1845), 22.

[101] *Ibid.*, VI (1850), 180.

from that of New York, or else that the common Syracuse or Onondaga salt sold in the west was not so well suited for butter making as West India salt.[102] A second and no less important reason for the inferiority of Ohio butter lay in careless handling by the store-keepers and the peddlers. The butter made by the farm wives, it was afterwards stated only too truthfully, "was taken in by storekeepers for merchandise, thrown in an old box or barrel, the best assorted over and sold at cost to the few who were compelled to buy, and the balance, after being tossed around for perhaps months, during which all the noxious gasses of the cellar penetrated it through and through, was packed up and sent to market, and then perhaps tossed about one or two months longer, and at last sold only to those who could only buy cheap butter, or else it was traded to the lard and tallow chandlers."[103] It is no wonder then, that as late as 1858, the best butter of Ohio to find its way into ordinary trade channels ranked "about with the second and third grades" of the butter of New York.[104]

Bad as Ohio butter was, it was no worse than that of other parts of the western country nor than that of most of the east, and therefore it could always be sold somewhere. Till the end of the 1840's the chief outlets were in the east and the south. It was stated in 1851, for example, that for several years past, a large proportion of the butter of Portage County had been bought up by one New Orleans dealer.[105] The gold rush resulted in the opening for a time of an important market in California. This was partly because little butter had ever been made by the Mexican inhabitants, and that little was dirty grey in color and disagreeable in flavor,[106] but mostly because the demands of the forty-niners and their successors vastly exceeded any theretofore known. Large amounts of butter were being exported from Ohio by 1852, to sell in some cases for as much as $1.50 a

[102] *Ibid.*, IV (1848), 93; *Western Agriculturist*, I (1851), 339; *Ohio Agricultural Report for 1855*, p. 256.

[103] *Ohio Agricultural Report for 1873*, p. 270.

[104] *Ohio Agricultural Report for 1858*, p. 299.

[105] *Ohio Legislative Documents*, Vol. XVI, Part II (1852), No. 2, p. 552.

[106] Alexander Forbes, *California: A History of Upper and Lower California from Their First Discovery to the Present Time, Comprising an Account of the Climate, Soil, Natural Productions, Agriculture, Commerce, &c.* (London, 1839), pp. 266–267.

pound.[107] One New York dealer announced in 1852 that he intended to buy butter to the amount of 405,000 pounds at his three agencies in Ohio, 230,000 pounds at Salem, 125,000 pounds at Wooster, and 50,000 pounds at Circleville, to repack it, and to ship it to San Francisco.[108] It was stated in 1858 that butter from the Western Reserve "has been largely shipped to California."[109] By this date, however, California was becoming increasingly independent of outside dairy supplies, so that Ohio butter was again being marketed mostly through its old eastern and southern channels.

Owing to the general increase in the consumption of butter which occurred throughout the nation in the late 1840's and the 1850's, butter was in greater demand in Ohio than it had been earlier. The coming of the railroads fostered this demand in regions which formerly had been isolated too much to engage in the industry to any extent, as, for example, Preble County.[110] It was reported from Portage County at the end of 1852 that "butter buyers have been so numerous the past season, that we find it impossible to ascertain the amount of butter exported."[111] The expansion in the production of butter which in consequence took place between the census of 1850 and that of 1860[112] was not, however, a phenomenon peculiar to Ohio, but was characteristic of most of the other states. The tendency to shift from cheese making to butter making, noticed in Mahoning County as early as 1850,[113] was likewise universal.[114]

The third branch of the dairy industry—that of furnishing fluid milk to urban consumers—was insignificant in comparison with cheese making and butter making prior to the Civil War. However, in the late 1840's raw-milk dairying was taking on local importance

[107] Patent Office Report for 1852, *Senate Executive Document*, 32nd Cong., 2d Sess., No. 55, Part II, p. 257; *Ohio Legislative Documents*, XVII, Part II (1853), No. 5, 284, 489.

[108] *Ohio Cultivator*, VIII (1852), 329.

[109] *Ohio Agricultural Report for 1858*, 299.

[110] *Ohio Legislative Documents*, XVIII, Part II (1854), No. 21, 649.

[111] *Ibid.*, XVII, Part II (1853), No. 5, 437.

[112] See above, note 91.

[113] *Ohio Agricultural Report for 1850* (Scott ed.), p. 267.

[114] For these general developments in the dairy industry, see Percy W. Bidwell and John I. Falconer, *History of Agriculture in the Northern United States, 1620–1860* (Washington, 1925), p. 429.

in the vicinity of Cincinnati and Cleveland. When the Little Miami Railroad came into operation, milk was shipped to the Cincinnati market from Warren County and even from Clark County; but until long after the Civil War at least ninety per cent of the dairies supplying Cincinnati were located in Hamilton County, just as those supplying Cleveland were almost entirely in Cuyahoga County.[115] It is scarcely necessary to mention that the need for sanitary handling of the milk was seldom recognized and that the day of regulation and inspection was still in the future.

The dairy industry in its several branches was so firmly established in Ohio by the outbreak of the Civil War that the introduction of the "Herkimer County factory system" of cheese making developed in upstate New York into Geauga County in the spring of 1862 and into other parts of the Western Reserve shortly thereafter involved no radical alteration in the farm economy of the State.[116] Subsequent innovations, such as the creamery method of butter making, similarly caused no furor in Ohio. Technological improvements were welcomed and adopted, it is true, but in an old dairying region they lacked the revolutionary implications they possessed in wheat-sick Iowa or Wisconsin or Upper Canada. By merely keeping abreast of changes in the industry, the sons and successors of the pioneer dairymen maintained the position of Ohio as one of the leading dairy states till the end of the century.[117]

[115] *Ohio Agricultural Report for 1849*, pp. 65, 79, 213; *Ohio Agricultural Report for 1851*, p. 271; *Ohio Agricultural Report for 1879*, p. 268; *Ohio Agricultural Report for 1883*, p. 306.

[116] For the introduction of the New York factory system into the Western Reserve, see *Ohio Agricultural Report for 1865*, Part II, pp. 171–174.

[117] In 1900 Ohio ranked sixth among the states in the farm value of its dairy produce. It was credited with $25,383,627, New York with $55,474,155, Pennsylvania with $35,860,110, Illinois with $29,638,619, Iowa with $27,516,870, and Wisconsin with $26,779,721. Cf. *Twelfth Census of the United States, Taken in the Year 1900* (Washington, 1902), V, *Agriculture*, Part I, clxviii.

IV

THE URBAN DIMENSION

Part IV
The Urban Dimension

"In the neighborhood of Cincinnati, the price of a well improved farm is sixty dollars per acre. Cincinnati is a noble looking town—I think the site is the finest I have ever seen, and the town is well laid out. It contains ten thousand inhabitants, and two thousand houses, with seven Churches and meeting houses, (one for Friends)—I think I never saw in Baltimore or in Philadelphia a market better supplied in quantity or quality of produce, than I saw at Cincinnati. . . . Building Lots and rents are however high—a lot for a Store was pointed out to me which sold for twenty-five thousand dollars."[1] This description of Cincinnati, penned by a traveler, is not striking in itself, except when one considers that it was written in 1819—only a few years after the period of "agrarian discontent" that Professor Taylor discussed in the essay reprinted earlier in this volume. That one of the western towns should have developed to this degree only two decades after the beginning of the nineteenth century alerts us to the fact that the "urban dimension" of the Old Northwest's growth cannot be neglected, even for the earliest period of settlement and development.

Richard C. Wade, professor of history at the University of Chicago, argues that the western towns were not merely a passive element in early development—rather they were "the spearheads of the American frontier."[2] Thus he assigns to early urban growth a key role in the process of community development in the Old Northwest, calling our attention to both the internal history of towns, and the relationships between towns and their hinterland. Louis Wirth,

[1] "From Pittsburgh to Shawnee Town, 1819: A Document," ed. William D. Hoyt, *OAHQ*, LVI (January, 1947), 94–97.

[2] The article reprinted here summarizes some of the leading themes in Professor Wade's full-scale study, *The Urban Frontier: The Rise of Western Cities* (Cambridge, Mass., 1959).

whose contributions to the sociology of regionalism have illuminated historians' understanding of regional phenomena, argued that urbanism (like regionalism) can be defined as "a way of life." As urban centers grow, he pointed out, "urbanites meet one another in highly segmental roles . . . . The contacts of the city may indeed be face to face, but they are nevertheless impersonal, superficial, transitory and segmental." For a city to function, it requires "proliferation of special tasks"; and so interpersonal relationships develop in the framework of functional specialization. Moreover, the constraints and opportunities of urban life have a profound impact upon class relationships; upon patterns of mobility, cohesion, and assimilation; and upon the organization of economic activity.[3] Sensitive to these special attributes of urban life, Professor Wade argues that to a large extent the culture and society of the early West—including the entire Ohio-Mississippi Valley and not merely the Old Northwest— were urban; and even country dwellers in the region, from the earliest period of settlement, were affected in nearly every facet of their lives by their relationships with the cities that grew amidst their rural settlements.

The questions left unanswered by Professor Wade's study (only because its terminal date is 1830) are crucial to an understanding of community building and community development in the Old Northwest. Did the patterns of urban development and urban-rural relationships in the Great Lakes country (which underwent its first surge of growth after 1830) follow lines similar to those exhibited by the Ohio-Mississippi Valley cities before 1830? Did these patterns in the Old Northwest diverge significantly from the pattern in other western frontier regions, most notably in the plantation South?[4] Did

[3] Wirth, "Urbanism as a Way of Life," *Louis Wirth on Cities and Social Life: Selected Papers*, ed. A. J. Reiss, Jr. (Chicago, 1964), pp. 68 ff. Eric E. Lampard, "American Historians and the Study of Urbanization," *American Historical Review*, Vol. LXVII (October, 1961); Oscar Handlin and John Burchard (eds.), *The Historian and the City* (Boston, 1963); Charles N. Glaab, "The Historian and the American City: A Bibliographic Survey," in *The Study of Urbanization*, ed. Philip M. Hauser and Leo F. Schnore (New York, 1965); and Roy Lubove, "Urbanization, Technology and the Historian" (pre-publication copy distributed 1966), are all important statements on the urban dimension in historical analysis.

[4] Important analyses of individual cities in the Old Northwest include: Bayrd Still, *Milwaukee* (Madison, 1948); Bessie L. Pierce, *A History of Chicago* (3 vols.; New

the impact of towns upon rural life (and conversely of the agricultural community on the towns) alter significantly as subregions of the Old Northwest underwent initial industrialization in the 1840's and 1850's?[5] Did the urban dimension of early life in the Old Northwest intensify a process whereby the region became more and more like the older-settled Northeast, or did the western urban tradition reinforce distinctive regional characteristics?

One key component of the "urban dimension" in the nineteenth-century Old Northwest was transportation. Probably more than any other single force, transportation conditioned the rate of growth for individual cities in the region, as the rivers and later the roads, canals, and railways devolved crucial trade advantages on some urban centers and deprived others of their market positions. Moreover, the prospect of gaining a place on a road, canal, or railroad galvanized urban forces in politics as perhaps nothing else could. The issues were perceived in terms of the life or death of towns. An Indiana newspaper editor expressed a common sentiment when he wrote of his city's project for a canal line: "With it our course will be upward, and without it our city will become a deserted village. . . . With it our streets will be the avenues of traffic; without, grass will grow upon the sidewalks. With it we will rival and

---

York, 1937–57); Floyd R. Dain, *Every House a Frontier: Detroit's Economic Progress, 1815–1825* (Detroit, 1956); and Edmund H. Chapman, *Cleveland: Village to Metropolis* (Cleveland, 1964). Among important articles, other than those cited in the two essays reprinted in this section, are F. D. Kershner, Jr., "From Country Town to Industrial City: The Urban Pattern in Indianapolis," *Indiana Magazine of History*, Vol. XLI (March, 1945); R. Richard Wohl, "Henry Noble Day," in *Men in Business*, ed. William Miller (Cambridge, Mass., 1952), on Hudson, Ohio, and its promotions; and Bessie L. Pierce, "Changing Urban Patterns in the Mississippi Valley," *JISHS*, Vol. XLIII (Spring, 1950). For comparisons with the city in developing areas of the South during frontier and early post-frontier periods, see the various works of Thomas Perkins Abernethy, especially *The Formative Period in Alabama, 1815–1828* (Southern Historical Publications, No. 8 [University, Ala., 1965]); and Charles Grier Sellers, Jr., "Who Were the Southern Whigs?" *American Historical Review*, Vol. LIX (January, 1954).

[5] See Bayrd Still, "Patterns of Mid-Nineteenth Century Urbanization in the Middle West," *MVHR*, Vol. XXVIII (September, 1941); Blake McKelvey, *The Urbanization of America, 1865–1915* (New Brunswick, N.J., 1963); and H. S. Perloff et al., *Regions, Resources, and Economic Growth* (Baltimore, 1960).

outstrip surrounding towns; without it they will leave us in the background."[6]

The second essay in this section, on "Urban Rivalry and Internal Improvements," discusses the leading role that towns and cities took in the political struggles over state transportation programs. Governor Thomas Ford of Illinois asserted that in his state, the urban centers generated most of the pressure for publicly financed improvements: the promotional meetings "were generally held in the towns, and mostly attended by the town people."[7] And so it was throughout the region. Indeed, so powerful were urban ambitions and urban rivalries that often the promoters of a still-unpopulated townsite speculation could muster more support in the state legislatures than could the settlers of developed rural communities.[8] When private transportation enterprise displaced public enterprise in the late 1840's, the urban focus remained just as strong as before. In an era characterized by rapid change in transport technology, business leaders in the towns and cities sought desperately to retain their established market advantages and to gain new advantages made possible by transport innovations.

[6] Richmond (Ind.) *Palladium*, April 9, 1842, quoted in Luther M. Feeger, *The History of Transportation in Wayne County, Indiana* (reprint from Richmond *Palladium-Item*, September 3, 1953).

[7] Ford, *A History of Illinois, . . . 1818 to 1847* (Chicago, 1854), p. 183.

[8] See, for instance, Paul W. Gates, *The Illinois Central Railroad and Its Colonization Work* (Cambridge, Mass., 1934), pp. 23–24; and John W. Weatherford, "The Short Life of Manhattan, Ohio," *OHQ*, Vol. LXV (October, 1956). The national context in which the urban struggle in the Old Northwest went forward is delineated well in Carter Goodrich, *Government Promotion of American Canals and Railroads, 1800–1890* (New York, 1960). An important study of the region is R. R. Russel, "A Revaluation of the Period before the Civil War: Railroads," *MVHR*, Vol. XV (December, 1928). See also the excellent study by Albert Fishlow, *American Railroads and the Transformation of the Ante-bellum Economy* (Cambridge, Mass., 1965). Victor M. Bogle, "Railroad Building in Indiana, 1850–55," *IMH*, Vol. LVIII (September, 1962) is a full analysis of promotion and construction in one state.

RICHARD C. WADE

8. Urban Life in Western America, 1790–1830

THE towns were the spearheads of the American frontier. Planted as forts or trading posts far in advance of the line of settlement, they held the West for the approaching population. Indeed, in 1763, when the British drew the Proclamation Line across the Appalachians to stop the flow of migrants, a French merchant company prepared to survey the streets of St. Louis, a thousand miles through the wilderness. Whether as part of French and Spanish activity from New Orleans or part of Anglo-American operations from the Atlantic seaboard, the establishment of towns preceded the breaking of soil in the transmontane West.

In 1764, the year of the founding of St. Louis, settlers made the first plat of Pittsburgh. Twelve years later and four hundred miles down the Ohio, Louisville sprang up at the Falls, and the following decade witnessed the beginnings of Cincinnati and Lexington. Before the century closed, Detroit, Buffalo, and Cleveland were laid out on the Great Lakes. In fact, by 1800 the sites of every major metropolis in the old Northwest except Chicago, Milwaukee, and Indianapolis had been cleared and surveyed.

Furthermore, these urban outposts grew rapidly even in their infant decades. By 1815 Pittsburgh, already a thriving industrial center, had 8,000 inhabitants, giving it a slight margin over Lexington. Cincinnati estimated its population at 4,000 at the end of the war with Great Britain, while farther west Louisville and St. Louis neared half that figure.

The speed and extent of this expansion startled contemporaries. Joseph Charless, the editor of the *Missouri Gazette*, who had made a trip through the new country in 1795, remembered the banks of the Ohio as "a dreary wilderness, the haunt of ruthless savages," yet twenty years later he found them "sprinkled with towns" boasting "spinning and weaving establishments, steam mills, manufactures in

229

various metals, leather, wool, cotton and flax," and "seminaries of learning conducted by excellent teachers."[1] The great transformation moved a Cincinnati bard to a somewhat heroic couplet:

> Here where so late the appalling sound
> Of savage yells, the woods resound
> Now smiling Ceres waves her sheaf
> And cities rise in bold relief.[2]

Not all the towns founded in the trans-Allegheny region in this period fared as well, however. Many never developed much beyond a survey and a newspaper advertisement. Others, after promising beginnings, slackened and settled down to slow and unspectacular development. Still others flourished briefly then faded, leaving behind a grim story of deserted mills, broken buildings, and aging people—the West's first harvest of ghost towns. Most of these were mere eddies in the westward flow of urbanism, but at flood tide it was often hard to distinguish the eddies from the main stream. Indeed, at one time Wheeling, Virginia, St. Genevieve, Missouri, New Albany, Indiana, and Zanesville, Ohio, were considered serious challengers to the supremacy of their now more famous neighbors.

Other places, such as Rising Sun, Town of America, or New Athens, were almost wholly speculative ventures. Eastern investors scanned maps looking for likely spots to establish a city, usually at the junction of two rivers, or sometimes at the center of fertile farm districts. They bought up land, laid it out in lots, gave the place a name, and waited for the development of the region to appreciate its value. Looking back over this period one editor called it a "city-making mania," when everyone went about "anticipating flourishing cities in vision, at the mouth of every creek and bayou."[3] This speculation, though extensive, was not always profitable. "Of the vast number of towns which have been founded," James Hall declared, "but a small minority have prospered, nor do we think that, as a general rule, the founders of these have been greatly enriched by their prosperity."[4]

---

[1] *Missouri Gazette* (St. Louis), July 13, 1816.
[2] *Liberty Hall* (Cincinnati), June 11, 1815.
[3] *Missouri Republican* (St. Louis), August 29, 1825.
[4] Hall, *The West: Its Commerce and Navigation* (Cincinnati, 1848), p. 227.

Despite many failures, these abortive attempts to plant towns were significant, for they reveal much about the motives of the people who came West in the early period. Many settlers moved across the mountains in search of promising towns rather than good land, their inducements being urban opportunities rather than fertile soil. Daniel Drake, who was among the earliest urbanites of the frontier, later commented on this process:

> It is worthy of remark, that those who made these beginnings of settlement, projected towns, which they anticipated would grow into cities. . . . And we may see in their origins, one of the elements of the prevalent tendency to rear up towns in advance of the country which has ever since characterized Ohio. The followers of the first pioneers, like themselves had a taste for commerce and the mechanic arts which cannot be gratified without the construction of cities.[5]

Proprietors competed for these urban migrants, most of whom came from "those portions of the Union which cherish and build up cities."[6] In fact, the preference of some settlers for towns was so great that in 1787 Lexington petitioned the Virginia legislature for incorporation to be "an inducement to well disposed persons, artizens [*sic*] and mechanics who from motives and convenience do prefer Town life."[7]

The West's young cities owed their initial success to commerce. All sprang from it, and their growth in the early years of the century stemmed from its expansion. Since the Ohio River was the chief artery of trade and travel, the towns along its banks prospered most. Pittsburgh, where the Allegheny meets the Monongahela, commanded the entire valley; Cincinnati served the rich farm lands of Kentucky and Ohio; Louisville fattened on the transshipment of goods around the Falls; and St. Louis, astride the Mississippi, was the focus of far-flung enterprises, some of which reached to the Pacific Ocean. Even Lexington, landlocked in a country of water highways, grew up as the central mart of Kentucky and Tennessee.

Though these cities were firmly established by the first decade

[5] Drake, "Dr. Drake's Memoir of the Miami County, 1779–1794," Beverley Bond, Jr. (ed.), in HPSO, *Quarterly Publications*, XVIII (1923), 58.

[6] *Ibid.*

[7] James R. Robertson (ed.), *Petitions of the Early Inhabitants of Kentucky to the General Assembly of Virginia, 1769–1792* (Louisville, Ky., 1914), p. 106.

of the century, the coming of the steamboat greatly enhanced their size and influence.[8] By quickening transportation and cutting distances, steam navigation telescoped fifty years' urban development into a single generation. The flow of commerce down river was now supplemented by a northward and eastward movement, giving cities added opportunities for expansion and growth. "The steam engine in five years has enabled us to anticipate a state of things," a Pittsburgher declared enthusiastically, "which in the ordinary course of events, it would have required a century to have produced. The art of printing scarcely surpassed it in beneficial consequences."[9] The "enchanter's wand" not only touched the established towns but created new ones as well. A French observer noted that "in the brief interval of fifteen years, many cities were formed . . . where before there were hardly the dwellings of a small town. . . . A simple mechanical device has made life both possible and comfortable in regions which heretofore have been a wilderness."[10]

As these commercial centers grew, some inhabitants turned to manufacturing. Indeed, this new interest spread so rapidly in Pittsburgh that in 1810 a resident likened the place to "a large workshop," and already travelers complained of the smoke and soot.[11] Between 1803 and 1815 the value of manufactured goods jumped from $350,000 to over $2,600,000, and the city's iron and glass products became known throughout the new country.[12] Watching this remarkable development, the editor of *Niles' Register* exclaimed: "Pittsburgh, sometimes emphatically called the 'Birmingham of America,' will probably become the *greatest manufacturing town in the world.*"[13] Lexington also turned increasingly to industry, her rope-

[8] Louis C. Hunter, *Steamboats on the Western Rivers, An Economic and Technological History* (Cambridge, Mass., 1949), pp. 27–32.

[9] Morgan Neville, "The Last of the Boatmen," *The Western Souvenir for 1829* (Cincinnati, Ohio, n.d.), p. 108.

[10] [Jean Baptiste] Marestier, *Mémoire sur les Bateaux à vapeur des États-Unis d'Amérique* (Paris, 1824), pp. 9–10.

[11] Zadock Cramer, *Pittsburgh Almanack for the Year of Our Lord 1810* (Pittsburgh, Pa., 1810), p. 52.

[12] Pittsburgh's industrial foundations are discussed in Catherine Elizabeth Reiser, *Pittsburgh's Commercial Development, 1800–1850* (Harrisburg, Pa., 1951), pp. 12–21.

[13] *Niles' Register*, May 28, 1814.

walks and textile mills supplying the whole West. Beginnings were more modest in other places, but every city had at least a few ambitious enterprises.

Some of this urban expansion rested on a speculative base, and the depression of 1819 brought a reckoning. Lexington, already suffering from its landlocked position, received fatal wounds, while Pittsburgh, the West's foremost city, was crippled for a decade. Elsewhere, however, the setback proved only momentary and the mid-twenties saw the old pace renewed. Population growth again provides a convenient index of development. Cincinnati quickly overtook its faltering rivals, the number of its residents leaping from 6,000 in 1815 to over 25,000 in 1830. By the latter date the census recorded Pittsburgh's recovery. Though the figure had dropped to 7,000 during the depression, it rose to 13,000 in 1830. Farther west Louisville and St. Louis enjoyed spectacular expansion, the former boasting over 10,000 inhabitants at the end of the period, while the Mississippi entrepôt passed the 6,000 mark. Lexington alone lagged, its population remaining stable for the next two decades.

Even these figures, however, do not convey the real growth. In most places municipal boundaries could no longer contain the new settlers, and many spilled over into the suburbs. For instance, Allegheny, Bayardstown, Birmingham, Lawrenceville, Hayti, and East Liberty added nearly 10,000 to Pittsburgh's population, bringing the total to 22,000.[14] The same was true of Cincinnati where 2,000 people lived in the Eastern and Northern Liberties.[15] In Louisville, Preston's and Campbell's "enlargements" and Shippingport and Portland swelled the city's total to 13,000.[16] Ultimately, the urban centers annexed these surrounding clusters, but in the meantime local authorities grappled with early manifestations of the suburban problem.

As the cities grew they staked out extensive commercial claims over the entire West.[17] Timothy Flint calculated that Cincinnati was

[14] *Pittsburgh Gazette*, November 16, 1830.

[15] *Cincinnati Advertiser*, August 18, 1830.

[16] United States *Census*, 1830, pp. 114–115.

[17] For an appreciation of the economic importance of the cities in the growth of the West, see Frederick Jackson Turner, *Rise of the New West, 1819–1829* ("The American Nation: A History," ed. A. B. Hart, XIV [New York, 1906]), 96–98.

the central market for over a million people, while a resident asserted
that its trade was "co-extensive with steamboat navigation on the
western waters."[18] Louisville's economic penetration was scarcely
less impressive. As early as 1821, a local editor declared that "the
people of the greater part of Indiana, all Kentucky, and portions of
Tennessee, Alabama, Illinois, Missouri, now report to this place for
dry goods, groceries, hardware and queensware."[19] St. Louis'
empire touched Santa Fe on the south, Canada on the north, and
the Pacific on the west. "It is doubtful if history affords the example
of another city," wrote Hiram M. Chittenden, "which has been the
exclusive mart for so vast an area as that which was tributary to St.
Louis."[20]

In carving out these extensive dependencies, the young metro-
polises overwhelmed their smaller neighbors. The rise of St. Louis
destroyed the ambitions of Edwardsville across the Mississippi, which
once harbored modest hopes of importance. Pittsburgh's recovery in
the late twenties condemned Wheeling and Steubenville to minor
roles in the upper Ohio region. And Louisville's development
swallowed two Kentucky neighbors while reducing Jeffersonville
and New Albany on the Indiana side of the river to mere appendages.

Not satisfied with such considerable conquests, the cities reached
out for more. Seeking wider opportunities, they built canals and
turnpikes and, even before 1830, planned railroads to strengthen
their position. Cincinnati, Pittsburgh, and St. Louis tried to tap the
increasing trade on the Great Lakes by water links to the North.
Pennsylvania's Iron City also hoped to become a major station on
the National Road, and for a decade its Washington representatives
lobbied to win that commercial bond with the East. Lexington,
suffocating in its inland position, frantically strove for better connections with the Ohio River. A turnpike to Maysville was dashed
by Jackson's veto, technical difficulties made a canal to the Kentucky
River impractical, but some belated hope rose with the possibility
of a railroad to Louisville or Cincinnati.

[18] Flint, "Thoughts Respecting the Establishment of a Porcelain Manufactory
at Cincinnati," *Western Monthly Review*, III (1830), 512; Benjamin Drake and
Edward W. Mansfield, *Cincinnati in 1826* (Cincinnati, Ohio, 1827), p. 71.

[19] *Louisville Public Advertiser*, October 17, 1829.

[20] Chittenden, *The American Fur Trade of the Far West* (2 vols.; New York, 1902),
I, 99.

The intensive search for new advantages brought rivalry and conflict. Though the commerce of the whole West lay untouched before them, the cities quarreled over its division. Thus Louisville and Cincinnati fought over a canal around the Falls of the Ohio. The Kentucky town, feeling that its strength depended upon maintaining the break in transportation, obstructed every attempt to circumvent the rapids. Only when Ohio interests threatened to dig on the Indiana side did Louisville move ahead with its own project. Likewise, harsh words flew between Wheeling and Pittsburgh as they contended for the Ohio River terminus of the National Road. Smaller towns, too, joined the struggle. Cleveland and Sandusky, for instance, clashed over the location of the Ohio Canal, the stake being nothing less than control of the mounting trade between the Valley and the lakes. And their instinct to fight was sound, for the outcome shaped the future of both places.

Urban rivalries were often bitter, and the contestants showed no quarter. In the late twenties when only the success of Transylvania University kept Lexington's economy from complete collapse, Louisville joined the attack which ultimately destroyed the school. In a similar vein Cincinnatians taunted their upriver competitor as it reeled under the impact of the depression of 1819. "Poor Pittsburgh," they exclaimed, "your day is over, the sceptre of influence and wealth is to travel to us; the Cumberland road has done the business." [21] But even the Queen City found her supremacy insecure. "I discovered two ruling passions in Cincinnati," a traveler remarked, "enmity against Pittsburgh, and jealousy of Louisville." [22] This drive for power and primacy, sustained especially by merchants and articulated by editors, was one of the most consistent and striking characteristics of the early history of Western cities.

As they pursued expansive policies, municipalities also ministered to their own growing pains. From the beginning, urban residents had to contend with the problems of living together, and one of their first acts was to petition the territory or state for governing authority to handle them. The legislatures, representing rural interests and generally suspicious of towns, responded with charters bestowing narrow grants of power which barely met current needs and failed

[21] *Pittsburgh Gazette*, December 18, 1818.
[22] *Pittsburgh Gazette*, February 5, 1819.

to allow for expansion. As localities grew, however, they developed problems which could be met only with wider jurisdiction. Louisville's charter had to be amended twenty-two times before 1815 and Cincinnati's underwent five major changes between 1815 and 1827. Others, though altered less often, were adjusted and remade until finally scrapped for new ones. Reluctantly, and bit by bit, the states turned over to the cities the responsibility of managing their own affairs, though keeping them starved for revenue by strict tax and debt limitations.

Despite inadequate charters and modest incomes, urban governments played a decisive role in the growth of Western cities. Since these were commercial towns, local authorities paid special attention to mercantile requirements. They not only constructed market houses but also extended municipal regulation over a wide variety of trading activity. Ordinances protected the public against adulterated foods, false measurements, and rigged prices. Some municipalities went even farther and assumed responsibility for seeing that "justice is done between buyer and seller."[23] In search of this objective, officials fixed prices on some goods, excluded monopolies from the market, and tried to equalize opportunities for smaller purchasers. To facilitate access to the exchange center, they lavished time and money on the development of wharves and docks and the improvement of streets.

Municipalities also tackled a wide variety of other problems growing out of urban life. Fire protection, at first casually organized, was placed on a more formal basis. Volunteer companies still provided the manpower, but government participation increased markedly. Local councils legislated against many kinds of fire hazards, and public money furnished most of the equipment. Moreover, some places, haunted by the image of Detroit's disaster in 1805, forbade the construction of wooden buildings in the heart of the city, a measure which not only reduced fire risks but also changed the face of downtown areas. The development of adequate police was much slower. By 1830 only Lexington and Louisville had regular patrols, and these were established with the intent more of control of slaves than the general protection of life and property. In other towns law enforcement was lax by day and absent at night, though

[23] *Pittsburgh Gazette*, March 9, 1810.

the introduction of gas lighting in Pittsburgh and Cincinnati in the late twenties made the after-dark hours there less dangerous than before.

Congested living created new health hazards and especially increased the likelihood of epidemics. Every place suffered, but none like Louisville, which earned a grim reputation as the "Graveyard of the West" because of the constant visitations of yellow fever and malaria.[24] Cities took preventive measures, such as draining stagnant ponds and clearing streets and lots, and also appointed boards of health to preside over the problem. Municipal water systems, introduced in Pittsburgh and Cincinnati before 1830, made life healthier and certainly more comfortable, while the discussion of installing underground sewers pointed to still more extensive reform in sanitation.

In meeting urban problems, Western officials drew heavily on Eastern experience. Lacking precedents of their own, and familiar with the techniques of older cities, they frankly patterned their practice on Eastern models. There was little innovation. When confronted by a new question, local authorities responded by adopting tested solutions. This emulation characterized nearly every aspect of development—from the width of streets to housing regulations. No major improvement was launched without a close study of established seaboard practices. St. Louis' council, for example, instructed its water committee to "procure from the cities of Philadelphia and New Orleans such information as can be obtained on the subject of conveying water and the best manner of clearing it."[25] When Cincinnati discussed introducing underground sewers, an official group was designated to "ascertain from the city authorities of New York, Philadelphia, Baltimore and Boston, how far the sinking of common sewers is approved in those cities."[26] Pittsburgh undertook gas lighting only after exhaustive research and "very full enquiries at New York and Baltimore."[27]

[24] Benjamin Casseday, *The History of Louisville from Its Earliest Settlement till the Year 1852* (Louisville, Ky., 1852), p. 49.

[25] St. Louis City Council, Minutes, Court House, St. Louis, June 12, 1829.

[26] Cincinnati City Council, Minutes, City Hall, Cincinnati, October 6, 1827.

[27] Pittsburgh City Council, City Council Papers, City Hall, Pittsburgh, May 10, 1827. The extent of Western urban indebtedness to the East is perhaps best illustrated in the establishment of the high school in Louisville. The building was

Though the young towns drew upon the experience of all the major Atlantic cities, the special source of municipal wisdom was Philadelphia. Many Western urbanites had lived or visited there; it provided the new country with most of its professional and cultural leadership; it was the model metropolis. "She is the great seat of American affluence, of individual riches, and distinguished philanthropy," a Pittsburgh editorial declared in 1818. "From her . . . we have everything to look for."[28] Newspapers often referred to it as "our mother city."[29]

From street plans to cultural activity, from the shape of market houses to the habits of people, the Philadelphia influence prevailed. Robert Peterson and John Filson, who had a hand in the founding of Louisville, Lexington, and Cincinnati, borrowed the basic grid pattern of the original plats from the Pennsylvania metropolis.[30] Market location and design came from the same source, as did techniques for fire fighting and police protection. Western towns also leaned on Philadelphia's leadership in street lighting, waterworks, and wharving. Even the naming of suburbs—Pittsburgh's Kensington and Cincinnati's Liberties—came from the mother city. The result was a physical likeness which struck many travelers and which Philadelphians themselves recognized. Gideon Burton, for instance, remembered his first impression of Cincinnati in the 1820's: "How beautiful this city is," he remarked, "how much like Philadelphia."[31]

"mainly after the plan of the High School of New York, united with the Public School Rooms of Philadelphia." Most of the teachers came from the East, while the curriculum and even reading assignments derived from "the High School of New York and some of the Boston establishments." *An Account of the Louisville City School, Together With the Ordinances of the City Council, and the Regulations of the Board of Trustees for the Government of the Institution* (Louisville, Ky., 1830), pp. 5 ff.

[28] *Pittsburgh Gazette*, October 27, 1818.

[29] For example, see *Pittsburgh Gazette*, June 23, 1818.

[30] For example, see Rufus King, *Ohio, First Fruits of the Ordinance of 1787* (Boston, 1888), p. 209.

[31] Burton, *Reminiscences of Gideon Burton* (Cincinnati, Ohio, 1895). The strategic location of Western cities in the life of the new country reminded some visitors of the regional supremacy of Philadelphia. Lewis Condict, for example, referred to Lexington as "the Philadelphia of Kentucky." "Journal of a Trip to Kentucky in 1795," *Proceedings of the New Jersey Historical Society*, n.s., IV (1919), 120.

The Quaker City spirit, moreover, went beyond streets, buildings, and improvements, reaching into a wide range of human activity. Businessmen, yearly visitors in the East, brought marketing and promotion techniques from there;[32] young labor movements lifted their platforms from trade union programs in the mother city; employment agencies were conducted "principally on the Philadelphia plan."[33] The same metropolis trained most of the physicians of the West and a large share of the teachers and ministers. Caspar Wistar's famed Sunday evening gatherings of the intelligentsia provided the idea for Daniel Drake's select meetings of Cincinnati's social and cultural elite. Moreover, Philadelphia furnished the model of the perfect urbanite, for the highest praise that Western town dwellers could bestow upon a fellow citizen was to refer to him as their own "Benjamin Franklin."[34] In short, Philadelphia represented the highest stage of urban development, and progress was measured against this ideal.

Such borrowing was a conscious policy. In 1825 Mayor William Carr Lane of St. Louis, the most able urban statesman of the period, provided the justification. "Experience is the best guide . . . ," he told his councilmen. "The records of other towns are a source from which we may expect to derive useful hints. . . . It is therefore incumbent upon us to examine carefully what other communities similarly situated have done."[35] The process, however, was selective, not slavish. Investigation usually revealed a wide variety of possibilities, allowing Western cities to choose the most appropriate technique. Nevertheless, young towns preferred to meet their urban problems by adopting the established ways of the East. The challenge of the new country, far from producing a bold and fresh response, led to greater dependence on the older sections of the Union.

As transmontane cities developed they created societies whose ways and habits contrasted sharply with those of the countryside. Not only was their physical environment distinct, but their interests, activities, and pace of life also differed greatly. In 1811 a farmer near

---

[32] *Cincinnati Enquirer*, April 22, 1923.

[33] *Pittsburgh Mercury*, August 7, 1827.

[34] The phrase was constantly used in characterizing John Bradford of Lexington and Daniel Drake of Cincinnati, but it was applied to others as well.

[35] St. Louis City Council, Minutes, Court House, St. Louis, April 25, 1825.

Lexington expressed the conflict as contemporaries saw it in a dialogue between "Rusticus" and "Urbanus." The latter referred to the "rude, gross appearance" of his neighbor, adding: "How strong you smell of your ploughed ground and corn fields. How dismal, how gloomy your green woods .What a miserable clash your whistling woodland birds are continually making." "Rusticus" replied with the rural image of the town dweller. "What a fine smooth complexion you have Urbanus: you look like a weed that has grown up in the shade. Can you walk your streets without inhaling the noxious fumes with which your town is pregnant? . . . Can you engage in calm contemplation, when hammers are ringing in every direction —when there is as great a *rattling* as in a storm when the hail descends on our house tops?" [36]

One of the most conspicuous differences was in social structure. The stratification of urban societies was in marked contrast with the boisterous equality of the countryside. Social lines developed very quickly in the city. Though not as tightly drawn as in the East, they represented the meaningful distinctions in Western communities. The groupings were basically economic, though professional people were set apart by their interest and training, and Negroes by their color. No rigid boundaries divided the classes, and movement between them was constant. Yet differences did exist; people felt them and contemporaries thought them significant. It is suggestive in this regard that the first great literary product of the West, *Modern Chivalry*, satirized the notion of equality, and the author, Hugh Henry Brackenridge, was one of Pittsburgh's leading citizens.

These divisions deepened in the postwar years. As the cities grew the sense of neighborliness and intimacy diminished, giving way to the impersonality characteristic of urban living. To old-timers the changing social configuration bred a deep nostalgia and raised the image of happier, simpler days. "We cannot helping looking back with sorrowful heart, in that time of unaffected content and gaiety," a Pennsylvanian lamented, "when the unambitious people . . . in the village of 'Fort Pitt' in the yet unchartered town of Pittsburgh, were ignorant and careless of all invidious distinctions, which distract and divide the inhabitants of overgrown cities. Then all was peaceful heartfelt felicity, undisturbed by the rankling thorns of

[36] *Kentucky Reporter* (Lexington), July 2, 1811.

envy; and equality . . . was a tie that united all ranks and conditions in our community."[37] Town life in the West had never been that idyllic, but the distortion of the vision was itself a measure of the rapid change. "We have our castes of society, graduated and divided with as much regard to rank and dignity as the most scrupulous Hindoos maintain in defense of their religious prejudices," the same source admitted in 1826. Moreover, social distances were great. "Between the . . . classes . . . there are lines of demarcation drawn wide, distinct and not to be violated with impunity."[38] Nor was this stratification surprising. Having come from places where differences mattered, early city dwellers tried to re-create them in a new setting. The urge for status was stronger than the appeal of equality, and as the towns expanded cleavages deepened.

Urban ways were further distinguished from rural habits by the collective approach to many problems. City living created issues which could not always be solved by the highly individualistic methods of agrarian society. Local governments assumed an ever wider responsibility for the conduct of community affairs, and voluntary associations handled a large variety of other questions. Merchants formed chambers of commerce to facilitate cooperation on common problems; professional people organized societies to raise the standards of their colleagues and keep out the untrained. Working people, too, banded together in unions, seeking not only greater economic strength but also fraternity and self-improvement. Religious and philanthropic clubs managed most charity and relief work, while immigrants combined to help new arrivals. In addition, other associations grew up to promote literature and music, encourage debating, advocate social innovations, support public causes, and conduct the welter of amusements which larger cities required. Just as conditions in the countryside placed greatest emphasis on individual effort, so the urban situation made cooperative action seem more appropriate.

Rural and metropolitan West were also separated by distinctive social and cultural developments. The towns very quickly produced a surprisingly rich and diversified life, offering opportunities in many fields similar to those of Eastern cities but lacking on the farm or

[37] Samuel Jones, *Pittsburgh in 1826* (Pittsburgh, Pa., 1826), p. 43.
[38] *Ibid.*

frontier.[39] They enjoyed a virtual monopoly of printing presses, newspapers, bookstores, and circulating libraries. Theaters sprang up to encourage local players and traveling troupes, while in larger places museums brought the curious and the scientific to the townfolks.[40] In addition, every week brought numerous lectures and debates on all kinds of topics, keeping urban residents abreast of the latest discoveries and developments in every field. By 1815 these amenities had already lost their novelty. Indeed, some thought the civilizing process was getting out of hand. "Twenty sermons a week—," a Cincinnatian wearily counted, "Sunday evening Discourses on Theology—Private assemblies—state Cotillion parties—Saturday Night Clubs, and chemical lectures— . . . like the fever and the ague, return every day with distressing regularity."[41]

Of course, the whole transmontane region matured culturally in this period, but the towns played a strategic role. "Cities have arisen in the very wilderness . . . ," a St. Louis editor noticed in 1821, "and form in their respective states the *foci* of art and science, of wealth and information."[42] A Cincinnatian made a similar observation. "This *city*, in its growth and cultural improvements has anticipated the western country in general."[43] The hinterland, already bound to urban communities by trade, readily admitted its dependence. The *Pittsburgh Gazette* merely stated the obvious when it remarked in 1819 that the surrounding region "looks up to Pittsburgh not only as a medium through which to receive the comforts and luxuries of foreign commodities, but also a channel from which it can most naturally expect a supply of intellectual wealth."[44] Thus while the cities' merchants staked out markets in the countryside, their civic leaders spread a cultural influence into the same area.

[39] For a day-to-day account of the cultural offerings of a Western city between 1820 and 1830, see the highly informative but unpublished diary of William Stanley Merrill in the library of the Historical and Philosophical Society of Ohio (Cincinnati).

[40] The development of the theater in Western cities is outlined in Ralph Leslie Rush, *The Literature of the Middle Western Frontier* (New York, 1925), I, 352–400. For a detailed study of a single town, see William G. B. Carson, *The Theatre on the Frontier, The Early Years of the St. Louis Stage* (Chicago, 1932), pp. 1–134.

[41] *Liberty Hall* (Cincinnati), December 9, 1816.

[42] *Missouri Gazette* (St. Louis), December 20, 1820.

[43] *Liberty Hall* (Cincinnati), June 29, 1819.

[44] *Pittsburgh Gazette*, April 30, 1819.

This leadership extended into almost every field. For example, the educational opportunities of town children greatly exceeded those of their rural neighbors. Every municipality developed a complex of private tuition schools topped by an academy and, in every place except Louisville, a college. Moreover, the cities organized the movement for public schooling. Ohio's experience is illustrative. The movement for state legislation started in Cincinnati, received its major impetus from the local press, and was carried in the Assembly through the efforts of representatives from Hamilton county. It is also significant that the first superintendent of common schools in Ohio was Samuel Lewis of Cincinnati. Nor was this urban leadership surprising. The cities, as the great population centers, felt the educational pressure first and most acutely. In addition, they alone had the wealth needed to launch ambitious projects for large numbers of children. Hence the towns were ready for comprehensive public programs long before the countryside.

The most striking illustration of the cultural supremacy of the cities, however, was Lexington's unique reign as the "Athens of the West."[45] The area's largest town until 1810, it was early celebrated for its polish and sophistication and was generally conceded to be the region's capital of arts and science. But the coming of the steamboat and the depression of 1819 combined to undermine its economic position. To offset this commercial and industrial decline, Lexington's civic leaders inaugurated a policy of vigorous cultural expansion.[46] They built schools, subsidized Transylvania University, and advertised the many opportunities for advancement in learning and letters in the metropolis. Throughout the twenties this campaign was a spectacular success. The town became the resort of the most talented men of the new country. Educators, scientists, painters, lawyers, architects, musicians, and their patrons all flocked there. Transylvania University attained national eminence, attracting most of its faculty from the East and drawing students from better than a dozen states. Like a renaissance city of old Italy, Lexington provided the creative atmosphere for a unique flowering that for a

---

[45] For Lexington's growth and brief supremacy see Bernard Mayo, "Lexington, Frontier Metropolis," in *Historiography and Urbanization*, ed. Eric F. Goldman (Baltimore, Md., 1941), pp. 21–42.

[46] See, for example, *Kentucky Reporter*, October 4, 1820.

decade astonished travelers and stimulated the best minds of the West.

In its golden age the town boasted the most distinguished collection of intellectuals the new country had ever seen in a single city. The central figure in this awakening was Horace Holley, a Unitarian minister from Boston and the president of Transylvania. Though not an accomplished scholar himself, he recruited a remarkable faculty and raised the institution from a small denominational college to a university of the first rank. The medical department achieved a special distinction. Its dean was Charles Caldwell, one of Benjamin Rush's favorite pupils, who turned down important posts in New York, Philadelphia, and Baltimore to join the Kentucky experiment. Members of the staff included the botanist, Charles Wilkins Short, Daniel Drake, later the author of a pioneering study of diseases in the Mississippi Valley, and the surgeon, Benjamin Winslow Dudley. Among them, too, was the furtive and erratic, yet highly talented, Turkish-born naturalist, Constantine Rafinesque, whose most fruitful years were spent in Lexington.[47]

The graduating class of the medical school in 1826 demonstrated the extent of the university's reputation and influence. With sixty-seven degrees granted in that year, twenty-eight of the recipients came from Kentucky, ten from Tennessee, five each from Virginia, South Carolina, and Alabama, three from Ohio, two each from Mississippi, Illinois, and Louisiana, and one each from North Carolina and Georgia. During the twenties the college trained many of the West's most distinguished people. In politics alone it turned out at least seventeen congressmen, three governors, six United States senators, and the president of the Confederacy. In the same decade the school produced scores of lawyers, clergymen, and physicians, who did much to raise professional standards in the new country. Few universities have left such a clear mark on a generation; in its heyday Transylvania fully deserved its title of the "Harvard of the West."[48]

[47] Transylvania's "golden age" is treated in detail in Walter William Jennings, *Transylvania, Pioneer University of the West* (New York, 1955), pp. 99–124, and Niels Henry Sonne, *Liberal Kentucky, 1780–1828* (New York, 1939), pp. 160–242.

[48] The reputation of Lexington in Cincinnati is charmingly portrayed in the letters of young Ohioans attending Transylvania University to their friends back

The college was the center of this wilderness renaissance, but around it moved other figures—artists, architects, musicians, and poets—who gave added luster to the movement. In Matthew Jouett the city had the West's most famous painter. A student of Gilbert Stuart and a portraitist of considerable gifts, he made his studio the exciting headquarters for a group of promising young artists. Gideon Shryock provided Lexington with an architect equal to its enlightenment. After studying with William Strickland in Philadelphia, he brought the Greek revival across the mountains. His work, especially the state capitol at Frankfort and Morrison College at Transylvania, brought him immediate fame and has led a modern critic to assert that he "was almost a decade ahead of his time even when judged by sophisticated eastern standards." [49] Music shared the upsurge, and in 1817 townsfolk heard Anthony Phillip Hennrich conduct the first performance of a Beethoven symphony in the United States.

The glitter of this city drew young people from all over the transmontane region, including many from the countryside. In doing so, it provoked a familiar lament from the rural areas whose children succumbed to the bewitchment of Lexington. "We want our sons to be practical men," wrote a Kentucky farmer, "whose minds will not be filled with those light notions of refinement and taste, which will induce them to believe that they are of a different order of beings, or that will elevate them above their equals." [50] Later, agrarian representatives in the legislature joined the attack on Transylvania by voting to cut off state financial assistance.

No less striking than cultural cleavages were the differences in rural and urban religious development. Progress in the cities was steadier and more substantial—though less spectacular—than in the back country. Traveling ministers might refer to Pittsburgh as "a young hell, a second Sodom," [51] and Francis Asbury might complain in 1803 that he felt "the power of Satan in those little, wicked western

---

home. See especially the William Lytle Collection in the library of the Historical and Philosophical Society of Ohio (Cincinnati).

[49] Talbot Hamlin, *Greek Revival Architecture in America: Being an Account of Important Trends in American Architecture and American Life prior to the War between the States* (New York, 1944), p. 244.

[50] *Kentucky Reporter* (Lexington), February 16, 1824.

[51] *Pittsburgh Gazette*, September 23, 1803.

trading towns,"[52] but both churches and membership multiplied
rapidly in urban centers. Furthermore, the growth owed nothing to
the sporadic revivals which burned across the countryside at the
beginning of the century. These movements were essentially rural,
having their roots in the isolation of agricultural living and the
spiritual starvation of people unattended by regular services. The
city situation, with its constant contacts and settled church organizations, involved neither of these elements. Instead, religious societies
proliferated, sects took on such additional functions as charity and
missionary work, and congregations sent money back East to aid
their seminaries. Far from being sinks of corruption, Western cities
quickly became religious centers, supplying Bibles to the frontier,
assisting foreign missions, and, in the twenties, building theological
schools to provide priests and ministers for the whole region.

Political life also reflected the growing rural–urban division.
Though the rhetoric of the period often obscured them, differences
existed from the very beginning. Suspicion of the towns led states to
avoid economic and cultural centers when locating their capitals.
Nearly all these cities sought the prize, but none was successful. The
Missouri Gazette candidly stated the issue in 1820. "It has been said
that St. Louis is obnoxious to our Legislature—that its growth and
influence . . . are looked on with a jealous eye, and its pretensions
. . . ought to be discouraged."[53] The same clash had earlier occurred
in Kentucky, where state leaders virtually invented Frankfort to
keep the capital away from Louisville or Lexington.

As the region developed, however, the conflict became increasingly apparent, though it was still expressed cautiously. "We must
be permitted to say," an editor asserted in 1829, "that in Cincinatti
we have separate interests" from the countryside.[54] Likewise, a
Pittsburgher prefaced a strong attack on the neighboring areas by
declaring that "we think it wrong to stir up a jealousy between city
and county."[55] Nevertheless, the split represented one of the
fundamental facts of Western politics.

[52] Francis Asbury, *Journal of Rev. Francis Asbury, Bishop of Methodist Episcopal
Church* (n.p., 1821), III, 127.

[53] *Missouri Gazette* (St. Louis), December 6, 1820.

[54] *Cincinnati Advertiser*, September 16, 1829.

[55] *Pittsburgh Statesman*, August 26, 1823.

Of course, farm dwellers easily outnumbered urbanites, but the latter wielded disproportionate power. The case of Jefferson and Oldham counties in Kentucky was illustrative. In the mid-twenties the combined vote reached 3,200, Louisville residents casting roughly a quarter of them. Yet the state senator and both representatives came from the city. In 1829 when a third assemblyman was added, the rural interests pleaded with Louisville leaders to name someone from the surrounding area. "It may seem strange," wrote an observer, "that it would be necessary thus to ask for the liberality of 800 voters in favor of 2,400. . . . Nevertheless, the concentrated energies of 800 do entirely outweigh the scattered influence of the 2,400—that all past experience teaches."[56] The situation was the same elsewhere. At one time all of Missouri's representatives in Washington—two senators and one congressman—as well as its governor came from St. Louis.

The cities' political influence rested on their ability to produce leadership. As the economic and intellectual centers of transmontane life they attracted the talented and ambitious in all fields. Politics was no exception. Nearly all the great spokesmen of the West had important urban connections and their activity often reflected the demands of their town constituents. Henry Clay was one of Lexington's most prominent lawyers when he went to the United States Senate in 1806. Thomas Hart Benton held local offices in St. Louis before moving on to the national scene, and William Henry Harrison, though he lived in nearby North Bend, had deep roots in Cincinnati affairs through most of his long public life. Moreover, all were alive to the interests of their city. Benton's successful attack on government factories in the Indian territory culminated a long and intense campaign by St. Louis merchants to break federal trade control on the Missouri. Clay's enthusiasm for an ample tariff on hemp derived at least as much from the pressure of Lexington's manufactures as from that of the growers of the Blue Grass. And Harrison, as state senator, led the campaign for public schools in Ohio largely at the behest of his Cincinnati supporters. These were not isolated cases; an examination of the careers of these men demonstrates the importance of their urban connections.

By 1830, then, the West had produced two types of society—one

[56] *Louisville Public Advertiser*, July 28, 1824.

rural and one urban. Each developed its own institutions, habits, and living patterns. The countryside claimed much the larger population and often gave to transmontane affairs an agrarian flavor. But broadcloth was catching up with buckskin. The census of 1830 revealed the disproportionate rate of city growth. While the state of Ohio had four times as many inhabitants as it counted in 1810, Cincinnati's increase was twelvefold. The story was the same elsewhere. Louisville's figure showed a growth of 650 per cent compared with Kentucky's 50 per cent, and Pittsburgh tripled in size while Pennsylvania did not quite double its population. By 1830 the rise of these cities had driven a broad wedge of urbanism into Western life.

Though town and country developed along different paths, clashes were still infrequent. The West was large enough to contain both movements comfortably. Indeed, each supported the other. The rural regions supplied the cities with raw materials for their mills and packinghouses and offered an expanding market to their shops and factories. In turn, urban centers served the surrounding areas by providing both the necessities and comforts of life as well as new opportunity for ambitious farm youths. Yet the cities represented the more aggressive and dynamic force. By spreading their economic power over the entire section, by bringing the fruits of civilization across the mountains, and by insinuating their ways into the countryside, they speeded up the transformation of the West from a gloomy wilderness to a richly diversified region. Any historical view which omits this aspect of Western life tells but part of the story.

Reprinted from *The American Historical Review*, LXIV (1959), 14–30.

HARRY N. SCHEIBER

9. Urban Rivalry and Internal Improvements in the Old Northwest, 1820–1860

AT the very beginning of settlement in the Old Northwest urban communities developed in response to the commercial needs of the surrounding country. And almost as soon as they appeared, there was "urban rivalry," that is, competition among them for advantages that would promote their growth and enhance their attractiveness to emigrants and investors.[1] The earliest rivalries usually involved competition for advantages that government might bestow. Designation as the county seat or as the territorial or state capital marked the beginning of growth for many a rude village in the West, and the pursuit of these choice prizes was inevitably marked by keen political struggles. The presence of federal land offices, colleges and academies, or government installations such as arsenals and prisons was for many towns the only factor that permitted them to outdistance less favored rivals with equivalent natural or geographic endowments.[2]

Sustained urban growth and economic viability were in most cases dependent upon more than initial advantages that this sort of government patronage could provide. Probably the most important single requirement for urban growth and commercial development was adequate transportation. Without reliable transport facilities

[1] Richard C. Wade, *The Urban Frontier: The Rise of Western Cities, 1790–1830* (Cambridge, 1959), *passim.* It was a signal feature of western urban rivalry in the early nineteenth century that it often mattered little whether competing towns were populated or not. Given the nature of frontier politics and townsite speculation, the "paper village" might have great political strength in the territorial or state legislature, or even at Washington.

[2] Francis P. Weisenburger, "The Urbanization of the Middle West: Town and Village in the Pioneer Period," *Indiana Magazine of History*, LXI (1945), 19–30.

connecting a town with an expanding hinterland and with outside markets, there were oppressive limitations upon growth. The struggle for internal improvements therefore became the cause of the most vigorous and persistent rivalries among western urban communities —rivalries marked by intense ambitions, deeply rooted fear of failure, and ingenious employment of the instruments of political and economic leverage at the disposal of urban leaders.[3]

The period of early urban growth in the Old Northwest co-incided with the period of canal construction by the states. How, then, did urban rivalries influence state transport policy in the canal era, 1820–45? How did continued rivalry affect the planning and con-struction of western railroads when private promotion supplanted state enterprise, from the mid-forties to 1860? Before dealing with these questions, it must be noted that self-interested urban activities and urban consciousness cannot be strictly separated from the more embracing force of which they were manifestations, that is, from "localism," a collective consciousness and sense of common interests among the people of a given locality. The definition of common objectives and self-interest might find expression at many levels, and often urban aims and objectives were merely an intense reflection of regional aims.[4] Towns frequently spoke in state politics for the trade areas with which they were associated; yet within intrastate regions (as within interstate sections) cities might compete for hegemony. New transport facilities and redirection of trade—or even the pros-pect of such change—might alter drastically the regional identifica-tion of given urban centers.

The interplay of regional and local rivalries at the state level is illustrated in the history of Ohio's improvements policy. The movement for construction of a canal between Lake Erie and the Ohio River, which, it was hoped, would open eastern markets to

[3] Wade, *Urban Frontier*, p. 336.

[4] For useful discussions of regionalism, see Louis Hartz, *Economic Policy and Democratic Thought: Pennsylvania, 1776–1860* (Cambridge, 1948), pp. 14–21; and Louis Wirth, *Community Life and Social Policy: Selected Papers*, ed. E. W. Marvick and A. J. Reiss, Jr. (Chicago, 1956), *passim*, especially pp. 160–161, 166–169. See also Harvey S. Perloff *et al.*, *Regions, Resources, and Economic Growth* (Baltimore, 1960). Two seminal studies emphasizing the importance of regional factors are Frederick Jackson Turner, *The United States, 1830–1850* (New York, 1935); and Arthur M. Schlesinger, "The City in American History," *MVHR*, XXVII (1940), 43–66.

Ohio farmers and merchants, began to gather strength about 1820 in response to construction of the Erie Canal in New York. In 1822 the Ohio legislature assigned to a special commission the task of planning such a canal. The canal commissioners soon recognized that their problem was as much one of politics as of engineering. As long as the project remained a subject of discussion in general terms, optimistic business and political leaders throughout the state gave it their support. But once the project took precise form and the commission recommended specific routes, the virtue of vagueness was lost, and the towns and regions that would be bypassed united immediately in opposition to the proposal. Spokesmen for the disappointed communities evoked the specter of oppressive taxation, argued in principle against state intervention in the economy, and denounced the commissioners for alleged corruption. Yet some of the same men had earlier been among the most outspoken advocates of a state canal project.[5]

In 1825 the Ohio canal commission recommended, and the legislature adopted, a canal program that represented a fusion of several important regional interests within the state. Two canals were authorized, rather than the single work originally contemplated. One, the Miami Canal, satisfied Cincinnati's mercantile community and southwest Ohio; it was to run sixty-seven miles from the Queen City north through the Miami Valley to Dayton, with the understanding that it would later be extended northward to the Maumee Valley and Lake Erie. The second canal, the Ohio Canal, followed a wide-sweeping reverse-S-shaped route from the Ohio River to the lake, passing first up the heavily settled Scioto Valley, then arching eastward to the headwaters of the Muskingum, there turning northward again to its terminus on the lake shore at Cleveland.[6]

This canal program gave new focus to urban and regional ambitions, which adjusted quickly to take account of inter-regional connections and new trade relationships that the canals would create. In the first place, within regions through which the canals passed, there was an intensified struggle for positions on the projected

[5] Harry N. Scheiber, "The Ohio Canal Movement, 1820–1825," *OHQ*, LXIX (1960), 231–256.

[6] *Ibid.*, 249–250. The Portsmouth-Cleveland line was named the Ohio Canal; in 1849, the designation Ohio & Erie Canal was substituted.

works. Everywhere along the canal routes there was speculation in new town-sites. A Tuscarawas County promoter expressed the thoughts of hundreds like himself when he wrote to one of the canal commissioners: "I expect a new town will spring up [along the canal], which, from the great trade which must center there, from the country between us and the Ohio, must be a flourishing one. But *where* the spot is, I want *you* to tell *me*."[7] Sensitive to the potential threat to their own interests, established market towns in the interior petitioned for construction of feeder canals that would connect them with the main works. In many instances the townspeople offered to pay a portion of the cost. Several towns organized private canal companies to build feeder lines, not in expectation of direct profits, but rather to protect their commercial position.[8]

Events in the Scioto Valley, the southern route of the Ohio Canal, indicated the extremes to which localism might run. Piketon and Chillicothe had joined with other towns in the valley to support the canal bill of 1825 in the legislature. But as soon as it became necessary for the commission to set the exact canal location, each town advanced its own cause and all sense of regional unity dissolved. The Chillicothe interests were determined to obtain a canal connection. They forced through the legislature a resolution ordering the canal commission to build the canal through Chillicothe, even if it was necessary to build a dam or aqueduct across the river in order to bring the canal through the town. The canal commission complied, crossing the river to place the route through Chillicothe. To avoid further expenditure the commission decided not to re-cross the Scioto below Chillicothe. Piketon and other communities on the opposite bank downriver opposed this action bitterly, since it would prevent them from achieving a canal connection, but they were

[7] Jacob Blickensderfer to Micajah T. Williams, June 23, 1825, M. T. Williams Papers, Ohio State Library (Columbus). See also *Senate Journal*, 1832–1833, Ohio General Assembly, p. 340.

[8] Among the side-cuts aided by private contributions were the Granville Feeder and the Dresden Feeder. The Lancaster Lateral Canal, a twelve-mile feeder from Lancaster to the Ohio & Erie Canal, was built by a private company. There is evidence in the directors' minutes that direct profits were not anticipated. Minutes of the Lancaster Lateral Canal Company, John T. Brasee Papers, Ohio Historical Society.

unsuccessful in their protests.[9] Ironically, the state's accommodation of Chillicothe quieted the clamor there for only a few months. Once actual construction had begun, neighborhoods within the town vied with one another in what may be termed "neighborhood rivalry," various factions demanding that a particular street or section of town be designated as the canal route. Passions ran high for several months, and the mayor finally had to hold a referendum on "the *naked* and *abstract* question" of the canal route.[10]

State officials systematically exploited such local rivalries. Where the canal might be located on either side of a river, the Ohio commissioners solicited donations of land or cash from townspeople and landowners on opposite sides of the stream, indicating that the more generous communities would be favored when the canal was located. This practice often stimulated unreasonable expectations and resulted in bitter disillusionment.[11]

Once the initial canal undertaking was approved, the "disappointed" communities—those entirely outside the region of the canals—did not give up their quest for improved transportation. On the contrary, they proposed a multitude of new projects, many of them reflecting an effort by ambitious towns to overcome the lead of commercial rivals that had obtained places on the canals. "Shall narrow views and sectional feelings withhold our assistance from a work of such evident public utility?" the promoters of one new project asked the general assembly. "Shall we, palsied by untimely fears, stop mid-way in the career of public improvement, to calculate the cost, before our fellow citizens in other parts of the State participate in their advantages?"[12]

[9] *House Journal, 1825–1826*, Ohio General Assembly, pp. 280–281. Also, John C. Parish, *Robert Lucas* (Iowa City, 1907), p. 91; Ebenezer Buckingham to E. A. Brown, July 21, 1828, Ethan Allen Brown Papers, Ohio State Library.

[10] William Steele to Canal Commission, January 16, 1830, Micajah T. Williams to Mayor of Chillicothe, April 5, 1830, Jesse Fulton to Alfred Kelley, April 15, 1830, and 1829–1830 correspondence, *passim*, Ohio Canal Commission Papers, Ohio State Archives, Ohio Historical Society. For a later neighborhood rivalry, albeit of a somewhat different nature, see H. J. Stratton, "The Northern Cross Railroad," *JISHS*, XXVIII (1935), 17–19.

[11] Scheiber, "Ohio Canal Movement," p. 254; B. M. Atherton *et al.* to Alfred Kelley, May 17, 1826, Canal Commission Papers.

[12] See the report of the select committee on a Sandusky-Dayton railroad charter

Such new improvements schemes disrupted older regional alliances and introduced new forces into state politics. Sandusky's railroad project is a case in point. Only a few years after their town had lost to Cleveland in the struggle for designation as the lake-shore terminus of the Ohio Canal, a group of Sandusky promoters requested state aid for the Mad River and Lake Erie Railroad. The Mad River Railroad was planned in 1831 to run from Sandusky southwest to Dayton, which was then head of navigation on the Miami Canal, and ultimately to Cincinnati. When the first canal program had been debated in the legislature, six years earlier, the Miami Canal proposal had been supported by the western counties located north of Dayton—but only because of the understanding that the canal would be extended northward as soon as finances permitted. Having enjoyed the benefits of its position as head of navigation on the Miami Canal, Dayton now shifted its allegiance, and the town's representatives decided to support state aid for the Mad River Railroad instead of for extension of the canal.[13] This move threatened to strand the area to the north, and the towns in that region (especially Piqua) resented what they regarded as Dayton's treachery. "The Canal *must* be extended," Piqua's news-paper editor declared, despite "the selfish policy of those, who at a former period made such professions of friendship to us; but who, since *their* views have been accomplished, *forget* their obligations."[14]

The projects that blossomed forth in every part of the state also

---

in *Senate Journal, 1830–1831*, Ohio General Assembly, pp. 364 ff. Also, Ohio Auditor of State, *Annual Report, 1835*, p. 16; Ernest L. Bogart, *Internal Improvements and State Debt in Ohio* (New York, 1924), pp. 47 ff.; and C. P. McClelland and C. C. Huntington, *History of the Ohio Canals* (Columbus, 1905), pp. 38 ff.

[13] "The Dayton people are opposed to the extension of 'their Canal,'" a federal land officer reported in 1832. (Thomas Van Horne to Peyton Symmes, August 23, 1832, Miscellaneous Letters File, Ohio Auditor's Office, Records Room. See also Charles Anthony and Simpson Mason to Commissioners of the Canal Fund, a broadside dated March, 1833, *ibid.*) The regional voting pattern on the issue of the canal extension versus state aid to the railroad is confirmed by a vote of March 1, 1831, in *House Journal*, 1830–1831, Ohio General Assembly, pp. 600–601. For the Mad River Railroad, see Leola Stewart, "Sandusky: Pioneer Link between Sail and Rail," *OAHQ*, LVII (1948), 227–236.

[14] *Piqua Gazette*, March 2, 1831. The entire controversy may be traced in the *Gazette* from February, 1831, to December, 1833.

came into conflict with one another in the effort to secure the patronage of the legislature, which at this time commanded only limited funds. If logrolling was an important feature of the legislative process, so too was the log jam. The Ohio General Assembly was virtually stalemated for several years in the early 1830's because of conflicting demands for internal improvements.[15] The jam began to break when extension of the Miami Canal and construction of the Wabash and Erie Canal were authorized—but only because the federal government had provided land-grant aid for these projects. Finally, the pressure of local ambitions became too great to resist further. In 1836–37 the legislature approved a comprehensive system of new canals and state aid to railroad and turnpike companies, a program that within five years would bring Ohio to the verge of default on its enlarged debt. Every region had to be satisfied, it seemed; every little community able to advance half the cost was to receive state assistance in the construction of turnpikes or railways.[16]

With adoption of the enlarged improvements program, urban and regional ambitions adjusted rapidly to the new transportation developments. Many of the patterns of localism and rivalries witnessed a decade earlier now reappeared. In the Muskingum Valley, where a project to improve the river for steamboat traffic was undertaken, Zanesville and Dresden fought over which town should be the head of navigation, just as Dayton and Piqua had struggled for headship on the Miami Canal. Meanwhile, Marietta, situated at the mouth of the Muskingum, protested that the size of the locks was too limited. The vision of every town in the valley appeared to be one of infinite optimism and boundless growth. "We look forward," a petition of Marietta merchants declared glowingly,

> and [we] see our situation placed on the thoroughfare, between the Atlantic & the Medeterranean [*sic*] of the North, the Mississippi & the St. Lawrence. We look forward to the arrival of the Ohio & Chesapeake

[15] So reported by a member of the legislature, in letter of Leicester King to S. Perkins, February 11, 1835, Simon Perkins Papers, Western Reserve Historical Society (Cleveland).

[16] Bogart, *Internal Improvements*, pp. 47 ff. See also Carter Goodrich, *Government Promotion of American Canals and Railroads* (New York, 1960), pp. 134–138.

Canal and the Baltimore & Ohio Rail Road. . . . We look & expect to
see the Ohio made slackwater by Locks & dams, from Marietta to
Pittsburgh . . . & Lastly we expect to see the Locks, on the Muskingum
Improvement, increased. . . . We wish to convince you, that the dis-
criminating principle, attending the small locks, is derogatory to social
Commerce, & has been discarded by all civilized nations.[17]

In the Maumee Valley, then sparsely settled, the people of
several small towns—Toledo, Maumee, Perrysburg, and Manhattan
—and the absentee proprietors of the towns (including several of the
most prominent Ohio political leaders), all had favored construction
of the Wabash and Erie Canal, a project designed to continue
Indiana's Wabash and Erie Canal from the state line through the
Maumee Valley to the lake. But once the Ohio legislature had decided to undertake the project, these villages competed bitterly with
one another for designation as the terminus.[18] Among the instruments of rivalry employed were court injunctions, petitions to the
legislature and to congress, and pressure on the United States
General Land Office to limit the extent of the federal land grant by
designating one of the competing towns as head of lake navigation.
State officials finally decided to satisfy all the major competing
points by extending the canal to the mouth of the river, with
terminal locks and basins at Manhattan, Toledo, and Maumee. To
equalize the conditions of rivalry the state agreed also to open all the
terminal locks simultaneously.[19] Thus even after a major improvement had been authorized, the competition of rival communities
could serve to increase the costs of construction.

Roughly the same patterns of localism characterized the evolution of public transport policy in the other states of the Old Northwest. During the early promotional phase of internal improvements,
when state officials or private pressure groups were agitating for

[17] Joseph Barker et al. to Canal Commission, August 14, 1838, Ohio Canal
Commission Papers. On the Dresden-Zanesville conflict, see petition of July 31,
1838, ibid.; Ohio Canal Commission, 15th Annual Report (Columbus, 1839),
pp. 17–19.

[18] H. S. Knapp, History of the Maumee Valley (Toledo, 1876), pp. 557–558; John
W. Weatherford, "The Short Life of Manhattan, Ohio," OHQ, LXV (October,
1956), 381–382.

[19] Ibid.; M. T. Williams to E. A. Brown, September 2, 1836, Brown Papers;
id. to L. Ransom, August 1, 1840, Williams Papers.

projects in general terms, there tended to be divisions between the great trade regions of each state. In Indiana, for example, the southern river counties viewed with suspicion the proposal for the Wabash and Erie Canal, and they coalesced to press for roads and railways from the interior to the Ohio River.[20] In Illinois, too, the region tributary to the Mississippi River and southern markets adamantly opposed state aid exclusively for the proposed canal to Chicago. The towns on the eastern lake shore in Wisconsin (still a territory) all sought canal or railroad connections with the interior; but they were prevented from realizing their objectives because of opposition in the northern region, which demanded priority for the Fox and Wisconsin river improvement project, and in the western river towns.[21]

Once specific projects had been formulated, broad regional divisions gave way under pressure for more localized objectives. "Most of the members [of the legislature] vote for nothing which does not pass through their own county," the Indiana state engineer complained in 1835. Indiana's Michigan Road, supported in a general way by all the Ohio River counties, became an object of sharp urban rivalry when designation of the southern terminus had to be made. Similarly, the program that the state's engineers submitted to the legislature in 1835 was not rendered acceptable until it had been expanded elaborately, "to buy votes," a year later.[22] In Michigan all the lake shore towns demanded connections with the interior, yet no policy could command adequate support until one embracing the objectives of every competing town had been formulated. And so Indiana, Illinois, and Michigan all adopted comprehensive state programs that overextended their resources. In both Illinois and Indiana the political strength of localism was

[20] Indiana Canal Commission to B. Tappan, June 16, 1835, Ohio Canal Commission Papers; Logan Esarey, *Internal Improvements in Early Indiana* (Indiana Historical Society, *Publications*, V, No. 2 [Indianapolis, 1912]), 87–98.

[21] I. A. Lapham, *Wisconsin: Its Geography and Topography* (2d ed.; Milwaukee, 1846), p. 46; Calvin T. Pease, *The Frontier State, 1818–1848* ("Centennial History of Illinois," ed. C. W. Alvord, Vol. II [Chicago, 1922]), chap. x; John H. Krenkel, *Illinois Internal Improvements, 1818–1848* (Cedar Rapids, Iowa, 1958), pp. 34 ff.

[22] Jesse Williams to M. T. Williams, January 12, January 23, 1835, M. T. Williams Papers; see also John D. Barnhart and D. F. Carmony, *Indiana: From Frontier to Industrial Commonwealth* (New York, 1954), I, 291–292.

258 THE OLD NORTHWEST

further manifested in provisions of the law requiring simultaneous starts on all projects; in addition, each of the states' settled regions was granted representation on the boards of public works.[23] Once construction had begun, moreover, scores of proposals were put forward in each state for branch lines, feeder canals, and turnpike and railroad connections designed to satisfy the needs of towns outside the immediate areas of the main improvements.[24]

Still another feature of urban and regional rivalry as it affected state policy concerned canal tolls. Toll schedules were commonly established by state authorities on a protectionist basis. The states maintained two toll lists—one for "domestic," or in-state, manufactures and a higher schedule of tolls for "foreign," or out-of-state, commodities. In Ohio, for example, manufacturers of glassware, iron, salt, crockery, and other products were the beneficiaries of protectionist tolls.[25] As long as canals remained the sole means of cheap transport to the interior, manufacturers located inland from Lake Erie or the Ohio River enjoyed a form of tariff protection from out-of-state competition. Merchants at the terminal cities on the lake and the Ohio River condemned the protectionist policy as one which imposed artificial restrictions upon the canal commerce that was their economic lifeblood. The conflict between terminal cities and inland towns was expressed in the 1840's in a debate over wheat and flour tolls. The millers of the interior demanded tolls on unprocessed grain that were proportionally higher than tolls on flour. This, they argued, would encourage Ohio's milling industry and reduce the flow of Ohio grain to New York State mills. Merchants and millers at terminal cities opposed such action; they favored equivalent tolls on grain and flour (or even discrimination against flour) as a means

[23] R. Carlyle Buley, *The Old Northwest: Pioneer Period, 1815–1840* (Bloomington, 1954), II, 299–300; Goodrich, *Government Promotion*, pp. 138–147; Esarey, *Internal Improvements in Early Indiana*, pp. 105–106; Pease, *Frontier State*, pp. 216–217.

[24] For the manner in which projects promoted in response to initial undertakings of the states helped produce the "long swing" characteristic of canal construction, see Carter Goodrich *et al.*, *Canals and American Economic Development* (New York, 1962), pp. 176–179.

[25] Ohio Board of Public Works, *Special Report . . . relative to the Toll Charged on Salt . . . January 29, 1848* (Columbus, 1848), p. 5. For a full discussion of this problem, see Harry N. Scheiber, "The Rate-Making Power of the State in the Canal Era," *Political Science Quarterly*, LXXVII (1962), 397–413.

of fostering the milling industry of their cities or the export of increasing quantities of grain.[26]

Similarly, merchants at Cleveland, then gateway for import of salt from the East, fought discrimination in salt tolls that protected Ohio producers in the central portion of the state. Thus within the state there was a conflict between mercantile and manufacturing interests, comparable to the division in national politics over tariff policy. The issue of canal tolls cut across party lines, and special regional alignments were fostered by this important question. State officials were forced to mediate such conflicts, with no resolution possible that could fully satisfy all contending interests.[27]

In the period of canal construction, urban and regional ambitions were directed largely toward manipulation and control of state policy. The panic of 1837 and the post-1839 depression marked the end of the era of state canals in the Old Northwest. As the depression came to an end in the mid-forties a new internal-improvements movement gathered momentum, with a new set of conditions shaping the character of the movement. In the first place, there had been a revulsion against further large-scale construction by state government, the result of scandals in management of the public works, intolerable indebtedness, and default on their debt by several states in the depression period.[28] In the second place, the advantages of the railroad over the canal had been demonstrated. Construction of railways to meet local needs was a task that many communities believed they could undertake independently of state aid, particularly if municipal, township, or county governments extended assistance to private companies.[29] This enthusiasm for railroads was heightened

[26] Atkins & Blair to Board of Public Works, December 9, 1843, Cincinnati Chamber of Commerce petition, June 20, 1845, Collins Brown & Co. petition, January 1, 1848, G. W. Addams to John Waddle, February 19, 1859, Board of Public Works Papers, Ohio State Archives.

[27] Ohio Board of Public Works, *Special Report . . . January 29, 1848*, p. 7; correspondence with Ohio salt manufacturers, 1840–1849, *passim*, Ohio Board of Public Works Papers. See also Cleveland petition, October 2, 1858, *ibid*.

[28] Carter Goodrich, "The Revulsion Against Internal Improvements," *Journal of Economic History*, X (1950), 145–151.

[29] For example, Alfonso Taft, *A Lecture on Cincinnati and Her Rail-Roads* (Cincinnati, 1850), p. 12. See also Carter Goodrich, "Local Planning of Internal Improvements," *Political Science Quarterly*, LXVI (1951), pp. 431 ff.

by another force: the infusion of eastern capital into western railroad construction and reorganization after 1845–46. Foreign investors, too (particularly the English), showed renewed interest after 1852 in purchasing railroad bonds or local-government securities issued for railroad aid.[30] Moreover, in the canal states the railroad promised to liberate urban centers and regions that had formerly been at the mercy of geographic conditions. Limitations of terrain that had characterized canal planning were no longer relevant, a change that urban leadership was quick to comprehend. The new railroad technology reopened the critical question of which city would dominate trade in each region of the Old Northwest. As Chicago, Milwaukee, and St. Louis battled for control of the Mississippi Valley trade in the most spectacular western urban rivalry, so too in every area of the West towns competed for positions on the new railroads and for hegemony in local trade areas.[31]

Most of the projected western railroads were designed at first to serve primarily local needs and objectives. This fact explains the enthusiasm with which communities, small and large, supported private railroad companies with public aid.[32] Among the arguments of railroad promoters seeking local subscriptions and public assistance were many that had become familiar in the canal era. Multiple market outlets were a major objective of many communities, and numerous railroad schemes were designed to free towns from "monopoly" conditions, under which they were tributary to a single market; in the same way, the state canal programs had been designed to open alternate markets to western producers formerly dependent

[30] Alfred D. Chandler, Jr., "Patterns of American Railroad Finance, 1830–1850," *Business History Review*, XXVIII (1954), 258–259; R. W. Hidy and M. Hidy, "Anglo-American Merchant Bankers and the Railroads of the Old Northwest, 1848–1860," *ibid.*, XXXIV (1960), 154 ff.

[31] The St. Louis-Chicago-Milwaukee rivalry is discussed in W. W. Belcher, *The Economic Rivalry between St. Louis and Chicago, 1850–1880* (New York, 1947); and Bayrd Still, *Milwaukee, The History of a City* (Madison, 1948). For a discussion of Cincinnati and her railroads in the 1850's, see Sherry O. Hessler, "'The Great Disturbing Cause' and the Decline of the Queen City," HPSO, *Bulletin*, XX (1962), 169–185.

[32] This was a national, not merely a western phenomenon; see G. R. Taylor and Irene Neu, *The American Railroad Network, 1861–1890* (Cambridge, 1956), pp. 3–6; and Goodrich, "Local Planning," pp. 437 ff.

upon the New Orleans outlet. Established metropolitan centers, such as Cleveland and Cincinnati, extended municipal aid to railroads in an effort to multiply and extend their transport radii or to obtain all-rail connections with the East. Some railroad promoters even advertised their projects as potential links in transcontinental systems that would carry the trade of Asia and the Far West through a particular town or village. And by the early fifties there had emerged the well-known competition among major cities for designation as the eastern terminus of a land-grant transcontinental railway.[33] Less pretentious communities sought places on the new railroad lines merely to survive, or else to overcome advantages enjoyed by rival towns on canals or rivers.[34]

Indicative of the emphasis upon local objectives in railroad promotion was the ambivalent western attitude toward eastern influence. The western railroad promoter was usually quite willing to accept financial assistance from established railroad companies, and he eagerly solicited eastern investment in bonds or stock. But he generally had to rely in the first instance upon local resources, public and private; and the prospect that outsiders might control the enterprise could hinder seriously his efforts to raise funds locally. One Ohio railroad organizer, for example, argued with his fellow promoters in 1851 that it was inadvisable to employ an engineer from the East to locate the line. Local people would, he said, suspect "that this Eastern man would come here with Eastern habits, feelings, associations and *interests*, the effect of which must be, to give everything an Eastern aspect."[35] In the same vein, the president of the New Albany and Salem Railroad in Indiana wrote in 1852 that because most of the stockholders lived along the route, the company was protected from "the prejudice that exists in the public mind in

[33] *Ibid.*, pp. 437–438; Herbert W. Rice, "Early Rivalry among Wisconsin Cities for Railroads," *WMH*, XXXV (1951), 10–15; Carrie Cropley, "When the Railroads Came to Kenosh," *ibid.*, XXXIII (1949), 189–191; Dwight L. Agnew, "Beginning of the Rock Island Lines," *JISHS*, XLVI (1953), 413–415; Wylie J. Daniels, *The Village at the End of the Road* (Indianapolis, 1938), pp. 57–58; O. Morrow and F. W. Bashore, *Historical Atlas of Paulding County, Ohio* (Madison, 1892), pp. 24–25.

[34] For an example, see Thomas D. Brock, "Paw Paw versus the Railroads," *Michigan History*, XXXIX (1955), 129–131.

[35] Samuel Carpenter to John T. Brasee, May 17, 1851, Brasee Papers.

many places against [railroads], where they are looked upon as monopolies owned and managed by persons having no interests or sympathies in common with them."[36] Yet two of the strongest arguments employed by western railroad promoters to secure local support were that their roads might one day merge with others to form a large integrated system or that they might bring an eastern main line to the sponsoring communities.[37]

Western railroad entrepreneurs skillfully induced and exploited local rivalries, as state canal authorities had once done, by soliciting subscriptions or donations from communities on alternative routes. One may trace the routes of many early western railroads by naming the towns and counties (seldom on a straight line!) that extended public aid. Similarly, the major eastern trunk lines—notably the Pennsylvania and the Baltimore and Ohio—gave financial support to several parallel-running western railroads, thereby stimulating competition among rival communities on all the routes thus aided.[38]

Private financing and public aid at the local level were critical determinants of the pace and character of western railroad expansion. Urban rivalry continued to find expression, however, in the arena of the state legislatures. Debate over charters often involved bitter conflict over routes; and in some cases railroad interests would block altogether the chartering of rival companies.[39]

Opposition to local aid was scattered, and not until 1851 in Ohio and long afterward in other western states was it effective. Urban

[36] Quoted in Frank F. Hargrave, *A Pioneer Indiana Railroad* (Indianapolis, 1932), pp. 33–34.

[37] Daniel Kilgore to Thomas Swan, December 26, 1849, Kilgore Papers, Ohio Historical Society; Cleveland and Mahoning Railroad, *Annual Report, 1852* (Cleveland, 1853), p. 27; Fayette B. Shaw, "Transportation in the Development of Joliet and Will County," *JISHS*, XXX (1937), 119 ff.

[38] Hargrave, *Pioneer Indiana Railroad*, pp. 37 ff.; Walter R. Marvin, "The Steubenville and Indiana Railroad," *OHQ*, LXVI (1957), 17; William P. Smith, *The Book of the Great Railway Celebrations of 1857* (New York, 1858), *passim*; H. W. Schotter, *Growth and Development of the Pennsylvania Railroad Company* (Philadelphia, 1927), pp. 36–38; Ohio Commissioner of Railroads, *Report, 1870*, I, 477–492; Alice E. Smith (ed.), "Wisconsin's First Railroad: Linsey Letters, 1852," *WMH*, XXX (1947), 349.

[39] Paul W. Gates, *The Illinois Central Railroad and Its Colonization Work* (Cambridge, 1934), chap. iii; Agnew, "Beginning of the Rock Island Lines," p. 411; Daniels, *Village at the End of the Road*, pp. 65–68; Victor M. Bogle, "New Albany," *IMH*, L (1954), 160.

leaders did occasionally divide over the question of priority in allocation of funds among several companies competing for a town's patronage. A few opponents of aid took an ideological position, condemning public assistance of any kind. There were also some instances of urban-rural conflict, with farming areas opposing county aid to railroads which, they averred, would merely enhance the wealth of already affluent market towns. The farm-mortgage railroad subscriptions notorious in Wisconsin—and to a lesser extent in Illinois—testify eloquently, however, to the fact that rural opposition to railroads was by no means universal. Finally, there were some instances of rivalry involving towns within counties, with several vying for connections on the route of a railroad seeking county aid.[40]

The results of generous public and private support of western railroads were highly uneven. Whether or not their railroad stock paid dividends, many communities were amply rewarded by commercial advantages conferred by the new transport lines.[41] But precisely because the objectives of western railway promotion had been defined within a context of local ambitions, the reaction was severe when these ambitions were frustrated. Throughout the Old Northwest the people resisted payment on bonds and subscriptions that aided railroads never built or which once built had fallen victim to bankrupt reorganization. Sometimes there was violence, as in Athens, Ohio, where townspeople tore up the tracks of the Marietta and Cincinnati Railroad, which had bypassed the town even though its citizens had voted for county aid to the company.[42] In the 1850's

[40] Kathleen B. Jacklin, "Local Aid to Railroads in Illinois, 1848–1870" (Master's thesis, Cornell University, 1958), pp. 68 ff.; Luther M. Feeger, *The History of Transportation in Wayne County, Indiana* (reprinted from Richmond, Ind., *Palladium-Item*, 1953–1954), installment of September 3, 1953; Frederick Merk, *Economic History of Wisconsin during the Civil War Decade* (Madison, 1916), pp. 238–270.

[41] The citizens of Mansfield, Ohio, subscribed about $500,000 to railroad stock; nearly all of it was lost by 1870, yet a county official declared they were "unanimous in the opinion that it is money well spent." (Ohio Railroad Commissioner, *Report, 1870*, II, 322.)

[42] Thomas W. Lewis, *History of Southeastern Ohio* (Chicago, 1928), I, 612–613. See also Ohio Railroad Commissioner, *Report, 1870*, II, 321. Estimates of the amounts of local aid extended to railroads in the Old Northwest appear in Goodrich, *Government Promotion*, pp. 137–148.

there appeared anti-railroad sentiment that presaged the Granger movement, a sentiment stimulated by resentment against emergent eastern dominance over railroads built initially with local aid; the outsiders often imposed rates unfavorable to the western communities that had helped build the roads.[43]

Whether or not the objectives of westerners who supported early railroads were later frustrated, the debates over transportation heightened urban community consciousness and sharpened local pride in many western towns. The issues concerning internal improvements that dominated town politics over many years constantly forced farmers and urban residents alike to reexamine their local interests, needs, and hopes in a period of rapid change in the West.

What occurred in the Old Northwest in the period 1820–60 also characterized development of the national transportation system in the pre-Civil War years: localism and regionalism were so strong that they rendered impossible any comprehensive, rational planning of a system of internal improvements.[44] A glance at the transport map of the West in 1860 reveals the gross absurdities of parallel lines and over-dense construction in many areas. The highly rational response of western leaders to their communities' transport needs had led to a highly irrational result. But the western transport network included many lines of communication, built mainly with the resources of state and local government, that were vital in the development of a national economy. And the growth of this transport network had been influenced significantly by the effects of urban and regional rivalry.

Reprinted from *Ohio History*, Vol. LXXI, No. 3 (October, 1962), pp. 227–239.

[43] Thus the Cincinnati Chamber of Commerce complained of "the manner in which the great [railroads] discriminate against the city which helped to build them, on the ground they would help to build up her interests." *Annual Statement of the Trade and Commerce of Cincinnati, 1860* (Cincinnati, 1860), p. 25. See also *Kalida* (Ohio) *Venture*, March 3, 1854, and Ohio General Assembly, Senate, *Report of the Standing Committee on Railroads* (n.p., n.d. but 1861), p. 2.

[44] See review by Charles Francis Adams in *North American Review*, LI (1840), 320–321; and Goodrich, *Government Promotion*, p. 45.

V
THE PEOPLE—MOVING

Part V
The People—Moving

By definition, a frontier area undergoing settlement is an area whose society will be characterized by spatial mobility—people on the move. But American historians are still in rudimentary stages of research, so far as studying the precise character and effects of mobility is concerned. Few, I think, would be willing to accept one scholar's view that in the West, the mobility that marked pioneer communities "engendered a social environment unlike that of any other section" of the nation.[1] For on the one hand, few studies are available to us on specific western communities—we have only scattered data on population turnover, on immigrant origins and the destinations of out-migrants, or on age, social-class, and ethnic characteristics of migrants. And we do not yet know enough about the degree or type of mobility in older-settled areas to say with confidence that the social environment conditioned by mobility in the West was indeed "unique."[2] Nor would most students of nineteenth-century America, I think, assert flatly that "the severing of family and community ties changed behavioral patterns in individuals," causing "alterations in the traits of the people."[3] Yet such assertions are most useful as working hypotheses, providing a framework for the systematic investigation that is so obviously required for an understanding of mobility in American life. It can aid in determining whether any single pattern of mobility characterized all the Old Northwest, or whether different communities in the region were

[1] Ray Allen Billington, *America's Frontier Heritage* (New York, 1966), p. 193.

[2] See *ibid.*, chap. ix and its notes; and also the stimulating discussion of "The Frontiers of Migration" in Oscar Handlin, *The Americans: A New History of the People of the United States* (Boston, 1963), pp. 195 ff.

[3] Billington, *America's Frontier Heritage*, p. 193. The impact of migrations on character traits is considered in Everett S. Lee, "The Turner Thesis Re-examined," *American Quarterly*, Vol. XIII (Spring, 1961); and Allan G. Bogue, "Social Theory and the Pioneer," *Agricultural History*, Vol. XXXIV (January, 1960).

affected by different patterns. It can aid in assessing how deviant (if at all) the West really was, in terms of mobility and its impact on "the traits of the people" and on social development, as compared with the national norm.

Although major interpretive questions still remain unresolved, we can be certain that the process of migrations formed an important part of community life in the Old Northwest. Even communities that were relatively stable, after the initial period of their settlement, developed in a milieu of mobility; and it would be indeed surprising if there were no important relationship between spatial mobility—people moving—and patterns of social mobility in the region.

George B. Engberg's article is an intensive study of the lumber-jacks as an occupational group in the Great Lakes region. He is concerned with the origins of the group, the mechanisms whereby migration was expedited, and the mixing of ethnic groups in the lumber camps. Mr. Engberg's study provides a lively sense of the "mingling" process that was emphasized so strongly in Turner's writings on the Old Northwest; and its emphasis upon an industry that early in the region's history employed wage labor, and that stood outside the urban and farm-community societies that usually engage our exclusive attention, reminds us that the Old Northwest had its counterparts to the shantytowns and the labor force they housed in the mining and timber frontiers of the Far West.[4]

Peter Coleman's study of Grant County, Wisconsin, is a still more intensive examination of evidence on mobility. An economic and social historian on the University of Illinois (Chicago) faculty, Professor Coleman has studied the migrations into and out of Grant County—and more important still, he has considered the county township by township. Thus he identifies communities that became stable as time passed, while others retained only a small proportion of their early settlers and were characterized by a high degree of mobility several decades after their frontier period had ended. The Grant County story suggests too that migrants from town to town perhaps played as significant a role as migrants from farm to farm,

---

[4] See Robert F. Fries, *Empire in Pine* (Madison, 1951); and James Willard Hurst, *Law and Economic Growth: The Legal History of the Lumber Industry in Wisconsin* (Cambridge, Mass., 1964).

in the late nineteenth century.[5] Though systematic generalization about migration and its effects may not yet be possible, studies such as those reprinted here provide the empirical basis for reconsidering the larger questions first formulated by Turner and recently reexamined by such scholars as Ray Allen Billington and George W. Pierson.[6]

[5] Lewis Atherton, *Main Street on the Middle Border* (Bloomington, 1954) treats the decline of small towns.

[6] Billington, cited earlier; and three articles by Pierson, "The Moving American," *Yale Review*, Vol. XLIV (Autumn, 1954); "The M-Factor in American History," *American Quarterly*, Vol. XIV (Summer, 1962); "A Restless Temper," *American Historical Review*, Vol. LXIX (July, 1964).

GEORGE B. ENGBERG

10. Who Were the Lumberjacks?

AT Menomonie in west central Wisconsin James H. Lockwood started a sawmill in 1828 with a motley crew of discharged soldiers, French-Canadians, and half-breeds.[1] As pilot for his lumber rafts, he hired an old voyageur who knew the vagaries of the rivers which were the chief available means of transportation.[2] Although this was not the first lumbering venture in the three states which touch Lake Superior and have come to be known in the forest products industry as the Lake States, the early crew that put in the logs and manned the sawmill was somewhat typical of the thousands who were to follow.

In dealing with the origin of the labor supply for the Lake States lumber industry, we are concerned with the men who worked in the basic timber industry. This category includes the lumberjacks who cut the trees in the woods and moved the logs to streams or railroads, the river drivers who guided logs and lumber down stream, and the sawmill operatives who converted the logs into rough lumber. These workers performed an essential task in providing building material for the homes, barns, and factories of the Middle West and parts of the eastern states. They also aided in opening up the wilderness for the farmers who followed and in many cases became farmers themselves. During most of the past century, the wood products industry has been second only to farming in importance to the people who lived in the three states which were the center of the white pine industry.

This study is concerned with the source of the labor supply for the lumber industry. It deals with domestic migration, both that from

[1] This paper on the labor supply for the lake states lumber industry was presented to a joint meeting of the Mississippi Valley Historical Association, the Agricultural History Society, and the Economic History Association at Rock Island, Illinois, on April 23, 1948.

[2] George W. Hotchkiss, *History of the Lumber and Forest Industry of the Northwest* (Chicago, 1898), p. 475; Thomas E. Randall, *History of the Chippewa Valley* (Eau Claire, 1875), p. 17.

the eastern states to the Middle West and that within the Lake States. Canada and northwestern Europe must also be considered as important contributors to the logging camps and sawmills. The interchange of workers with other industries, especially farming, will be considered. This subject thus becomes largely a study of migration between different areas and different industries. An understanding of the problems of labor supply is important in the history of the forest products industry and also has something to contribute to the more general topics of population movement, labor, and the opening of the Middle West to settlement.

Many of the men who made lumbering their major occupation followed the northern pine belt across the continent from New England and the Middle Atlantic states.[3] They paid little attention to state lines and those who came through Canada showed almost equal indifference to national boundaries. New York, as the most populous state, was the heaviest contributor to this native immigrant stream. In 1880 persons born in New York accounted for eighteen per cent of the residents in selected Michigan lumbering counties and about ten per cent of those in similar counties in Wisconsin and Minnesota. Many people migrated from Ohio to these lumbering areas, especially those in Michigan, and its sons accounted for about three per cent of the total. Pennsylvania came next with two and one-half per cent.[4]

Although Maine did not contribute as many men as the large states just mentioned, those who did enter the lumber industry in the Lake States were outstanding for their ability and leadership. Some of the Maineites moved to the Great Lakes region by way of Canada. Others cut timber in Pennsylvania before migrating farther west, but the largest numbers went to the Lake States where the supply of timber was greatest and most like that along the north Atlantic coast.[5] The number of persons born in Maine who lived in Wisconsin and Minnesota in 1880 bore about the same relation to

[3] Ellis B. Usher, "Cyrus Woodman, a Character Sketch," *WMH*, II (June, 1919), 405.

[4] *Statistics of the Population of the United States at the 10th Census (1880)* (Washington, 1883), I, 480–483, 513–515, 534–535. Hereafter cited as *10th Census: Population*.

[5] Richard G. Wood, *A History of Lumbering in Maine, 1820–1860* (University of Maine, *Studies*, Ser. 2, No. 33 [Orono, 1935]), pp. 227–234.

the number of immigrants from other northeastern states as the population of Maine bore to those same states, but the proportion of Maineites in selected lumbering counties of Minnesota was over six times as great as in the state as a whole and more than double for a group of ten Wisconsin counties. In other words, Maine men were concentrated in the logging counties.[6]

These displaced Yankees attracted special attention because many of them became leaders in the lumber industry, and some of them, such as Senator Isaac Stephenson of Wisconsin, became prominent in other fields. Their success and their need for additional skilled and dependable workers were factors in enlarging the stream of migrant Maine lumbermen. Stephenson, born in New Brunswick and educated in Maine, was one of several men from that area who came to the Green Bay region to work for the firm of Sinclair and Wells. In turn he recruited loggers in Maine when he was operating camps in the woods near Escanaba in the Upper Peninsula.[7]

The migration of men from Maine was encouraged by employers who favored the experienced woodsmen from the Pine Tree State with backgrounds similar to their own. One man who had been told by Ard Godfrey in Minneapolis that no more men were needed went back the next day and announced himself as being from Maine, whereupon Godfrey welcomed him like a brother and immediately offered him a job.[8]

The men who came from other sections of the country to work in the forests and mills of the northwest did jobs requiring all degrees of skill. Maine supplied not only camp and mill foremen, but also axmen, teamsters, and other less skilled laborers.[9] Toward the turn of the century there was an influx of Kentucky and Tennessee men into the Upper Peninsula, many of whom were relatively unskilled wood-cutters. Middle western metropolitan centers such as Chicago and St. Louis frequently contributed unskilled men on a seasonal basis.[10]

In addition to this intersectional migration there was within the

[6] *10th Census: Population*, I, 480–483, 515, 534–535.

[7] Isaac Stephenson, *Recollections of a Long Life, 1829–1915* (Chicago, 1915), 79–81, 104, 109; Marinette and Peshtigo *Eagle*, July 8, 1882.

[8] D. W. Snell, "An Introduction to the History of Lumbering in Minnesota" (Master's thesis, University of Minnesota), p. 66.

[9] Wood, *Lumbering in Maine*, p. 234.

[10] Interview with Carl H. A. Schultz at Hermansville, August 16, 1947.

Lake States a considerable amount of migration which supplied workers for the forest products industries. During the first part of the nineteenth century many of the lumberjacks and sawmill men moved into the area by way of the rivers and lakes from other frontier settlements. After the signing of the treaty with the Chippewa in 1837, Hercules L. Dousman, Henry H. Sibley, and other agents of the American Fur Company brought laborers and materials from Prairie du Chien, in order to build and operate a sawmill at the falls of the Chippewa River.[11]

In the latter part of the nineteenth century the migration of lumber workers within the Lake States was often the result of the exhaustion of timber resources in the older areas. Men who helped log off the Saginaw River pineries moved on to western Michigan, the Upper Peninsula, Wisconsin, or Minnesota.[12] Even as early as 1880, Wisconsin ranked third among the states as a place of birth for nonnative workers in Minnesota lumbering counties, and by the opening of the twentieth century the new logging operations in northern Minnesota were attracting men from the camps of the Upper Peninsula.[13]

Such cities of the Northwest as Milwaukee, Minneapolis, St. Paul, and Duluth also provided large numbers of employees for the forest products industry, either from their own regular labor supply or from the men who came in from neighboring areas.[14] A Works Progress Administration study in the 1930's indicated that the migration of lumber workers in and out of the cities of the northwest was still continuing, although its volume had fallen off with the decline in the industry.[15]

[11] *History of Northern Wisconsin* (Chicago, 1881), p. 193.

[12] Willis C. Ward, "Reminiscences of Michigan's Logging Days," *Michigan History Magazine*, XX (1936), 310; *Mississippi Valley Lumbermen*, XXV (December 14, 1894), 1; Michigan Bureau of Labor and Industrial Statistics, *9th Annual Report, 1892*, p. 372, quoting from a Ludington newspaper of September 12, 1891; Hotchkiss, *Lumber and Forest Industry*, p. 542.

[13] *10th Census: Population*, I, 481; Marquette *Mining Journal*, October 19, 1901.

[14] St. Paul and Minneapolis *Daily Minnesota Tribune*, January 9, 1883; *Mississippi Valley Lumberman*, XXVI (October 25, 1895), 19; Wisconsin Industrial Commission, *Labor Camps in Wisconsin* (n.p., n.d. but issued in 1913), p. 16.

[15] J. M. Webb, *The Migratory-Casual Worker* (Works Progress Administration, Division of Social Research [Washington, 1937]), pp. 45–46.

The largest single group of foreigners in the Lake States lumber industry came from Canada. In fact, the French-Canadians can be classed as pioneers in the industry, since they operated mills in the Detroit area in the middle of the eighteenth century and helped to open up the forests of the Mississippi Valley in the course of the shift from fur trading to logging.[16] The reduction in timber duties as Great Britain moved toward free trade in the 1840's allowed Baltic timber to re-enter the British market and to displace New Brunswick timber. The result was that many of the New Brunswick lumber workers, both employers and laborers, migrated to the Lake States. The higher wages paid in the western pineries were also an attraction, especially in the 1860's when there was a wartime labor shortage.

Migration from Canada to the Lake States was also encouraged by the availability of both water and railroad transportation. The Saginaw Valley was close to Canada, and Bay City became a center for Canadian lumbermen. Sarnia, opposite Port Huron, was a funnel through which many Canadians, especially those of French descent, entered Michigan. Some were seasonal laborers but many remained in the United States. About 1880 the net annual migration to the United States through Sarnia was over seven thousand.[17] Of the tickets which an Ottawa agent sold to fellow Canadians bound for the western states, two-thirds were for points in the Lake States.[18] In 1880 there were nearly forty thousand persons of Canadian birth living in a group of lumbering counties in the Lake States where the total population was slightly over three hundred thousand.[19]

It is difficult to estimate how many Canadians migrated to the Lake States, since many of them returned home after shipping opened in the spring and their re-entry was often not recorded. The Canadian government became so alarmed that official investiga-

[16] *Michigan Pioneer and Historical Collections*, II (1880), 102.

[17] Canada, Parliament, House of Commons, "Report of the Select Standing Committee on the Immigration and Colonization," *Journals*, Sess. 1884, Appendix No. 1 (Ottawa, 1884), p. 3.

[18] *Id.*, "Report of the Select Standing Committee on the Immigration and Colonization," *Journals*, Sess. 1880–1881, Appendix No. 1 (Ottawa, 1881), pp. 16–17.

[19] *10th Census: Population*, I, 480–483, 513–515, 534–535.

tions were made of the movement of population across the border
into the United States during the 1880's and 1890's.[20] These investigations indicated that about seventy-five per cent of those going to
Michigan were lumbermen, large parties going in the fall for the
logging season and other sizable groups entering in the spring to take
part in the drives.[21] One of the most famous of the migrating lumbermen was Robert Dollar, who came from Scotland to Canada in 1858
and moved to Michigan in 1882, where he ran a sawmill for five
years before going on to California to become better known as the
owner of the Dollar Steamship Company.[22] There were so many
Scotsmen entering the Michigan camps from Canada that the camp
clerks faced real problems of identification. The many MacDonalds
with the same given name in one camp were entered on the payroll as
Big Dan, Black Dan, Curley Dan, Dirty Dan, and Dan-with-the-
Gold-Watch.[23] Federal census returns indicate that the number of
Canadians employed in the logging camps, on the drives, and in the
saw and planing mills of the Lake States increased from nearly four
thousand in 1870 to over twelve thousand five hundred in 1890.
This was one fourth to one fifth of the total number of lumber
industry employees in the area.[24]

The logging and sawmill crews in the Lake States also included a
large number of men of European birth, especially from the countries
of northwestern Europe. Certain nationalities predominated in some
areas and in some crews, while others contained men of many nationalities. German and Irish employees were particularly common in the
1840's and 1850's, a reflection of the heavy immigration from those

[20] Canada, Department of Agriculture, "Report of the Minister of Agriculture
... 1880," House of Commons *Sessional Papers*, Sess. 1880–1881 (Ottawa, 1881),
VII, No. 12, xxxix; Canada, Department of the Interior, "Annual Report ...
1892," *ibid.*, Sess. 1893 (Ottawa, 1893), XXVI, No. 13, 101; Canada, Parliament,
House of Commons, "Report of the Select Standing Committee on Immigration
and Colonization," *Journals*, Sess. 1880–1881, Appendix No. 1 (Ottawa, 1881),
pp. 17, 25, 76; *id.*, Sess. 1884, Appendix No. 1 (Ottawa, 1884), pp. 3, 101.

[21] *Id.*, House of Commons, *Journals*, Sess. 1880–1881, Appendix No. 1, p. 25.

[22] Robert Dollar, *Memoirs* (San Francisco, 1917), I, 2–27.

[23] Marian V. Loud, "No Winter Came," Ms, p. 141, Burton Historical Collection of the Detroit Public Library.

[24] *Statistics of the Population of the U.S. at the 9th Census (1870)* (Washington,
1872), I, 740–741, 764; *10th Census: Population*, I, 829–830, 853; *Report on Population
of the U.S. at the 11th Census (1890)* (Washington, 1897), Part II, 570–573, 624–625.

countries in that period.[25] Scandinavians began to arrive before 1850 and became increasingly prominent in Wisconsin and Minnesota, both as laborers and as managers.[26] Between 1870 and 1890 the German contribution to the labor force in the Lake States lumber industry declined from twelve per cent to ten per cent and the Irish element fell from five per cent to two per cent. These declines were due in part to the increased immigration of other nationality groups. The Scandinavians, for instance, increased from six per cent to fifteen per cent of the total during the same two decades.[27]

Other nationality groups played an important part in more localized areas. Belgians settled on the Door Peninsula in northeastern Wisconsin and worked in the lumber and shingle mills of that area.[28] Polish sawmill workers were important in the strikes around Bay City in the 1880's.[29] The Finns contributed heavily to the work in the Upper Peninsula and in the northern part of Minnesota.[30]

Many of the men who were hired by the Lake States lumber operators were employed for only part of the year and may be regarded as coming to the industry from other occupations. Large numbers of axmen, raftsmen, mill hands, and teamsters were pioneer farmers who worked in the woods or mills when farm work was slack. Some farmers also cut and hauled logs from their own land to near-by mills during the winter when there was time for such work and frozen ground and snow made transportation easy.[31] Early

[25] Stephenson, *Recollections*, pp. 87, 105. Also, Henry H. Crapo to William W. Crapo, April 12, 1858, April 17, 1859, in the Henry H. Crapo Papers, Michigan Historical Collections (Ann Arbor); Frank H. Gillmor to Lucile Kane, December 16, 1947, in the files of the Forest Products History Foundation, Minnesota Historical Society (St. Paul).

[26] Stephenson, *Recollections*, pp. 105–106; Hotchkiss, *Lumber and Forest Industry*, p. 533; Walker, Judd, and Veazie Papers (Mss), Minnesota Historical Society.

[27] *9th Census: Population*, I, 740–741, 764; *10th Census: Population*, I, 829–830, 853; *11th Census: Population*, II, 570–573, 624–625.

[28] Xavier Martin, "The Belgians in Northeast Wisconsin," *WHC*, XIII (1895), 381–391.

[29] Sidney Glazer, "Labor and Agrarian Movements in Michigan, 1876–1896" (Unpublished Ph.D. dissertation, University of Michigan, 1932), p. 5.

[30] *Mississippi Valley Lumberman*, XXIII (May 5, 1893), 1; C. M. Oehler, *Time in the Timber* (St. Paul, 1948), p. 33.

[31] Joseph Shafer, *A History of Agriculture in Wisconsin* (Madison, 1922), pp. 130–131; William A. Henry, *Northern Wisconsin: A Handbook for the Home Seeker* (Madison, 1896), pp. 154–165.

settlers located in timbered areas for other reasons than the obvious convenience of ample supplies of lumber and fuel. Such location meant that they would be near logging camps and sawmills where they could earn cash wages that could be used to buy goods they could not produce and to make payments on the land which they were occupying.[32]

The amount of farm labor available was dependent in part on the amount of prosperity which the farmers were enjoying. If times were good the farmers were less anxious to work and were more easily discouraged by bad roads or weather.[33] The logging and farming occupations dovetailed nicely in that their busy periods came in different seasons. This was also true of harvest hands who followed the ripening wheat crop in a northward movement that left them near the pineries when the logging season was about to open. The great harvest demand in the Northwest came at a time of year when many sawmills were beginning to exhaust their supply of logs, which was probably a fortunate circumstance, for the mills could hardly compete with the wages paid in the harvest fields.[34]

There was also frequent seasonal rotation between railroad construction work in the summer and logging in the winter. This rotation became especially important in the latter half of the nineteenth century while the railroad net of the northwest was being built.[35] Then, too, there was some flow of labor back and forth between the pineries and the iron and copper mines of the Lake Superior country. This movement was likely to be accelerated during times of depression, since although the mines were shut down, work in the woods went ahead, even though at a reduced volume.[36] Hard times also sent city workers into the woods, since many of the jobs in and

[32] Kate A. E. Levi, "Geographical Origin of German Immigration to Wisconsin," *WHC*, XIV (1898), 356–383; *Mississippi Valley Lumberman*, XXVII (December 11, 1896), 13; Muskegon *Daily Chronicle*, July 30, 1906.

[33] *American Lumberman*, I (February 18, 1899), 31.

[34] *Mississippi Valley Lumberman*, XXX (September 22, 1899), 14; Stillwater (Minnesota) *Gazette*, July 24, 1878.

[35] Alvin H. Hansen *et al.*, *The Duluth Casual Labor Group* (Employer Stabilization Research Institute, University of Minnesota, *Bulletin*, I, No. 3 [Minneapolis, 1932]), 15.

[36] *Mississippi Valley Lumberman*, XXV (October 12, 1894), 16.

around logging camps did not require much skill and could be learned quickly.[37]

There were also some other small additions to the labor force which should be mentioned. A few Indians forsook their blankets and rifles long enough to try their hands with the ax and saw, although they were never an important source of labor, except in some of the lumbering operations on Indian lands which were managed under the watchful eye of the Indian Bureau. Although most of the workers in the lumber industry were men, some women and children were employed, especially in doing lighter work around the mills. The census reports indicate that about five hundred women were working in the various parts of the basic lumber industry in the Lake States from 1870 to 1890. There were over a thousand children so employed in 1870 and nearly double that number in 1880.[38]

The labor supply for the lumber industry in the Lake States, then, did not come from any one source, but rather from many areas in North America and from northwestern Europe. Many of the men who worked in the woods and in the mills came to the industry from other occupations. In dealing with the sources of the labor supply for the Lake States lumber industry, it has been practicable to refer only slightly to many phases of the labor problem that are closely related to supply. Other parts of the story have not even been mentioned. The size of the labor force, the types of work which the men did, and the training they received are important parts of the picture. The conditions under which the work was done and the hours and wages are factors which cannot be ignored in any well-rounded discussion of the labor supply. The same might also be said of such factors as accident rates, laws which affected the workers, and the related problems of unionization and strikes. Consideration of these topics will give us an answer not only to the question of who the lumberjacks were, but also to the equally important questions of what they did, why they did it, and what were the results of their work.

Reprinted from *Michigan History*, XXXIII (1948), 238–246.

[37] F. E. Cummings, "Lumbering in the Chippewa Valley," Eau Claire *Daily Telegram*, April 21, 1916.

[38] *Report on Manufacturing Industries in the U.S. at the 11th Census (1890)*, Part III: *Selected Industries*, pp. 610–611.

PETER J. COLEMAN

11. Restless Grant County: Americans on the Move

IF only in a general way, American historians have long been conscious of the role of population mobility in shaping the nation's development and spirit. With Frederick Jackson Turner they have followed the waves of settlers moving westward toward the setting sun. And since the close of the frontier at the end of the nineteenth century they have watched the drift of population to the cities. More recently, political scientists and sociologists have observed the impact of latter-day migration to the Pacific Coast, to the South West, and to parts of the Old South. They have also become students of that most recent of American phenomena, the decay of the old city and the exodus to suburbia. But though there is at present less willingness than there once was to accept Turner's simplistic frontier-cum-free-land explanation for the restlessness apparently deeply embedded in the American soul, the pervasive influence of population mobility can not be denied. Indeed, Professor George W. Pierson has argued that the "moving American" has so profoundly molded folkways that society has become stabilized in its own instability.[1]

Despite this broad recognition of the importance of population mobility, the precise nature, extent, and significance of American restlessness remains unplumbed. Perhaps this is because most scholars have generalized from published census data. They have supposed that communities with a fairly constant population from census to census were relatively stable entities. But this is not necessarily the case. For behind this facade of apparent demographic stability lurk hitherto unsuspected degrees of population mobility. They are of primary significance to an understanding of American social history. Conditions in Grant County, Wisconsin, in the late nineteenth century substantiate this assertion.

[1] George Wilson Pierson, "The Moving American," *Yale Review*, XLIV (1954), 99–112.

Bounded by Illinois to the south and by the Mississippi and Wisconsin rivers to the west and north, Grant County grew, according to the published census records, from some 31,000 inhabitants in 1860 to almost 39,000 in 1900.[2] The county's modest annual growth rate of a mere 0.7 per cent reflected, apparently, the gradual stabilization of the jurisdiction's economy. Lead mining, which was the initial catalyst in the region's pre-Civil War development, was gradually supplanted in importance by pioneer farming. By the last quarter of the nineteenth century a relatively prosperous and stable agricultural economy was firmly established. Thus, Grant County appears as a classic example of Turner's concept of the stage-like growth of frontier communities. Each phase of development was seemingly reflected in a rising level of economic and demographic stability.

An examination of the demographies of five of the county's thirty-one townships, however, reveals considerable disparity in growth rates. Between 1860 and 1890 the population of Bloomington increased at about the same rate as the county, twenty-five per cent, but Cassville almost doubled in size, and Muscoda increased by nearly 80 per cent. The two other townships, Hazel Green and Potosi, declined, the first by more than half, the second only slightly. With the exception of Hazel Green, all five townships grew sharply in the sixties but either declined or expanded slowly during the final three decades of the nineteenth century. The reader of the *published* census data, therefore, might be excused for supposing that after 1870 these were lethargic communities which had reached their point of maximum growth. For apparently these townships could anticipate little further expansion until the introduction of fundamental changes in the agricultural arts, or until industrialization injected a dynamic new factor into their economies.

The villages within these five townships exhibited an equally striking pattern of demographic disparity. Differences stemmed primarily from their social and economic individuality. Hazel Green and Bloomington were located in the interior of the county, one in

[2] The mobility data which follow have been compiled from the Ms Tenth Census of the United States, 1880, Schedule One, Grant County, Wisconsin Volume; and Ms Wisconsin Census, 1885 and 1895, Heads of Households, Grant County.

the southeast, the other in the west central. Each served the needs of a flourishing agricultural region. Though Bloomington, ethnically the most American of the five villages, was only a few miles beyond the northern extremity of the lead region, neither its original location nor its subsequent growth depended upon the mining industry. Rather, small enterprises such as an iron foundry, a regional bank, meat-packing houses, and butter-making plants enabled the village to grow, if only slowly, between 1870 and 1900.[3] By contrast, Hazel Green, a community with a fairly large contingent of British-born residents, declined rapidly when the lead mining industry which had formerly sustained it began to falter. Its population fell from 723 in 1870 to only 442 in 1900. A similar fate might well have overtaken Potosi, which had also enjoyed a lively though brief prosperity from its lead deposits, had it not been for the brewery established by the Barvarian, Gabriel Hail, in 1855. By 1880 it was a substantial enterprise with a capital of more than $10,000 and an extensive physical plant. Nevertheless, population declined from 466 in 1880 to 434 in 1900.[4] Cassville and Muscoda owed their initial growth to their favorable locations, the one on the Mississippi between Dubuque and Prairie du Chien, the other on the Wisconsin. Transportation was the key to Muscoda's success. Until the construction of a railroad in 1856, a ferry across the Wisconsin, and later a bridge, the village faced an apparently gloomy future. Completion of these improvements, however, enabled the village to extend its interests into Richland and Iowa counties, and enlarged the prosperous agricultural region it served. However, the limits of growth were reached soon after the Civil War. Despite an increase in the number of families of Bohemian origin in the eighties, between 1880 and 1900 village population remained static at about 743 inhabitants.[5] Like Muscoda, Cassville quickly pre-empted a hinterland which it provided with transportation, banking, and mercantile services. The

[3] See Schedules One, Three, and Five to Nine, Grant County, Wisconsin Volume, Ms Industrial Census of the United States, 1880; Bloomington's population grew from 364 inhabitants in 1870 to 611 in 1900.

[4] Compare Anonymous, *History of Grant County, Wisconsin* (Chicago, 1881), p. 768, and Costello N. Holford, *History of Grant County, Wisconsin* (Lancaster, 1900), p. 538.

[5] Joseph Schafer, *The Wisconsin Lead Region* (Madison, 1932), pp. 195–196.

firm of Klindt, Geiger and Company was the largest and most successful. It transacted banking business for its customers, sometimes with banks in northern Illinois or eastern Iowa; it held the local agency for the K. N. L. Packet Company's paddle steamers plying the Mississippi; it conducted a real estate business; it operated as a grain and livestock broker; and it sold general merchandise both at retail and at wholesale.[6] Cassville also benefited from railroad construction in the upper Mississippi Valley. But unlike Muscoda, it continued to grow after the Civil War. Partly because of continued German immigration, village population rose from 551 in 1870 to 979 in 1900.

These differences in locale and social and economic structure help to explain the demographic disparities both between the several towns and between the several villages. They also help to account for differences in the growth rates of the various county communities. With the exception of Hazel Green, where urban population declined more rapidly than rural population, between 1870 and 1900 most villages increased their proportion of the townships' total populations. Thus the proportion of the township population residing in the village of Bloomington rose from 29 per cent in 1870 to 49 per cent in 1900. Urban growth in Cassville was less marked but was nevertheless significant. The proportion of village population rose from 40 to 60 per cent. The change in Muscoda and Potosi, by contrast, was very slight. But in no case is there any evidence of a direct correlation between urban and rural growth rates. Villages did not expand at the expense of townships, and townships, did not, even in the case of Hazel Green, drain village populations.

There is nothing particularly striking or noteworthy about these demographic patterns. Changes from decade to decade were modest and entirely unspectacular. Indeed, with local variations in the pattern, these undramatic population changes could probably be duplicated throughout the rural Midwest in the late nineteenth century. Seemingly, an era of rapid economic growth had ended and a relatively mature and stable agricultural economy had come into being.

[6] See Ms Otto F. Geiger Papers, State Historical Society of Wisconsin. Many of the firm's brokerage connections were with St. Louis.

TABLE 11–1

ORIGINAL FAMILIES REMAINING IN SELECTED VILLAGES IN GRANT COUNTY,
WISCONSIN, 1880–1895

	Number of Original Families, 1880	Number of Original Families Reported in 1885 Census, and Percentage Remaining	Number of Original Families Reported in 1895 Census, and Percentage Remaining
Bloomington	98	58 (59.2)	32 (32.7)
Cassville	132	63 (47.7)	39 (29.6)
Hazel Green	151	57 (37.6)	29 (19.2)
Muscoda	156	54 (34.6)	17 (10.9)
Potosi	100	47 (47.0)	20 (20.0)
TOTALS	637	279 (43.8)	137 (21.5)

However, when the outer shell is stripped away from the *published* data these Wisconsin communities assume a wholly different character. For the *manuscript* census records show that seemingly stolid and static villages were, in reality, undergoing processes of change perhaps only somewhat less dynamic than Turner's fresh-born frontier outposts. The level of emigration from, and immigration to, Grant County villages was strikingly higher than students have supposed. Indeed, the exodus was so great between 1880 and 1895 that villages maintained their spurious facades of stability only by virtue of an influx of residents sufficient to conceal the high level of emigration.

More than half (56 per cent) of all the households reported in the five villages in 1880 had disappeared from the census rolls by 1885. Almost four-fifths (78 per cent) of the original families were likewise not reported ten years later in 1895. As Table 11–1 demonstrates, the two villages which grew most substantially, Bloomington and Cassville, retained the highest proportion of households. Nevertheless, the turnover was extremely high. Bloomington lost over 40 per cent of its families between 1880 and 1885. By 1895 only one-third of the original families were still residents of the village. During the same period the community had grown from 403 to 552 inhabitants or by almost 37 per cent. Though Cassville grew even more rapidly in the fifteen years after 1880, by 52 per cent, it retained an even smaller proportion of its residents than Bloomington. Almost half of its families were lost over the first five years and a further 18 per cent from 1885 to 1895. In all, over 70 per cent of Cassville's original households were disbanded. Muscoda and Potosi, whose total populations were virtually the same in 1880 and 1895, fared even worse. Muscoda lost almost two-thirds (65 per cent) of its families between 1880 and 1885, and by 1895 almost nine-tenths (89 per cent) of the original families were no longer reported in the census. Potosi was somewhat more successful than Muscoda in retaining its households intact. Even so, over half the families (53 per cent) had disappeared from the census rolls by 1885, and by 1895 the proportion had risen to four-fifths. Hazel Green also lost a high proportion of its original households. Over three-fifths (62 per cent) disappeared during the first five years. By 1895 over four-fifths or 81 per cent of the households were no longer located in the village. Thus Hazel Green, though its population declined by about a quarter during the fifteen years from 1880 to 1895, retained a higher portion of its original families than did Muscoda, whose population declined by less than 1 per cent during the same fifteen year period. But whether the villages were growing, static, or declining, the rate of population turnover seems extraordinarily high. Certainly, the published census statistics give no hint of its enormity.

That this situation was not some temporary social aberration or the consequence of a natural or economic disaster can be judged from the behavior of new immigrant families. Households first reported in the census of 1885 proved to be no more stable than the original ones. On the average, barely a fifth of these families located permanently in the village of their choice. Like the original households, there was considerable disparity from community to community. As Table 11–2 shows, Bloomington, Hazel Green, and Potosi retained approximately one family out of four. Cassville, by contrast, retained more than every third family, but Muscoda was able to retain less than one in ten. Thus the facade of demographic stability was again maintained only by new families moving into these villages to replace those who emigrated.

The remarkable degree of population mobility revealed in these Grant County villages at the close of the frontier period of American history calls attention to a number of significant but unexplored problems in American social history. Were these five villages typical of southwestern Wisconsin, of Wisconsin as a whole, of the upper

TABLE 11–2

IMMIGRANT FAMILIES REMAINING IN SELECTED VILLAGES IN GRANT COUNTY,
WISCONSIN, 1885–1895

	Number of Immigrant Families, 1885	Number of Immigrant Families Reported in 1895 Census, and Percentage Remaining	Number of New Families Reported in 1895 Census
Bloomington	89	23 (25.8)	78
Cassville	75	27 (36.0)	187
Hazel Green	51	12 (23.5)	73
Muscoda	171	17 (9.9)	77
Potosi	49	11 (22.5)	69
TOTALS	435	90 (20.7)	484

Middle West, or of rural America generally in the late nineteenth century? Did these migratory families eventually send down roots elsewhere? Or did they continue to move from village to village, never staying anywhere long enough to contribute more than a transient's mite to the community's culture or economy? Where had the families come from that arrived after 1880? What were they seeking? Why were they attracted to Grant County? Why did they leave again? Were they simply touched by a restlessness, even an aimlessness, that always militated against permanent settlement? A number of factors working either independently or in conjunction with each other probably explain the pattern of movement.[7]

The overriding consideration appears to be the region's economic sluggishness. Once the initial phases of development had been completed—once the lead deposits had been exhausted and the land had been broken in to farming—the economy was incapable of expanding rapidly enough to absorb the natural increase of population. In varying degrees, therefore, each community was subjected to the pull of external forces.

The free land of the frontier, for example, may have been a potent lure. Undoubtedly Turner was premature in supposing that the frontier as he understood it had closed. His revisionists have been quick to point to the vast acreage that was settled after 1890 and to the fact that the rate of land entry was, if anything, rising in the last

[7] Records in the custody of the Grant County Registrar of Deeds, and headstones in the Bloomington village cemetery, show that death accounted for only a minor fraction of the families whose names disappeared from the census rolls.

decade of the nineteenth century. Nevertheless, even if the frontier were to have closed at some point later than the data presented here, these villages were too remote from the public land that was being settled in the eighties and nineties to account for more than a fraction of the undercurrent of restlessness abroad in Grant County. Some families, successful no less than unsuccessful, emigrated to Iowa, Nebraska, or to the Dakotas, but they were petty merchants, artisans, and laborers rather than land seekers. Like those who replaced them in Wisconsin, their interests were urban, not rural. And since the county's farming economy had already become stabilized at a mature level, it is unlikely that Turner's idea of pioneer farmers being displaced by later waves of immigrants provides an explanation. For only a modest amount of land changed hands in the county in the eighties and nineties. Of course, Turner's apologists might argue that frontier habits died hard, that this restlessness reflected a deeply ingrained American tradition. But the rate of mobility appears to be too high to be explained by mere habit. And since immigrant groups were as deeply affected as native-born settlers, they could only have acquired the habit with indecent rapidity.

A more plausible explanation seems to lie in the unsettling influence of the profound social and economic transformation sweeping America in the late nineteenth century. Industrialization, urbanization, the influx of new ethnic groups, and the exodus from the farms both contributed to and were a product of this revolution. Nearby urban centers, such as the county seat of Lancaster, or the Iowa commercial center of Dubuque, exerted the strongest attraction; but Grant County villages were also within the orbit of cities like Chicago, Milwaukee, Madison, and Minneapolis-St. Paul. Thus migratory families, having concluded that these economically static Grant County villages held out little hope for the realization of the American dream, sought security or status elsewhere. Their places were taken by new families who, before long, met with similar disappointments. And so the pattern was repeated. There is some evidence to substantiate this view. Most of the original families which emigrated, or the new families which replaced them, owned, bought, or acquired little taxable property. The households were generally headed by men of little substance and, frequently, of limited skill. They were wage-earners rather than petty entrepreneurs and they found opportunities for newcomers severely limited. Most well-established mercantile or professional families, by contrast, made no attempt to move, even when business slackened, though their children sometimes moved away, generally to small western towns where they engaged in such crafts as blacksmithing and wagonmaking or became dealers in hardware and dry goods.

Five villages constitute too small an example to have intrinsic meaning, nor has a control sample been studied. Comparisons are therefore impossible at this time. Nevertheless, the Grant County data suggest that a whole chapter of American social history remains to be explored. Until that is done, the nature and meaning of a vital segment of the American history will continue to be an enigma.

Reprinted from the *Wisconsin Magazine of History*, XLVI (1962), 16–20.

VI

GOVERNMENT AND POLITICS

Part VI
Government and Politics

It was in the realm of government and politics that the issues of community-building became most explicit. Under the Northwest Ordinance, the autonomous powers of self-government were severely circumscribed; moreover, Congress mandated the basic legal framework within which community-building proceeded—laws governing land disposal, resource use, migration, and so on. Even at the threshold of statehood, the proposed state constitution had to be submitted to Congress for approval. But the people of the Old Northwest never accepted passively their formal status as "colonials." Conflict frequently marked relations between the territorial legislatures and the Federal governors and judges; and the western citizenry kept up continual pressure for such policy concessions as liberalization of land laws and Congressional subsidies for internal improvements. The territorial statutes, petitions to Congress from the territorial legislatures and from settlers, and expressions of western opinion in newspapers of the region all provided striking evidence of tension between the governors and the governed. Though often divided among themselves on specific questions, the people of the Old Northwest were always alert to the fundamental issue: What kind of political and social order should be built?[1]

Once statehood had been achieved, westerners' autonomy over their own affairs was, of course, considerably increased. But still Federal-regional tensions persisted. To achieve some of their most

[1] See the monumental collection edited by Clarence E. Carter, *Territorial Papers of the United States* (Washington, 1934–   ). The richest case study available, illustrating the Federal-regional dimension of territorial politics, is Howard R. Lamar, *Dakota Territory, 1861–1889* (New Haven, 1956). Also valuable are two other studies of a region outside the one here considered: Robert W. Johannsen, *Frontier Politics and the Sectional Conflict: The Pacific Northwest on the Eve of the Civil War* (Seattle, 1955); and Earl Pomeroy, *The Pacific Slope: A History of California, Oregon, Washington, Idaho, Utah, and Nevada* (New York, 1965).

important policy goals, western men remained dependent upon action by Congress—most notably, expensive river and harbor improvements, roads, and canals were still beyond the fiscal resources of the younger states. As long as frontier defense remained a problem, Federal military installations and troops were essential; and even when development passed beyond the frontier phase, Federal land law governed the pace and quality of new settlement within state borders.

The informal political process also reflected the complexities of Federal-regional relationships. Organized political parties in the Old Northwest necessarily dealt in issues of local importance, but the need to maintain cohesiveness within the national organization often became a constraint on freedom of action in the state political arena —just as was true of local parties in the eastern states. On the other hand, special-interest groups in the West (and also the West as a whole, on issues that were sectional in character) tried to work through the national parties to achieve their aims.[2]

Historians in the Turnerian tradition have stressed still another dimension of western politics: that of ideology. Turner argued that "the West believed in the rule of the majority," whereas the East was more conservative and feared "an unchecked democracy." Moreover, he asserted that there was a fundamental continuity in the history of "pioneer ideals." From the early days of teiritorial politics, when a Jeffersonian faction first emerged in Ohio, through the period of antislavery agitation in the Old Northwest, and on through the Granger, Populist, and Progressive periods, egalitarian-democratic ideals continually conditioned western politics.[3] All these movements, Turner argued, derived their strength from the democratic faith that had first been articulated and acted out in the West; and that faith was the product of the frontier environment.

Turner himself conceded that sometimes he drew "too sharply contrasted a picture" as between eastern and western political

<hr>

[2] See Eugene E. Roseboom, *The Civil War Era, 1850–1873* ("History of the State of Ohio," ed. Carl Wittke, IV [Columbus, 1944]), 219–372; and Don E. Fehrenbacher, *Prelude to Greatness: Lincoln in the 1850's* (New York, 1964).

[3] F. J. Turner, *Frontier and Section*, ed. Ray Billington (Englewood Cliffs, N.J., 1961), p. 116. See also *ibid.*, pp. 154 ff.

ideals.[4] The four essays that follow illustrate well the multiple facets
of western politics that Turner thus recognized but never stressed in
his own studies. The first essay, by Merton Lynn Dillon of Northern
Illinois University, a leading student of American abolitionism, lends
no support to the Turnerian notion of a peculiarly western radical
ideology as the basis of abolitionist sentiment. (Indeed, it would be
most surprising to find such evidence in Illinois, where settlers from
the South left a heavy imprint on politics and where slavery itself
long persisted under the guise of "voluntary" indentured servitude,
despite the terms of the Northwest Ordinance.) Instead, Professor
Dillon portrays a strikingly *illiberal* vision of community goals, as
expressed by some articulate citizens of Illinois: they supported
Negro colonization not so much because they detested slavery on
egalitarian grounds as because they hoped thereby to expel an
undesirable element from their community.[5] Also, we find that
national antislavery groups sent into the West their field agents to
build support for their programs; and all the diverse strains of the
Illinois movement were affected by the need to adjust reformist
hopes to political realities.[6]

This is not to say that Illinois lacked any radical tradition. For in
Professor Stanley L. Jones's essay on the 1862 constitutional convention is ample evidence that ideology was sometimes a critical factor
in politics. The 1862 division pitted one group which (in terms much
like those Turner described as typically "western," and which are
recognizable in any case as "Jacksonian") denounced "chartered
monopolies" and "monied aristocrats," against an opposing group
that was pushing for a "Whiggish" constitution that would expedite
rapid economic development. But ideology did not tell the whole
tale. There was also a north-south regional split in Illinois that over-
lay the ideological division, with Chicago's interests standing as a

[4] *Ibid.*, p. 117.

[5] On a similar theme, see David B. Davis, "Some Themes of Counter-subversion:
An Analysis of Anti-Masonic, Anti-Catholic, and Anti-Mormon Literature,"
MVHR, XLVII (September, 1960), 205–224.

[6] For an exposition of the view that the Old Northwest founded antislavery, see
Dwight L. Dumond, *Antislavery Origins of the Civil War in the United States* (Ann
Arbor, 1939), chap. vii. But see also Avery Craven's provocative analysis, in *The
Coming of the Civil War* (rev. ed.; Chicago, 1966), chaps. xiii–xiv; and Louis Filler,
The Crusade Against Slavery (New York, 1960).

distinct third party to intrastate regional disputes. In any event, one still needs to ask whether the Jacksonian-agrarian view was as uniquely "western" as Turner averred.[7]

In his essay on opposition to President Lincoln's war policies in the Old Northwest, Professor Frank L. Klement of Marquette University similarly stresses the vital role of ideology, tempered by regional self-consciousness. Klement demonstrates that Jacksonian ideals and western suspicion of modern industrialism formed a bridge between the politics of the 1830's and events of the Granger era after the Civil War. But his analysis also makes clear that the persistent appeal of agrarian ideals was closely linked to specific regional problems and concrete economic payoffs—such questions as the freight rates that westerners must pay the railroads, or how much corporate, absentee control of their community life westerners were prepared to accept as the cost of growth. One cannot lose sight of the anti-war or anti-Negro motivations of some Copperhead leaders; but Professor Klement indicates that the context of the movement was in large measure pro-western and not exclusively pro-southern.[8]

The study of the "Wisconsin Idea" by Vernon Carstensen, professor of history in the University of Washington, carries us to the era when the modern industrial economy so feared by the Illinois "agrarians" in 1862 had already triumphed in the region. By the late 1890's, it was no longer an open question whether the Old Northwest should be assimilated into industrial America: the region already was producing a fourth of the nation's manufacturing output and had a fourth of its manufacturing employees. But how the people of the

[7] Recent interpretive controversies are reviewed in Alfred A. Cave, *Jacksonian Democracy and the Historians* (University of Florida Monographs: Social Sciences, No. 22 [Gainesville, 1964]); see also Chester McA. Destler, *American Radicalism, 1865–1901* (Chicago, 1966), pp. 1–31.

[8] Some important re-evaluations of sectionalism and party, based largely on study of Congressional roll calls, are: Glenn Linden, "Radicals and Economic Policies: The Senate, 1861–1873," *Journal of Southern History*, Vol. XXXII (1966); Linden, "Radicals and Economic Policies: The House of Representatives, 1861–1873," *Civil War History*, Vol. XIII (1967); and Allan G. Bogue, "Bloc and Party in the United States Senate, 1861–1863," *ibid.*, Vol. XIII (1967). See also the revisionist study by David Donald, *The Politics of Reconstruction, 1863–1867* (Baton Rouge, 1965); and J. Voegeli, "The Northwest and the Race Issue, 1861–1862," *MVHR*, Vol. L (1963).

region could maintain control over the new industrial order was a question by no means settled.

As Turner recognized, the principal trend in western politics during the 1880's and 1890's was toward increased use of government as an instrument of social control, even at the expense of individualistic mores.[9] The most important innovations of the period were associated with the "Wisconsin Idea," during Robert M. La Follette's governorship in Wisconsin. La Follette made his state government what Theodore Roosevelt termed "literally a laboratory for wise experimental legislation." Wisconsin government mobilized the expertise of modern science and pioneered in social engineering, to match development in the private sector with equally powerful instruments of control. The La Follette era fascinated Turner mainly because it seemed to mark a new beginning in western politics, closing out the tradition of pioneer-style individualism and parochialism. "Even Western states like Wisconsin," he wrote, were sending commissions to England and the European Continent "to study their systems of taxation, workingmen's insurance, old age pensions," and the like.[10] Such alien ideas had become acceptable in the West, Turner postulated, partly because of urgent new requirements—but also because heavy infusions of European immigration had tempered traditional western politics, for the Europeans were accustomed to active, large-scale government. Thus Turner came to modify his portrait of fundamental continuity in "pioneer ideals" from early western beginnings to the Progressive era. Ironically, Professor Carstensen makes a persuasive case for understanding the Wisconsin Idea in more indigenous terms, finding its origins in the history of the state's own system of higher education and in university extension work that dated from the 1860's.

[9] Turner, *Frontier and Section*, pp. 161–162.
[10] *Ibid.*, p. 101.

MERTON LYNN DILLON

12. The Antislavery Movement in Illinois: 1824–1835

THE proposal made in 1823 to call a state constitutional convention precipitated a full-scale antislavery movement in Illinois. Since it was popularly believed that the purpose of holding the convention was to legalize slavery in the state, the months before the vote on the question witnessed an intensive and searching discussion of the merits of Negro slavery. Practically every religious, moral, economic and political argument that was ever to be presented against that institution was heard during those years. Antislavery pamphlets and antislavery newspapers were printed; antislavery sermons were delivered and antislavery societies established; eventually the antislavery forces were organizing for direct political action, not only to prevent alteration of the state constitution but also to elect antislavery men to public office.

All of this agitation was vigorous, widespread and effective; but however critical men at that time were of slavery, their avowed purpose was not so much to destroy slavery in the United States as it was to prevent the extension of the slave system into Illinois. On August 2, 1824, the voters by a majority of 1,668 votes decided that the constitution of 1818 should not be revised.[1] For most people in Illinois that vote settled the matter. Having prevented an alteration in their constitution, they ceased their agitation against slavery. Although a letter appearing in the *Edwardsville Spectator* three months later urged Governor Edward Coles to continue to press for the total abolition of the slavery and indentured servitude already existing within the state,[2] and the Baptist Friends of Humanity in their circular address of 1824 warned that "there is still a great deal more

---

[1] Theodore C. Pease (ed.), *Illinois Election Returns, 1818–1848* (Illinois Historical Collections, XVIII, Springfield, 1923), 27. The vote was 6,640 to 4,972.
[2] *Edwardsville Spectator*, November 2, 1824.

to do," [3] the political leaders in Illinois took little aggressive action against slavery during the next decade.

To be sure, Governor Coles—though quite without success—continued his efforts to abolish the state's indenture system by which Negroes were bound to labor for periods far exceeding the normal life span of a human being. His messages of November 16, 1824 and December 5, 1826 [4] were ignored. Indeed, the General Assembly appeared to be solidly in favor of retaining the current conditions regarding slavery and indentured servitude. The antislavery bloc which had existed in the Assembly in the years immediately before 1824 had practically disappeared as an effective force two years later. In the Assembly elections of 1826, such stalwart anticonventionists as Jacob Ogle, John Messinger, Daniel Stookey, William H. Bradsby, Daniel Parker, Moses Lemen and Augustus Collins were defeated. [5] The most active of the anticonventionists withdrew from public life. Hooper Warren sold the antislavery *Edwardsville Spectator* and moved north to sparsely settled Sangamon County, where his influence was small indeed. [6] Morris Birkbeck, the antislavery pamphleteer, was drowned in 1825 while fording a river on his way home to Wanborough from a visit with Robert Owen at New Harmony, Indiana. [7] Governor Coles, in view of the antipathy he had aroused among his powerful political opponents, could do little else than retire from public life. [8] A declining interest in slavery was evident even among the Baptist Friends of Humanity, the only religious sect in Illinois which had thus far taken a united stand against it. After 1826, their

[3] *Ibid.*, September 14, 1824.

[4] Illinois, General Assembly, Senate, *Journal, 1824*, 1st Sess. (Vandalia, 1824), p. 16; *ibid.*, 1826, pp. 21–22.

[5] Pease, *Illinois Election Returns*, pp. 219–220, 226–227.

[6] Warren to Ninian Edwards, March 24, 1828, *The Edwards Papers*, ed. E. B. Washburne ("Chicago Historical Society Collections," Vol. III [Chicago, 1884]), p. 330.

[7] *Dictionary of American Biography*. Hereafter cited as *DAB*.

[8] Coles was considered a candidate for the Senate in 1826, but lost to Elias Kent Kane. Theodore C. Pease, *The Frontier State, 1818–1848* ("Centennial History of Illinois," II [Chicago, 1919]), 124–125. In 1831 he ran for representative in Congress and lost to Joseph Duncan, receiving but 14 per cent of the votes cast. Pease, *Illinois Election Returns*, pp. 70–73.

energies were diverted to other reforms and to other religious interests.[9]

But the citizens of Illinois were not quite so uniformly unconcerned about slavery during the decade following the convention controversy as the record of their official bodies might indicate. Although the crusading drive against slavery was notably lacking from 1824 to 1835, the issue was at no time lost sight of nor did opposition to the continued existence of slavery completely disappear. The nature of the population made that impossible. Many persons had come to Illinois even before 1824 specifically because they wished to escape from a slave society.[10] It was not to be expected that they should have welcomed proposals to make Illinois a slave state in 1824 or, after having defeated those plans, that they should have completely ignored the fact that slavery still existed.

The Presbyterians of Shoal Creek in Bond County, who in 1824 had opposed the movement to amend the state constitution,[11] had migrated to Illinois from South Carolina after a period of living among antislavery groups in Ohio.[12] By 1831, they were issuing violent denunciations of slavery and of the Presbyterian Church for failing to take a determined stand against it.[13] By 1835, one of their number, William M. Stewart, was included among the foremost abolitionists in the state, if not in the nation.[14]

Methodist circuit riders, many of whom had but recently arrived from slave states, continued to present their listeners with charges of the iniquities of slavery much as their colleagues had done during

[9] William W. Sweet (ed.), *The Baptists, 1783–1830* ("Religion on the American Frontier," I [New York, 1931]), 99–101.

[10] Arthur C. Boggess, *The Settlement of Illinois, 1778–1830* ("Chicago Historical Society Collections," V [Chicago, 1908]), 91–92; W. P. Strickland (ed.), *Autobiography of Peter Cartwright, the Backwoods Preacher* (New York, 1857), p. 168; James Leaton, *History of Methodism in Illinois from 1793 to 1832* (Cincinnati, 1883), p. 31; *Edwardsville Spectator*, April 12, 1823; Chicago *Western Citizen*, December 30, 1842; Carrie P. Kofoid, *Puritan Influences in the Formative Years of Illinois History* (Springfield, 1906), p. 25.

[11] Pease, *Illinois Election Returns*, p. 27.

[12] Wilbur H. Siebert, *The Underground Railroad from Slavery to Freedom* (New York, 1898), p. 14.

[13] Vandalia *Illinois Intelligencer*, February 19, 1831.

[14] See his speech to the General Assembly of the Presbyterian Church, in the *Liberator*, June 7, 1835.

the convention controversy.[15] The Rev. Peter Cartwright, the best known of all early Illinois preachers, came to the state in 1824 from the South to escape from slavery.[16] In 1825, the Rev. George Locke was transferred from the Kentucky Conference to the Illinois Conference because of his dislike for slavery.[17] The Rev. Jesse Haile of Tennessee, who preached in Illinois intermittently before 1827 and regularly after that time, was a reader of the antislavery *Genius of Universal Emancipation* and distributed that journal in the South when he took a trip to Texas.[18] In 1831, the Rev. John Sinclair, a circuit rider in the Kentucky Conference, asked to be transferred to Illinois in order to live in a free state.[19] Many Methodists in Illinois in the years after 1824 must, therefore, have listened to men like the Rev. Peter Axley, who is said often to have preached in Illinois against the "trinity of devils"—"superfluous dress, whisky, and slavery."[20]

The effect of antislavery preaching on Methodist laymen during this period of supposed apathy on the question of slavery was sufficient to make them so sensitive to the subject that the introduction of the issue of slavery into political campaigns was sometimes urged in order to sway Methodist votes.[21] It is true that the Illinois Conference of the Methodist Episcopal Church long remained noncommital on the subject, and that the internal harmony of the Methodist churches in Illinois was never seriously disturbed by discussions of the merits of slavery. But not even the rather conservative Illinois Conference could altogether avoid the complications produced by slavery; nor could it remain totally unaffected by the all-pervading influence of the developing cleavage between the free and the slave states.

[15] For Methodist circuit rider activity in 1823, see *Illinois Intelligencer*, July 5, August 23, 1823.

[16] *DAB.*

[17] Leaton, *Methodism in Illinois*, pp. 284–285.

[18] Thomas Earle, *The Life, Travels and Opinions of Benjamin Lundy* (Philadelphia, 1847), p. 244.

[19] Stephen R. Beggs, *Pages from the Early History of the West and North-west* (Cincinnati, 1868), pp. 306–307.

[20] Cartwright, *Autobiography*, p. 95.

[21] Ninian Edwards to Cyrus and Benjamin Edwards, July 15, 1830, *Edwards Papers*, pp. 530–531.

In the session of the Illinois Conference held in Edwardsville in October, 1828, the subject of co-operating with the Missouri Annual Conference in establishing a Methodist seminary for the West was considered. The arrangement committee appointed by the Illinois Conference was composed of John Dew, Peter Cartwright and John Strange, of whom the first two are known to have possessed anti-slavery sentiments.[22] The two conferences having agreed on a plan of operation, two sites were suggested for the seminary: Lebanon, in northeastern St. Clair County in Illinois, and Mount Salubria, a village in Missouri. When the vote on selecting the site was taken, it was found that Mount Salubria had been chosen. The Illinois Conference then voted to reconsider the favorable report of the joint committee, which it had previously approved, recommending co-operation with the Missouri Conference. It now refused to adopt the proposed plan.[23] According to an early historian of the Methodist Church of Illinois, this procedure was prompted by the unwillingness of the Illinois Methodists to support a seminary located in a slave state. Peter Cartwright is said to have declared, in what must for him have been the ultimate expression of disapproval, that he would rather send his children to a Calvinistic school than to one in a slave state.[24]

Not only did people in Illinois feel impelled to continue their opposition to slavery in the abstract; to an increasing extent after 1824 they were aware of the problems arising from the presence in their own state of a by-product of the slave system, the free Negro. The census of 1820 recorded 457 free Negroes in Illinois. By 1830 their number had increased to 1,637, and by 1840 to 3,598.[25] Free Negroes were in constant peril of being kidnapped and returned to slavery in the South,[26] a fact as certain to arouse the sympathy of humanitarians as the very presence of the growing population of free Negroes was certain to arouse the misgivings of others. Given this

[22] Washington, D.C., *African Repository and Colonial Journal*, IX (1833–34), 217; *DAB*.

[23] "The Journals of the Illinois Conference, 1824–1831," in William Warren Sweet (ed.), *The Methodists, 1783–1840* ("Religion on the American Frontier," IV [Chicago, 1946]), 305–306, 311, 321, 326–327, 329, 333–334, 336.

[24] Leaton, *Methodism in Illinois*, pp. 306–307.

[25] *Seventh Census of the U.S.:. 1850* (Washington, 1853), p. 719.

[26] *Edwardsville Spectator*, September 21, October 12, 1822.

situation, it was only natural that such active opposition to slavery as existed after the defeat of the convention proposal should have been absorbed in measures for colonizing free Negroes. Actually, however, interest in colonization was not a new development in Illinois. As early as 1817, a territorial newspaper had given publicity to the activities of a colonization society in the East;[27] and Daniel Pope Cook, Illinois' second representative to Congress, when speaking to a committee of the House of Representatives on the Missouri Compromise, had endorsed colonization societies as "sound" and emancipation accompanied by colonization as the only proper solution to the racial problem in the United States.[28]

Opposition to slavery in Illinois before 1835 was expressed in a colonization movement, but sentiment for Negro colonization, as is well known, is not always to be equated with sentiment against slavery itself.[29] Prejudice against free Negroes was high in Illinois and was a powerful motive working in favor of colonization. One of the reasons William Bradsby had given in the Illinois territorial legislature in 1817 for advocating the repeal of the indenture laws was that he wished to prevent the accumulation of free Negroes in Illinois which he believed must result from that "cob web of legislation."[30] The suggestion that free Negroes be sent out of the United States also attracted the interest of many of the men who had been devoted opponents of the convention.[31]

The attempt to introduce slavery into Illinois in 1824 had been resisted for a variety of reasons. Among the most powerful had been the belief that slavery was contrary to the law of God and to the principles of the Declaration of Independence. But mingled with that conviction had been a genuine distrust of the Negro race. One of the strongest arguments used against extending slavery to Illinois had been that the slave population of the United States must in the fullness of time rise in revolt against its white masters. Morris

[27] Kaskasia *Western Intelligencer*, January 15, 1817.

[28] *Edwardsville Spectator*, May 16, 1820.

[29] The most vigorous modern indictment of the colonization movement is in Dwight L. Dumond, *Antislavery Origins of the Civil War in the U.S.* (Ann Arbor, 1939), pp. 10–20.

[30] *Western Intelligencer*, December 18, 1817.

[31] *Illinois Intelligencer*, March 19, 1831; Vandalia *Illinois Advocate*, January 19, 1833.

Birkbeck's distrust of Negroes arose from his belief that they were depraved and dangerous. He attributed their evil character, however, to the fact that they lived in a state of slavery.[32] Some persons, on the other hand, assumed that Negroes were inherently inferior to members of the white race and therefore constituted a menace to the society of the United States.

Such racial prejudice continued to operate in the General Assembly. Early in 1829, that body passed a law designed to prevent the further settlement of free Negroes in the state. The committee in the senate which considered the bill recognized slavery to be a "national calamity, and slavery in any form as contrary to the genius of our government." It also reported, however, that the residence of Negroes in Illinois even when they were controlled as slaves was "productive of moral and political evil," and free Negroes the committee considered to be still "more objectionable." "The natural difference between them and ourselves," the committee continued, "forbids the idea that they should ever be permitted to participate with us in the political affairs of our government." It therefore recommended that means be found to free all of the slaves in the country and transport them to Africa.[33]

One group of men in Illinois, then, favored colonization because it would rid the country of an undesirable racial element. Another group, however, regarded colonization as a means of extending humanitarian aid to an unfortunate part of the population. Indeed, so far as such people were concerned, the colonization phase of the antislavery movement had its origin in the same benevolent, religious spirit which had prompted the clergy and church members to work in opposition to the convention proposal in 1823 and 1824. In the 1826 circular letter of the Friends of Humanity, the Rev. George Clark was enthusiastic about colonization. This approval was clearly associated with a genuine hatred of slavery. His deep moral convictions on the subject could not be altered by any apology or justification the slave owner might offer. Dismissing as the most blatant hypocrisy all statements made by church members that they treated their slaves well, worked them moderately, and neither

[32] *Edwardsville Spectator*, November 8, 1823.

[33] Illinois, General Assembly, Senate, *Journal, 1828* (Kaskaskia, 1829), pp. 182–183.

bought nor sold them, he insisted that the laws of God required not merely the kind treatment of slaves but rather the complete abandonment of slavery.[34]

These two beliefs—(1) that slavery was an iniquitous system by which human beings had been wronged and corrupted and (2) that the nature of Negroes made them a dangerous element in the population—led to proposals in Illinois that the Negroes of the United States be returned to Africa.

The humanitarians' approval of colonization was ordinarily given only upon the condition that colonization be voluntary.[35] In contrast, those persons who hated free Negroes simply because they were Negroes were quite willing to support compulsory deportation. Probably few persons in the 1820's recognized that the colonization of free Negroes might be operating as a means of safeguarding slavery; yet some men in Illinois at an early date concluded that the colonization of the Negro population was perhaps not the most humane method of solving the problems of slavery. On December 9, 1824, the resolutions of the Ohio legislature recommending to the states and Congress a system of emancipation by which freedom would be granted to all slaves at the age of twenty-one upon the condition that they accept transportation to Africa were reported in the Illinois House of Representatives. Risdon Moore, Sr., speaking for the committee which had considered the Ohio plan, stated that deeply as the committee lamented the existence of slavery and anxious as its members were to effect emancipation they were not willing to approve Ohio's plan of compulsory colonization. It seemed unreasonable to them to impose upon the persons to be emancipated the condition that they consent to be transported to Africa in order to enjoy their freedom. "This at best," wrote Moore, "would seem to be a bad alternative." The committee was "induced to believe that slavery at home would often be preferred to freedom in an unknown and foreign land."[36]

[34] Sweet, *The Baptists*, pp. 595–596. See also address by Benjamin Bond to the Clinton County Colonization Society, in *Illinois Advocate*, July 20, 1833.

[35] *Illinois Intelligencer*, March 19, 1831; Shawneetown *Illinois Gazette*, September 4, 1830.

[36] Illinois, General Assembly, House of Representatives, *Journal, 1824* (Vandalia, 1824), pp. 97–98.

The same sympathies and fears which operated in Illinois had led to the organization of the American Colonization Society in Washington in the winter of 1816–1817.[37] Although the society was eventually to be active in Illinois, the first attempt on the part of a resident of Illinois actually to colonize Negroes was made independently of the national society by George Flower, an immigrant from England.

Flower, one of the founders of the English settlement in Edwards County, was much concerned about the existence of slavery and the problems of the free Negro. As early as 1819, he considered forming a communitarian society modeled on that of the Rappites of New Harmony, Indiana, for the purpose of freeing slaves and employing free Negroes.[38] He was able to carry out his plans at least to the extent of settling some free Negroes on his farm in Edwards County, but opposition to his scheme was so prevalent and the danger of kidnapping of the Negroes so great that he persuaded them to leave Illinois and settle in Haiti. Flower obtained the approval of the President of Haiti for his plan, and on June 8, 1823, the Negroes arrived in Haiti where they were established on a plantation.[39] Letters from Flower's Haitian colony were later printed in the *Illinois Gazette* with a view to encouraging the colonization of other free Negroes in the same place.[40]

The impetus for Flower's second plan for the emancipation of slaves came indirectly from Robert Owen's colony at New Harmony through the person of Frances Wright, who consulted with Flower on the subject at his home. The trustees of the venture were to buy slaves who would work on the lands of the colony at Nashoba in Tennessee until they had repaid their purchase price, at which time they would be freed. George Flower did not remain resident at the colony, but he retained his connection as trustee at least as late as

[37] Early Lee Fox, *The American Colonization Society, 1817–1840* ("Johns Hopkins University Studies in Historical and Political Science," XXXVII [Baltimore, 1919]), 46–50.

[38] William Faux, *Memorable Days in America* ("Early Western Travels," ed. R. G. Thwaites, XI [Cleveland, 1905]), 259.

[39] George Flower, *History of the English Settlement in Edwards County, Illinois* ("Chicago Historical Society Collections," I [Chicago, 1882]), 265–269.

[40] *Illinois Gazette*, August 7, 1824. In the *Edwardsville Spectator* of December 7, 1822, Flower had given publicity to the advantages of Haiti for Negro colonization.

February 1, 1827.[41] The Nashoba colony was soon transformed by Miss Wright from being simply a means of freeing slaves into an experiment designed to provide not merely emancipation for slaves but religious and sexual emancipation for whites as well. As such it failed. In 1830 she acknowledged the collapse of the scheme by taking the Negroes still living at Nashoba to Haiti.[42]

The first Illinois experiments in freeing slaves had obviously been of little success. The more orthodox plans of the American Colonization Society had yet to be tried. The first auxiliary to the national society to be formed in the area was organized at St. Louis in 1825 by the Rev. Salmon Giddings of St. Louis and the Rev. John Mason Peck of Illinois.[43] The St. Louis society was evidently designed to operate in both Missouri and Illinois, for John Mason Peck, then living at Rock Spring in St. Clair County, Illinois, was appointed its agent and representative to the parent society, and Governor Edward Coles was chosen as one of its four vice-presidents.[44] It is uncertain, however, what activities, if any, the society carried on within Illinois.

Even though colonization continued to receive favorable notice in Illinois, no formal colonization society was organized within the state until 1830. No agent for Illinois was provided by the American Colonization Society until the appointment of Josiah F. Polk on July 29, 1829, as agent for Indiana, Illinois, Tennessee and Alabama. Polk made a ten-month tour of the West in 1829–1830 and established state societies in Indiana, Tennessee and Alabama, but he failed to reach Illinois.[45] Nonetheless, the society was not completely lacking in representation in the state. Edward Coles was acting as an informal agent and during the first quarter of 1829 collected $168 in Illinois for the use of the national society.[46]

[41] *New-Harmony Gazette* (New Harmony, Ind.), II (1827), 173, 215.

[42] Arthur E. Bestor, Jr., *Backwoods Utopias* (Philadelphia, 1950), pp. 219–226.

[43] Communication from Peck, February 8, 1856, in William B. Sprague, *Annals of the American Pulpit . . . to the Year 1855* (9 vols.; New York, 1859–1869), IV, 508; *African Repository and Colonial Journal*, II (1826–1827), 120.

[44] Rufus Babcock (ed.), *Forty Years of Pioneer Life: Memoir of John Mason Peck, D. D.* (Philadelphia, 1864), pp. 210–211; *African Repository and Colonial Journal*, II (1826–1827), 63.

[45] *Ibid.*, VI (1830–1831), 71–72, 74.

[46] *Ibid.*, IV (1828–1829), 383.

In 1830, Cyrus Edwards, brother of ex-governor Ninian Edwards, was formally commissioned agent for Illinois. He called a meeting of the citizens of Madison County on July 3, and after explaining the plans of the American Colonization Society to the twenty persons who attended, he organized them into the Madison County Colonization Society, the first in Illinois. Shortly afterward, he assisted in forming the Lebanon Colonization Society of St. Clair County. He then began a tour of the state for the purpose of furthering the cause of colonization. At Belleville in St. Clair County his plans for forming a society were defeated by "the unkind imputations of a prominent individual," but he was listened to by an otherwise sympathetic audience. At Waterloo in Monroe County he spoke on the subject of colonization and developed what he called a "plan of operations" but did not attempt to form a society. He was successful also in forming organizations in Randolph, Clinton, Morgan, Sangamon and Greene counties. Although he met with positive opposition only in Belleville, he reported that there was "much of chilling indifference to encounter." The society could not expect, he said, to receive much in contributions because of the state's sparse population and limited resources.[47]

Cyrus Edwards' crowning achievement as agent was the formation in Vandalia on December 9, 1830, of the Illinois State Colonization Society.[48] In his address at the statehouse preceding the organization of the society, he described the "dangerous and baneful influence on all around them" of free Negroes. The motive for colonization, as he saw it, was to rid the state of a hopelessly inferior people. "No matter how great their industry," he told his audience, "or how abundant their wealth—no matter what their attainments in literature, science or the arts—no matter how correct their deportment or what respect their characters may inspire, they can never, no, never be raised to a footing of equality, not even to a familiar intercourse with the surrounding society!" Of the plan of immediate abolition, which apparently was already being discussed in Illinois, he said, "No wild dream of the wildest enthusiast was ever more extravagant than that of turning loose upon society two

[47] *Ibid.*, VII (1831–1832), 114–115; *The Home Missionary and American Pastor's Journal*, III (New York, 1830–1831), 159.
[48] *Illinois Intelligencer*, March 19, 1831.

millions of blacks, idle and therefore worthless, vicious and therefore dangerous, ignorant and therefore incapable of appreciating and enjoying the blessings of freedom." His appeal was obviously based on racial prejudice and notions of the biological inferiority of the Negro race, but that was not his only argument. Illinois, he said, should support the American Colonization Society for benevolent reasons. Its operations would spread civilization to Africa; more than that, Africa would thereby become both a source of supply and a market for American industry.[49] These varied arguments were compelling enough and resulted in the formation of the Illinois State Colonization Society, whose officers included many of the most prominent men in the state.[50]

Edwards had formed a network of societies in seven counties plus a state society for co-ordinating the work of all. He had apparently created the framework for an effective humanitarian movement; yet almost as soon as he had withdrawn from the field as agent, his organization collapsed. Although in 1831 the Rev. John M. Ellis of Jacksonville, an agent of the American Home Missionary Society, referred to the colonization society of Morgan County as the "most popular society we have,"[51] the situation seems to have been otherwise with the societies Edwards had established elsewhere. When the Rev. James Latta of the Methodist Church was appointed as the American Colonization Society's agent for Illinois late in 1832, he found that many of the societies formed by his predecessor only two years before had ceased to operate. Latta attributed their failure to a lack of popular interest in the project, but he suggested an additional factor in their decline when he reported that he himself had been hindered in beginning his work as agent by the Black Hawk War and a depression during the spring of 1832 which, taken together, had made it impracticable "to say anything on the subject."[52]

He began his agency in earnest in 1833. His first task was to

[49] *African Repository and Colonial Journal*, VII (1831–1832), 97–109.

[50] According to the *Illinois Intelligencer*, March 19, 1831, members included Samuel D. Lockwood, of the Illinois Supreme Court; James Hall, editor of the *Illinois Intelligencer*; Henry Eddy, editor of the *Illinois Gazette*; Joseph Duncan, soon to be governor; A. F. Hubbard, lieutenant governor; Ninian Edwards and Edward Coles, both former governors.

[51] *Home Missionary and American Pastor's Journal*, IV (1831–1832), 84.

[52] *African Repository and Colonial Journal*, IX (1833–1834), 24, 125.

revive the state society. At its January meeting it resumed its work by agreeing to subscribe $100 for ten years to aid in carrying out the plan of Gerrit Smith of New York for transporting Negroes to Africa. Latta organized a new society at Greenville in Bond County. At Carlyle in Clinton County, he revived the society which Edwards had started. He was successful also in re-establishing the lapsed society at Lebanon in St. Clair County. At Belleville, where Edwards had encountered opposition, Latta was able to organize a society with no less a dignitary than Governor John Reynolds as president. He formed other societies in Waterloo, Monroe County; Salem, Marion County; and in Hillsboro, Montgomery County. His efforts were unsuccessful in Macoupin, Macoupin County; in Alton, Madison County; and in Nashville, Washington County. In those places, he left the actual formation to others who were instructed to act when the time seemed more propitious.[53]

Latta reported that he found nearly all ministers favorable to the work of the colonization societies and that most of them had agreed to take collections in their churches on July 4 for the furtherance of the work.[54] Obviously the churches were identifying colonization with the other major reform movements of the day to which they also gave their support. Members of the three major denominations in Illinois—Baptists, Methodists and Presbyterians—approved of colonization at this time. One of the churches officially endorsed it: the Presbytery of Illinois at its meeting of September 18, 1833, passed a resolution expressing its "high approval" of the American Colonization Society and recommended that member churches offer that society their prayers, co-operation, and financial contributions.[55] When the Randolph County Colonization Society was organized at Kaskaskia on August 18, 1830, it listed four ministers among its members.[56] The Rev. John Brich, a Presbyterian, bequeathed five hundred dollars to the American Colonization Society when he died in 1836; Charles R. Matheny, an active Methodist and former circuit rider and an opponent of the convention in 1823–1824, was

[53] Latta's complete report, *ibid.*, pp. 125–126.

[54] *Ibid.*, p. 126.

[55] Minutes of the Presbytery of Illinois, McCormick Theological Seminary, Chicago, II, 69–70.

[56] *Illinois Gazette*, September 4, 1830.

elected president of the Sangamon County Colonization Society in 1833; the Rev. Thomas Lippincott, a Presbyterian who was later to become a fervent abolitionist, was made a life member of the American Colonization Society in 1832.[57]

Although soon after 1830 it was recognized by some people in Illinois that support of colonization represented a safe alternative to abolition,[58] the colonization societies at their formation were not at all the declared foes of abolition which they were to become when antislavery societies were formed in Illinois after 1835. Since people like Thomas Mather, Thomas Lippincott, David Blackwell, Edward Coles, William H. Brown, Moses Lemen and Peter Cartwright, all of whom are known to have been sincerely opposed to slavery, belonged to the colonization societies of Illinois at this period,[59] one must conclude that colonization was viewed by many men in Illinois as a sincere effort to benefit those free Negroes who wished to leave a country which had no place for them. Neither the doubts which Daniel Pope Cook had expressed in 1820 over the sincerity of certain Southern advocates of colonization nor the disappointment which Benjamin Lundy had experienced from the inconsistency of such prominent colonizationists as Bushrod Washington, Henry Clay and Charles F. Mercer was shared by many people in Illinois, even though the views of both Cook and Lundy were given publicity in the state.[60]

Even as late as 1831, the American Colonization Society was not generally recognized in Illinois as being a hindrance rather than a help to emancipation. A meeting of the Shoal Creek Presbyterian Church of Bond County on January 29, 1831, which declared slavery to be "a scandal to the Presbyterian Church" and inconsistent

[57] Charles G. Davis, "The Reverend John Brich: His Life and Tragic Death," *JISHS*, XXXVIII (June 1945), 236. The bequest was never fulfilled because of legal technicalities. Paul M. Angle, *Here I Have Lived: A History of Lincoln's Springfield, 1821–1865* (Springfield, 1935), p. 52; *Alton Spectator*, February 27, 1832.

[58] *Alton Spectator*, May 11, 1832, expressed approval of colonization and wrote against "incendiary" publications by abolitionists. See also *Illinois Intelligencer*, March 19, 1831, and letter from "a distinguished Baptist clergyman in Illinois" (probably John M. Peck) in *African Repository and Colonial Journal*, IX (1833–1834), 349.

[59] *Illinois Gazette*, September 4, 1830; *Illinois Advocate*, January 19, 1833.

[60] *Edwardsville Spectator*, May 16, 1820, December 11, 1821.

with both Christianity and republicanism, also heard an address by the Rev. Solomon Hardy on the progress of the American Colonization Society.[61] On July 4, 1833, Benjamin Bond delivered to the recently formed Carlyle Colonization Society in Clinton County an address which would not have been much out of place at an abolitionist meeting. He declared that slavery was not only unjust but that it was also illegal and had no basis in law. The institution of slavery seemed to him incompatible with the doctrines of the American Revolution: "Can we who have solemnly declared 'that all men are created equal...,' be unmindful of the injuries wrought in our land to a portion of Adam's long line of posterity?"[62]

The first reaction of the more earnest members of colonization societies in Illinois to criticism from the abolitionists of the East was one of hurt dismay. The Rev. John Dew of the Methodist Church presented to the Waterloo Colonization Society in Monroe County resolutions which were passed unanimously "That this Society view with deep and solemn concern and with painful regret the opposition raised to the American Colonization Society by the ... Abolition Societies of the Eastern States—and that this organized opposition ... should only serve to arouse its friends to more bold and vigorous efforts in its support."[63]

Despite this brave statement, interest in colonization declined rapidly in Illinois after 1833; indeed, its efforts were never very "bold and vigorous." The tangible results of the movement during its first period of operation in Illinois were some small contributions to the parent society and the freeing of a very few slaves.[64] Colonization activity in Illinois never aroused sufficient enthusiasm to prevent the auxiliary societies from languishing whenever no agent was present to encourage the work. Probably no active colonization society existed in the state by the end of 1834,[65] and none was to be

[61] *Illinois Intelligencer*, February 19, 1831.

[62] *Illinois Advocate*, July 20, 1833.

[63] *African Repository and Colonial Journal*, IX (1833–1834), 217.

[64] *Ibid.*, IV (1828–1829), 383; VII (1831–1832), 31, 96, 350; VIII (1832–1833), 64, 351; IX (1833–1834), 126; X (1834), 288.

[65] John M. Peck to the Rev. Dr. Proudfit, November 14, 1837, *ibid.*, XIII (1837), 379: "Circumstances ... have called up our citizens to the subject of African Colonization; and an effort will be made to revive the cause, which, for three or four years, has been suffered to languish."

formed again until 1837 when the conservative element saw danger in the activities of the abolitionists. The initiative by then had passed from the colonizationists to the abolitionists, who sought to restore immediately the rights of the slave and to improve his condition while retaining him within the boundaries of the United States.

A lack of money seems to have contributed to the early failure of the colonization movement in Illinois. The colonization project, unlike the later abolitionist societies, required money to be effective. When by picturing the sufferings of the free Negro and the slave, it generated moral fervor, it channeled that fervor away toward what was essentially a side issue, rather than directing it against the institution which was the source of the suffering. Since not enough money was available in Illinois to make the colonization idea work, the moral reformers remained ineffective so long as their activity was limited to colonization.

The rise of the abolitionist phase of the antislavery movement in Illinois was made possible by an influx of new settlers from both North and South who thoroughly hated slavery and wished to see the system ended. They were not interested merely in extending aid to Negroes who suffered from racial prejudice. Many of these people possessed stern religious ideas which left them no easy alternatives when moral decisions were involved. For that reason few of them could become adherents of the colonization movement, and for that reason abolition doctrines which urgently required difficult moral action had for them a special appeal. It is obvious, however, that when they moved to Illinois they were not entering an area where antislavery doctrines were a novelty. Although little had been accomplished from 1824 to 1835 toward ending slavery, antislavery sentiment had been kept alive during those years among significant groups of the population who were aware of the problem but favored a less extreme manner of solving it than did the abolitionists. The ten-year period following the defeat of the convention proposal was, therefore, an important stage in the evolutionary development of the antislavery movement in Illinois.

Reprinted from the *Journal of the Illinois State Historical Society*, XLVII (1954), 149–166.

13. *Agrarian Radicalism in Illinois' Constitutional Convention of 1862*

THE state constitutional convention that met at Springfield in January, 1862, was the rallying point for the last outburst of Jacksonian agrarian radicalism in Illinois. As such it illustrated the vitality of the Jacksonian movement in the West, while it was also a portent of the Granger and Populist movements. The most important of the many facets of this agrarian radicalism was its opposition to banks and corporations.[1]

Since territorial days Illinois had experimented with banking systems in periods of prosperity only to have them fail in time of depression. Recurring panics and bank failures had caused acute hardship throughout the state and had convinced the people that banks were, indeed, nefarious instruments of a group of ruthless monopolistic capitalists, as asserted by the followers of Jefferson and later by the Jacksonian Democrats.

Illinois farmers, particularly in the southern part of the state, saw state banking systems as contributing to the growth of a commercial and industrial society in which the small farmer and businessman would be at a great disadvantage. Conversely, in the eyes of the inhabitants of urban areas, particularly in northern Illinois, rapid commercial and industrial growth was the paramount object. Therefore they tended to favor the establishment of banks, which were needed to achieve this. The Democratic Party was frequently associated with the anti-bank movement, while most Whigs and Republicans favored banks.

The delegates to the previous constitutional convention, in 1847, were still experiencing the effects of a long and severe depression. The banking system created in the mid-thirties had failed, and since 1842 there had been no bank in operation in the state. The anti-bank

---

[1] Thomas Ford, *History of Illinois . . . 1818 to 1847* (Chicago, 1854), p. 282.

faction had advocated the election as delegates [of] men who were opposed to banks.[2] In the convention an intense struggle occurred between pro-bank and anti-bank groups; and the new constitution provided that banks should not be set up in Illinois unless the legislation providing for them should be approved by the people at a general election.[3] No action was taken until 1851, when a general law permitting the creation of banks with the power of issuing circulating notes based on state and national government securities was passed by the General Assembly and approved by the electorate.[4] Democratic Governor Augustus C. French's veto of this bill was the signal for a concerted attack upon it by anti-bank groups.

With but few exceptions the counties south of Sangamon County voted against the banking bill in 1851, while those north of Sangamon rolled up heavy majorities for it.[5] The controversy over the bill split the Democratic Party in Illinois, as northern Democrats hesitated to follow French's lead in his attack upon it. The pro-bank faction gained control of the party's nominating convention in 1852, and signalized its ascendancy by nominating Joel A. Matteson of Joliet for governor.[6] In the next few years a number of banks appeared in Illinois under the provisions of the general banking law; the people of the state were more prosperous; and anti-bank sentiment subsided.

The agrarian radicalism of which it had been a part, however, continued to assert itself in the political life of the state. Illinois farmers had always distrusted corporations. In the prosperous mid-1850's the General Assembly created by special act scores of new corporations at each session, although the Constitution of 1848 denied them the power to establish corporations by special legislation except "in cases where, in the judgment of the General Assembly, the objects of the corporation cannot be attained under general

[2] *Chicago Weekly Democrat*, August 27, September 24, 1845; Springfield *Illinois State Register* (hereafter cited as *ISR*), October 16, 1846.

[3] Arthur C. Cole (ed.), *Constitutional Debates of 1847* ("Illinois Historical Collections," XIV [Springfield, 1919]), 694.

[4] *Public Laws of Illinois, 1851*, pp. 163–175.

[5] Official election returns, November 24, 1851 (Ms), Archives, Illinois State Library.

[6] *Chicago Daily Democrat*, April 28, 1852; Springfield *Illinois Journal*, May 10, 12, June 13, 1852.

laws."[7] Representatives from agricultural areas looked upon the growth of these corporations with suspicion.[8]

Another important issue during this decade was the Illinois Central Railroad. The most urgent problem related to the road's financial obligation to the state.[9] It was suspected of attempting to evade the payments required by the charter of 1851. In the 1858 campaign the supporters of both Lincoln and Douglas attempted to discredit the opposing candidate by suggesting that he had helped the Illinois Central to attain a privileged position in Illinois.[10] Other railroads, too, were accused of refusing to pay debts which they had incurred for wages or materials. There was already widespread discontent with the freight rates of the railroads, and they were accused of charging unequal rates between equidistant points. As a result demands were made for state control.[11]

The panic of 1857 caused the failure of many Illinois banks and revived anti-bank sentiment. The secession movement following the election of 1860 produced a situation which destroyed confidence in the Illinois banking system. The amount of bank money in circulation had been increased rapidly after 1857, chiefly through the issues of poorly supervised banks located in isolated rural areas.[12] A large share of this paper was based on the securities of the seceding southern states.[13]

The General Assembly of 1861 attempted to reform the Illinois

[7] Emil J. Verlie (comp.), *Illinois Constitutions* ("Illinois Historical Collections," XIII [Springfield, 1919]), 84.

[8] *ISR*, January 30, 1861; *Illinois State Journal*, February 6, 1861.

[9] W. H. Osborn to Thomas E. Walker, December 19, 1861, President's Letter-Book, Illinois Central Railroad Company Manuscripts, Newberry Library (Chicago); *ISR*, January 7, 1862. [EDITOR'S NOTE: See also Frank L. Klement, "Middle Western Copperheadism and the Genesis of the Granger Movement," *infra*; and Charles Fairman, "The So-called Granger Cases, Lord Hale, and Justice Bradley," *Stanford Law Review*, V (July, 1953), 592 ff., for later development of regulation in the state's constitutional and statutory law.]

[10] *ISR*, October 20, 1858; *Greenville Advocate*, October 28, 1858.

[11] Petition of citizens of Town of Atlanta, Logan County, to General Assembly, 1859, Archives, Illinois State Library; *Chicago Journal*, February 11, 1859.

[12] *Bankers' Magazine*, XV (New York, 1861), 585. [EDITOR'S NOTE: See also George W. Van Vleck, *The Panic of 1857: An Analytic Study* (New York, 1943).]

[13] John Trible to Lyman Trumbull, December 18, 1860, Trumbull Papers, Illinois State Historical Library; *Chicago Journal*, December 31, 1860.

banking system and adopted an act for the creation of a new system of branch banking on a specie basis.[14] The constitution required the submission of the latter measure to the people in the next general election. Since this legislature also provided for the election in November of delegates to a constitutional convention to convene early in 1862, the people preferred to leave reforms in the banking structure to the convention and rejected the new banking law.[15]

In the early agitation for a constitutional convention it was evident that many wanted to incorporate in a new constitution sections concerning banks, the Illinois Central, and other economic problems.[16] After a convention was approved in the election of 1860, and the legislature of 1861 provided for the election of its members, the radical elements concentrated their efforts upon securing the election of anti-bank delegates. The conservatives admitted the need of banking reform, but did not advocate the abolition of banks then in operation.

The Republican Party requested that partisanship be abandoned during the election, but the Democrats claimed that the failure of the "no party" advocates to take a firm stand on major economic issues required the continuance of their party organization. Sensing the welling discontent accompanying depression and bank failure, the Democrats prepared to regain authority in the state by a radical economic program.[17] This program found a ready response among the people. Of seventy-five delegates elected to the convention forty-five were Democrats, twenty Republicans, and ten Union Party candidates, most of whom voted with the Democrats on economic issues.[18]

Three members of this convention had been in the constitutional convention of 1847: James W. Singleton of Adams County, Anthony Thornton of Shelby, and Thomson R. Webber of Champaign. Others who could look back on careers of public service were ex-Governor

[14] *Ibid.*, January 19, 31, February 18, 1861; *ISR*, January 11, 1861.

[15] *Ibid.*, October 29, 1861; *Canton Register*, October 29, 1861.

[16] Canton *Fulton County Ledger*, February 15, 1859; *Jonesboro Gazette*, February 12, 1859.

[17] *Chicago Democrat*, July 24, 1861; *ISR*, July 28, August 13, 16, October 3, 1861.

[18] O. M. Dickerson, *The Illinois Constitutional Convention* (Urbana, 1905), pp. 7–8.

Augustus C. French; John Wentworth, Chicago editor and politician; William A. Hacker, president of the convention; and Alexander Campbell of La Salle, a Republican with radical agrarian views. The convention was controlled by a bipartisan group who had grown up in the Jacksonian tradition and were prepared to apply these principles to the problems of Illinois in 1862.

The ascendancy of Democrats and radicals in the convention did not at first alarm the conservatives in the state. On January 7 the *Illinois State Journal* of Springfield (Republican) characterized the assembling delegates as "leading citizens of the State, of well known ability and conservative tendencies," and did not believe that "any radical movement will be attempted." After the convention had been in session a few days, however, the *Journal* concluded that it was "not a *Constitutional*, but a *revolutionary* Convention . . . to make the Convention a mere machine for resuscitating and re-organizing the Democratic party in the State." [19]

The convention had in a very short time brought forth strikingly radical proposals on economic issues. This has been overlooked because of its attempts to interfere with the war program of Governor Richard Yates. The published reports of the convention make it evident that the Democratic majority in the convention was determined to embarrass and discredit Yates, criticizing his war administration and investigating the state's war finances; but there is little evidence upon which to conclude that they planned to usurp the governor's powers. In the field of banking their obstructive interference with Yates' administration was motivated by the desire to forestall impending financial disaster. In fact, one of the chief advocates of such interference was not a Democrat but the Chicago Republican, John Wentworth. [20]

In the weeks immediately before the delegates assembled the banking structure of Illinois had reached its nadir. When the state failed to control the circulation of depreciated bank notes, Chicago businessmen adopted the practice of accepting such notes at their approximate market value rather than their face value, and periodically issued lists indicating the rate at which these notes would

[19] *ISR*, January 14, 1862.

[20] Dickerson, *Constitutional Convention of 1862*, p. 52; Richard Yates to Russell Ward, March 24, 1862, Yates Papers, Illinois State Historical Library.

be accepted.[21] Under this pressure, combined with a demand from the state auditor's office that banks whose note issues were based on the bonds of seceded states either replace these bonds with reliable securities or suspend operations, the circulation of Illinois bank notes declined from $12,320,000 on December 1, 1860, to $1,933,686 in January, 1862.[22]

Under these circumstances it was inevitable that a large share of the attention of the convention should be directed toward framing the banking article of the new constitution. The question of prohibiting or permitting banks occasioned but slight debate. On January 21 the chairman of the committee on banks and currency, Norman H. Purple of Peoria, submitted an article providing that

> No bank or banking corporation, nor any association or corporation with any banking powers, shall hereafter be created in this State. This section shall take effect and be in force immediately, as a portion of and as an amendment to the constitution of this State.[23]

Though other sections of the bank article were drastically altered during the course of the debates, this section and the following one prohibited the renewal or extension of bank charters previously granted stirred up little controversy and went into the final draft of the constitution as originally presented.

There was heated controversy over section three, stating that no paper money of a denomination less than $10 could circulate in Illinois after the adoption of the constitution. The more radical anti-bank men wanted the circulation of all paper money prohibited at once. The convention adopted a compromise by which gradually within four years all paper money, except United States Treasury notes, would be barred from the state.[24]

The radical anti-bank majority easily passed the banking article on March 3, 1862.[25] This article was to be submitted to the people

[21] *Chicago Democrat*, May 18, 1861; W. H. Osborn to Thomas E. Walker, May 29, 1861, Illinois Central Railroad Manuscripts.

[22] Auditor's statement, in *Illinois State Journal*, January 6, 1862.

[23] *Journal of the Constitutional Convention of the State of Illinois, Convened at Springfield, January 7, 1862* (Springfield, 1862), pp. 130–131. (Hereafter cited as *Convention Journal*.)

[24] *Ibid.*, pp. 566–568; *Illinois State Journal*, February 3, 4, 5, 6, 12, 26, 27, 1862.

[25] *Ibid.*, March 14, 1862.

separately, thus giving the electorate an opportunity to reject it without defeating the entire constitution.

In the early part of the convention the anti-bank men were confused about the position that they should take on the new treasury notes being issued by the federal government. These appeared dangerous because they were paper money and issued by a Republican administration; on the other hand, the people, particularly in rural areas, were having difficulty in raising specie to pay taxes and clamored for the acceptance of treasury notes for that purpose. Faced with this demand, many anti-bank Democrats tried to persuade the convention to authorize the payment of taxes in the new medium. The state treasurer also asked the convention's committee on revenue about accepting treasury notes for taxes, but the committee refused to make a recommendation; and when a resolution of the convention directed the committee to prepare a report approving such acceptance, the committee reported that since Congress had not yet made treasury notes legal tender, the convention should not act. Although Congress did make the treasury notes legal tender before the adjournment of the convention no further action was taken.[26]

The convention's suspicion of railroads was fully equal to its suspicion of banks. Most of the hostility was directed toward the Illinois Central, which had delayed its payments to the state. Its officers explained that because of reduced revenues caused by the war they could not pay until Illinois and the United States paid the I. C.'s claims against them. The payment proffered by the road was discounted in proportion to the depreciated value of the paper bank notes which it had accepted in the course of business.[27] The belief that these actions constituted a refusal to comply with the provisions of the railroad's charter increased the popular distrust of its motives. The Illinois Central, anticipating an extended discussion of the road in the convention, retained two agents at Springfield during most of the session.[28]

[26] *Ibid.*, January 30, February 20, 1862; *ISR*, February 10, 13, 19, May 6, 8, 1862.

[27] *Convention Journal*, pp. 115–119.

[28] W. H. Osborn to Thomas E. Walker, December 19, 1861, January 29, 1862, President's Letter-Book, Illinois Central Railroad Manuscripts.

The members who feared the Illinois Central insisted upon a constitutional provision requiring the road to comply with all the terms of the charter. After much maneuvering on the part of the railroad and extended debate in the convention, the article which was adopted stated that the General Assembly could not release the Illinois Central from money payments or taxes due the state under its charter. This left the way open for the railroad to seek legislative action concerning the sale of its lands, but in matters of finance and taxation it was left in the same position as before.[29]

The practice by counties and towns of mortgaging themselves to finance the building of railroads resulted in the adoption of a provision denying the legislature the power to permit any county, city, town, township or school district of the state to give financial aid to any individual or corporation, and prohibiting such local jurisdictions from making subscriptions to the stock of any incorporated or other business association.[30]

Complaints that railroad rates were unjustly high and discriminatory as between places led to resolutions asking that the convention consider ways and means of controlling rates and services. The convention refused to set up an instrument for railroad regulation, but the attention directed to this problem suggested that the delegates' constituents had strongly felt grievances against the railroads.[31]

The legislature was directed to enact general laws for incorporation and was denied the power of incorporating by special laws.[32] It was also empowered to alter, amend or repeal charters granted under the new constitution.[33] Also, any corporation previously

[29] Osborn to A. S. Hewitt, March 24, 1862, *ibid.*

[30] *Convention Journal*, pp. 1081–1082.

[31] *Illinois State Journal*, January 16, 22, February 6, March 28, 1862. On January 23, Perry A. Armstrong introduced the following resolution: "*Resolved*, That the committee on railroad corporations be instructed to inquire into the expediency of creating a board of railroad commissioners, who shall have the supervision of tariffs and fare on the several railroads of this state, and may also regulate, as far as practical, the time tables and connections of the several railroads, and perform such other duties as may, from time to time, be required of them by law." (*Convention Journal*, p. 148.)

[32] *Ibid.*, pp. 1092–1093.

[33] *Ibid.*, pp. 832–833.

chartered which did not begin operations within one year after the adoption of the constitution was to forfeit its charter.[34] The legislature was directed to pass a law to exempt from forced sale or levy "a homestead to every householder having a family."[35] There was discussion of the advisability of requiring the legislature to enact laws to control the rate of interest, but no action was taken.[36]

Republican opposition both inside and outside the convention gradually stiffened. An attempt at the end of January to adjourn the convention to a later date received only slight support. As the end neared most of the Republican members withdrew, despairing of any success in writing their views into the constitution. On March 22, when the convention voted on the question of accepting or rejecting the completed constitution, only forty-six members were present, forty-two of whom voted for it.

Eventually fifty-four delegates signed the constitution, but the remaining twenty-one (mostly Republicans) refused to affix their signatures.[37] This was consistent with the Republican strategy of discrediting the Democratic majority by treating their work as disloyal and treasonable. The Democrats attempted to gain public approval of the constitution by emphasizing the provisions for economic reform, calling it the "People's Constitution."[38] Both parties were aware of the economic discontent in Illinois, but the Republicans feared "that in the zeal of our people to kill the Banks they will swallow all the enormities which have been concocted."[39] The *Peoria Union* summed up the economic arguments of the advocates of the new constitution:

> Well may it be called the "poor man's constitution," for it protects him against chartered monopolies and monied aristocracies, chartered privileges and special legislation, peculations and plundering; it puts all

[34] *Ibid.*, pp. 1045–1046, 1092–1093.

[35] *Ibid.*, pp. 610, 614, 867, 897, 978, 1095.

[36] *Ibid.*, pp. 410, 900. [EDITOR'S NOTE: On the general subject of interest-rate regulation, cf. Lawrence M. Friedman, "The Usury Laws of Wisconsin: A Study in Legal and Social History," *Wisconsin Law Review*, Vol. 1963 (July, 1963), 515–565.]

[37] *Convention Journal*, pp. 1114–1115; *Illinois State Journal*, April 2, 1862.

[38] Bloomington *Illinois Statesman*, April 11, 1862.

[39] S. M. Willson to Richard Yates, March 19, 1862, Yates Papers.

men upon an equal footing. . . . By it the mechanic is secured for his labor, the poor man his homestead and all their just rights, allowing no one special privileges to the exclusion of others.[40]

The opponents of the constitution rarely attempted to criticize its banking and corporation articles; but when they did, it was on the principle that the state could not advance commercially or industrially without banks, paper currency, and corporations with charter privileges. The *Chicago Post* editorialized:

> We are a great commercial State. This Constitution fetters commerce; cuts off the avenues of trade; blocks up the channels of communication with other States; discourages the investment of capital; drives away manufacturers; stops internal improvements; paralyzes enterprise; turns away from us the tide of immigration, and scandalizes us before the world.[41]

At the election on June 17, 1862, Chicago gave heavy majorities for the constitution and the article banning banks. The *Chicago Journal* stated that the cry "Down with stumptail!" had caused the people to vote for the constitution.[42] When it became known that both the constitution and the banking article had been defeated, the *Journal* and *Tribune* both attributed it to the superior intelligence of the "rural voters."[43] The rural counties in southern and central Illinois, however, like the Chicago workingmen, had voted for the banking article and the constitution.

In general the pattern of voting on the banking issue in 1862 was like that of 1851. In 1862, however, Jo Daviess, Cook, Will, Sangamon and a tier of counties in western Illinois as far north as Peoria also gave majorities for the banking article; while sixteen counties[44] south of Springfield voted against it. There were fewer votes cast on the banking article than on the constitution, but the former received more votes than did the constitution and had many less cast against it. The majority against the constitution was 16,051, but the

---

[40] Reprinted in *ISR*, May 16, 1862.

[41] Reprinted in *Illinois State Journal*, June 16, 1862.

[42] *Chicago Journal*, June 18, 1862.

[43] *Ibid.*; *Chicago Tribune*, June 20, 1862.

[44] These counties were Bond, Clay, Coles, Douglas, Edgar, Edwards, Hardin, Jefferson, Lawrence, Massac, Perry, Pope, Richland, Wabash, Wayne, and White.

banking article was defeated by only 3,181 votes out of a total of 256,877.[45] The attempt to restore Illinois to an agrarian economy modeled on the economic ideals of Jacksonian Democracy had almost succeeded.

Reprinted from the *Journal of the Illinois State Historical Society*, XLVIII (1955), 271–282.

[45] Official election returns, June 17, 1862 (Ms), Archives, Illinois State Library.

FRANK L. KLEMENT

14. Middle Western Copperheadism and the Genesis of the Granger Movement

NATIONALISM as a force and apotheosis as a process have tempted writers to laud Abraham Lincoln and to denounce his enemies.[1] Lincoln cultists and nationalist historians have wielded a weighty whip when chastising Copperheads, who were midwestern malcontents and opponents of the Lincoln administration. Investigators of the Copperhead theme have busied themselves in unearthing Copperhead quotations from newspapers, letters, and speeches and hanging them upon the line of treason. They have denounced these administration critics as traitors pure and simple—in effect, as men whose hearts were black, whose blood was yellow, and whose minds were warped.

Cause and effect as a principle of history has seldom been applied to the Copperhead theme. Northern critics of administration policy have been removed from their setting to be publicly pilloried. But Clement L. Vallandigham's views were not bolts out of the blue. He truly represented the majority views of his district. Nor was it an accident that Edward G. Ryan of Wisconsin headed the Copperhead clan of his state during the Civil War—the same Ryan who wrote the Jacksonian antibank clause into the proposed state constitution of 1846 and who, as chief justice of the Wisconsin Supreme Court, rendered in 1874 the greatest of the state decisions against the railroads.[2] Samuel Medary believed that his editorials in the Columbus

---

[1] Presented in part as a paper at the joint session of the Mississippi Valley Historical Association and the Economic History Association at Oklahoma City, April 21, 1950.

[2] In handing down the decision in Munn v. Illinois, 94 U. S. 113 (1876), Chief Justice Morrison R. Waite followed the argument of Edward G. Ryan in Pike v. The Chicago, Milwaukee & St. Paul Railway Company, 40 Wis. 583 (1876). [EDITOR'S NOTE: See Alfons J. Beitzinger, *Edward G. Ryan* (Madison, 1960); and

Crisis preached the same Jeffersonian and Jacksonian doctrines as his paper's earlier motto: "Unawed by the influence of the rich, the great, or the noble, the people must be heard and their rights protected." In fact, a good case could be prepared to prove that consistency created Copperheads and that midwestern Copperheadism linked Jacksonian Democracy and Grangerism. Times changed, but the views of the Copperheads did not. They were malcontents because they protested against the dwindling influence of agriculture, the nationalization of business, and the centralization of the federal government.

Midwestern Copperheadism was compounded out of a half dozen complex ingredients. At times Democratic partisans flavored it with political opportunism and sordid party tactics. At times religious hopes and fears served as a condiment, for a tinge of Know-Nothingism colored the Republican party and drove Irish and German Catholics into the ranks of the opposition.[3] The Wisconsin draft riots of 1862 were caused, in part, by the anti-Catholic policy followed in the naming of chaplains.[4] Frederick W. Horn's predictions that New England Puritanism would "war upon certain religious denominations" and that the region would try to establish its "sectional church" as a "national one" were based upon religious fears.[5]

Copperheadism in the Middle West also possessed social aspects. The designation "Butternut," used interchangeably with the term

---

Charles Fairman, "The So-called Granger Cases, Lord Hale, and Justice Bradley," *Stanford Law Review*, V (July, 1953), 587–679.]

[3] Milwaukee *See-Bote*, October 31, 1860. This German-language newspaper, the unofficial organ of German Catholics of Milwaukee and vicinity, continuously reminded its readers that many Republicans had been Know-Nothings. Ekkehard Eickhoff of Braunschweig, Germany, a graduate student and research assistant at Marquette University in 1949–1950, aided the author in examining the editorial columns of the *See-Bote* and other Milwaukee German-language newspapers. The author hereby expresses his appreciation to Mr. Eickhoff and the University for the aid both have given—one by helping in research and the other by furnishing the helper.

[4] Peter L. Johnson, "Port Washington Draft Riot of 1862," *Mid-America*, I (January, 1930), 212–220.

[5] Frederick W. Horn to Gov. Alexander Randall, April 18, 1861, Wisconsin Governor's Letters, Civil War Period, Manuscripts Collection, Wisconsin State Historical Society Library (Madison).

"Copperhead," suggested its rural and democratic basis. It was, in the main, a small farmer movement—for the Cooperhead country was characterized by small homesteads, poor soils, and widespread illiteracy.[6] David Ross Locke, through his fictitious character Petroleum V. Nasby, ridiculed a social class and his economic inferiors as well as an opposition political party.

The ingredient usually referred to as "humanitarian sentiment" left occasional evidence of its presence. Mothers whose love of sons exceeded devotion to country, and those who feared the effects of conscription, endorsed the antiadministration arguments. Medary's Quaker heritage encouraged his pro-peace pleading. Marcus M. Pomeroy, a small-city editor who had given the war qualified support, visited the Arkansas sector in 1863 and returned to La Crosse to become an ardent peace advocate and a vociferous Lincoln critic because rotting coffins, ravenous buzzards, and "cotton crusades" were an integral part of the war.[7]

Western sectionalism—so much a part and parcel of Grangerism[8]—was another ingredient out of which midwestern Copperheadism was compounded. Westerners, generally, sought to promote their own and their section's well-being. They were as section conscious as were the southern planters or the New England Yankees. They were desirous of promoting their section's economic welfare, political aspirations, and cultural development. Vallandigham openly averred, "I became and am a Western sectionalist,"[9] and he restated that contention more expressively upon the floor of the House of Representatives: "I am as good a western fire-eater

[6] John L. Stipp, "Economic and Political Aspects of Western Copperheadism" (Unpublished Ph.D. dissertation, Ohio State University, 1944), confines his study almost wholly to the Copperhead country of Ohio; it is a work which deserves more recognition and circulation.

[7] Marcus M. Pomeroy, *Journey of Life: Reminiscences and Recollections of "Brick" Pomeroy* (New York, 1890), pp. 182–194; *La Crosse* (Wis.) *Weekly Democrat*, February 10, March 3, 17, 1863.

[8] The sectional aspects are emphasized in James D. McCabe (Edward Winslow Martin, pseud.), *History of the Grange Movement: or, The Farmer's War Against Monopolies* (Chicago, 1873), and the Easterner's answer is convincingly presented in Charles Francis Adams, Jr., "The Granger Movement," *North American Review*, CXX (April, 1875), 394–424.

[9] Clement L. Vallandigham, *Speeches, Arguments, Addresses, and Letters of Clement L. Vallandigham* (New York, 1864), p. 211.

as the hottest salamander in this House."[10] The same sectional sentiments were repeated in all parts of the Midwest. A prewar Chicago *Times* editorial warned Easterners: "The great Northwest will not submit to be a vassal to New England."[11] Samuel S. Cox repeatedly expressed his distrust of Puritan culture, the Puritan character, and New England industrialism.[12] His tactless colleague Vallandigham also resented the fact that New York and New England regarded "the western man . . . to be a sort of outside barbarian," and he stated that he was "inexorably hostile to Puritan domination in religion or morals or literature or politics."[13] Horn, the prominent Wisconsin Democrat whose name was closely tied to the state draft riots, understood the economic conflict which existed between western farmers and eastern industrialists; he early decried the "plundering of the Midwest" for the benefit of "Pennsylvania's Iron Mongers and New England manufacturers."[14] The editorial columns of the *Crisis* constantly voiced these sectional views. The Milwaukee *See-Bote*'s editor condemned the industrial and "codfish aristocracy," and often threw sharp editorial darts at New England.[15] The Cincinnati *Enquirer*, one of the principal Copperhead sheets, repeatedly spoke in terms of western advantages and interests.[16] Daniel W. Voorhees, capable Indiana Copperhead, often exploited the same sectional theme. So did Orlando B. Ficklin, later a prominent Illinois Granger, but he expressed himself more vividly;

[10] *Congressional Globe*, 36 Cong., 1 Sess., Appendix, p. 43. Hereafter cited *Cong. Globe*, followed by Congress and Session.

[11] Chicago *Times*, December 10, 1860.

[12] Samuel S. Cox, *Puritanism in Politics: Speech of Hon. S. S. Cox of Ohio . . . January 13, 1863* (New York, 1863).

[13] *Cong. Globe*, 36 Cong., 1 Sess., Appendix, pp. 43–44; Vallandigham, *Speeches, Arguments, Addresses*, p. 7.

[14] Horn to Gov. Randall, April 18, 1861, Wisconsin Governor's Letters, Civil War Period.

[15] Milwaukee *See-Bote*, April 23, 30, October 1, December 15, 1862.

[16] Washington McLean, co-owner of the Cincinnati *Enquirer*, was the Democratic boss of Hamilton County, the political ally of Samuel Medary, and political patron of Vallandigham. McLean, always expressing pro-western sentiments, owned several boiler-plate factories and resented the competition of the Pennsylvania interests. Editorial opinions have been adequately examined in Charles R. Wilson, "The Cincinnati *Enquirer* and Civil War Politics: A Study in Copperhead Opinion" (Unpublished Ph.D. dissertation, University of Chicago, 1934).

he was thankful "that God made the world before He made the Yankees, for they would have interfered with His business and destroyed the beautiful world in which we live."[17] Illinois Copperheads, acting in concert in the legislature, accused the Republican governor of pandering to New England capitalists.[18]

More than one midwestern critic of New England and its influence in the nation's capital asked for separation from the Northeast and the protection of western interests.[19] Sectional sentiment gave substance to the anti-New England resolution adopted at a Democratic meeting in Brown County, Indiana: "our interests and inclinations will demand of us a withdrawal from political association in a common government with the New England States, who have contributed so much to every innovation upon the constitution, to our present calamity of civil war, and whose tariff legislation must ever prove oppressive to our agricultural and commercial pursuits."[20]

Repeatedly midwestern Copperheads contended that New England caused the war and benefited from it while the West paid in money and men as well as in services and subserviency. Many malcontents insisted that the war elevated New England's "galvanized Federalism" to the driver's seat while western agriculturists pulled the heavy load.[21] Truly, middle western Copperheadism makes sense only when it is viewed as a prowestern rather than a prosouthern movement.

The sectional loyalty of the Copperheads was accentuated by the long list of economic grievances which they recited. The collapse of the banking systems in several states bore heavily upon the farmers. Bank notes, based upon southern bonds, depreciated in

---

[17] O. B. Ficklin, quoted in the Springfield *Illinois State Journal*, January 9, 1863.

[18] Illinois, House of Representatives, *Journal, 1863* (Springfield, 1863), p. 279.

[19] Chicago *Daily Tribune*, January 9, 1863.

[20] Indianapolis *Indiana Daily State Sentinel*, January 9, 1863.

[21] Typical are the claims of the editorial writer of the Milwaukee *See-Bote*, October 1, 1862: "It is the tender yoke of the factory barons, the blessed working of the Puritan oligarchy which now dispose of us. New England is really now our ruler and master; nay it is more—it is the creditor, we are its debtors. To her we are tributary. New England has the bonds in her hands which the other states have to pay. . . . The money monopoly of New England is absolutely controlling and the labor of the others, especially the Western states, is tributary to it."

value and institutions closed their doors in rapid succession as a bank panic gripped the Northwest when secession and war became a reality. In Illinois only 17 of the state's 112 banks remained solvent by the end of 1861. Nearly half of Wisconsin's banks closed their doors and scores failed in other midwestern states. Bankers, merchants, and employers passed on to farmers and workingmen most of the depreciating state bank notes. An official of the Illinois Central Railroad suspected that the bankers were interested in keeping "the present trash afloat until such time as they can clean their vaults of it." [22] Farmers who held the stock of defunct banks as well as worthless currency complained bitterly. Furthermore, there was a shortage of currency to handle the fall harvest.

The closing of the Mississippi River trade also affected the farmers of the Midwest adversely. Although the growing eastbound trade severed, in part, the economic ties of the West and the South, the river trade was still necessary to the western farmers' welfare in 1860. Agricultural statistics and trade reports proved that southern states bordering the mighty Mississippi depended upon the upper Midwest, in large part, for foodstuffs.[23] An article entitled "Illinois Corn and Secession" in the December, 1860, issue of the *Prairie Farmer* reported that the New Orleans market had contracts for a million bushels of grain in 1861.[24] In fact, the year 1860 witnessed the heyday of the down-river traffic.[25] Cincinnati alone shipped 105,332 sacks of corn, 47,801 bushels of wheat, and 158,592 barrels

[22] General Superintendent William R. Arthur to William H. Osborn, April 24, 1861, "President's Letter-Book: W. H. Osborn," Illinois Central Railroad Company Manuscripts, Newberry Library (Chicago).

[23] *Eighth Census of the U.S. (1860): Agriculture* (Washington, 1864), pp. xxix, xxxi, cxxix, 6–9, 84–87.

[24] *Prairie Farmer* (Chicago), XXII (December 27, 1860), 406.

[25] Henry C. Hubbart, *The Older Middle West, 1840–1880* (New York, 1936), p. 82. Those interested in the commercial ties of the West should not bypass such works as Albert L. Kohlmeier, *The Old Northwest as the Keystone of the Arch of the American Federal Union* (Bloomington, 1938); E. Merton Coulter, "Effects of Secession upon the Commerce of the Mississippi Valley," *MVHR*, III (December, 1916), 264–285; Charles R. Wilson, "Cincinnati a Southern Outpost in 1860–1861?" *ibid.*, XXIV (March, 1938), 473–482; R. B. Way, "The Commerce of the Lower Mississippi in the Period 1830–1860," Mississippi Valley Historical Association, *Proceedings*, X, Part I (1920), 57–68; and Thomas Senior Berry, *Western Prices before 1861: A Study of the Cincinnati Market* (Cambridge, 1943).

of flour southward in 1860.[26] Many manufactured items such as Cincinnati beer and Belleville whisky, produced from farm surpluses, went down the river.

The closing of the river trade forced farm prices downward, and flour, packed pork, and distilled spirits went begging for buyers. Corn commanded less than ten cents a bushel; potatoes could be had by the hundred bushels for the asking; butter was a drug on the market, and hog prices were more than halved in 1861.[27] It was not prosouthern sympathy but economic reality which prompted an Illinois newspaperman to entitle an editorial "Western Farmers, What Are Your Interests," to deplore administration measures which erased the southern market, and to ask the question, "Will the fighting farmers of the Upper Mississippi ever find out that it is the Lincoln blood-and-murder party who has killed their 'goose with the golden eggs'?"[28]

As farm prices dived downward, household necessities skyrocketed in price. The Morrill tariff of February 20, 1861, and the supplementary act of the following August levied duties on tea, coffee, sugar, spices, and other items. Anticipating the effect, wholesalers and retailers raised their prices: before the end of 1861 sugar doubled in price and coffee, which had sold for eleven cents a pound before Lincoln's election, brought more than three times as much by the end of 1862. A Wisconsin editor suggested to his Republican opponents that the best way they could support a "mistaken President" was by "drinking lots of coffee at . . . thirty-five cents a pound."[29] The same Illinois legislature which considered a national convention as a way of ending the war, whimpered because Lincoln had "given sanction to a measure known as the Morrill Tariff, under which the East is enriching itself at the expense of the West."[30] In

---

[26] *Eighth Census of the U.S. (1860): Agriculture*, p. clviii. Russell H. Anderson, "Agriculture in Illinois during the Civil War Period, 1850–1870" (Unpublished Ph.D. dissertation, University of Illinois, 1929) contends that probably one fourth of the surplus agricultural produce of the Northwest went southward in the late fifties.

[27] Columbus (Ohio) *Crisis*, November 28, 1861; *Cong. Globe*, 37 Cong., 2 Sess., p. 170.

[28] Carlyle (Ill.) *Constitution and Union*, October 3, 1863.

[29] Sheboygan (Wis.) *Journal*, February 18, 1862.

[30] Illinois, House of Representatives, *Journal, 1863*, p. 279.

his editorial columns Medary thundered, "The West has been sold to Eastern manufacturers by the politicians; the tariff is not a war measure, but a New England protective measure by which she expects to lay the great agricultural West tributary at the feet of her cotton and woolen mills."[31]

Farmers could not see the justice in requiring "four bushels of corn to buy one pound of coffee."[32] Their depressed spirits and deflated pocketbooks encouraged them to turn their backs upon the Lincoln administration in the fall elections of 1862 and the spring voting of 1863. When the economic shoe pinched, midwestern farmers transposed their economic grievances into political arguments, personal pessimism, and open opposition.

The malcontents also directed a barrage of criticism against the railroads. The closing of the Mississippi had put midwestern farmers at the mercy of the railroads which made the most of their opportunity. "The railroads have put up their tariff on freights to almost an embargo price," moaned Medary in the columns of the *Crisis*; "they are literally skinning the West alive by advantage of the Mississippi blockade."[33] Immense purchases of American foodstuffs for the European market affected the western farmer but slightly, for prohibitory transportation rates of the trunk line railroads and lake freighters deprived western agrarians of the benefits they should have received.[34] In July, 1861, barley commanded more than two and a half times as much in New York as in Chicago, and much more in Chicago than at the local railway depots.

Complaints against excessive rail rates echoed from all parts of the Middle West. Iowans pointed out "that it cost more than *five times* as much to transport a bushel of wheat from Iowa to New York as the farmer received for it."[35] It seemed unfair to Southern Illinois farmers that railroads which charged $1.10 to $1.20 per barrel to ship produce to New York in July, 1861, should raise their rates to $3.00 per barrel by January 15, 1862—and that while farm

<hr />

[31] Columbus *Crisis*, August 15, 1861.

[32] *Cong. Globe*, 37 Cong., 2 Sess., p. 169; Vallandigham, *Speeches, Arguments, Addresses*, p. 326.

[33] Columbus *Crisis*, November 28, 1861.

[34] *Ibid.*, October 24, 1861, January 23, 1862.

[35] *Eighth Census of the U.S. (1860): Agriculture*, p. xli.

prices spiraled downward. A downstate Copperhead Democrat asserted that Randolph County farmers paid $36,000 in increased freight rates in the last six months of 1861 and that Illinois residents paid a total of $18,000,000 in increases during the same period.[36] Vallandigham, self-styled "western fire-eater," gave a sectional interpretation to the freight problem: "Cut off as we are from all other means of outlet . . . and with our railroads leading to the East, for the most part in the hands of eastern directors or bondholders, the tariff on freights has at the same time been fully doubled, thus increasing the burden upon our trade both ways, so largely as to amount in a little while longer to absolute prohibition."[37] Medary stated his sectional views more bluntly, asserting that administration policy would make Westerners victims of the "skinning, brutally skinning despotism of Eastern railroads, and make us Western people paupers and slaves forever."[38] General John A. McClernand, in reporting reasons why the Northwest repudiated the administration in the elections of late 1862, ascribed the general discontent to high freight rates.[39] The Great Lakes carriers were also included when the farmers protested against excessive freight rates. Even rail lines which brought farm surpluses to lake ports recognized that water transportation rates were so high that they pained and provoked the farmer and "reduced the nett [*sic*] price of his products . . . to so low a point as to leave no margin of profit."[40]

Grangerlike arguments against monopoly, discriminatory rates, pooling, stock watering, lobbying, and fraudulent promotion reverberated from many parts of the Midwest. Charges of coalescence between lake-port railroads and elevators appeared in many newspapers. One Copperhead spokesman, in an "Address to the People of Illinois," stated that the "aggregate indebtedness of counties, cities and towns for railroad companies has been ascertained to

[36] "Proceedings of the Illinois State Constitutional Convention . . . January 21, 1862," Springfield *Illinois State Journal*, January 22, 1862.

[37] *Cong. Globe*, 37 Cong., 2 Sess., p. 170.

[38] Columbus *Crisis*, January 28, 1863.

[39] *War of the Rebellion: A Compilation of the Official Records of the Union and Confederate Armies* (130 vols.; Washington, 1880–1901), Series I, Vol. XVII, Pt. 2, p. 333.

[40] Illinois Central Railroad Company, *Annual Report, 1861* (Chicago, 1862).

exceed fifteen millions" in his state.[41] Most of the charges which Grangers made in the 1870's were a repetition of the antirailroad arguments of the early 1860's.

Prominent "Peace Democrats" lampooned the "vested interests," condemning eastern capital and western railroad promoters. Republicanism, to them, was "revitalized Whiggery" or "Hamiltonian doctrine" galvanized to new life. Vallandigham preached that gospel, contending that the moneyed powers "found the nucleus of such an organization [Republican party] ready-formed to suit their hands—an organization . . . founded upon the most powerful passions of the human heart."[42] The correspondent of the London *Times*, in touring the West, found evidence of the economic ties of Lincoln's party when he observed, "Wherever wealth is prevalent, there you have the stronghold of the Republican party."[43] Copperheads, generally, hated New England influence, opposed "vested interests," and asserted faith in Jeffersonian principles.

Republican bigwigs, on the other hand, often deplored western sectionalism. "Palsied be the hand," stated Governor Richard Yates of Illinois, "that would sever the ties which bind the East and West."[44] Indiana's aggressive wartime governor, Oliver P. Morton, shadowboxed with "traitors" in his state and used emotional pleas to quash Copperhead sentiment. The Chicago *Tribune*, unofficial spokesman for the Lincoln administration, injected emotion into its editorials while tarring as traitors all critics of the party in power. While these and other champions of Radical Republicanism attributed "disloyal sentiments" to black hearts and blank minds, a more competent observer gauged Copperhead causation more rationally. William H. Osborn, competent president of the Illinois Central Railroad Company during the years of civil conflict, spent much time in Chicago and Springfield and noted that farmer discontent was closely tied to the question of high freight rates. In a series of letters he contradicted the views of his Republican colleagues, attributing the farmers' dissatisfaction to economic rather than

[41] Quoted in Chicago *Times*, June 3, 1863.

[42] Vallandigham, *Speeches, Arguments, Addresses*, p. 278.

[43] Chicago *Times*, October 31, 1863.

[44] Richard Yates, "Message to the Legislature, January 5, 1863," Chicago *Daily Tribune*, January 7, 1863.

biological or emotional factors. He scored the excessive tolls charged by the Erie Canal and trunk line operators, saying that "The West cannot consent to be held by the throat any longer to enrich Albany and Buffalo."[45] "The people of this State," he wrote from Chicago, "are bound to have an outlet to the Sea; this leaning towards Canada is a natural consequence of the apathy and indifference manifested by the State of New York touching a fair division of the spoils of the products of the prairies— $\frac{7}{8}$ to forwarders and $\frac{1}{8}$ to the poor devil who raises the corn. It is grievous."[46] The disgusted Westerners, wrote Osborn, have paid "thirty-five to fifty cents per bushel to get their grain to market; it makes them grit their teeth." Then he pithily added: "*It is not a question of loyalty, but . . . one of bread and butter.*"[47]

The Illinois state constitutional convention of 1862 illustrated the tie of midwestern Copperheadism and Grangerism. The Chicago *Tribune*, Republican party whip in Illinois, criticized the downstate Democratic delegates as "Copperheads," "secession conspirators," and "Southern sympathizers." Other administration papers followed suit. The *Tribune* charged that Democrats "who were members of, or sympathizers with, the Knights of the Golden Circle," controlled the convention and that treason was in process.[48] State Treasurer William Butler, a Republican, predicted that the partisan delegates would "attempt to take the State out of the Union."[49]

Four prominent Copperheads, Orlando B. Ficklin, Samuel Buckmaster, William J. Allen, and James W. Singleton, dominated the so-called "Copperhead Convention." Antirailroad arguments and action occupied the major share of its time—even the "Granger idea" that public utilities were subject to state regulation was forcefully promoted. The attack upon the railroads came from every

[45] Osborn to "My dear Sir," February 18, 1863, "President's Letter-Book: W. H. Osborn," Illinois Central Railroad Company Manuscripts.

[46] Osborn to David Dowst Company, New York, February 18, 1863, *ibid*.

[47] Osborn to H. V. Poor, New York, February 18, 1863, *ibid*. The italics are the author's.

[48] Chicago *Tribune*, June 5, 1862. Criticism of the *Tribune*'s charges was voiced from the floor of the convention. See *Journal of the Constitutional Convention of the State of Illinois convened at Springfield on January 7, 1862* (Springfield, 1862), pp. 941–944.

[49] William Butler to Lyman Trumbull, February 4, 1862, Lyman Trumbull Manuscripts (microfilm in Illinois State Historical Society, Springfield).

quarter. Delegate Daniel Reilly, the miller who spoke for the farmers of Randolph County, asserted that the closing of the Mississippi gave the railroads an opportunity to defraud the farmers by excessive freight rates.[50] Delegate R. B. M. Wilson of Tazewell County resented the practice which forced local governments to buy railroad bonds or stock in order to determine the course of the line; he pointed out that every county from Terre Haute to St. Louis went into debt between $80,000 and $100,000 by subscribing for railroad stock. Morgan County, he said, subscribed to stock in two railroads and issued bonds to cover the $200,000 indebtedness. Foreclosures wiped out the stock and left the farmers shouldering a heavy yet empty bag. Too many farmers and too many local governmental units, complained Wilson, "have been bitten by this monster of appropriations for railroads."[51]

Downstate delegates from the "Copperhead country" denounced the free pass system as a form of bribery. They desired an oath from incoming state officials that they had never "received or accepted any free ticket, gift, or gratuity from any railroad company." Copperheads candidly condemned railroad officials who authorized bribes in the form of free travel, champagne suppers, or outright gifts.[52] Some complained that outsiders, representing "foreign capital," dictated "when we may ride and how much we shall pay per mile."[53] Others, continuing the Grangerlike arguments, insisted that it was the right and "the duty of a State" to control all corporations created by it and to relate restrictions to public welfare.[54] They weighed a demand for uniform rates per mile for both passengers and freight, but failed in the effort to write such a requirement into the state's fundamental law.[55] They discussed the desirability of disqualifying all railway corporation officials from membership in the legislature.[56]

[50] "Proceedings of the Illinois State Constitutional Convention, January 21, 1862," Springfield *Illinois State Journal*, January 22, 1862.

[51] Springfield *Illinois State Journal*, February 11, 12, 18, 1862.

[52] *Ibid.*, February 6, 1862.

[53] *Ibid.*, January 22, 1862. See also D. C. Wilbur in *Transactions of the Illinois State Agricultural Society, 1861–1864* (Springfield, 1865), p. 631.

[54] *Ibid.*

[55] *Journal of the Constitutional Convention of the State of Illinois . . . 1862*, p. 55.

[56] *Ibid.*, p. 593.

The newly drafted constitution was loaded with provisions aimed at the railroads. It contained a clause, Jeffersonian and Grangerlike, that all private property was "subservient to the public welfare." It guaranteed to railway mechanics a lien upon the product of their work. Another section declared that rolling stock of railroads was "personal property and liable to execution as such." It prohibited local governments which were willing to lend their credit to chartered companies from becoming, in any way, subscribers to the stock of such corporations. Another clause bound the Illinois Central to its charter obligations and forbade any future legislature to release the company from them—nullifying the vigorous lobbying activities of William H. Osborn and John M. Douglas, president and attorney, respectively, of the railroad.[57] The convention membership tried to reduce the influence of lobbyists by increasing legislators' salaries. It tried to check "private and special legislation" by providing that bills should be read at large on three separate days and by specifying that only general laws should be passed on certain subjects—for special legislation had become a "crying evil" under the old state constitution.[58] The agrarian spokesmen were bold in contending,

[57] Osborn's correspondence, November 19, 1861—July 1, 1862, "President's Letter-Book: W. H. Osborn," Illinois Central Railroad Company Manuscripts, reveals the fears of the road's chief executive and shows the company's interest in the convention's daily deliberations. Osborn's letter of March 12, 1862, to John D. Caton expresses the President's disgust: "To add to our troubles the Constitutional Convention stirs up something every week—and I sometimes wish I could go away as fast as a telegraph message." Another letter of March 12, 1862, to Thomas E. Walker proves that the lobbying activities concerning the Illinois Central constitutional clause were not wholly futile: "The resolution as at first adopted would have been almost fatal to us. D. [Douglas, chief lobbyist for the road] succeeded in getting out the fatal word—and as at last determined we are in the same position we have always been in. I think we may yet improve the resolution, but . . . [it is] hazardous to touch it." Much earlier Osborn had written to the treasurer: "We have muzzled the only mischievous fellow who has appeared thus far." (Osborn to Walker, February 7, 1862, *ibid.*) Douglas' lobbying activities on behalf of the road are revealed in "Letter-Book, J. M. Douglas, Attorney, March 6, 1860—January 25, 1864," J. M. Douglas Out-Letters file, Illinois Central Railroad Company Manuscripts. See esp. Douglas to John Barnard, February 19, 1862, *ibid.*

[58] *Journal of the Constitutional Convention of the State of Illinois . . . 1862*, p. 27; Oliver M. Dickerson, *The Illinois Constitutional Convention of 1862* (Urbana, 1905), p. 27; Chicago *Times*, June 3, 1862.

"There are other interests in the State besides commerce and industry."[59]

The agrarian-controlled convention undid its own work by an exhibition of rank partisanship, base politics, slipshod leadership, and inopportune extension of its authority into outlying fields. It halved the terms of the incumbent Republican state officials, and it gerrymandered when reapportioning the legislative and congressional districts. It busied itself with diverse and sundry investigations and played politics in wartime.

Governor Yates's Republicans capitalized upon Copperhead errors of judgment. Editor Joseph Medill led the attack upon the newly drafted constitution with its many antirailroad provisions. It was, he contended, a "secession swindle" and an "infamous fraud," engineered and supported by the "traitorous Knights of the Golden Circle."[60] Illinois Central officials opposed the new constitution, but they refused to proclaim their opposition openly for fear of a popular reaction.[61] But William B. Ogden, on the way to becoming "Railway King of the Northwest," campaigned actively for the defeat of the proposed constitution. He pointed out that railroads had contributed much to Illinois' development and declared that the old constitution was adequate. "We do not require a change in the present Constitution," Ogden told a Chicago audience on the eve of the election, "and we should hesitate ere we make one, lest we might apply to ourselves the inscription on the tombstone: 'I was well; I took medicine, and here I am.'"[62]

The new constitution failed of ratification, at least in part, because the banks, the express companies, and the railroads threw their weight against the document.[63] Douglas, the Illinois Central's efficient lobbyist, was "jubilant over the results."[64] Medill's *Tribune*,

[59] "Proceedings of the Illinois State Constitutional Convention . . . January 21, 1862," Springfield *Illinois State Journal*, January 22, 1862.

[60] Joseph Medill's paper continued to preach against the "Springfield abomination" which the editor contended was "conceived in sin and brought forth in iniquity." (Chicago *Daily Tribune*, June 2, 5, 6, 7, 9, 14, 16, 1862.)

[61] Osborn to Walker, March 19, 1862, "President's Letter-Book; W. H. Osborn," Illinois Central Railroad Company Manuscripts.

[62] Chicago *Daily Tribune*, June 17, 1862.

[63] Chicago *Times*, June 20, 1862.

[64] John F. Tucker to Osborn, June 20, 1862, "President's Letter-Book: W. H. Osborn," Illinois Central Railroad Company Manuscripts.

ignoring the economic issues, headlined an editorial, "Illinois Saved from the Grasp of Traitors," and expressed delight that "the traitors of Illinois and their infamous schemes are buried out of sight."[65]

The Illinois legislature of 1863—accused of "secesh sympathies" by the Republican press—again revealed the tie between Copperheadism and Grangerism. In this unusual session, prorogued by Governor Yates for its peace proposals and stigmatized as "traitorous,"[66] the antirailroad element was again active. Senator William Berry, McDonough County Democrat, introduced a significant resolution on January 9:

> *Resolved*, That the committee on Judiciary be instructed to examine whether or not the present exorbitant and ruinous rates of charges for transportation on the railroads of this state, can be restrained by law, and if so, to report a bill effectually guarding the interests of the country and the people against the same.[67]

The Senate soon passed a bill which threatened to put this "Granger idea" of the postwar era into law. The proposal restricted railroad earnings to 10 per cent, and it set up a three-member commission with rate-making powers.[68] Ogden, who was then planning the consolidation of a number of lines into the Chicago and Northwestern Railroad system, gave the ablest speech against it, although he had capable support from a Republican colleague, William H. Underwood.[69] Railroad companies increased their activity at Springfield.[70] Edward L. Baker, president of the Chicago, Burlington & Quincy, opposed the bill and presented the railroaders' views:

> The idea of establishing a uniform system of fares and freights on the railroads is as preposterous as it would be to compel all your legislators

[65] Chicago *Daily Tribune*, June 21, 1862.

[66] Chicago *Weekly Journal*, January 16, June 19, 1863; Springfield *Illinois State Journal*, June 16, 1863; *Western Railroad Gazette* (Chicago), Vol. VII (May 30, 1863); Chicago *Tribune*, February 12, 1863.

[67] Illinois, *Journal of the Senate, 1863* (Springfield, 1863), pp. 70–71.

[68] "Proceedings of the Legislature, 1863," summarized in Springfield *Daily Illinois State Journal*, January 14, 1863; Chicago *Weekly Journal*, February 13, 1863; Illinois *Journal of the Senate, 1863*, pp. 89, 193–194, 210–211.

[69] Chicago *Weekly Journal*, February 13, 1863; Chicago *Tri-Weekly Tribune*, February 5, 6, 1863.

[70] Charles Butler (president of the St. Louis, Alton & Terre Haute) to W. D. Griswold, January 9, 1863, "St. Louis, Alton & Terre Haute Out-Letters," Illinois Central Railroad Company Manuscripts.

—big men and little men—to eat the same quantity of roast beef and plum pudding daily, winter and summer, & to wear pen jackets of the same size all the year around.[71]

The *Western Railroad Gazette*, circulating by its own admission "with the especial view to subserve the interests of Railroad men,"[72] waged a vicious war upon "the fire in the rear scoundrels"—those "miserable, sneaking, God-forsaken, pusillanimous Copperheads" of the 1863 legislature. Governor Yates weakly defended the railroad against the monopoly charges,[73] while the Chicago *Journal*, the Chicago *Tribune*, and the *State Journal* aided the cause of the railroads by slandering the legislators as "pro-Southern schemers," "treason mongers," and "secessionist-disunionists." "Our Springfield dispatches," warned the keeper of the Republican party conscience, "say that the leaders of the copperheads intend revolution against the authority of the General Government."[74] It accused them of perfecting a "secession movement under the auspices of the Knights of the Golden Circle."[75]

Meanwhile, the railroad commission bill found the going heavier in the lower house as the opposition organized and strengthened its lines. But the bill finally passed the preliminary hurdles and was made the special order for June 10.[76]

The legislature, however, had been concerned with more than the railroad commission bills. The Copperheads had adulterated their antirailroad brew with impure ingredients—poisonous politics and peace proposals. Popular opinion, framed and fanned by the Radical Republican press, Governor Yates's supporters, and the railroad interests, deserted the Copperhead legislators. On the morning of June 10, minutes before the railroad bill was scheduled for "special order" discussion in the lower house, Yates prorogued the legislature. This tactical and parliamentary victory of the

[71] Edward L. Baker to Amos T. Hall (treasurer), January 17, 1863, "E. L. Baker Out-Letters," Chicago, Burlington & Quincy Railroad Manuscripts, Newberry Library.

[72] *Western Railroad Gazette*, Vol. VII (May 30, June 13, 1863).

[73] Yates, "Message to the Legislature, January 5, 1863," Chicago *Daily Tribune*, January 7, 1863.

[74] Chicago *Daily Tribune*, January 7, February 12, 16, 1863.

[75] Chicago *Tri-Weekly Tribune*, February 6, 1863.

[76] Illinois, *Journal of the House of Representatives, 1863*, pp. 117, 502–503, 681.

Governor and his partisans quashed the Copperhead plan to endorse a national peace convention and it nullified the schemes of Democratic plotters—plans to take army patronage out of Yates's hands and a conspiracy to reapportion in favor of the antiadministration party. But it also killed the railroad commission bill and invalidated the work of the antirailroad interests. While the railroad men applauded, Republican chieftains congratulated Governor Yates for his "brilliant coup d'etat" in proroguing "the copperhead swell mob late known as the Illinois Legislature."[77] The Democratic malcontents, meanwhile, were left stewing in their own juice, a bitter compound of Copperhead incompetency combined with venal politics.

Administration strategy, highlighted by the attempt to tie the tail of treason to the Democratic kite, placed the opposition party at a disadvantage. Rising farm prices in late 1863, the pressure of patriotism, soldier-voting laws and practices, military-political control of the border states, and Copperhead clumsiness combined to render the protest of the midwestern malcontents ineffective. Vallandigham's persecution complex and his distasteful deportment also nullified the protests of the western sectionalists. New England's industrialism held the whip hand in the later phases of the Civil War and the objections of the dissenting Democrats of the Midwest were overruled. The Jeffersonian protests of the western sectionalists against "revitalized Whiggery" and "galvanized Federalism," ably expressed by Illinois Copperheads in the constitutional convention of 1862 and the "Copperhead Legislature" of 1863, were hushed until revived in the postwar years by the Greenbackers and Grangers.

Midwestern Copperheadism had much in common with Grangerism. Both were sectional protests. Both were grounded in economic grievances. Both flaunted the banner of state rights, emphasized civil liberties and individual rights, and muttered Jeffersonian phrases. They spoke of human rights and of opposition to the vested interests. Grangerism, yet unnamed, was evident in the claims and language of that lesser known Copperhead who represented Schuyler County at the Illinois constitutional convention and who succinctly stated, "I believe this doctrine of vested rights is a great humbug—a cobweb—gotten up by the lawyer to confuse the

[77] *Western Railroad Gazette*, Vol. VII (June 13, 1863).

common man."[78] It was evident in the words of the Democrat Daniel Reilly, Copperhead from lower Illinois, when he lustily proclaimed:

> We believe down in Egypt—in that part of Egypt I have the honor of representing—that all our railroad corporations are creatures of the State; that what rights and immunities they have were all derived from the State; that they have derived their existence from the State. And we believe also, that railroad corporations are a power in the State not to be despised, but rather to be treated with favor; but that these great establishments are not worthy of favor if they do not favor the interests of the people. . . .[79]

Truly, Grangerism existed in the Middle West before Oliver Hudson Kelly contributed the name, the organic structure, and the organizing zeal.

Not all Copperheads were antirailroad men, nor were all antirailroad men Copperheads. But it was no coincidence that Illinois Copperheads in session, whether in the constitutional convention of 1862 or the legislature of 1863, took measures to check the railroad abuses and to proclaim the Granger doctrine of state control and regulation.

Reprinted from the *Mississippi Valley Historical Review*, XXXVIII (March, 1952), 679–694.

[78] *Journal of the Constitutional Convention of the State of Illinois . . . 1862*, p. 438.

[79] "Proceedings of the Illinois State Constitutional Convention . . . January 21, 1862," Springfield *Illinois State Journal*, January 22, 1862.

VERNON CARSTENSEN

15. The Origin and Early Development of the Wisconsin Idea

THE Wisconsin Idea is a term that has had and still has both national and international currency. Indeed, in 1952, the Democratic nominee for the presidency of the United States characterized it as one of the truly creative ideas of the twentieth century. Others both before and since have spoken as rapturously about it. With the current celebration of the fiftieth anniversary of the Extension Division, an agency intimately associated with the early flowering of the Wisconsin Idea, it is appropriate to examine briefly some of the elements involved in its origin and early development.

In 1912 Charles McCarthy wrote a book entitled *The Wisconsin Idea*, devoted to a description of the background, spirit, aims, and processes of reform legislation in Wisconsin. McCarthy declared that "no one categorical explanation of the Wisconsin idea can be given." He warned the reader that he would not find in the book "vivid pictures of perfect legislation or administration or clear-cut philosophy. He will find, on the contrary, a seemly comprehension of the difficulties of the problem as above outlined and a groping after and testing of one device after another to serve in combating the tendencies considered. He will find that patient research and care have been the watchwords used everywhere."[1] The same year Frederick C. Howe declared that Wisconsin was "an experiment station in politics, in social and industrial legislation, in the democratization of science and higher education. It is a state-wide laboratory in which popular government is being tested in its reaction on people, on the distribution of wealth, on social well-being."[2] Theodore Roosevelt in his introduction to McCarthy's book spoke

[1] Charles McCarthy, *The Wisconsin Idea* (New York, 1912), pp. 16–17.
[2] Frederick C. Howe, *Wisconsin: Experiment in Democracy* (New York, 1912), p. vii.

about Wisconsin's having become "literally a laboratory for wise experimental legislation aiming to secure the social and political betterment of the people as a whole." [3]

It would probably be impossible to get complete agreement on a detailed statement of what the Wisconsin Idea embraced, even in 1912, but many persons would agree that experimental reform based upon detailed research, the extensive use of academic and other experts in government, agriculture, and industry, and an enlightened electorate were all prominent elements. All would agree that the University of Wisconsin played an important part, directly through the work of faculty members on various advisory and administrative boards and agencies, and indirectly through the extension work of the University.

Some observers might explain the origin of the Wisconsin Idea wholly in terms of the work and personalities of three men: Robert M. La Follette, Sr., leader of the progressive Republicans in Wisconsin for a quarter of a century; Charles R. Van Hise, President of the University from 1903 to 1918; and Charles McCarthy, legislative reference librarian from 1901 to 1921. Others might insist that geography would explain it. The Capitol and the main University building are located just one mile apart, each standing on its respective section corner. State Street, laid out along the section line, connects what William Ellery Leonard called the "twin domes of law and learning." These are very important factors, but probably more important in the origin and early development of attitude and practices that comprised the Wisconsin Idea was the way in which the University had developed.

That a state-supported university should contribute directly to improved farming, more efficient industry, and better government was not a new idea in the United States even when the University of Wisconsin was created in 1848. The founders of many a nineteenth century college or university spoke and wrote about such objectives. The Iowa Constitution of 1846, for example, directed the general assembly to encourage "by all suitable means, the promotion of intellectual, scientific, moral and agricultural improvement." The early Regents of the University of Wisconsin again and again

---

[3] McCarthy, *Wisconsin Idea*, p. vii.

stated similar hopes. In 1858, a legislative committee declared that the people of Wisconsin

> have an unquestioned right to demand that . . . [the University] shall primarily be adapted to popular needs, that its course of instruction shall be arranged to meet as fully as possible, the wants of the greatest number of our citizens. The *farmers, mechanics, miners, merchants, and teachers* of Wisconsin . . . have a right to ask that the bequest of the government shall aid them in securing to themselves and their posterity, such educational advantages as shall fit them for their pursuits in life, and which by an infusion of intelligence and power, shall elevate those pursuits to a dignity commensurate with their value.[4]

But it was one thing to propose such a program; it was quite another thing to do something about it. Indeed, it was precisely at this point that general failure occurred. Several decades passed before the devices were created to translate these aspirations into educational programs. At Wisconsin the successful creation of such educational agencies rested in part upon the almost complete early failure of the University to find a way of carrying on effective agricultural education.

In 1866 at the request of the Regents, the Legislature had attached the College of Agriculture and Mechanic Arts to the University. The Regents then acquired a farm and, after some delay, hired a professor of agriculture and chemistry. The professor was little interested in agricultural education. He and other members of the faculty thought that any young man wanting to study agriculture must first complete a number of courses in natural and physical science, mathematics, law, and literature, as well as a host of other not very closely related subjects. Naturally, few students enrolled. The faculty and the president of the University justified the failure of the College to attract farmers' sons in various ways, often by implying that farmers did not want to learn.[5]

It is true that the farmers were often opposed to the new agricultural colleges and indifferent to the efforts that were being made

[4] Wisconsin Assembly, *Journal, 1858*, II, 1523.

[5] W. H. Glover, *Farm and College: The College of Agriculture of the University of Wisconsin—A History* (Madison, 1952), chaps. vi, ix; Merle Curti and Vernon Carstensen, *The University of Wisconsin: A History* (2 vols.; Madison, 1949), I, chap. xvi.

in their behalf by social reformers and professional educators, but they were not as hostile to change, as contemptuous of learning as some of the sponsors of the new colleges claimed. Their willingness to change their methods was reflected in the zeal with which they adopted farm machinery; their desire to learn was registered in their support of such institutions as the annual fairs, in their support of the state departments of agriculture and of the agricultural press. The slow rise in the popularity of agricultural education was only partly explained by the farmers' reluctance to learn the lessons of science. Through the centuries, the farmer had learned his lessons from observation. The accumulated learning of his craft was less in books, as in the professions of law and medicine and theology, than in what a father taught his son. To win the farmer, the college must find other than the bookish devices used for the instruction of lawyers, ministers, and doctors. Yet, during the early and ineffective years of agricultural instruction the farmer continued to be wooed with promises of mental discipline and theoretical knowledge.

At the annual meetings of the state agricultural organizations the farmers lambasted the University for its failure to provide agricultural education. Few had precise recommendations on what ought to be done, but they agreed, year after year, that they did not like what was being done. In the middle 1880's, a movement was launched by farm groups to separate the agricultural college from the University. A bill was introduced in the Legislature in 1883, but failed. By 1885 it looked as if the farmers might succeed. The University Regents, of course, opposed this move to chop up their domain. They met with farmer representatives, but the farmers refused to abandon their plans for a separate agricultural college.[6] The Regents then appointed a committee to study the matter. The committee brought in a report which inaugurated the famous Short Course in agriculture, a vocational educational device which was to be tremendously successful at Wisconsin and to be imitated throughout the country. It provided merely for two short winter sessions, to which anyone with a common school education would be admitted. The course was devoted exclusively to agricultural subjects. The Short Course was established by the Regents without the approval of the director of the agricultural department or the

[6] Glover, *Farm and College*, chap. vi.

faculty.[7] The attempt of the Regents to provide for utilitarian agricultural education probably reduced some of the farmer support for a separate college. More important was another bill providing $5,000 for farmers' institutes, to be managed by the Regents of the University. The one to three day institutes, which were to be held throughout the State during the winter months, gave the professors a chance to talk to the farmers and, what was perhaps more important, gave the farmers a chance to talk back. It could also connect the college with the numerous farmers' clubs then in existence. These two innovations, one imposed by the Regents on an unwilling faculty, the other by the Legislature on a surprised Board of Regents, gave the University an opportunity to have a direct influence upon farming.

The farmers' institutes quickly became popular. During the first winter an estimated 50,000 farmers attended. In 1887 the Legislature raised the appropriation for this work to $12,000 a year. When Charles Dudley Warner, an editor of *Harpers*, visited Wisconsin in 1888, he was deeply impressed by the effectiveness of the institutes. He wrote:

> The distinguishing thing about the State University is its vital connection with the farmers and agricultural interests. . . . I know of no other State where a like system of popular instruction on a vital and universal interest of the State, directed by the highest educational authority, is so perfectly organized and carried on with such unity of purpose and detail of administration; no other in which the farmer is brought systematically into such direct relations to the university.

He testified, as something less than an expert to be sure, that the institutes were a powerful influence in changing Wisconsin from a one-crop to a diversified agriculture. An agricultural revolution, he said, was taking place "greatly assisted, if not inaugurated, by this systematic, popular instruction from the University as the centre."[8] Four years later, Frederick Jackson Turner declared that "it is not too much to say that the rapid progress made by the State in the direction of dairying, horticulture and improved stock raising is in

[7] *Ibid.*, pp. 367–377, for a copy of the Vilas-Hitt report on which the Short Course was based.

[8] Charles Dudley Warner, "Studies of the Great West," *Harpers*, LXXVI (April, 1888), 771–774.

no small degree owing to the work of the institutes. Farmers are becoming more intelligent and more prosperous."[9]

A year after the institutes were launched Thomas C. Chamberlin came to the University as president. Chamberlin was quick to see the larger possibilities of this experiment in agricultural education. A geologist by training, Chamberlin was a man of originality and boldness and his mind was unfettered by commitment to any one type of learning or one discipline as the single road to educational salvation. It seemed to matter little to him whether an educational program had been tried before or whether it conformed to traditional usage. He was concerned primarily with whether it promised useful results and how it could be carried out.[10] On one occasion he declared: "Scholarship for the sake of the scholar is simply refined selfishness. Scholarship for the sake of the state and the people is refined patriotism."[11]

Chamberlin sought not only to extend the institutes and the Short Course, but urged that what was being done for the farmers could be done for the mechanics in the rising industrial cities of the State and that what could be done in the field of practical education could be done in the field of liberal education. In this he had also been influenced by the success of the English university extension work and the Chautauqua movement in the United States. In 1889 he declared to the Board of Regents:

> I have given further consideration . . . to the broader subject of rendering University aid to the various local associations who are endeavoring to extend educational influence among the people, and I would recommend the adoption of a general policy on the subject, and would advise that the University offer all the aid which the faculty can give consistent with their duties in the University to local associations or organizations engaged in endeavoring to educate the people in any industry or calling or in general culture or in any useful line, and that only the necessary expense attending such aid be charged.[12]

[9] Frederick Jackson Turner, "Extension Teaching in Wisconsin," *Handbook of University Extension*, ed. G. J. James (Philadelphia, 1893), p. 314.

[10] See Curti and Carstensen, *University of Wisconsin*, I, chap. xix, for a fuller discussion of Chamberlin's educational philosophy.

[11] *The Coming of Age of the State Universities* (n.p., 1890), p. 9.

[12] Chamberlin to the Regents, *Reports to the Regents*, Vol. C, pp. 29–30, June 18, 1889, University of Wisconsin Archives, Memorial Library.

Again the same year he declared: "The view is rising into recognition that it is also a function of a university to seek a universal educational influence in the community tributary to it." "It is no more impracticable," he asserted, "to extend the popular range of university education than to extend the sweep of the university courses."[13]

Mechanics' institutes were organized in a number of Wisconsin towns, but they met with little success. In 1891 a program of general University extension courses was inaugurated. During the first year it was estimated that some 8,500 people attended these lectures. Interest continued during the next few years, and in the middle 1890's President C. K. Adams, who had succeeded Chamberlin in 1892, reported that various reform movements had been launched in some communities as a result of the University extension lectures. But the general support of extension lectures was already beginning to dissolve. By the end of the decade this experiment in extension work had, like the mechanics' institutes, virtually disappeared. Nevertheless, by the end of the century, the farmers' institutes and other popular educational devices of the College of Agriculture were flourishing. A summer school for science teachers, begun largely as an extension project, had become so successful that it was incorporated into the regular University program.[14]

At this juncture several important events occurred. Robert M. La Follette was elected to the governorship in 1900. A graduate of the University in 1879, he had been profoundly influenced by President John Bascom, Chamberlin's immediate predecessor. He declared that Bascom's teaching was "among the most important influences in my early life." Of the University, he said: "For myself, I owe what I am and what I have done largely to the inspiration I received while there."[15] In 1901 Charles McCarthy was appointed to a minor post in the Wisconsin Free Library Commission. In 1903 Charles R. Van Hise became President of the University. Van Hise had been a classmate of La Follette's at the University and was a friend and supporter. He, too, had studied under Bascom and had been both student and colleague of Chamberlin.

In his inaugural address Van Hise proposed that professors be

---

[13] *University Catalogue*, 1888–1889, pp. 50–51.
[14] Curti and Carstensen, *University of Wisconsin*, I, 721 ff.
[15] Robert M. La Follette, *Autobiography* (Madison, 1911), pp. 26–27.

used as technical experts by the state government. He felt that professors had knowledge that might be useful in helping to solve social and political problems. Nor did he propose in vain. Governor La Follette had already begun to use them in state positions. In his *Autobiography*, he wrote:

> I made it a . . . policy, in order to bring all the reserves of knowledge and inspiration of the university more fully to the service of the people, to appoint experts from the university wherever possible upon the important boards of the state—the civil service commission, the railroad commission and so on—a relationship which the university has always encouraged and by which the state has greatly profited.[16]

In 1912, Charles McCarthy listed forty-six men who were serving both the University and the State.[17] It is impossible to measure the effect of the University professors upon legislation and state government, but it is clear that some of these men for a time exercised a strong influence. John R. Commons was the author of the act establishing the Industrial Commission and served for a period as one of the commissioners. T. S. Adams, who helped write the Wisconsin income tax law, served on the tax commission, and a number of other professors held prominent positions.[18] The fact that University professors were advising the governor and the Legislature and serving in administrative and other posts in the state government presented a novelty certain to be commented upon by reporters sent to spy out La Follette's state.

Equally important was the revival of University extension work. When Van Hise first became president, he showed very little interest in this activity. The evidence suggests that the agitation for the revival of general University extension was the work of Frank Hutchins and others connected with the Free Library Commission. Hutchins had come to Madison as a member of the staff of the superintendent of public instruction in the early 1890's. He had been instrumental in the creation of the Free Library Commission in 1895 and had become its secretary. The commission was created to assist

---

[16] *Ibid.*, p. 31.

[17] McCarthy, *Wisconsin Idea*, pp. 313–317.

[18] Howard J. McMurray, "Some Influences of the University of Wisconsin on the State Government of Wisconsin" (Unpublished Ph.D. dissertation, University of Wisconsin, 1940), pp. 39–40.

small libraries. Its functions were quickly expanded under Hutchins' leadership. It contrived and popularized the package library, it gave various assistance to small libraries, and perhaps most striking of all, it created the Legislative Reference Bureau. Such a library was made necessary because the library of the Historical Society, which for many years had been used by the Legislature, had been moved in 1900 from the Capitol to the new building on the University campus. Thus in 1901 an appropriation was made to the commission for the establishment and maintenance of a working library at the Capitol for the use of the Legislature, the executive departments, and citizens. To the post thus created Hutchins brought Charles McCarthy, one of Frederick Jackson Turner's students, whose doctoral dissertation had won the Justin Winsor prize in history. With Hutchins' aid and support McCarthy quickly expanded the services of the library to make it uniquely successful as a legislative reference bureau. At first it sought to provide legislators with all the information available on the problems on which they wished to legislate. In 1907, provision was also made to offer legislators a bill drafting service.[19]

It was the men of the Free Library Commission, Hutchins, McCarthy, and later Henry Legler, who urged Van Hise to re-establish general University extension work on a broad basis. In the summer of 1906 McCarthy had surveyed the activities of the private correspondence schools in the State. He found that some 35,000 people in the State were enrolled in such schools and that approximately $800,000 was paid annually for this instruction. At the same time Legler and McCarthy solicited comment from leading Wisconsin businessmen and politicians on the worth of University extension work. Almost unanimously they approved it.[20]

Meanwhile Van Hise had become converted. Late in 1905 he told a Washington audience that "a state university should not be above meeting the needs of the people, however elementary the instruction necessary to accomplish this."[21] The words echoed those

[19] Curti and Carstensen, *University of Wisconsin*, II, 552 ff.; Edward A. Fitzpatrick, *McCarthy of Wisconsin* (New York, 1944), pp. 41 ff.

[20] Fitzpatrick, *McCarthy*, pp. 250, 287.

[21] Charles R. Van Hise, Address to the Association of State Universities, Washington, D.C., November, 1905 (Ms), Presidents' Papers, University of Wisconsin Archives.

of his old teacher and colleague, T. C. Chamberlin. The next year University extension work was begun again on a small scale. The Legislature of 1907 was asked for a grant of $20,000 for this work and so well had the groundwork been laid that the bill passed both houses by unanimous vote. Later that year Van Hise declared to the Regents: "Too much cannot be said as to the importance of University extension under which the University goes out to the people." The farmers' courses, he felt, were fully justified, "if the fundamental conception be correct, that the University is to be managed in such a way as to be of the greatest possible service to the state." [22]

Thus provision was made for a large program of general University extension work. Louis E. Reber, then dean of the college of engineering of Pennsylvania State College, was brought to Wisconsin to direct the new department. The position, Van Hise told Reber, would be one of "developing a new line of education in state universities which I believe in the future is likely to become one of very great importance." [23]

It was Reber, a trained engineer, who implemented and expanded Van Hise's ideas. He outlined an ambitious program. He told an audience in 1915:

> Right or wrong you find here a type of University extension that does not disdain the simplest form of service. Literally carrying the University to the homes of the people, it attempts to give them what they need— be it the last word in expert advice, course of study carrying University credit, or easy lessons in cooking and sewing. University extension in Wisconsin endeavors to interpret the phraseology of the expert and offers the benefits of research to the household and the work shop, as well as to municipalities and state.[24]

Reber sought to make the Extension Division into an agency by means of which all or any knowledge not only could but would be transmitted to those who sought it or those who ought to have it.

[22] Report of the President, *Regents Biennial Report*, 1905–1906, pp. 35, 37–38.
[23] Van Hise to Reber, August 17, 1905, Presidents' Papers, University of Wisconsin Archives.
[24] Louis E. Reber, "The Scope of University Extension and its Organization and Subdivision," First National University Extension Conference, *Proceedings*, March 10–12, 1915, p. 25.

Although called University Extension, and organized to give University credit, only a small part of the work was along conventional University lines. Indeed, the division was, at its best, a people's university, designed to appeal to the people it was intended to serve. Reber and Van Hise conceived the function of the division to be largely outside the area of customary University work and, whatever might be said about it to the contrary, in terms of social or cultural benefits and the rest, its main purpose was to offer utilitarian courses at virtually any level.

Consciously patterned after the privately owned correspondence schools, aimed at being all things to all men, evangelical in outlook, unreservedly committed to the assumption that one sure way to earthly salvation lay through education, the new Extension Division developed quickly, energetically, and conspicuously. The ideas involved were not themselves unusual. The remarkable thing was that an organization was conceived and created, a staff assembled, trained, and made effective. The division consisted initially of four departments: correspondence study, instruction by lectures, debating and public discussion, and general information and welfare. The State was divided into districts and a field organization created. Textbooks were written to meet the specific need of the division. The success of the experiment was reflected in the quickly increased legislative support, in the large enrollments, and in the wide publicity. In 1915 Van Hise pointed out that in the preceding year Wisconsin devoted almost twice as much money to University Extension as did any other institution in the country. Meanwhile the College of Agriculture had broadened its extension program. The formal organization of various extension services of that college was brought about after 1909. Short courses for farmers' wives were added to those for farmers and farmers' sons. In 1910 the dean reported that over 1,000 farmers and 400 farm women had attended short courses offered by the college at Madison. The college also established a weekly press service intended to reach all state newspapers as well as the agricultural press. After 1912 another effective link between the college and the farmers was formed in the creation of the office of county agricultural representatives or county agents.[25]

[25] The foregoing paragraphs rest upon Curti and Carstensen, *University of Wisconsin*, II, 562–577.

The frank dedication of the University to service and the lines the service took won enthusiastic although not always well-informed acclaim. The times were propitious. During these years Wisconsin was experiencing a reform movement while throughout the nation various groups sought to make government more responsive to the will of the people, to bring the growing industrial and financial associations under the control of government, and to correct or at least to ameliorate the conditions of the workers in industrial cities.

For reformers generally the first step consisted of spreading information among the people. For them, as for many others, knowledge and virtue were indivisible. Given knowledge, the people would be virtuous and just. The way to correct evils was to expose them.

In 1907 William Hard in an article in *Outlook* described how the University faculty served the State. But, he contended, the University was not in politics; it simply furnished facts. "The University of Wisconsin has become a kind of 'consulting engineer' in the public life of the State. . . ." [26] The next year Lincoln Steffens published an article in the *American Magazine* entitled, "Sending a State to College." Steffens observed that most of the work of the University was utilitarian and, like Turner twenty years before, he saw the promise of better things to come. "Madison is using the conscious demand for 'utilitarian' instruction to develop the unconscious demand that exists in the American people today for light." He looked forward to the time when the University would "distribute scientific knowledge and the clear truth in plain terms to all the people for their self-cultivation and daily use." Like many another reporter who came to Madison, Steffens assumed that the Legislative Reference Library was a part of the University. This institution, he declared, was the

> most remarkable example of state service by the university. . . . Creeping into the minds of the children with pure seed, into the debates of youth with pure facts, into the opinions of voters with impersonal, expert knowledge, the state university is coming to be a part of the citizen's own mind, just as the state is becoming a part of his will. And that's what this whole story means: the University of Wisconsin is a highly conscious

[26] *Outlook*, LXXXVI (July 21, 1907), 667.

lobe of the common community's mind of the state of the people of Wisconsin.[27]

A year later E. E. Slosson declared that "it is impossible to ascertain the size or location of the University of Wisconsin. The most that one can say is that the headquarters of the institution is at the city of Madison and that the campus has an area of about 56,000 square miles." Like Lincoln Steffens, he found the influence of the University both universal and good. "Under the influence of university men, Wisconsin has become the recognized leader in progressive and practical legislation, the New Zealand of the United States."[28] In 1913, F. P. Stockbridge published an article in *World's Work* under the title, "A University that Runs a State," and the *Independent* editorialized on the state-wide forum in Wisconsin.[29] Many observers thought they saw, beyond the courses in sanitary sewerage, highway construction, and shop mathematics offered by the Extension Division, the promise of a new, completely informed, progressive America.

All of these elements, the large program of legislative reform, the expert work of the professors, the work of the Legislative Reference Library, the vigorous extension work of the University, and the staunch devotion of the University to the principle that the professors should be untrammeled in their pursuit of truth, were part of the Wisconsin Idea. Political and social reform legislation probably reached its high point in the work of the Legislature of 1911. Within the next year La Follette, McCarthy, and Howe had all written books intended, at least in part, to explain Wisconsin to the nation. Ironically, 1912 also witnessed a serious split within the ranks of the Wisconsin Progressives. McGovern, the Progressive governor, supported Roosevelt for the presidential nomination and followed him into the Bull Moose Party. Two years later a conservative Republican was nominated for the governorship, and elected. During the war the University faculty condemned La Follette for his stand on the war. The Progressives returned to power in 1920, but the old magic was gone. Van Hise died shortly after the Armistice, McCarthy in

[27] *American Magazine*, LXVII (February, 1909), 361–364.

[28] E. E. Slosson, *Great American Universities* (New York, 1910), pp. 210–244.

[29] *World's Work*, XXV (April, 1913), 699–708; *Independent*, LXXVI (November 6, 1913), 245.

1921, and La Follette in 1925. No men stepped forth immediately to take their places.

Although the agencies these men had created continued in existence, the great energy of the reform movement subsided. Perhaps the influence of the University in the fields of social and political behavior was neither as large nor as lasting as many had claimed, but for a decade and a half under the leadership of La Follette, Van Hise, and McCarthy, Wisconsin had enjoyed what William B. Hesseltine has called a successful wedding of soil and seminar, a fruitful joining of research and reform. The mark of the Wisconsin Idea is still on the State and Nation.

Reprinted from the *Wisconsin Magazine of History*, **XXXIX** (1956), 181–188.

VII

THE TENSIONS OF INDUSTRIALIZATION

Part VII
The Tensions of Industrialization

By the 1880's the Old Northwest had become part of industrialized America. The seat of the giant Standard Oil empire was at Cleveland; throughout the region, large-scale mining firms, many of them tied into railroad and metals-industry complexes, employed armies of workers; and giant ships carried iron ore and coal on the Great Lakes where four decades earlier the grain trade had dominated the waters. On the Ohio River, which half a century previously had been the highway for an armada of farmers' flatboats, plied steam vessels towing barges with the materials of heavy industry. The entire Old Northwest was crisscrossed with railroads, most of them owned by national companies whose boardrooms were located in New York and Philadelphia, where decisions were made that affected every aspect of economic life in the western states.

Despite the swiftness of industrialization, the modern order did not fasten itself, unheralded and full-blown, on the region in the post-Civil War years. In a sense, the people of the Old Northwest had been preparing the way for an industrial order since the earliest years. The territorial legislatures had granted land and water rights to gristmills and distilleries; later, the states had awarded corporate privileges and exemption from taxes to railroads and manufacturing corporations; large-scale lumbering had begun to thrive in the Great Lakes region as early as the 1850's, stimulated by favorable laws that impelled the stripping of forests and the use of streams for floating logs and for milling; and the region's cities had competed aggressively with one another to encourage local capital to move out of commerce and into manufacturing, and to attract manufacturing capital from the East.[1]

[1] See James Willard Hurst, *Law and the Conditions of Freedom in the 19th-Century United States* (Madison, Wis., 1964); and Hurst, *Law and Economic Growth: The Legal History of the Lumber Industry in Wisconsin* (Cambridge, Mass., 1964). Also, there are

Nor were the people of the Old Northwest entirely unaware that they were changing their social order dramatically. In the 1862 constitutional debate, the people of Illinois seemed to understand well enough that they were debating the future of their state as an industrial commonwealth. And as we have seen, the Copperheads of the Civil War years and the Grangers of the following decade dramatized the fact that complexes of private economic power had already established a firm grip on social and economic life in their West. Moreover, the promoters of urban growth, who championed this city or that and articulated a vision of "a West of cities" did not pretend that such growth would leave basic social institutions untouched.[2] "If I can read the signs of the times," a conservative Democratic leader in Ohio declared as early as 1850, "there is to be a contest in this country—a legislative one—between capital and labor, between the capitalists and the working men. That contest has hardly begun, and this generation may not know which will have the mastery."[3] And yet, despite such forebodings, when fierce contests between labor and capital wracked the West in the 1870's, many seemed taken by surprise—astonished to realize how thoroughly their old social order had crumbled.

In his analysis of labor strife in the seventies, Herbert G. Gutman, professor of history in the University of Rochester, argues that the social structure and the prevailing ideology in small industrial communities vitally affected the balance of power between capitalists and their employees. His essay is not concerned exclusively with the Old Northwest, though much of its evidence is drawn from the

---

abundant references to early public economic policy in Beverley W. Bond, Jr., *The Civilization of the Old Northwest* (New York, 1934).

[2] See articles by Stanley Jones and Frank L. Klement in this volume. Also, Charles N. Glaab, "Jesup W. Scott and a West of Cities," *Ohio History*, Vol. LXXIII (Winter, 1964); and James C. Malin, *The Contriving Brain and the Skillful Hand* (Lawrence, Kan., 1955), pp. 199 ff.

[3] Judge Joseph R. Swan, quoted in Ohio Constitutional Convention, 1850, *Official Reports of the Debates and Proceedings*, ed. J. V. Smith (Columbus, 1851), p. 368. In *The Search for Order, 1877–1900* (New York, 1967), Robert H. Wiebe provides a brilliant analysis of the small-town and rural responses to the new social-economic order. As indicated in the Gutman essay and in the studies by Jones and Klement reprinted in this volume, there were important lines of continuity between the responses to industrialization in the pre-Civil War and postwar eras.

region, for his data indicate that the differences among geographic regions in postwar America were less important than the differences between small towns and the large urban centers. The ideology that he cites as a major factor in class relationships is not a uniquely "western" ideology but rather a "pre-industrial" ideology, which stressed the imperative need for humane, face-to-face relationships among men in society, and which was reinforced by the strong sense of community that prevailed in the industrial towns. Whereas the middle class in the large cities had lost contact with the workers in mine and factory, in the towns the shopkeepers and professionals (including newspaper editors and even local police officials) still adhered to pre-industrial morality: they could not easily treat the distressed condition of their worker-neighbors in terms of *laissez-faire* abstractions.

Professor Gutman stresses that the industrial towns were remarkably homogeneous, despite ethnic diversity of the population in some, because so large a portion of the population was engaged as wage laborers. He stresses further that there was a high degree of participation by workers in the political process: the workers were voters, many held public office, and they did not hesitate to mobilize their governments for community purposes. Finally, he underlines the fact that when unemployment or a prolonged labor strike occurred, the entire population of the industrial town responded to the emergency as a community problem. When such a "time of troubles" came, cohesiveness was reinforced and genuinely community-wide action followed. All the key elements in Gutman's analysis parallel the components of the recent reformulation by Stanley Elkins and Eric McKitrick of the Turner thesis respecting the frontier's effects on democratic political institutions and behavior. In the Elkins-McKitrick model, the high degree of participation and "widespread sense of personal competence to make a difference" by action through politics, manifest in frontier communities, is explained by two major factors. First, the frontier settlement characteristically was faced with a wide range of problems; and second, such communities were basically homogeneous in the Old Northwest (with fewer class distinctions prevailing, for example, than in less "democratic" frontiers such as the plantation country of the new Southwest). Therefore times of troubles—the need for problem-solving in community fashion—

mobilized men in politics and in privately organized groups.[4] More-over, Elkins and McKitrick argue that political mobilization on dem-ocratic lines was most striking in the towns (the "urban frontier") of the Old Northwest: there, men associated their private economic welfare, and linked their individual hopes and aspirations, most con-cretely to the community. "Every town was a promotion.... Everyone understood that success must depend upon the town's prosperity."[5]

Professor Gutman's study suggests that political and social development in the small industrial communities of post-Civil War America was in many ways comparable to the processes that Elkins and McKitrick describe on the Old Northwest's early frontier. Nor can one say that the industrial towns responded to emergencies as they did because of their "frontier tradition"—for some of them were not even founded until the 1860's; they were built up in an industrial landscape, not in an unblemished wilderness, and they were factory or mining towns from the start. Instead, one can probably explain the striking resemblances between them and the early towns of the West by reference to their pre-industrial ideology, their social structure, and the powerful sense of community: here, as in frontier Cincinnati or Sandusky, "everyone understood that success must depend upon the town's prosperity," and prosperity was not a concept divorced from the workers' welfare. The postwar industrial towns were not vestiges of an agrarian-frontier era, but rather were vestiges of pre-industrial America. By the 1870's, cities such as Chicago and Cleveland were part of a new industrial-urban order—and the heavy-handed suppression of labor disorders in those cities indicated that they had reached a new stage of development. In the smaller towns, however, the older social order remained.[6] It was

[4] Stanley Elkins and Eric McKitrick, "A Meaning for Turner's Frontier," *Political Science Quarterly*, LXIX (September, 1954), 321–330 *et passim*.

[5] *Ibid.*, pp. 342–343. They stress the "setting in which the people are close enough together to make common efforts possible, and a social texture thick enough to make it not only feasible but crucial to organize for a variety of objects." (*Ibid.*, p. 340.)

[6] There is remarkable similarity too between the response of the small towns and cities that Professor Gutman treats and the way in which a rural county in Michigan reacted to the loss of livestock caused by railroad accidents on an unfenced Michigan Central Railroad track in the 1840's. Professional and middle-class people coalesced with the small farmers who were being hurt, against the

under attack to be sure; and in some of the small communities, social cohesiveness proved no match for forces that could be mobilized from outside: infusions of strikebreakers, the appearance of the state militia, and the like. But even in postwar America the concepts of community welfare and community defense were still vital.

---

corporation; local juries refused to indict; and the corporation exerted what leverage it could mainly by going outside the local environment, using private detectives and mobilizing state officials friendly to its interests. This fascinating episode in pre-Civil War anti-railroad agitation is treated at length in Charles Hirschfeld, *The Great Railroad Conspiracy* (East Lansing, 1953).

For analysis of urbanization and industrialization in the states of the Old Northwest, see Harvey S. Perloff *et al.*, *Regions, Resources, and Economic Growth* (Baltimore, 1960), pp. 9 ff., 109–221. There is much on the area's growth, too, in Edward C. Kirkland, *Industry Comes of Age: Business, Labor, and Public Policy, 1860–1897* ("Economic History of the United States," ed. Henry David *et al.*, Vol. VI [New York, 1961]). See also George R. Taylor and Irene D. Neu, *The American Railroad Network, 1861–1890* (Cambridge, Mass., 1956); W. B. Gates, Jr., *Michigan Copper and Boston Dollars* (Cambridge, Mass., 1951); Harold F. Williamson and Arnold Daum, *The American Petroleum Industry: Age of Illumination* (Evanston, Ill., 1959); Edith Abbott, *The Tenements of Chicago* (Chicago, 1936); and William T. Hutchinson, *Cyrus Hall McCormick: Harvest, 1856–1884* (New York, 1935). Also, Henry David, *The History of the Haymarket Affair* (New York, 1936); and Almont Lindsey, *The Pullman Strike* (Chicago, 1942), on labor crises. A path-breaking reinterpretation of Progressive responses to the new urban social order is provided by Samuel P. Hays, in his "The Politics of Reform in Municipal Government in the Progressive Era," *Pacific Northwest Quarterly*, LV (October, 1964), 157–169.

16. The Workers' Search for Power: Labor in the Gilded Age

UNTIL very recent times, the worker has never seemed quite so glamorous or important as his counterpart, the entrepreneur. This is especially true of the Gilded Age, where attention focuses more readily and with greater delight upon Jim Fisk or Commodore Vanderbilt or John D. Rockefeller than on the men whose labor built their fortunes to dizzying heights. Furthermore, those studies devoted to labor in this period have devoted too much attention to too little. Excessive interest in the Haymarket riot, the "Molly Maguires," the great strikes of 1877, the Homestead lockout, the Pullman strike, and close attention to the violence and disorder attending them has obscured the deeper and more important currents of which these things were only symptoms. Close attention has also focused on the small craft unions, the Knights of Labor, and the early Socialists, thus excluding the great mass of workers who belonged to none of these groups, and creating an uneven picture of labor in the Gilded Age.[1] Surely it is time to broaden the approach into a study of labor in the society of the time as a whole.

Labor history in the Gilded Age had little to do with those matters traditionally and excessively emphasized by scholars. Too few workers belonged to trade unions to make them that important; it is that simple. There is a fundamental distinction between the wage-earners as a social class and the small minority of the working population that belonged to labor organizations. The full story of the wage-earner in that era is much more than the tale of struggling craft unions and the exhortations of committed trade-unionists and assorted reformers and radicals. The dramatic events that rise up out of that generation's labor history mask significant underlying developments. Finally, the national perspective emphasized by so

[1] See John R. Commons *et al.* (eds.), *A Documentary History of American Industrial Society* (New York, 1958), IX, i–viii.

many labor historians often blurs and misrepresents those issues important to large segments of the post-bellum working population and to other economic and social groups who had contact with the wage-earner.[2] Most of the available literature about labor in the Gilded Age is excessively thin and suffers from serious and fundamental deficiencies. There are huge gaps in our knowledge of the entire period.[3] Little of the secondary literature is concerned with the workers themselves, their communities, and the day-to-day occurrences that shaped their outlook. The narrow institutional development of trade unions has been emphasized more than the way the social and economic structure and the ideology of a rapidly industrializing society affected workers and employers. Excessive concern with craft workers has meant the serious neglect of the impact of a new way of life, industrial capitalism, upon large segments of the population.

A rather stereotyped conception of labor and of industrial relations in the Gilded Age has gained widespread credence. Final and conclusive generalizations about labor abound. A labor economist describes industrial conflict in the 1870's in an authoritative fashion:

> During the depression from 1873 to 1879, employers sought to eliminate trade unions by a *systematic* policy of lock outs, blacklists, labor espionage, and legal prosecution. The *widespread* use of blacklists and Pinkerton labor spies caused labor to organize *more or less* secretly, and *undoubtedly* helped bring on the violence that *characterized* labor strife during this period. [Emphasis added.][4]

[2] See Thomas C. Cohran, "The Social Sciences and the Problem of Historical Synthesis," in Fritz Stern (ed.), *The Varieties of History* (New York, 1956), pp. 352–356; Frank Tannenbaum, *A Philosophy of Labor* (New York, 1952), p. 68; John Hall, "The Knights of St. Crispin in Massachusetts, 1869–1878," *Journal of Economic History*, XVII (June, 1958), 174–175.

[3] The literature is voluminous, if not always accurate or comprehensive; see Harold Williamson (ed.), *The Growth of the American Economy* (New York, 1951), p. 462; Anthony Bimba, *The Molly Maguires* (New York, 1932); J. Walter Coleman, *The Molly Maguire Riots* (Richmond, Va., 1936); George McNeil (ed.), *The Labor Movement* (New York, 1892), pp. 241–267; Andrew Roy, *A History of the Coal Miners of the United States* (Columbus, 1903); John R. Commons *et al.*, *History of Labor in the United States* (New York, 1918), II, 179–180; McAlister Coleman, *Men and Coal* (New York, 1943), pp. 42–44; Arthur Suffern, *Conciliation and Arbitration in the Coal Industry of America* (Boston, 1915), pp. 7–17.

[4] Richard Lester, *Economics of Labor* (New York, 1947), p. 545.

A labor historian asserts, "Employers *everywhere* seemed determined to rid themselves of 'restrictions upon free enterprise' by smashing unions."[5] The "*typical* [labor] organization during the seventies," writes another scholar, "was secret for protection against intrusion by outsiders."[6] Such seemingly final judgments are very questionable. How *systematic* were lockouts, blacklists, and legal prosecutions? How *widespread* was the use of labor spies and private detectives? Was the secret union the *typical* form of labor organization? Did violence *characterize* industrial relations?

It is widely believed that the industrialist exercised a great deal of power and had almost unlimited freedom of choice when dealing with his workers after the Civil War. Part of this belief reflects the weakness or absence of trade unions. Another justification for this interpretation, however, is somewhat more shaky. It is the assumption that industrialism generated new kinds of economic power which, in turn, *immediately* affected the social structure and the ideology of that time. The supposition that "interests" rapidly reshaped "ideas" is entirely too simple and therefore misleading. "The social pyramid," Joseph Schumpeter pointed out, "is never made of a single substance, is never seamless." There is no single *Zeitgeist*, except in the sense of a construct. The economic interpretation of history "would at once become untenable and unrealistic . . . if its formulation failed to consider that the manner in which production shapes social life is essentially influenced by the fact that human protagonists have always been shaped by past situations."[7] Too often, the study of industrial development and industrial relations in the Gilded Age has neglected these pertinent strictures.

Careful study of a number of small industrial communities in this era suggests that the relationships between "interest" and "ideology" was very complex and subtle. In this period, industrial capitalism was relatively new as a total way of life and therefore was not fully institutionalized. Much of the history of industrialism at that time is the story of the painful process by which an old way of

[5] Herbert Harris, *American Labor* (New Haven, 1938), p. 75.

[6] Selig Perlman, "Upheaval and Reorganization Since 1876," in Commons *et al.*, *History of Labor*, II, 196.

[7] J. A. Schumpeter, "The Problem of Classes," in Reinhard Bendix and Seymour Lipset (eds.), *Class, Status and Power* (Glencoe, 1953), p. 79.

life was discarded for a new one. The central issue was the rejection or modification of an old set of "rules" and "commands" which no longer fit the new industrial context. Since so much was new, traditional stereotypes about the popular sanctioning of the rules and values of industrial society either demand severe qualification or entirely fall by the wayside. Among questionable commonly held generalizations are those that insist that the worker was isolated from the rest of society; that the employer had an easy time and a relatively free hand in imposing the new disciplines; that the spirit of the times, the ethic of the Gilded Age, worked to the advantage of the owner of industrial property; that workers found little if any sympathy from nonworkers; that the quest for wealth obliterated nonpecuniary values; and that industrialists swept aside countless obstacles with great ease. The usual picture of these years portrays the absolute power of the employer over his workers and emphasizes his ability to manipulate a sympathetic public opinion as well as various political, legal, and social institutions to his advantage.

The story is not so simple, however, as intensive examination of numerous strikes and lockouts shows. The new way of life was more popular and more quickly sanctioned in large cities than in small towns dominated by one or two industries. Put another way, the social environment in the large American city after the Civil War was more often hostile toward workers than was that in the smaller industrial towns. Employers in large cities had more freedom of choice than their counterparts in small towns where local conditions of one kind or another often hampered the employer's decision-making power. The ideology of many nonworkers in these small towns was not entirely hospitable toward industrial, as opposed to traditional, business enterprise. Strikes and lockouts in large cities seldom lasted as long as similar disputes outside of these urban centers. In the large city, there was almost no sympathy for the city worker from the middle and upper classes. At the same time, a good deal of pro-labor and anti-industrial sentiment (the two are not necessarily the same) flowed from similar occupational groups in the small towns. It is a commonplace that the small-town employer of factory labor often reached out of his local environment for aid of one kind or another in solving industrial disputes, but insufficient attention has been given to those elements in the contemporary social structure and ideology which shaped such decisions.

Though the direct economic relationships in large cities and in small towns and outlying industrial regions were essentially similar, the social structure in each of these areas was profoundly different. Here is the crucial clue to these distinct patterns of thought and behavior. Private enterprise was central to the economy of the small industrial town as well as to that of the large metropolitan city, but it functioned in a different social environment. The social structure and ideology of a given time are not derived only from economic institutions.[8] In the Gilded Age, a time of rapid economic and social transformation and a time when industrial capitalism was still young and relatively new to the United States, parts of an ideology that were alien to the new industrialism retained a powerful hold on the minds of many who lived outside the large cities.

Men and their thoughts were different in the large cities. "The modern town," John Hobson wrote of the large nineteenth-century cities, "is a result of the desire to produce and distribute most economically the largest aggregate of material goods: economy of work, not convenience of life, is the object." In such an environment, "anti-social feelings" were exhibited "at every point by the competition of workers with one another, the antagonism between employers and employed, between sellers and buyers, factory and factory, shop and shop."[9] Persons dealt with each other less as human beings and more as "things." The *Chicago Times*, for example, argued that "political economy" was "in reality the autocrat of the age" and occupied "the position once held by the Caesars and the Popes."[10] According to the *New York Times*, the "antagonistic . . . position between employers and the employed on the subject of work and wages" was "unavoidable. . . . The object of trade is to get as much as you may and give as little as you can."[11] The *Chicago Tribune* celebrated the coming of the centennial in 1876 by observing, "Suddenly acquired wealth, decked in all the colors of

[8] *Ibid.*

[9] See Adna Weber, *The Growth of Cities in the Nineteenth Century* (New York, 1899), pp. 433–434.

[10] *Chicago Times*, May 22, 1876.

[11] *New York Times*, November 20, 1876.

the rainbow, flaunts its robe before the eyes of Labor, and laughs with contempt at honest poverty." The country, "great in all the material powers of a vast empire," was entering "upon the second century weak and poor in social morality as compared with one hundred years ago."[12]

More than economic considerations shaped the status of the working population in large cities after the Civil War, for the social structure there unavoidably widened the distance between the various social and economic classes. Home and job often were far apart. A man's fellow workers often differed from his friends and neighbors. Face-to-face relationships became less meaningful as the city grew larger and as production became more diverse and more specialized. "It has always been difficult for well-to-do people of the upper and middle classes," wrote Samuel Lane Loomis, a Protestant minister, in the 1880's, "to sympathize and to understand the needs of their poorer neighbors." The large city, both impersonal and confining, made it even harder. Loomis was convinced that "a great and growing gulf" lay "between the working-class and those above them."[13] A Massachusetts clergyman saw a similar void between the social classes and complained: "I once knew a wealthy manufacturer who personally visited and looked after the comforts of his invalid operatives. I know of no such case now."[14] All in all, the fabric of human relationships was cloaked in a kind of shadowed anonymity that became more and more characteristic of urban life.[15]

Social contact was more direct in the smaller post-Civil War industrial towns and regions. The *Cooper's New Monthly*, a reform trade-union journal, insisted that while "money" was the "sole measure of gentility and respectability" in large cities "a more democratic feeling" prevailed in small towns.[16] "The most happy

[12] *Chicago Tribune*, July 4, 1876.

[13] Samuel Lane Loomis, *Modern Cities and Their Religious Problems* (New York, 1887), pp. 60–61, 63–66.

[14] See Massachusetts Bureau of Labor Statistics, *Second Annual Report, 1870–1871* (Boston, 1871), p. 475.

[15] For example, see Louis Wirth, "Urbanism as a Way of Life," in Paul Hatt and Albert Reiss, Jr. (eds.), *Cities and Society* (Glencoe, 1957), pp. 36–63; Bert F. Hoselitz, "The City, the Factory, and Economic Growth," *American Economic Review*, XLV (May, 1955), 166–184.

[16] "The Distribution of Wealth," *Cooper's New Monthly*, I (July, 1874), 7–9.

and contented workingmen in the country," wrote the *Iron Molder's Journal*, "are those residing in small towns and villages. . . . We want more towns and villages and less cities."[17] Except for certain parts of New England and the mid-Atlantic states, the post-Civil War industrial towns and regions were relatively new to that kind of enterprise. The men and women who lived and worked in these areas in the Gilded Age usually had known another way of life and doggedly contrasted the present with the past. They grasped the realities of the new industrialism for a simple reason: the nineteenth-century notion of enterprise came quickly to these regions after the Civil War, but the social distance between the various economic classes that characterized the large city came much more slowly and hardly paralleled industrial developments. In the midst of the new industrial enterprise with its new set of commands, therefore, men often clung to an older ("agrarian") set of values. They often judged the economic and social behavior of local industrialists by these older and more humane values. The social structure of the large city differed from that of the small industrial town because of the more direct human relationships among the residents of the smaller towns. Although many of these persons were not personally involved in the industrial process, they always felt its presence. Life may have been more difficult and less cosmopolitan in these small towns, but it was also less complicated. This life was not romantic, for it frequently meant company-owned houses and stores as well as conflicts between workers and employers over rights that were taken for granted in agricultural communities and large cities.[18] Yet, the non-urban industrial environment had in it a kind of compelling simplicity. Its inhabitants lived and worked together, and a certain sense of community threaded their everyday lives. Men knew each other well, and the anonymity that veiled so much of urban life was not nearly so severe. There was of course more than enough economic hardship and plain despair in these towns, but the impersonal social environment of the large city in the Gilded Age was almost entirely lacking.

The first year of the 1873 depression suggests sharply the differences between the large urban center and the small industrial town.

[17] *Iron Molder's Journal* (January, 1874), p. 204.

[18] See Ohio Bureau of Labor Statistics, *First Annual Report, 1877* (Columbus, 1878), pp. 156–192.

There is no question about the severity of the economic crisis. Its consequences were felt throughout the entire industrial sector, and production, employment, and income fell sharply everywhere.[19] The dollar value of business failures in 1873 was greater than in any other single year between 1857 and 1893.[20] The deflation in the iron and steel industry was especially severe: 266 of the nation's 666 iron furnaces were out of blast by January 1, 1874, and more than 50 per cent of the rail mills were silent.[21] A New York philanthropic organization figured that 25 per cent of the city's workers, nearly 100,000 persons, were unemployed in the winter months of 1873–74.[22] "The simple fact is that a great many laboring men are out of work," wrote the *New York Graphic.* "It is not the fault of merchants and manufacturers that they refuse to employ four men when they can but one, and decline to pay four dollars for work which they can buy for two and a half."[23] Gloom and pessimism settled over the entire country, and the most optimistic predicted only that the panic would end in the late spring months of 1874.[24] James Swank, the secretary of the American Iron and Steel Association, found the country suffering "from a calamity which may be likened to a famine or a flood." "The nation," he sourly observed, "is to have a period of enforced rest from industrial development. Let the causes be what they may, the fact that we *are* resting is patent to all men."[25]

A number of serious labor difficulties occurred in small industrial towns and outlying industrial regions during the first year of the

[19] A. Ross Eckler, "A Measure of the Severity of Depression, 1873–1932," *Review of Economic Statistics*, XV (May, 1933), 75–81; O. V. Wells, "The Depression of 1873–1879," *Agricultural History*, XI (July, 1937), 237–249; Rendigs Fels, "American Business Cycles, 1865–1879," *American Economic Review*, XLI (September, 1951), 325–349; Alvin Hansen, *Business Cycles and National Income* (New York, 1951), pp. 24–26, 39–41.

[20] T. E. Burton, *Financial Crises and Periods of Industrial and Commercial Depression* (New York, 1908), p. 344.

[21] *Annual Report of the Secretary of the American Iron and Steel Association of the Year 1874* (Philadelphia, 1875), pp. 4–5.

[22] New York Association for Improving the Condition of the Poor, *Thirty-first Annual Report* (New York, 1874), p. 28.

[23] *New York Graphic*, January 14, 1874.

[24] *American Manufacturer*, October 30, 1873.

[25] *Annual Report of the Secretary of the American Iron and Steel Association for the Year 1874*, pp. 12, 81–82.

depression, revealing much about the social structure of these areas. Although each of these incidents had its own unique character, a common set of problems shaped all of them. The depression generated difficulties for employers everywhere. Demand fell away and industrialists necessarily cut production as well as costs in order to sell off accumulated inventory and retain a hold on shrinking markets. This general contraction caused harsh industrial conflict in many parts of the country. "No sooner does a depression in trade set in," observed David A. Harris, the conservative head of the Sons of Vulcan, a national craft union for puddlers and boilermen, "than all expressions of friendship to the toiler are forgotten."[26] The *New York Times* insisted that the depression would "bring wages down for all time," and it advised employers to dismiss workers who struck against wage reductions. This was not the time for the "insane imitations of the miserable class warfare and jealousy of Europe."[27] The *Chicago Times* found that strikers were "idiots" and "criminals," while its sister newspaper, the *Chicago Evening Journal*, said the economic crisis was not "an unmixed evil" because labor would finally learn "the folly and danger of trade organizations, strikes, and combinations . . . against capital."[28] *Iron Age* was similarly sanguine. "We are sorry for those who suffer," it explained, "but if the power of the trade unions for mischief is weakened . . . the country will have gained far more than it loses from the partial depression of industry." After employers withdrew "every concession" made to the unions and "forced wages down to the lowest rates, . . . simple working-men" would learn they were misled by "demagogues and un-principled agitators." Trade unions "crippled the productive power of capital" and retarded the operation of "beneficent natural laws of progress and development."[29] James Swank was somewhat more generous. Prices had fallen, and it was "neither right nor practicable for all the loss to be borne by the employers." "Some of it," he ex-plained, "must be shared by the workingmen. . . . We must hereafter

[26] See *Vulcan Record*, I (September, 1874), 12–14.

[27] *New York Times*, October 27, November 2, 15, 1873.

[28] *Chicago Times*, October 3, November 3, 1873.

[29] See *Iron Molder's Journal*, I (December, 1873), 161; *Iron Age*, May 26, 1874, p. 14.

be contented with lower wages for our labor and be more thankful for the opportunity to labor at all."[30]

In cutting costs in 1873 and 1874, many employers faced difficult problems, but a central trouble emerged when they found that certain aspects of the social structure and ideology in small industrial towns hindered their freedom of action. It proved relatively easy for them to announce a wage cut or to refuse publicly to negotiate with a local trade union, but it often proved quite difficult to enforce such decisions easily and quickly. In instance after instance, and for reasons that varied from region to region, employers reached outside of their local environment to help assert their local authority.

Industrialists used various methods to strengthen their local positions with their workers. The state militia brought order to a town or region swept by industrial conflict. Troops were used in railroad strikes in Indiana, Ohio, and Pennsylvania; in a dispute involving iron heaters and rollers in Newport, Kentucky; in a strike of Colorado ore diggers; in two strikes of Illinois coal miners; and in a strike of Michigan ore workers.[31] At the same time, other employers aggravated racial and nationality problems among workers by introducing new ethnic groups in their towns as a way of ending strikes, forcing men to work under new contracts, and destroying local trade unions. Negroes were used in coal disputes.[32] Danish, Norwegian, and Swedish immigrants were brought into mines in Illinois, and into the Shenango Valley and the northern anthracite region of Pennsylvania. Germans went to coal mines in northern Ohio along with Italian workers. Some Italians also were used in western Pennsylvania as coal miners and in western and northern New York as railroad workers.[33] A number of employers imposed

[30] *Annual Report of the Secretary of the American Iron and Steel Association for the Year 1874*, pp. 81–82.

[31] See Herbert Gutman, "Trouble on the Railroads in 1873–1874: Prelude to the 1877 Crisis?" *Labor History*, II (Spring, 1962), 215–235; *Cincinnati Enquirer*, February–March, 1874; *Chicago Times*, November 12, 1873; *Chicago Tribune*, November 10–20, 1874.

[32] *Workingman's Advocate*, March 28, June 27—July 4, 1874; John James, "The Miner's Strike in the Hocking Valley," *Cooper's New Monthly*, I (July, 1874), 4.

[33] *Chicago Tribune*, April 23, 1874; *Workingman's Advocate*, July 11–18, 1874; *New York World*, July 23, 1874.

their authority in other ways. Regional and local blacklists were
tried in the Illinois coal fields, on certain railroads, in the Ohio
Valley iron towns, and in the iron mills of eastern Pennsylvania.[34]
Mine operators in Pennsylvania's Shenango Valley and Tioga coal
region used state laws that allowed them to evict discontented workers from company-owned houses in mid-winter.[35]

In good part, the social structure in these small towns and the
ideology of many of their residents, who were neither workers nor
employers, shaped the behavior of those employers who reached
outside their local environments in order to win industrial disputes.
The story is different for every town, but has certain similarities.
The strikes and lockouts had little meaning in and of themselves,
and it is of passing interest to learn whether the employers or the
workers gained a victory. The incidents assume broader significance
as they shed light on the distribution of power in these towns and
on those important social and economic relationships which shaped
the attitudes and actions of workers and employers.

One neglected aspect of the small industrial town after the
Civil War is its political structure. Because workers made up a large
proportion of the electorate and often participated actively in local
politics, they were able at times to influence local and regional
affairs in a manner not open to wage-earners in the larger cities.
There is no evidence in 1874 that workers held elected or appointed
offices in large cities. In that year, nevertheless, the postmaster of
Whistler, Alabama, was a member of the Iron Molder's International Union.[36] George Kinghorn, a leading trade-unionist in the
southern Illinois coal fields, was postmaster of West Belleville,
Illinois.[37] A local labor party swept an election in Evansville, Indiana.[38] Joliet, Illinois, had three workers on its city council.[39] A
prominent official of the local union of iron heaters and rollers sat

[34] *Workingman's Advocate*, March 28, 1874; *Chicago Times*, November 7–9,
1874; *Cincinnati Commercial*, February 11, 1874; *Iron Age*, August 13, 1874, p. 14.

[35] See Herbert G. Gutman, "Two Lockouts in Pennsylvania, 1873–1874,"
The Pennsylvania Magazine of History and Biography, LXXXIII (July, 1959), 317–318,
322–326.

[36] *Iron Molder's Journal* (December, 1874), p. 138.

[37] *Chicago Tribune*, November 19, 1874.

[38] *Workingman's Advocate*, April 14, 1874.

[39] *Ibid.*

on the city council in Newport, Kentucky.[40] Coal and ore miners ran for the state legislature in Carthage, Missouri, in Clay County, Indiana, and in Belleville, Illinois.[41] The residents of Virginia City, a town famous to western mythology, sent the president of the local union of miners to the national Congress.[42] In other instances, town officials and other officeholders who were not wage-earners sympathized with the problems and difficulties of local workers or displayed an unusual degree of objectivity during local industrial disputes.

It was the same with many local newspapers in these towns, for they often stood apart from the industrial entrepreneur and subjected his behavior to searching criticisms. Editorials in these journals defended *local* workers and demanded redress for their grievances. Certain of these newspapers were entirely independent in their outlook, and others warmly endorsed local trade-union activities.

The small businessmen and shopkeepers, the lawyers and professional people, and the other nonindustrial members of the middle class were a small but vital element in these industrial towns. Unlike the urban middle class they had direct and everyday contact with the new industrialism and with the problems and the outlook of workers and employers. Many had risen from a lower station in life and intimately knew the meaning of hardship and toil. They could judge the troubles and complaints of both workers and employers by personal experience and by what happened around them and did not have to rely on secondary accounts. While they invariably accepted the concepts of private property and free entrepreneurship, their judgments about the *social* behavior of industrialists often drew upon noneconomic considerations and values. They saw no necessary contradiction between private enterprise and gain on the one hand, and decent, humane social relations between workers and employers on the other. In a number of industrial conflicts, segments of the local middle class sided with the workers in their communities. A Maryland weekly newspaper complained in 1876, "In the changes of the last thirty years not the least unfortunate is the separation of personal relations between employers

[40] *Cincinnati Commercial*, January 18, 1874.

[41] *Workingman's Advocate*, September 5–12, November 7, 28, 1874.

[42] *Iron Molder's Journal* (December, 1874), p. 138.

and employees."[43] At the same time that most metropolitan newspapers sang paeans of joy for the industrial entrepreneur and the new way of life, the *Youngstown Miner and Manufacturer* thought it completely wrong that the "Vanderbilts, Stewarts, and Astors bear, in proportion to their resources, infinitely less of the burden incident to society than the poorest worker."[44] The *Ironton Register* defended dismissed iron strikers as "upright and esteemed . . . citizens" who had been sacrificed "to the cold demands on business."[45] The *Portsmouth Times* boasted, "We have very little of the codfish aristocracy, and industrious laborers are looked upon here with as much respect as any class of people."[46]

Detailed illustrations of the difficulties certain employers faced when they sought to enforce crucial economic decisions in small towns reveal a great deal about the social structure of these areas and the outlook of many residents. These illustrations also tell something of the obstacles industrialists often encountered in their efforts to deal with workers.

In 1873 when the depression called a temporary halt to the expansion of the Illinois mining industry, Braidwood, Illinois, was less than a dozen years old.[47] Coal mining and Braidwood had grown together, and by 1873, 6,000 persons lived in the town. Except for the supervisors and the small businessmen and shopkeepers, most of the residents were coal miners and their families. Braidwood had no "agricultural neighborhood to give it support" and "without its coal-shafts" it would have had "no reasonable apology for existing." The town had three coal companies, but the Chicago, Wilmington and Vermillion Coal Company was by far the largest, and its president, James Monroe Walker, also headed the Chicago, Burlington, and Quincy Railroad. This firm operated five shafts and employed 900 men, more than half the resident miners. Most of the owners did not live in the town: Walker, for example, resided in Chicago. The miners were a mixed lot, and unlike most other small

---

[43] *Frostburg Mining Journal*, November 25, 1876.

[44] *Cooper's New Monthly*, I (January, 1874), 16.

[45] *Iron Age*, March 5, 1874; *Cincinnati Commercial*, January 29, February 3, 1874.

[46] *Portsmouth Times*, February 7, 1874.

[47] See Herbert G. Gutman, "The Braidwood Lockout of 1874," *JISHS*, LIII (Spring, 1960), 5–28.

industrial towns in this era Braidwood had an ethnically diverse population. About half the miners came from Ireland. Another 25 per cent were English, Welsh, and Scotch. A smaller number were Swedes, Italians, and Germans, and still others came from France and Belgium and even from Poland and Russia. There were also native-born miners. "The town of Braidwood," a contemporary noted, "is . . . nearly akin to Babel as regards the confusion of tongues."

Although they came from diverse backgrounds, the miners were a surprisingly cohesive social community. A trade union started in 1872 was strong enough to extract a reasonable wage agreement from the three coal firms. A hostile observer complained that nearly all the voters were miners and that a majority of the aldermen and justices of the peace "are or have been miners."

The depression cut the demand for coal and created serious problems for the operators. By March, 1874, at least 25 per cent of the miners were unemployed, and the town was "dull beyond all precedent." In late May the operators, led by the Chicago, Wilmington, and Vermillion firm, cut the rate for digging coal from $1.25 to $1.10 a ton and reduced the price for "pushing" coal from the work wall to the shaft nearly in half. They announced that the mines would close on June 1 unless the men accepted the new contract for a full year. The miners' efforts at compromise and suggestions of arbitration were summarily rejected, and the mines closed. The general superintendent of the largest company displayed "a haughty indifference as to whether the mines 'run' or not" and would not listen to the miners' bitter complaints that they could not have received "worse treatment in the old country" and that the "Wilmington fellows" were "right up and down monopolists." Instead, the Chicago, Wilmington, and Vermillion company contacted private labor contracting agencies in Chicago and recruited a large number of unskilled laborers, most of whom were Scandinavian immigrants and were not miners. Three days after the strike began, 65 Chicago workers arrived. More came two weeks later, and from then on a small number arrived daily until the end of July when the number increased sharply. At the same time, anticipating trouble in putting the new men to work, the operators brought special armed Chicago Pinkerton police to the town.

Difficulties plagued the operators from the start. The miners realized they had to check the owners' strategy in order to gain a victory. As soon as new workers arrived, committees of miners explained the difficulty to them. "We ask the skilled miners not to work," the leader of the strikers explained. "As to green hands, we are glad to see them go to work for we know they are . . . a positive detriment to the company." All but three of the first 65 new workers agreed to return to Chicago, and since they lacked funds the miners and other local residents paid their rail fare and cheered them as they boarded a Chicago-bound train. By mid-July one shaft that usually employed 200 men had no more than ten workers. At the end of July, only 102 men worked in the mines, and not one of them was a resident miner. The disaffected miners also met the challenge of the Pinkerton men. The miners appointed a 72-man committee to prevent violence and to protect company property. The mayor and the sheriff swore in twelve of these men as special deputies, and, with one exception (when the wives of certain miners chased and struck Allan Pinkerton), the miners behaved in a quiet and orderly manner.

Time and again, Braidwood's tiny middle class—the businessmen, the storekeepers, and the public officials—strengthened the striking miners. According to one reporter, they "all back[ed] the miners." They denied complaints by the owners that the miners were irresponsible and violent. One citizen condemned the coal companies for creating "excitement so as to crush the miners" and declared that "public sympathy" was "entirely" with the workers. The *Chicago Tribune* reporter found that "Braidwood is with the strikers root and branch." The attitude of the local publicly elected officials, for example, is of great interest. The operators wanted Pinkerton and his men appointed "special deputies" and made "merchant police" with power to arrest persons trespassing on company properties, but the mayor and the sheriff turned them down and deputized the strikers. Mayor Goodrich forbade parading in the streets by the Pinkerton men, and the sheriff ordered them to surrender their rifles and muskets. The sheriff did not want "a lot of strangers dragooning a quiet town with deadly weapons in their hands," and he said he feared the miners "a good deal less than . . . the Chicago watchmen."

The operators faced other troubles. Local judges and police officials enforced the law more rigorously against them and their men than against the resident miners. In one instance, two new workers who got into a fight one Sunday were arrested for violating the Sabbath law and fined $50 and court costs. Unable to pay the fine, they were put to work on the town streets. One of them, jailed for hitting an elderly woman with a club, was fined $100 and court costs. A company watchman was arrested four times, twice for "insulting townspeople." Frustrated in these and other ways by the miners and the townspeople, the operators finally turned for help to the state government, and E. L. Higgins, the adjutant general and head of the state militia, went to Braidwood to see if troops were needed. Higgins openly supported the mine owners. He tried to prevent union men from talking with new workers, and although he asked the mayor to meet him in the office of the Chicago, Wilmington, and Vermillion firm, he "never went to see the officers of the city . . . to gain an unprejudiced account of the strike." "If this is what the military forces and officers are kept for," one miner observed, "it is high time . . . such men [were] struck off the State Government payroll and placed where they belong." Mayor Goodrich reminded Higgins that neither the Braidwood nor the Will County authorities had asked for state interference. In a bitter letter to the *Chicago Times*, Goodrich wondered whether Higgins had come "in his official capacity or as an agent of the coal company," and firmly insisted that "the citizens of this city were not aware that martial law had been proclaimed or an embargo placed upon their speech."

Unable fully to exercise their authority in the town and worried about the possibility of losing the fall trade, the operators confessed their failure and surrendered to the strikers fourteen weeks after the conflict had started. The final agreement pleased the miners, and they were especially amused when the Chicago, Wilmington, and Vermillion company agreed to send all the new workers back to Chicago. A spokesman for the operators, however, bitterly assailed the Braidwood mayor and other public officials for their failure to understand the meaning of "peace, order, and freedom." Surely the operators had further cause for complaint in 1877 when Daniel McLaughlin, the president of the miners' union, was elected mayor of Braidwood, other miners were chosen aldermen, and one was chosen police magistrate.

Manufacturers in the small industrial iron towns of the Ohio Valley such as Ironton and Portsmouth, Ohio, and Newport and Covington, Kentucky, had troubles similar to those of the Braidwood coal operators in 1873 and 1874.[48] Several thousand men and fifteen iron mills were involved in a dispute over wages that lasted for several months. The mill owners who belonged to the Ohio Valley Iron Association cut the wages of skilled iron heaters and roller men 20 per cent on December 1, 1873. After the workers complained that the manufacturers were taking "undue advantage" of them "owing to the present financial trouble," their wages were cut another 10 per cent. The valley mill owners worked out a common policy; they decided to close all the mills for a month or so in December and then reopen them under the new scale. Hard times would bring them new workers.

Although the mill owners in large cities such as St. Louis, Indianapolis, and Cincinnati found it easy to bring in new workers from the outside, it was another story in the small towns. They could hire new hands in Pittsburgh, Philadelphia, and other eastern cities, but the social environment in Covington, Portsmouth, Newport, and Ironton made it difficult for them to hold on to these men. The locked-out workers found sympathy from other townspeople. In such an environment they were a relatively homogeneous group and made up a large part of the total population of the town. When workers agitated in small towns, paraded the streets, or engaged in one or another kind of collective activity, their behavior hardly went unnoticed.

The difficulties faced by the small-town iron manufacturers beset especially Alexander Swift, owner of the Swift Iron and Steel Works in Newport, Kentucky. Although his workers suffered from almost indescribable poverty after the factory closed, they would not surrender. When Swift reopened his mill, he had it guarded by armed "special policemen." Some of the new workers left the town after they learned of the conflict, and the "police" accompanied the rest to and from their work. The old workers made Newport un-

---

[48] See Herbert G. Gutman, "An Iron Workers' Strike in Ohio Valley, 1873–1874," *Ohio Historical Quarterly*, LXVIII (October, 1959), 353–370.

comfortable for the new hands. There was no violence at first, but many strikers and their wives, especially the English and Welsh workers, gathered near the mill and in the streets where they howled at the "black sheep" as they went to and from work. The Newport workers exerted pressure on them in "the hundred ways peculiar to workingmen's demonstrations." Swift was embittered, for at the end of January only a few men worked in his mill.

Swift was not alone in his troubles; mill owners in Covington, Ironton, and Portsmouth were in similar difficulty. Early in February, therefore, the Ohio Valley Iron Association announced that unless the men returned to work on or before February 20 they would lose their jobs and never again be hired in the valley iron mills. When most of the workers refused to return, they were fired. New workers were quickly brought to the towns, and Swift demanded special police protection for them from the Newport City Council, but it assigned only regular police to guard them. Crowds jeered the new men, and there were several fights. A large number of new workers again left Newport. Swift appealed to the police to ban street demonstrations by the workers and their families, but his plea was rejected. "We never went any further with those fellows," a striker explained, "than calling them 'black sheep' and 'little lambs.' . . . When they'd be going to work in the morning with the policemen on each side of them, we'd cry 'Ba-a-a-a.'" Swift armed his new workers with pistols. When the strikers and their supporters gathered to jeer these men, one of the new workers shot wildly into the crowd and killed a young butcher's helper. The enraged crowd chased Swift's men out of the city, and Swift, after blaming the shooting on the failure of the Newport authorities to guard his men properly, closed the mill.

These events did not go unnoticed in the Ohio Valley. The *Portsmouth Times* leveled a barrage of criticism at Swift and the other manufacturers. It asked whether or not they had a "right" to circulate the names of strikers in the same manner as "the name of a thief is sent from one police station to another." Such action was "cowardly . . . intimidation," and the *Times* asked: "Does not continued and faithful service deserve better treatment at the hands of men whose fortunes have been made by these workmen they would brand with the mark of CAIN? . . . Is this to be the reward for men who have grown gray in the service of these velvet-lined aristocrats? . . . Out on such hypocrisy!" After the shooting in Newport, the *Times* turned on Swift and called him a "blood-letter." Violence was wrong, the *Times* admitted, "wrong in theory and practice," but it nevertheless advised the striking iron workers: "If the gathered up assassins from the slums and alleys of the corrupt cities of the East are brought here to do deeds of lawlessness and violence, the stronger the opposition at the beginning the sooner they will be taught that the city of Portsmouth has no need of them."

Immune from such criticism, Swift continued to try to break down the strength of the Newport workers. In the end he succeeded. He realized that the only way to weaken the strikers was to suppress their power of public demonstration and therefore urged the Newport mayor to enforce local ordinances against dangerous and "riotous" crowds, asked the Kentucky governor to send state militia, and even demanded federal troops. Although the mayor banned "all unusual and unnecessary assemblages" in the streets, Swift still asked for state troops, and on March 5, the Kentucky governor ordered twenty-five members of the Lexington division of the state militia to Newport. The arrival of the militia weakened the strikers and created a favorable environment for Swift and his plans. Street demonstrations were banned. The police were ordered to arrest "all persons using threatening or provoking language." When a number of unskilled strikers offered to return at the lower wage, Swift turned them away. He also rejected efforts by a member of the city council to effect a compromise with the old workers. A week after the troops arrived, and three and a half months after the start of the lockout, Swift fully controlled the local situation. New men worked in his factory, and the strikers admitted defeat.

The use of troops, however, was bitterly condemned in the Ohio Valley. A reporter for the *Cincinnati Enquirer* found that the "general opinion" in Newport was that Swift's maneuver was "little else than a clever piece of acting intended to kindle public sentiment against the strikers and . . . gain the assistance of the law in breaking up a strike." A Newport judge assailed the Kentucky governor, and a local poet sang of the abuse of state power:

> Sing a song of sixpence
> Stomachs full of rye,

> Five-and-twenty volunteers,
>   With fingers in one pie;
> When the pie is opened
>   For money they will sing,
> Isn't that a pretty dish
>   For the City Council Ring?

There was less drama in the other Ohio Valley iron towns than in Newport, but the manufacturers in Portsmouth, Ironton, and Covington faced similar trouble. The old workers persuaded many new hands to leave the region. "A few men who try to work," wrote an Ironton observer, "are 'bah-d' at from the cross streets as they go to and from the shops. To have a lot of boys follow one up with cries of 'bah, black sheep' is a torment few workmen can endure." When fourteen Philadelphia workers arrived in Ironton and learned of the troubles for the first time, they left the city. Strikers paid their return rail fare. In Portsmouth, the same happened, and the departing workers publicly declared, "A nobler, truer, better class of men never lived than the Portsmouth boys . . . standing out for their rights." Nonstrikers in these towns also acted contrary to the manufacturers' interests. Each week the *Portsmouth Times* attacked the mill owners. "We are not living under a monarchy," the *Times* insisted, and the "arbitrary actions" of the employers were not as "unalterable as the edicts of the Medes and Persians." A Covington justice of the peace illustrated something of the hostility felt toward the companies. Three strikers were arrested for molesting new hands, but he freed one of them and fined the other men a dollar each and court costs. A new worker, however, was fined twenty dollars for disorderly conduct and for carrying a deadly weapon. He also had to post a $500 bond as a guarantee that he would keep the peace.

In the end, except in Newport where Swift had successfully neutralized the power of the workers, a compromise wage settlement was finally worked out. Certain of the mills succeeded in bringing in new men, but some manufacturers withdrew the blacklist and rehired their striking workers. Commenting on the entire dispute, a friend of the Ohio Valley iron manufacturers bitterly complained: "Things of this sort make one ask whether we are really as free a people as we pretend to be." Convinced that the workers had too much power and that the manufacturers were not fully free entrepreneurs, this devotee of classical laissez faire doctrine sadly concluded: "If any individual cannot dispose of his labor when and at what price he pleases, he is living under a despotism, no matter what form the government assumes."

Although hardly any Negroes worked in coal mines before 1873, soon after the depression started mine operators in the Ohio Hocking Valley recruited hundreds of Negroes from border and southern cities. Some Negroes had been sparingly employed in certain Indiana and Ohio mines, but they attracted little attention. It was different in the Hocking Valley in 1874. A large number of white miners struck and showed an unusual degree of unanimity and staying power. They found support from members of the local middle classes, and the operators, unable to wear down the strikers, brought in Negroes. Although the miners were defeated, the problems they raised for their employers indicated much the same social environment as in Braidwood and in the Ohio Valley iron towns.

The railroad revolutionized the Hocking Valley economy after the Civil War, for it opened new markets for bituminous coal, and the years between 1869 and 1873 were a time of great prosperity and economic development. Production figures shot up spectacularly: in 1870, 105,000 tons left the valley and in 1873 just over one million tons were shipped. Two years later, more than 20 per cent of the coal mined in Ohio came from the Hocking Valley. Although entry costs were low, the ten largest firms in 1874 employed nearly two-thirds of the valley's miners.[49]

The miners fell into two social groupings. Those born in and near the valley had spent most of their lives in the mines and often held local positions of public trust and esteem. A Cincinnati reporter found that miners held "a good position in society . . . as a class" and filled "a fair number of municipal, church, and school offices." These men had watched the region develop and had seen their status depersonalized as they quickly became part of a much larger labor force dependent on the vicissitudes of a distant and uncontrollable market. They unavailingly complained when operators brought in many more miners than needed for full-time work. A perceptive observer found that many of the older miners "have

[49] See Herbert G. Gutman, "Reconstruction in Ohio: Negroes in the Hocking Valley Coal Mines in 1873 and 1874," *Labor History*, III (Fall, 1962), 243–264.

worked in these mines since they were boys and feel they have an actual property right to their places." Most of the new men who flocked to the valley after 1869 came from distant areas, and a good number were from England, Wales, and Ireland. The rapid growth of the industry made it difficult to support trade unions in the valley.[50]

Economic crisis in 1873 suddenly punctured the prosperity of the entire region. At best, miners found only part-time employment, and cash wages were less common than usual, for working miners received mostly 90-day notes and store credit. The operators complained that labor costs were too high and made the selling price of coal in a competitive but depressed market prohibitive. Talk of wage cuts, however, turned the miners toward trade-unionism, and in December, 1873, they founded several branches of the newly established Miners' National Association. The operators responded by forming a region-wide trade association, and each of them posted a $5,000 bond as proof he would follow its directives. They also announced a sharp wage cut effective April 1, 1874, and entirely proscribed the new union. Prominent union leaders lost their jobs. One operator closed his supply store "for repairs," and another locked his men in a room and insisted that they sign the new wage agreement. But the union thrived. Only nine "regular" miners favored the new contract, and no more than twenty-five or thirty regulars refused to join the union. The union men agreed to the lower wage but refused to abandon their organization. The operators remained adamant and insisted that the "progress or decay" of the region hinged on the destruction of the new union—"a hydra too dangerous to be warmed at our hearth." A strike over the right of labor organization started on April 1.[51]

The strike brought trouble for the operators. Except for the *Logan Republican*, the weekly valley newspapers either supported the strikers or stood between them and the operators. The *Nelsonville Miner* time and again antagonized the powerful operators. The *Hocking Sentinel* and the *New Lexington Democratic Herald* defended the

[50] *Cincinnati Commercial*, May 23, June 4, 1874; Edward Wieck, *The American Miners' Association* (New York, 1940), p. 141.

[51] *Cincinnati Commercial*, May 23, 1874; *Hocking Sentinel*, December 25, 1873, January 8, 22, February 12, 26, March 5, 1874.

miners and criticized reporters from Columbus and Cincinnati who uniformly wrote in support of the operators. Unions were essential, insisted the *Athens Journal*, when capitalists made "extortionate" demands of their workers.[52]

The operators had other troubles. No more than thirty regular miners accepted the new contract on April 1 and only seventy men entered the mines that day. Local public officials declined to do the bidding of prominent operators. The New Straitsville police deputized strikers, and after Governor William Allen sent the state inspector of mines to investigate reported miner violence, county and town officials assured him there was no trouble and a committee of merchants and "other property owners" visited Allen "to give him the facts." New Straitsville town officials joined the miners to check the effort of operator W. B. McClung to bring in from Columbus "a posse" of nine special police armed with Colt revolvers and Spencer rifles. The miners felt it "unnecessary" for armed police to come to "their quiet town," and men, women, and children paraded the streets in protest. They made it uncomfortable for McClung's police, and he promised to close his mine and return the men to Columbus. But the mayor on the complaint of a miner issued a warrant for their arrest for entering the town armed, for "disorderly conduct," and for "disturbing the peace and quiet." Ordered to stand trial, the nine left town after McClung's superintendent posted their bond. "At the depot, there was a large crowd of miners, and one of their leaders wanted to give the Columbus party three cheers on their departure," but the much abused men "declined the honor." Except for the Nelsonville operators, the other mine owners closed their mines on April 1 for two months and just waited out the strikers. Toward the end of May, the operators divided among themselves. A few settled with strikers, but the largest operators rejected suggestions of arbitration and rebuked the union.[53]

Compromise was out of the question, insisted the more powerful operators. They attacked the governor for not sending militia to aid them and to protect private property. The triumph of the union would soon lead to the "overthrow" of "our Government and bring

[52] *Logan Republican*, April 4, 1874.

[53] *Cincinnati Commercial*, May 23, 1874; *Workingman's Advocate*, May 23, 1874.

upon us anarchy and bloodshed that would approach, if not equal, the Communism of Paris." [54]

Unable to exert their authority from within, the operators brought in between 400 and 500 Negroes in mid-June. Most of the Negroes came from cities such as Memphis, Louisville, and Richmond; few, if any, had had experience as coal miners. They were told nothing of the dispute and were generally misinformed about conditions in the valley. They also were offered high wages. One operator admitted that "the motive for introducing the negro was to break down the white miners' strike." Another boasted of his "great triumph over Trades-Unions" and called the use of Negroes "the greatest revolution ever attempted by operators to take over their own property." Gathered together in Columbus, the Negroes then were sped by rail to one of the mines which was turned into a military camp. The county sheriff, twenty-five deputies, and the governor's private secretary were there, too. Apparently with the approval of these officials, the operators armed the Negroes with "Government muskets," bayonets, and revolvers, and placed them on "military duty" around the property. No one could enter the area unless endorsed "by the operators or police." In the meantime, state militia were mobilized in nearby Athens, in Chillicothe, and in Cincinnati. [55]

Anger swept the Hocking Valley when the strikers learned of the coming of the Negroes. The first day 1,000 miners and their families stood or paraded near the Negro encampment. No violence occurred, but the miners made their displeasure known by calling across the "picket lines" of armed Negroes and urging them to desert the operators. The second day even more miners paraded near the encampment and urged the Negroes to leave. Small numbers of Negroes left the operators. The miners succeeded in "raiding" the operators with an "artillery of words." In all, around 120 Negroes went back on the operators. Two of the Negro defectors addressed the miners and admitted they had been "led by misrepresentations to come North" and "wouldn't interfere with white folks' work." They defended unions as "a good thing" and advocated

[54] *Athens Messenger*, May 7, 1874.
[55] *Hocking Sentinel*, April 1, 1874; *Chicago Tribune*, June 30, 1874.

"plenty of good things" for everyone. The strikers housed the Negroes in their union lodge rooms, and with the help of some local citizens raised about $500 to help them return South. But this was just a small victory for the union miners. Enough Negroes remained to strengthen the hand of the operators and to demoralize the union men. Negroes went to other mines even though strikers begged them not to work and "mothers held their children in their arms pointing out the negroes to them as those who came to rob them of their bread."[56]

Outside of the Hocking Valley, the press applauded the operators. The *Cleveland Leader* found the strikers were "aliens" who would not understand their rights and duties as Americans for another fifty or sixty years. The leading correspondent for the *Cincinnati Commercial* called the strikers drunkards, thieves, and assassins. In the Hocking Valley, however, some residents complained of the "mercenary newspaper men and their hired pimps." The valley newspapers especially criticized the operators for using Negroes. Some merchants and other business folk also attacked the operators. Certain Nelsonville businessmen offered aid to the strikers and unsuccessfully pleaded with the operators to rehire all the miners. They even talked of starting a new company to "give employment to miners who are citizens and who have lost their places." The Nelsonville police also were friendly to the miners, and the New Straitsville mayor prevented the sending of militia to his town.[57]

Destruction of the union and the introduction of Negro workers did not bring industrial harmony to the Hocking Valley. There were strikes over wage cuts in 1875 and 1877, and there also was conflict between the Negro and white miners. In 1875, when the miners resisted a wage cut, the operators tacitly admitted that their power in the valley still was inadequate. Two of them, W. F. Brooks and T. Longstreth, visited Governor Allen and pleaded that he "restore order" in the valley towns. The governor was cautious, however, and would not be used as a tool by the owners. Allen sent no troops and the operators returned empty-handed to Nelsonville.

[56] *Cincinnati Commercial*, June 13, 14, 15, 1874; *New Lexington Democratic Herald*, June 18, 1874.

[57] *Cleveland Leader*, July 7, 1874.

But their plea revealed the employers' anxieties, and their need for outside power to control their men as well as their businesses.[58]

Nothing better illustrates the differences between the small town and large city in this period than attitudes toward public works for the unemployed. Urban newspapers frowned upon the idea, and relief and welfare agents often felt that the unemployed were "looking for a handout." The unemployed, one official insisted, belonged to "the degraded class . . . who have the vague idea that 'the world owes them a living.'" Unemployed workers were lazy, many said, and trifling.[59]

Native-born radicals and reformers, a few welfare officers, ambitious politicians, responsible theorists, socialists, and relics from the pre-Civil War era all agitated for public works during the great economic crisis of 1873–74. Protest meetings boasted craft-unionists, agitators of all hues, and responsible citizens as well as the unemployed workers themselves as they aired their demands for remedial public works. The earliest advocates urged construction of city streets, parks and playgrounds, rapid transit systems, and other projects to relieve unemployment. These schemes, in most cases, depended on borrowed money or fiat currency, or issuance of low interest rate bonds on both local and national levels. Public assistance was necessary because the job was too big for private enterprise, which could not deal with the "present gigantic difficulty." The government had aided the wealthy classes in the past, and now it was time to "legislate for the good of all not the few." Street demonstrations and meetings by the unemployed occurred in November and December of 1873 in Boston, Cincinnati, Chicago, Detroit, Indianapolis, Louisville, Newark, New York, Paterson, Pittsburgh, and Philadelphia. In December, Chicago and Cincinnati workers paraded the streets with placards that read: "Work or Bread" and "Death to Starvation." The *Chicago Tribune* found the city "entirely unprepared for anything of the kind." The plea of aid struck "like

[58] *Cincinnati Commercial*, October 3, 1874, March 22, 1875; *New Lexington Democratic Herald*, March 25, 1875; *Hocking Sentinel*, March 4, 25, 1875; *Ohio State Journal*, April 1, 1875.

[59] *New York Graphic*, November 10, 1873; *Chicago Tribune*, December 23, 1873; New York Association for Improving the Condition of the Poor, *Thirtieth Annual Report, 1873* (New York, 1873), pp. 41 ff.

lightning from a clear, blue sky." More than 4,000 persons jammed into Cooper Institute on December 11, and despite a heavy rainfall, thousands milled outside. Indianapolis witnessed the largest labor meeting in its history, and on December 21 an overflow crowd of between 5,000 and 7,000 packed into Chicago's Turner Hall. The dominant theme at all these gatherings was the same: unemployment was widespread, countless persons were without means, charity and philanthropy were poor substitutes for work, and public aid and employment were necessary and just.[60]

The reaction to the demand for public works contained elements of surprise, ridicule, contempt, and genuine fear. The Board of Aldermen refused to meet with committees of unemployed Philadelphia workers. Irate Paterson taxpayers forced an end to a limited program of street repairs that the city government had started. "When the question of economy comes before the citzens," explained the *Cincinnati Gazette* of the rejection of public works programs by the Board of City Improvements, "the plea of love for the laborer will not be received." Chicago public officials and charity leaders told the unemployed to join them "in God's work" and "rescue the poor and suffering" through philanthropy not public employment.[61]

The urban press rejected the plea for public works and responsibility for the unemployed. Public employment was "sheer unadulterated bosh," and men demanding such aid were "disgusting," "crazy," "loud-mouthed gasometers," "impudent vagabonds," and even "ineffable asses." They were ready "to chop off the heads of every man addicted to clean linen." They wanted to make "Government an institution to pillage the individual for the benefit of the mass." Hopefully, "yellow fever, cholera, or any other blessing" would sweep these persons from the earth. Depressions, after all, were normal and necessary adjustments and workers should only "quietly bide their time till the natural laws of trade" brought renewed prosperity. Private charity and alms as well as "free land" were adequate answers to unemployment. "The United States," said the *New York Times*, "is the only 'socialistic,' or more correctly 'agrarian,' government in the world in that it offers good land

[60] *New York Sun*, October 23, November 4, November 20—December 20, 1873; *Chicago Times*, December 1–31, 1873.

[61] *New York World*, December 27, 1873; see sources in note 60.

at nominal prices to every settler" and thereby takes "the sting from Communism." If the unemployed "prefer to cling to the great cities to oversupply labor," added the *Chicago Times*, "the fault is theirs." [62]

None of the proposals of the jobless workers met with favor, but the demand by New York workers that personal wealth be limited to $100,000 was criticized the most severely of all. To restrict the "ambition of building up colossal fortunes" meant an end to all "progress," wrote the *Chicago Times*. The *New York Tribune* insisted that any limitation on personal wealth was really an effort "to have employment without employers" and that was "almost as impossible . . . as to get into the world without ancestors." [63]

Another argument against public responsibility for the unemployed identified this notion with immigrants, socialists, and "alien" doctrine. The agitation by the socialists compounded the anxieties of the more comfortable classes. Remembering that force had put down the Paris Communards, the *Chicago Times* asked: "Are we to be required to face a like alternative?" New York's police superintendent urged his men to spy on labor meetings and warned that German and French revolutionaries were "doing their utmost to inflame the workingman's mind." The *Chicago Tribune* menacingly concluded, "The coalition of foreign nationalities must be for a foreign, non-American object. The principles of these men are wild and subversive of society itself." [64]

Hemmed in by such ideological blinders, devoted to "natural laws" of economics, and committed to a conspiracy theory of social change so often attributed only to the lower classes, the literate nonindustrial residents of large cities did not identify meaningfully with the urban poor and the unemployed. A Chicago Unitarian minister warned his congregation: "There are thousands who . . . are ready to become the writhing body of any monster mob that can find a head, like the *sans-culotte* of the French Revolution." And Thurlow Weed, the aged but wise Republican politician, saw only danger from the unemployed. He urged an enlarged program of private relief and charity. "It is not a question of duty, of sympathy, or of interest but one of *safety*," Weed warned New Yorkers. The matter

[62] *New York Tribune*, December 12, 1873.

[63] *Ibid.*, December 12, 1873.

[64] *Chicago Times*, December 23, 30, 1873; *Chicago Tribune*, December 23–30, 1873.

concerned "the rich far more deeply than the poor," but he feared that the wealthy class would "draw its purse strings too tightly." Most well-to-do residents of large cities in 1873 and 1874 believed that men rose or fell solely through individual effort. They viewed the worker as little more than a factor of production. They were sufficiently alienated from the urban poor to join the *New York Graphic* in jubilantly celebrating a country in which republican equality, free public schools, and cheap western lands allowed "intelligent working people" to "have anything they all want."[65]

The extreme reaction against the concept of public responsibility for the unemployed by the residents of large cities was not just a response to the radical character of that demand. The attitude displayed toward the unemployed reflected a broader and more encompassing attitude toward labor. Unlike similar groups in small towns, the urban middle and upper income groups generally frowned upon labor disputes and automatically sided with employers. Contact between these persons and the worker was casual and at best indirect. Trade unions, moreover, were abstractions. Labor unions, therefore, did little more than violate certain immutable "natural and moral laws" and deter economic development and capital accumulation.[66] The *Chicago Times* put it another way in its discussion of workers who challenged the status quo: "The man who lays up not for the morrow, perishes on the morrow. It is the inexorable law of God, which neither legislatures nor communistic blatherskites can repeal. The fittest alone survive, and those are fittest, as the result always proves, who provide for their own survival."[67]

Unions and all forms of labor protest, particularly strikes, were condemned. The *New York Times* described the strike as "a combination against long-established laws" especially "the law of supply and demand." The *New York Tribune* wrote of "the general viciousness of the trades-union system," and the *Cleveland Leader* called "the labor union kings . . . the most absolute tyrants of our day." Strikes,

---

[65] See *Chicago Tribune*, December 29, 1873; Thurlow Weed to the Editor, *New York Tribune*, December 20, 1873; *Cumberland* (Maryland) *Civilian and Times*, February 12, 1874.

[66] *New York Tribune*, June 22, 1874.

[67] *Chicago Times*, August 26, 1874.

insisted the *Chicago Tribune*, "implant in many men habits of indolence that are fatal to their efficiency thereafter." Cleveland sailors who protested conditions on the Great Lakes ships were "a motley throng and a wicked one," and when Cuban cigar makers struck in New York, the *New York Herald* insisted that "madness rules the hour." City officials joined in attacking and weakening trade unions. The mayor forbade the leader of striking Philadelphia weavers from speaking in the streets. New York police barred striking German cigar workers from gathering in front of a factory whose owners had discharged six trade-unionists including four women. Plain-clothes detectives trailed striking Brooklyn plasterers. When Peter Smith, a nonunion barrel maker, shot and wounded four union men, killing one of them, during a bitter lockout, a New York judge freed him on $1,000 bail supplied by his employers and said his employers did "perfectly right in giving Smith a revolver to defend himself from strikers."[68]

A brief review of three important labor crises in Pittsburgh, Cleveland, and New York points out different aspects of the underlying attitude toward labor in the large cities. The owners of Pittsburgh's five daily newspapers cut printers' wages in November, 1873, and formed an association to break the printers' union. After the printers rejected the wage cut and agreed to strike if nonunion men were taken on, two newspapers fired the union printers. The others quit in protest. The *Pittsburgh Dispatch* said the strikers "owe no allegiance to society," and the other publishers condemned the union as an "unreasoning tyranny." Three publishers started a court suit against more than seventy union members charging them with "conspiracy." The printers were held in $700 bail, and the strike was lost. Soon, Pittsburgh was "swarming with 'rats' from all parts of the country," and the union went under. Though the cases were not pressed after the union collapsed, the indictments were not dropped. In 1876, the *Pittsburgh National Labor Tribune* charged, "All of these men are kept under bail *to this day* to intimidate them from forming a Union, or asking for just wages." The weekly organ of the anthracite miners' union attacked the indictment and complained

---

[68] *New York Herald*, November 2, 1873; *New York Times*, June 3, 1874; *Cleveland Leader*, June 18, 1874; *Chicago Tribune*, April 15, 1874.

that it reiterated "the prejudice against workingmen's unions that seems to exist universally among office-holders." [69]

In May, 1874, Cleveland coal dealers cut the wages of their coal heavers more than 25 per cent, and between 400 and 500 men struck. Some new hands were hired. A foreman drew a pistol on the strikers and was beaten by them. The foremen and several strikers were arrested, and the coal docks remained quiet as the strikers, who had started a union, paraded up and down the docks and neither spoke nor gestured to the new men. Police guarded the docks, and a light artillery battery of the Ohio National Guard was mobilized. Lumber heavers joined the striking workers, and the two groups paraded quietly on May 8. Nearly one hundred police led by the mayor patrolled the docks, and the light artillery battery waited in the armory with seventy-five rounds of cannister. Although the strikers were orderly, the police jailed several of their ring-leaders. The strikers did not resist and dispersed when so ordered by the law. In their complaint to the public, the strikers captured the flavor of much of urban industrial conflict:

> The whole thing is a calumny, based upon the assumption that if a man be poor he must necessarily be a blackguard. Honest poverty can have no merit here, as the rich, together with all their other monopolies, must also monopolize all the virtues. We say now . . . we entertain a much more devout respect and reverence for our public law than the men who are thus seeking to degrade it into a tool of grinding oppression. We ask from the generosity of our fellow citizens . . . to depute [sic] a commission of honest men to come and examine our claims. . . . We feel confident they will be convinced that the authorities of Cleveland, its police force, and particularly the formidable artillery are all made partisans to a very dirty and mean transaction.

The impartial inquiry proved unnecessary; a few days later several firms rescinded the wage cut, and the strikers thanked these employers. [70]

Italian laborers were used on a large scale in the New York building trades for the first time in the spring of 1874. They were cheap, unskilled labor and were used to break strikes. They lived

[69] *Pittsburgh Post*, November 21–30, 1873.
[70] *Cleveland Plain Dealer*, May 7–11, 1874.

"piled together like sardines in a box" and worked mainly as rag pickers and street cleaners. They were men of "passionate dispositions" and, "as a rule, filthy beyond the power of one to imagine." "Their mental condition," a doctor insisted, "somewhat corresponds to their physical condition." Irish street laborers and unskilled workers were especially hard on the Italians, and numerous scuffles between the two groups occurred in the spring of 1874. In spite of the revulsion toward the Italians as a people, the *New York Tribune* advised employers that their "mode of life" allowed them to work for low wages.[71]

Two non-Italians, civil engineers and contractors, founded the New York Italian Labor Company in April, 1874. It claimed 2,700 members, and its superintendent, an Italian named Frederick Guscetti, announced: "As peaceable and industrious men, we claim the right to put such price upon our labor as may seem to us best." The firm held power of attorney over its members, contracted particular jobs, provided transportation, supplied the "gangs" with "simple food," and retained a commission of a day's wages from each monthly pay check. Guscetti said the company was started to protect the Italians from their Irish "adversaries," and he said the men were ready and willing to undertake work "at panic prices." The non-Italian managers announced the men would work for 20 per cent less in the building trades. Employers were urged to hire them "and do away with strikes."[72]

Protected by the city police and encouraged by the most powerful newspapers, the New York Italian Labor Company first attracted attention when it broke a strike of union hod carriers. Irish workers hooted and stoned the Italians, but the police provided them with ample protection. The *Cooper's New Monthly* complained that "poor strangers, unacquainted with the laws and customs and language of the country," had been made "the dupes of unprincipled money sharks" and were being "used as tools to victimize and oppress other workingmen." This was just the start. The firm advertised its services in *Iron Age*. By the end of July, 1874, it had

---

[71] *New York Toiler*, August 22, 1874; *New York Sun*, July 6, 1874; Board of Health of the City of New York, *Fourth Annual Report, May 1, 1873, to April 30, 1874* (New York, 1874), pp. 96–97.

[72] *New York Times*, June 25–30, 1874; *New York Tribune*, June 2–24, 1874.

branched out with work gangs in New York, Massachusetts, and Pennsylvania.[73]

There is much to say about the attitude toward labor that existed in large cities, but over all opinion lay a popular belief that iron laws governed not only the economy but life itself, and that he who tampered with them through social experiments or reforms imperiled the whole structure. The *Chicago Times* was honest if perhaps callous in saying: "Whatever cheapens production, whatever will lessen the cost of growing wheat, digging gold, washing dishes, building steam engines, is of value. . . . The age is not one which enquires when looking at a piece of lace whether the woman who wove it is a saint or a courtesan." It came at last almost to a kind of inhumanity, as one manufacturer who used dogs as well as men in his operation discovered. The employer liked the dogs better than the men. "They never go on strike for higher wages, have no labor unions, never get intoxicated and disorderly, never absent themselves from work without good cause, obey orders without growling, and are very reliable."[74]

The contrast between urban and rural views of labor and its fullest role in society and life is clear.[75] In recent years, many have stressed "entrepreneurship" in nineteenth-century America[76] without distinguishing between entrepreneurs in commerce and trade and entrepreneurs in industrial manufacturing. Reflecting the stresses and strains in the thought and social attitudes of a generation passing from the old agricultural way of life to the new industrial America, many men could justify the business ethic in its own sphere without sustaining it in operation in society at large or in human relationships. It was one thing to apply brute force in the market place, and quite another to talk blithely of "iron laws" in operation when men's lives and well-being were at stake.

[73] *New York Sun*, June 2, 10, 1874; *New York World*, July 23–24, 1874.

[74] *Chicago Times*, May 22, 1876; *Iron Age*, April 27, 1876, p. 24.

[75] See Herbert Gutman, "Two Lockouts in Pennsylvania, 1873–1874," *loc. cit.*, note 35, above; and Herbert Gutman, "Trouble on the Railroads in 1873–1874: Prelude to the 1877 Crisis?" *loc. cit.*, note 31, above.

[76] See Louis Hartz, *The Liberal Tradition in America* (New York, 1955), pp. 110–113, 189–227; Richard Hofstadter, *The American Political Tradition and the Men Who Made It* (New York, 1948), pp. v–ix; John Higham (ed.), *The Reconstruction of American History* (New York, 1962), pp. 21–24, 119–156.

Not all men had such second thoughts about the social fabric which industrialism and commercialism were weaving, but in the older areas of the country, still susceptible to the cries of an ancient conscience, the spirits of free enterprise and free action were neither dead nor mutually exclusive. As the story shows clearly, many elements of labor kept their freedom of action and bargaining even during strikes. And the worker was not without shrewdness in his appeal to public opinion. There is a certain irony in realizing that rural, or at least small-town America, supposedly alien and antagonistic toward the city and its ways, remained in this period a stronghold of freedom for the worker seeking his economic and social rights.

But perhaps this is not so strange after all, for rural America, whatever its narrowness and faults, had always preached individualism and personal freedom. It was the city, whose very impersonality would one day make it a kind of frontier of anonymity, which often preached personal restriction and the law of the economic and social jungle. As industrialism triumphed, the businessman's powers increased, yet it is significant that in this generation of genuine freedom of action, he was often hindered and always suspect in vast areas of the nation which cheered his efforts toward wealth even while often frustrating his methods.[77]

Facile generalizations are easy to make and not always sound, but surely the evidence warrants a new view of labor in the Gilded Age. The standard stereotypes and textbook clichés about its impotence and division before the iron hand of oppressive capitalism do not fit the facts. Its story is far different when surveyed in depth, carrying in it overtones of great complexity. And it is not without haunting and instructive reminders that even in an age often dominated by lusts for power, men did not forget or abandon old and honored concepts of human dignity and worth.

Reprinted from *The Gilded Age: A Reappraisal*, ed. H. Wayne Morgan (Syracuse: Syracuse University Press, 1963).

[77] See Thomas C. Cochran, *Railroad Leaders, 1845–1890: The Business Mind in Action* (Cambridge, 1953), p. 181.